Worcester County Maryland
Marriage Licenses
1795-1865

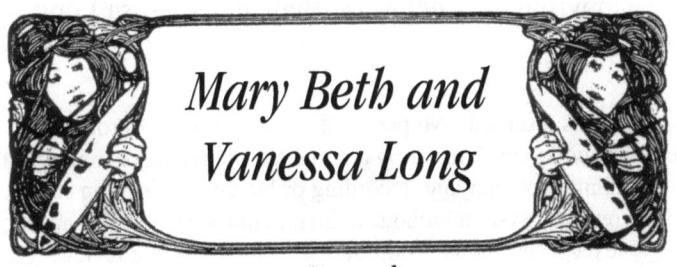

Mary Beth and Vanessa Long

HERITAGE BOOKS
2008

HERITAGE BOOKS
AN IMPRINT OF HERITAGE BOOKS, INC.

Books, CDs, and more—Worldwide

For our listing of thousands of titles see our website at
www.HeritageBooks.com

Published 2008 by
HERITAGE BOOKS, INC.
Publishing Division
100 Railroad Ave. #104
Westminster, Maryland 21157

Copyright © 1990 Mary Beth and Vanessa Long

All rights reserved. No part of this book may be reproduced or transmitted in any form or by any means, electronic or mechanical, including photocopying, recording or by any information storage and retrieval system without written permission from the author, except for the inclusion of brief quotations in a review.

International Standard Book Numbers
Paperbound: 978-1-58549-180-3
Clothbound: 978-0-7884-7254-1

PREFACE

This is a collection of the earliest known marriage licenses issued in Worcester County. Copies are available at the courthouse in Princess Anne and the State Archives, Annapolis. The dates given are the dates that the license was issued and not the dates of the marriage. In fact one can not assume that the marriage necessarily took place. Nevertheless the probability is great that the couple were married within a few days of the date of the license. There is a series of records of the actual marriages which begins for Worcester County in 1865.

When licenses were first recorded in Worcester County, licenses were not necessary if the bride and groom announced their intentions in a recognized church service for three successive meetings preceding the actual ceremony. This was called the posting of banns.

Records of early marriages can be found in found in the series, Maryland Eastern Shore Vital Records, published by Family Line Publications. These include church records of Worcester County and its parent County, Somerset, and records of marriages found in the land records of Somerset County, prior to the formation of Worcester County. Unfortunately many of the marriage records of the churches have been lost to fires, carelessness and the ravages of time. Somerset County marriage licenses were published by Roy C. Pollit in Somerset County, Maryland, Marriag Records, 1796-1871 (Somersett House, 1986)

A few marriages are found in the publication, Marriage and Deaths of the Lower Delmarva, 1835-1840 which includes marriages and deaths from newspapers, The Borderer, The Worcester Banner and Worcester Sentinel, all printed at Snow Hill. Following are the announcements of the marriages found in issues of the above mentioned newpapers with the date of marriage license when known:

Date of marriage/minister/Groom and bride/date of marriage license if known
7 Jan 1835   Mustard   Robert S. Mills and Miss Ann Q. Dennis of Snow Hill - marriage license dated same day.
7 Jan 1835   Mustard   Peter Rook and Miss Elizabeth Dorathy of Worcester Co. - no Worcester Co. or Somerset Co. marriage license.
21 Jan 1835   Mustard   William Brown and Miss Elizabeth dau of Edward Knock of Worcester Co. - marriage license dated same day.
21 Jan 1835   Mustard   Capt. John D. Fields and Miss Elizabeth Ann McMaster, Accomac Co. VA. - no Worcester Co. or Somerset Co. marriage license.
4 Mar 1835   Mustard   Littleton Taylor and Miss Hester Cropper of Worcester Co. - Worcester Co. marriage license dated two days earlier.
11 Mar 1835   Wiley   William B. Stuart of Snow Hill and Miss Ellen P., youngest dau of Nathaniel Dixon, of Somerset Co. - Somerset Co. marriage license dated same day.
2 Apr 1835   Laird   John W. Rider of Salisbury and Miss Sarah Ann, dau of late Major George Hayward of Worcester Co. - Somerset Co. marriage license dated same day.

8 Jul 1835   Wiley   William Johnston of Princess Anne and Miss Rosina M. Upshur of Snow Hill. - marriage license dated same day.
29 Jul 1835   Mustard   John P. Robins, Esq., and Margaret E., eldest dau of Lem. P. Spence, Esq., both of Snow Hill. - Worcester Co. marriage license dated same day.
14 Mar 1836   Henderson   Henry Boston and Miss Leah Adams. - Worcester Co. marriage license dated same day.
14 Mar 1836   Foreman   George Bowden and Miss Esther Morris. - Worcester Co. marriage license dated same day.
31 Jul 1839   Robins   Jesse B. Truitt and Miss Sally, dau of Parker Selby of Worcester Co. - Worcester Co. marriage license dated previous day.
24 Sep 1839   Mustard   James Laird Vallandigham, Esq. of New Lisbon, OH, and Miss Mary Eliza, dau of Lemuel P. Spence of Snow Hill. - Worcester Co. marriage license dated same day.
13 Nov 1839   Mustard   Thomas Stevenson of Snow Hill and Miss Ann Maria Bell of Pitts' Creek. No Worcester Co. or Somerset Co. marriage license.
8 Jan 1840   Watts   John K. Truitt, Inn Keeper, Horn Town, VA, and Miss Rosa Hall. No Worcester Co. or Somerset Co. marriage license.
10 Jan 1840   Watts   Diar Ward and Miss Elizabeth Lewis. - Worcester Co. marriage license dated same day.

WORCESTER COUNTY MARRIAGES
1795 - 1865

1795

April 14	Robert TOWNSEND	Nancy KERNYL
April 28	Sewell TURPIN	Betty RACKLIFFE
May 1	Nehemiah DAVIS	Abigail HARRIS
May 1	Selby PRUITT	Rebecca PEPPER
May 2	Sevasten LANKFORD	Elizabeth GUTHERY
May 8	James SMITH	Frankey NELMO
May 27	Jonathan STEVENSON	Lydia MILLS
June 2	John WILKINS	Elizabeth CHRISTIE
June 11	George JOHNSON	Catherine SELBY
June 12	Joseph HOUSTON	Bridgat PATTERSON
June 22	William SCHOFIELD	Sarah LAYFIELD
June 23	Belitha GRIFFEN	Mary SMITH
July 3	Edward BURBAGE	Mary SMACK
July 3	George TWILLEY	Priscilla TAYLOR
July 11	Hezekiah WRIGHT	Elizabeth RILEY
July 16	Dennis HUDSON	Polly MELVIN
July 17	Edward HAMMOND	Nancy TRUIT
July 24	Rives R. TOWNSEND	Sarah SCARBOURGH
Aug. 5	George RICE	Mary Ann SMITH
Aug. 11	J. Jno HOLLAND	Polly RICHARDSON
Aug. 13	Edward MORRIS	Sarah ROBERTS
Aug.	Not Legible	Nancy BRITTINGHAM
Sept. 9	Thomas CALHOON	Nancy TAYLOR
Sept. 11	Leonard JOHNSON	Aralanta BRITTINGHAM
Sept. 12	Phillip MORRIS	Nancy MUMFORD
Oct. 20	Josiah DUNCAN	Martha M. DALE
Oct. 22	Robert GIVANS	Rosanna BUTLER
Nov. 30	Angelo ATKINSON	Sarah HUDSON
Nov. 30	William BAYNUM	Betsey CAREY
Dec. 4	John BRATTEN	Piercey GRAY
Dec. 8	Milby PURNELL	Amelia PARKER
Dec. 11	James TAYLOR	Peggy AYDELOTT
Dec. 11	Absolom WYATT	Nancy PENNEWELL
Dec. 18	Archebald SMITH	Mary HAMMOND
Dec. 18	James TRIP	Jane PURNELL
Dec. 19	William BAKER	Martha EVANS
Dec. 22	Ezekiel HENDERSON	Hannah TIMMONS
Dec. 25	McKenny HUDSON	Hannah DYMOCK
Dec. 25	Levi JONES	Rachell LONG

1796

Jan. 4	Abijah DAVIS	Catherine PARKER
Jan. 9	Rouse GRAY	Bridgett CATHELL
Jan. 14	William PORTER	Naomi STURGIS
Jan. 29	Stephen DRYDEN	Catherine DRYDEN
Jan. 29	Caleb POWELL	Elizabeth BETHARDS
Feb. 4	William TINGLE	Sarah LONG
Feb. 8	John HENDERSON	Sally HENDERSON
Feb. 9	George HALL	Hesse BROWN

1796

Feb. 12	Nehemiah HOLLAND	Martha RICHARDSON
Feb. 18	Belitha JARMAN	Rachel ADKINS
March 1	John K. TRUITT	Mary TEAGUE
March 8	Thomas HARRIS	Sarah MILLS
March 10	Daniel COTTINGHAM	Polly TILGHMAN
March 15	Josiah NELSON	Margaret SMITH
March 25	Benjamin HUDSON	Elizabeth WILLIAMS
Arril 11	William S. WHITE	Betsey S. WAGGERMAN
April 15	Elgate DRISKLE	Anna DYKES
April 18	Annania BRADFORD	Nancy RICHARDS
April 23	Littleton RILEY	Sally TOWNSEND
April 25	William LAW	Polly MILLER
May 3	Eli CHRISTOPHER	Lotte DRISKELE
May 10	John TAYLOR	Polly POWELL
May 11	Levin GODFREY	Ann T. TRUITT
May 19	Edward HAMMOND	Nancy HOWARD
May 31	Robert HUDSON	Mary ATKINSON
June 20	Staphen TOWNSEND	Esther BENSON
June 23	Thomas COTTINGHAM	Rhoda TOWNSEND
June 30	Tho FRANKLIN	Charlotte KIRBY
July 8	John SCARBOROUGH	Elizabeth SMULLEN
July 12	Benjamin GUNBY	Esther STURGIS
July 15	Charles HARRIS	Hannah NOBLE
July 25	John WILSON	Sarah ENNIS
July 26	Peter EVANS	Nancy HUDSON
July 26	Benjamin HAMMOND	Janet COTTINGHAM
July 30	Wm. BRITTINGHAM	Polly GOOTEE
Aug. 6	John PARKER	Nancy PARKER
Aug. 7	John GOWTEE	Polly DISHAROON
Aug. 20	Thomas WHITE	Sarah NAIRN
Aug. 26	Samuel BLADES	Tabitha JONES
Sept. 2	William CLAYVILLE	Rachel JOHNSON
Sept. 5	George TAYLOR	Polly TIMMONS
Sept. 29	Isaac BRITTINGHAM	Betsey TOWNSEND
Oct. 1	Sylvanus Uriah ROBERTS	Sarah GILLETT
Oct. 6	John TUNNELS	Mary SELBY
Oct. 6	Parker LUCAS	Rhoda BOWEN
Oct. 10	Samuel BISHOP	Mary SMITH
Oct. 10	John JACKSON	Elizabeth BURBAGE
Oct. 13	Zadock LONG	Leah WHITTINGTON
Oct. 22	Ephraim TOWNSEND	Rachel CULTER
Oct. 25	John SLOCOMB	Polly McCREDDY
Oct. 25	Jabez BRUMLEY	Martha TARR
Nov. 18	Josa BEACHBOARD	Wealthy PAINE
Nov. 23	James EASHUM	Delliah PARKER
Nov. 25	Zadock MARSHALL	Peggy COSTEN
Nov. 28	Zadock WHEELER	Martha B. DICKERSON
Nov. 30	Thomas WILSON	Elizabeth FISHER
Nov. 30	John ALLEN	Lucretia BRUMBLY

1796
Dec. 9	Thomas REYNOLDS	Dolly BOWEN
Dec. 9	John CATHELL	Priscilla WARD
Dec. 13	Benjamin JARMAN	Elizabeth TIMMONS
Dec. 15	George HOUSTON	Rhoda BRATTEN
Dec. 16	Jonathan MILLS	Leah TULL
Dec. 16	Ephraim TIMMONS	Patty HOLLOWAY
Dec. 21	John JOHNSON	Sally CROPPER
Dec. 21	Turner DAVIS	Mary BOWEN
Dec. 21	Warren HADDER	Polly JOHNSON
Dec. 22	Jacob TEAGUE	Zapporah ROUNDS
Dec. 24	William HUGHS	Mary HOUSTON
Dec. 29	Thomas TINDALE	Agnes MELVIN

1797
Jan. 4	John WEBB	Mary HANCOCK
Jan. 7	Lazarus COTTMAN	Betsey BISHOP
Jan. 10	Charles PARKER	Tabitha JOHNSON
Jan. 10	David McDANIEL	Elizabeth CAREY
Jan. 10	John PURNELL	Dolly BENNETT
Jan. 11	William HAMMOND	Betsey GIBBS
Jan. 23	William BROWN	Leah WILSON
Jan. 24	John STURGIS	Tabitha BRUMLY
Jan. 25	John STURGIS	Nancy BISHOP
Jan. 30	Henry WHITE	Sally LISTER
Jan. 31	John TARR	Peggy ALLEN
Jan. 31	William NELSON	Sally STURGIS
Jan. 31	James JOHNSON	Patty BAKER
Feb. 1	William BELL	Polly PITTS
Feb. 8	James COLLINS	Polly WHITE
Feb. 10	Jesse MUMFORD	Betsey RICHARDSON
Feb. 16	Severn PRUITT	Polly MERRITT
Feb. 17	William DIXON	Leah DIKES
Feb. 21	James DAVIS	Hannah Jenkins ADKINS
Feb. 22	Hanson BRION	Nancy HOLLAND
Feb. 22	Isaac HENDERSON	Sally DAVIS
Feb. 22	Arthur HUDSON	Nancy TAYLOR
Feb. 27	Thomas WILLIAMS	Nancy PARKER
Feb. 28	Joseph SCHOOLFIELD	Esther GUNBY
Feb. 28	Andrew SIMPSON	Patty HOLLAND
March 1	Alexander FRANKLIN	Rachel RILEY
March 7	Jesse FARLOW	Sarah LAWS
March 8	John GREEN	Betsey TOWNSEND
March 22	James GIVANS	Betsey LINDZEY
April 10	Benjamin LEVINGSTON	Sarah JONES
April 17	James DAVIS	Hannah BIRCH
April 17	George STATEN	Rachel TURNER
April 24	Samuel TURNER	Sally TAYLOR
May 2	Edward SCARBOROUGH	Nancy SELBY
May 10	James KING	Nancy KENNETT

1797

Date	Groom	Bride
May 12	Philip MARSH	Polly SELBY
May 19	Teague DONOHOE	Elizabeth HANDY
May 26	Levi DUNCAN	Leah PURNELL
May 27	Joshua EVANS	Betsey NELSON
June 6	James Hall JONES	Margaret DALE
June 13	Jacob RICHARDS	Sarah RAGGAN
June 14	John ROCK	Polly MITCHELL
June 14	Barneby BERNARD	Mary R. DICKERSON
June 21	Matthias DAVIS	Betsey HANDY
July 6	Handy DAVIS	Rhoda BURBAGE
July 10	Alexander LOW	Nancy BREWINGTON
July 18	McKemmy PORTER	Nancy PARKER
July 18	Walton COLLINS	Martha TOWNSEND
July 18	William FRANKLIN	Anna RILEY
Aug. 3	William FERGUSON	Eunice DAVIS
Aug. 17	Stephen ROACH	Mary LAMDEN
Aug. 18	Robert MITCHELL	Elizabeth MUMFORD
Aug. 22	Layfield COLLIER	Sally WHITE
Aug. 29	William HOSHIER	Nancy TRADER
Sept. 8	William SCHOOLFIELD	Rosanna MERRILL
Sept. 15	Isaac DREADEN	Mary ALEXANDER
Sept. 22	William TARR	Hannah GUTHERY
Sept. 28	John BITTS	Sally TRUITT
Oct. 10	Soloman K, PRICE	Elizabeth HARRIS
Oct. 12	John Gibbs TAYLOR	Hannah AYDELOTTE
Oct. 17	Robert GIVANS	Ruth ROBERTSON
Oct. 23	Barneby HENDERSON	Margaret KNOX
Oct. 30	George TRUITT	Sally BISHOP
Nov. 4	Edmund EVANS	Rachel P. MILBOURN
Nov. 8	William CAUDRY	Sally BOWEN
Nov. 8	John PURNELL	Patty PURNELL
Nov. 14	Southy STERLING	Rachel DRYDEN
Nov. 22	David WALSTON	Polly MOOR
Nov. 24	James REID	Betsy DAVIS
Nov. 24	Elijah PRUITT	Betsey BISHOP
Nov. 29	John REDDEN	Hesse TAYLOR
Nov. 30	Joseph STEVENSON	Elizabeth STEVENSON
Dec. 5	Levi NELSON	Hannah MILLS
Dec. 8	William GORDY	Betsey MITCHELE
Dec. 13	Isaac LONG	Charlotte GRIFFEN
Dec. 14	Caleb HOUSTON	Betsy MILLS
Dec. 18	Esme WALLER	Sally ELZEY
Dec. 19	Jesse SMACK	Sally TRUITT
Dec. 19	Lemuel TURNER	Sally PARKER
Dec. 20	William NELSON	Sarah BROTHERY
Dec. 20	Joseph CROPPER	Amelia BOWEN
Dec. 20	Thomas BIRD	Anna FLEMING
Dec. 20	George SELBY	Betsy Curtis STURGIS
Dec. 22	Edward LAMBDEN	Polly MERRILL

1797			
Dec. 26		Issac BEATHARDS	Sally RICHARDS
1798			
Jan. 2		Holland SMACK	Betsey SMACK
Jan. 2		Robert SMITH	Sarah MARTIN
Jan. 3		Isaac COLLINS	Tabitha STEVENSON
Jan. 3		James HINMAN	Sarah SCARBOROUGH
Jan. 4		Elijah NELSON	Sophia MELVIN
Jan. 5		John BOTHAM	Polly LAYFIELD
Jan. 9		William JONES	Catherine HADDER
Jan. 12		Outten ENNIS	Polly GLADDEN
Jan. 16		Levin LAYFIELD	Nancy BRITTINGHAM
Jan. 19		Henry GARNWELL	Mary J. HENMAN
Jan. 23		John GUNBY	Amelia CHAILLE
Jan. 23		John BOWEN	Polly CAUDRY
Jan. 23		Levi MERRILE	Elizabeth WHEELER
Jan. 31		John BRATTEN	Polly QUINTON
Feb. 5		Isaac MARSHALL	Polly COLLYER
Feb. 6		Lott WRIGHT	Esther EVANS
Feb. 7		Jacob JOHNSON	Nancy ARMSTRONG
Feb. 9		John SMITH	Anne SMITH
Feb. 16		Matthew JONES	Joanna JOHNSON
Feb. 19		David ADKINS	Mary WALLER
Feb. 21		Ebenezer HEARN	Betsey ROACH
Feb. 28		Josiah HILL	Polly FRANKLIN
March 7		William HUDSON	Comfort KNOX
March 16		Henry THORNTON	Euphama TOWNSEND
March 26		Benjamin TRUITT	Eleanor JOHNSON
March 27		William DUNCAN	Esther HOLLAND
April 7		George KNOX	Hetty MERRILL
April 17		Levin HILL Jr.	Catherine JOHNSON
April 27		Eli SHOCKLY	Betsy COLIBOURN
April 27		Thomas SHOCKLY	Nancy COLEBOURN
May 11		Nath BISHOP	Nancy FRESHWATER
May 21		James REDDEN	Sarah BENSTON
May 22		Thomas NEWBOLD	Polly TAYLOR
May 22		Eli WILLIAMS	Euphamy JONES
May 25		Bowden HAMMOND	Amelia JONES
June 9		James BLADES	Sarah MELVIN
June 21		Joseph URBUSH	Polly WILLIAMS
June 22		Timothy IRONS	Sarah DORMAN
June 25		John WALKER	Selvina CROPPER
June 26		Levin MATTHEWS	Charlotte WILLIS
June 26		Benjamin RICHARDSON	Catharine BRATTEN
July 4		Arthur TRAZY	Sally JOHNSON
July 12		Jesse GRAY	Sarah LAWRENCE
July 31		Arthur TAYLOR	Polly LESTER
Aug. 3		George TRUITT	Elizabeth HOLLOWAY
Aug. 5		Martin A. DAVIS	Nancy BAILY

1798

Aug. 28	Warrington DAVIS	Polly SMACK
Sept. 4	William DAVIS	Mary PARKER
Sept. 11	Richard CLARK	Nancy BELL
Sept. 11	Kirk GUNBY	Hannah DUNCAN
Oct. 2	Cannon LANK	Mary PRICE
Oct. 9	Thomas McCORMACK	Eleanor WALTER
Oct. 16	Phillip MORRIS	Eleanor BURBAGE
Oct. 22	Stephen ANDERSON	Nancy CAHOON
Oct. 22	William HILL	Rebecca HILL
Oct. 23	Hope TAYLOR	Rachel BURNETT
Oct. 26	Andrew TULE	Susanna DICKERSON
Nov. 4	Ebben CHRISTOPHER	Polly STURGIS
Nov. 8	Samuel ENNIS	Elizabeth WRIGHT
Nov. 10	William PRICE	Jemima WILSON
Nov. 15	Curtis KELLAM	Leah DUNSTON
Nov. 20	James TUBBS	Kesiah RAIN
Nov. 22	Gilbert TOWNSEND	Nancy HANDY
Dec. 12	Matthias LINDZEY	Nancy BROWN
Dec. 17	Armel Showele HOLLOWAY	Ann Maria GODFREY
Dec. 17	Abil HICKMAN	Sally BRATTEN
Dec. 18	James COTTINGHAM	Grace COTTINGHAM
Dec. 18	Richard STURGIS	Leah GUNN
Dec. 18	Jacob WHITE	Polly WILSON
Dec. 19	Bavqilla PARKER	Sally WRIGHT
Dec. 19	John STEVENSON	Elizabeth TOWNSEND
Dec. 22	Jonathan HUDSON	Sarah Kirk TOWNSEND
Dec. 22	John MARCHANT	Nancy HUDSON
Dec. 28	Eliakem JOHNSON	Charlotte WARTERS
Dec. 31	Mills BEAVANS	Barshaba RICHARDS

1799

Jan. 7	Selby FRANKLIN	Mary B. VANDOME
Jan. 7	Levi SMACK	Andesiah CROPPER
Jan. 8	Thomas MILBOURN	Tabitha SELBY
Jan. 8	Jacob PAYNE	Elizabeth PAYNE
Jan. 9	John TURPIN	Henrietta QUINTON
Jan. 10	Edward BONNAWELL	Patzy BARN
Jan. 11	James NOBLE	Hetty JOHNSON
Jan. 15	Elijah COLEBOURN	Hetty AUSTIN
Jan. 15	Henry WHITE	Polly JONES
Jan. 16	Mager LINDSY	Hetty TOWNSEND
Jan. 11	William QUINTON	Sarah HOUSTON
Jan. 23	John BLEZARD	Leah BURBAGE
Jan. 23	Lemuel HOSHIER	Elizabeth TRUITT
Jan. 29	Isaac COTTINGHAM	Susanna LAMDEN
Jan. 29	Moses PILCHARD	Elizabeth BLADES
Feb. 6	William DENNIS	Polly DUKES
Feb. 6	Robert NAIRNE	Polly OSTON
Feb. 6	Gilliam WATERS	Sarah BOLING

1799

Date	Groom	Bride
Feb. 11	Henry WHITE	Sarah TRADER
Feb. 12	Stoutten SMITH	Elizabeth PARMORE
Feb. 13	Wm TAYLOR	Nancy STURGIS
Feb. 25	William WARWICK	Nelly FLEMMING
Feb. 26	James COLLINS	Martha DAVIS
Feb. 27	Littleton GRAY	Peggy SMITH
March 12	Purnell WILLIAMS	Peggy COLLINS
March 19	Handy BLADES	Comfort BLADES
March 22	John RADISH	Elr JOHNSON
March 26	James SELBY	Mary RANKAN
March 27	James BEAVANS	Paggy KELLAEM
April 9	Edward STEVENSON	Nancy WILLIAMS
May 3	John McDANIEL	Rachel SMALLWOOD
May 3	Esme PURNELL	DOLLY CHAILLE
May 7	William HUDSON	Peggy HUDSON
May 7	John WHITE	Polly SELBY
May 8	William STEVENSON	Nancy NAIRN
May 10	Lemuel SELBY	Sally SELBY
May 28	Stephen WALTON	Rebecca HUDSON
June 1	Thomas WEBB	Mary HOLLOWAY
June 1	Jesse POWELL	Caty WHITTINGTON
June 6	William COVINGTON	Sarah TINGLE
June 10	Zadok TOWNSEND	Mary TOWNSEND
June 11	James ROBERTSON	Rhoda CLAYWELE
June 12	Levin TOWNSEND	Nancy TOWNSEND
June 18	Jonathan HAMMOND	Patsy PEPPER
June 21	Thomas E. NUTTER	Nancy NELMO
July 5	Jonathan SHOCKLEY	Polly SAVAGE
July 9	William KENNETT	Sally RIGGAN
July 10	Archibald BAKER	Anna WAIT
July 23	John PAYNE	Sally PRUIT
July 24	John WARD	Euphame MARSHALL
July 26	Samuel GRAY	Levy HUDSON
July 26	Edward HAMMOND	Molly BAKER
Aug. 5	Matts WARREN	Elizabeth MITCHELL
Aug. 13	George WILLIS	Mary FELDMAN
Aug. 27	Levi CROPPER	Mary CAREY
Aug. 27	James HUGHES	Anna ALLEN
Aug. 29	Coulbourn LONG	Mary DAVIS
Sept. 5	William DICKERSON	Hetty GIVANS
Sept. 6	Belitha TIMMONS	Rebecca TAYLOR
Sept. 16	Peter LESTER	Annaretta TAYLOR
Oct. 1	George DIKES	Dolly EVENS
Oct. 5	Col. George DASHIEL	Sally Dennis LANE
Oct. 10	Holland SMACK	Ann WILLIAMS
Oct. 22	Frederick DAVIS	Martha HAMMOND
Oct. 28	Levi OLIVER	Polly REED
Nov. 1	Jacob ROUND	Martha RICHARDSON
Nov. 1	James PARSONS	Mary DAVIS

1799
Nov. 23	Benjamin JOHNSON	Sarah DASHIELL
Nov. 25	Elisha HILL	Elizabeth TAYLOR
Nov. 29	Levin STURGIS	Nancy TAYLOR
Dec. 3	James STURGIS	Gaty Purnell JONES
Dec. 3	James TARR	Betsey JOHNSON
Dec. 6	Elijah SMITH	Sally DAILEY
Dec. 10	Marshall SMITH	Ama TIMMONS
Dec. 16	John SMITH	Mary JONES
Dec. 17	Ephraim K. WILSON	Sally JONES
Dec. 18	William H. TAYLOR	Sally JOHNSON
Dec. 20	George CHRISTOPHER	Major WILLING
Dec. 20	George PATTERSON	Elizabeth MERRILL
Dec. 31	William HOLLAND	Sally BOWEN

1800
Jan. 3	Jonathan FOOKS	Eleanor ROACH
Jan. 7	Belitha COLLINS	Comfort IRONS
Jan. 8	John DUKES	Tabitha ALLEN
Jan. 13	Eli HUDSON	Nancy ENNIS
Jan. 14	John BEAVANS	Polly ROUNDS
Jan. 22	James TRUITT	Molly TAYLOR
Jan. 22	John VENABLES	Martha SHOCKLEY
Jan. 28	William PITTS	Sally HILL
Jan. 28	John H. HILL	Nancy JOHNSON
Feb. 6	John GOUTY	Nelly TRUITT
Feb. 26	William DALE	Sarah GODFREY
March 4	James BARRETT	Catharine LAYFIELD
March 4	Elijah CHRISTOPHER	Sarah BRATTEN
March 10	Samuel BUTLER	Nancy ANDERSON
March 10	Richard HUTSON	Polly COLLINS
March 14	Benjamin LOKEY	Polly TAYLOR
March 19	John REDDEN	Sarah SCHOOLFIELD
March 22	William LAYFIELD	Amelia DRYDEN
March 21	Francis MURRY	Hetty TULL
March 28	William Purnell BENNETT	Dolly JOHNSON
March 29	Jacob DALE	Charlotte TRUITT
April 9	Arthur PRICE	Sally BRADFORD
April 12	James DREADIN	Dolly HOLSTON
April 23	John HUTSON	Leah BRIDDLE
April 26	Thomas FASSETT	Sarah FASSETT
May 6	John RICHARDS	Mary TRUITT
May 6	Seth RUARK	Sally HENDERSON
May 10	Jesse HUDSON	Mary COLLINS
May 16	Annanias EVANS	Priscilla ADKINS
June 7	William TOWNSEND	Betsey HOOKE
June 8	Isaac LEWIS	Nanny RAIN
June 10	Elisha GIBB	Hessy MERRITT
June 20	John FASSETT	Anna BRAVARD
June 25	Peter S. CORBIN	Molly STOCKLY

1800

July 5	John BENSON	Sophia CROPPER
July 11	James ARMWOOD	Gertrude HARPER
July 15	John COLLINS	Betsey DAVIS
July 15	William DONNAWAY	Sophia WILKINS
July 25	Johnson RUARK	Sally WESTERHOUSE
July 29	Benjamin Dingley SMITH	Nancy COARD
July 29	William SMITH	Rebecca BATTS
July 30	Josiah HOPKINS	Polly BURBAGE
Aug. 13	John WILLS	Polly CHRISTOPHER
Aug. 13	Milby ATKINSON	Polly TRAYHEARN
Aug. 18	Nat WHITE	Patty GRAY
Aug. 19	Belitha GRIFFIN	Mary GALT
Sept. 9	Jno M. KNOX	Mary HENDERSON
Sept. 16	William SMITH	Polly GUNN
Sept. 16	Caleb WILLIAMS	Hetty WILLIAMS
Sept. 19	Elisha TRUITT	Comfort TAYLOR
Sept. 19	William H. HENDERSON	Tabitha DIXON
Sept. 23	David SMITH	Hannah NELSON
Sept. 23	Geo LIVINGSTON	Susannah ENNIS
Sept. 23	Benjamin SCOTT	Sally ANDERSON
Sept. 30	William MELVIN	Sarah TULL
Oct. 5	Cornelius CROPPER	Leah C. KENNETT
Oct. 17	Joseph CALLAHAN	Nancy HENDERSON
Oct. 29	Robert PURNELL	Betsey REED
Oct. 30	Robert BLAIR	Nancy RICHARDSON
Nov. 1	Jno WILLIAM	Henrietta TURPIN
Nov. 17	Samuel ENNIS	Rachel MARSHALL
Nov. 24	John MELVIN	Mary REDDEN
Nov. 25	Robert J.H. HANDY	Molly SELBY
Nov. 25	Jacob HENDERSON	Elizabeth ABBOTT
Dec. 2	John BOUNDS	Nancy NUTTER
Dec. 8	William J. HOUSTON	Sally CHAILLE
Dec. 12	Jonathan BAKER	Polly HICKMAN
Dec. 12	Soloman TULL	Esther ONLY
Dec. 15	George Howard GRAY	Sally LAW
Dec. 16	Handy JONES	Leah HAMMOND
Dec. 17	Jacob HENDERSON	Sarah BENNETT
Dec. 19	William CLARK	Mary WEBB
Dec. 22	Jesse HENDERSON	Molly White LONG
Dec. 25	Levin William COLLICK	Amy BLACK
Dec. 27	Annanias HUDSON	Luretta BENSON
Dec. 30	Coulbourne LONG	Sarah PRICE
Dec. 31	James HANDCOCK	Rachel WARD

1801

Jan. 2	John WILLIAMS	Lydia TURNER
Jan. 5	Evans MUMFORD	Nancy WELDON
Jan. 6	Samuel MILES	Sally SELBY
Jan. 6	Thomas TAYLOR	Rebecca TARR

1801

Date	Groom	Bride
Jan. 7	George VENSON	Polly DISHAROON
Jan. 7	Obediah QUILLEN	Mutey? FRANKLIN
Jan. 7	John TINGLE	Sarah MESSICK
Jan. 9	Sampson DAVIS	Patty DAVIS
Jan. 13	John CLOG	Sarah PILCHARD
Jan. 13	John BISHOP	Anna BISHOP
Jan. 17	David LONG	Sally BURNETT
Jan. 19	John HILL	Peggy GAULT
Jan. 20	Sampson BURBAGE	Leah HANDCOCK
Jan. 26	James (JARMAN)?	Rachael GIVANS
Jan. 26	Samuel DAVIS	Rachel RICHARDSON
Jan. 26	William PARKER	Hannah PARSONS
Jan. 27	John WEBB	Susanna HUDSON
Jan. 27	James HOUSTON	Mary PARRAMORE
Jan. 27	Henry COTTINGHAM	Lucretia TOWNSEND
Jan. 30	Samuel DORMAN	Margaret BIRD
Feb. 2	Littleton DAVIS	Polly BELL
Feb. 7	George PURNELL	Mary PURNELL
Feb. 20	James HOOK	Polly MUMFORD
Feb. 21	William COTTMAN	Hetty BISHOP
Feb. 27	Edward STEVENSON	Sally HOUSTON
March 3	Elijah ENNIS	Mary CHRISTOPHER
March 9	Tubman LOWE	Anne HITCH
March 20	Leonard TIMMONS	Eliza ADKINS
March 23	Henry POWELL	Hetty CROPPER
March 28	James MARSHALL	Polly STEVENSON
April 1	Samuel MERRILL	Nancy PAINE
April 2	John SMITH	Hannah JONES
April 3	Cabel TILGHMAN	Sally HALL
April 10	Devin PILCHARD	Agnes WATSON
April 14	John SMITH	Scarbourgh BENNETT
April 18	Robert M. RICHARDSON	Nancy SCHOOLFIELD
April 21	Anthony BACON	Henrietta Done CHAILLLE
April 22	James ANGAVINE	Esther JOHNSON
April 23	Riley BOWEN	Hessey WRIGHT
April 29	George JOHNSON	Polly RICHARDSON
May 8	George FOOKS	Polly FOOKS
May 18	Daniel ROWLEY	Sally Kendell BELL
May 16	John CAMRON	Polly FISHER
May 18	George BELL	Nancy MITCHELL
May 27	Timothy IRONS	Peggy BRITTINGHAM
June 15	John LANE	Sally GRAY
June 18	Peter RICHARDSON	Sally OUTTEN
June 22	Jesse HUDSON	Betsey PARKER
June 23	James BOWEN	Molly RILEY
June 26	Josiah LONG	Sarah HENDERSON
June 26	James MADDUX	Comfort SPION
June 27	John COOPER	Nancy POSTLY

1801
July	1	Milby BOWEN	Sophia CROPPER
July	7	James MARRITT	Nancy GIBBS
July	17	Sampson WTIGHT	Betsey SMITH
July	17	Charles HARRIS	Catherine STURGIS
July	26	Isaac WARREN	Sally BRADFORD
Aug.	7	Pressgrave WILLIAMS	Martha HOLLAND
Aug.	7	Moses CAREY	Betsey HILL
Aug.	7	John DRISKELL	Catherine MORRIS
Aug.	11	Benjamin BLADES	Leah BLADES
Aug.	19	Isaac RILEY	Betsey TOWNSEND
Sept.	4	John POWELL	Sally JONES
Sept.	16	Saml. BOSTON	Leah MERRILL
Sept.	18	Edward DAVIS	Betsey WALKER
Sept.	22	James H. HUTSON	Mary CROPPER
Sept.	29	Josiah HUBBEL	Polly TOWNSEND
Sept.	29	Cyre TRUITT	Fanny POWELL
Oct.	13	William RICHARD	Betsey SHOCKLEY
Oct.	13	Thomas DOROTHY	Sally ROACH
Oct.	14	James HOUSTON	Catharine DAVIS
Oct.	20	Kendall BRADFORD	Caty SMACK
Oct.	20	Charles BENNETT	Sarah PURNELL
Oct.	28	Fisher RICHARDSON	Elizabeth HOLLAND
Nov.	13	Elisha CAREY	Rhoda TIMMONS
Nov.	15	James TRIPPAND	Mary PURNELL
Nov.	17	Abel TEACKLE	Polly BRATTEN
Nov.	20	Daniel WAILES	Betsey CATHELL
Nov.	30	Sacker TAYLOR	Betsey GRAY
Dec.	6	Monze BISHOP	Zetta LEWIS
Dec.	7	John STEVENSON	Betsey WILLIAMS
Dec.	8	Elijah DAVIS	Sally SELBY
Dec.	12	Natl. BRITTINGHAM	Molly BASSETT
Dec.	12	James COLLINS	Polly PREDEAUX
Dec.	15	William WILLIS	Sarah CLOG
Dec.	15	Beauchamp CARMEAN	Hetty TRUITT
Dec.	18	Marshall HAMBLIN	Oma RICHARDSON
Dec.	23	John FREENEY	Martha BREWINGTON
Dec.	24	William CAMPBELL	Peggy FINNERY
Dec.	25	John SELBY	Rebecca JONES
Dec.	29	David PRICE	Polly NEWTON
Dec.	30	Levin HENDERSON	Nancy LAYFIELD

1802
Jan.	1	George PARSONS	Sarah BASSETT
Jan.	5	William TURNER	Rachel JONES
Jan.	8	James MURRAY	Nancy HOLLOWAY
Jan.	11	Ambrose WHITE	Peggy PERKINS
Jan.	11	Elijah STEVENSON	Esther HENDERSON
Jan.	12	William SELBY	Nancy BOWLES
Jan.	14	John STEEL	Nancy CHRISTIE

1802

Date	Groom	Bride
Jan. 18	Joseph PORTER	Catherine COULBOURNE
Jan. 20	John RICHARDS	Sally HAMMOND
Jan. 20	Kendall CROOPER	Nancy WHITE
Jan. 25	William Bell WHITE	Susanna TAYLOR
Jan. 29	Lazarus MADDUX	Rachel RIGGAN
Feb. 2	John WHITE	Elizabeth CONNER
Feb. 5	John PORTER	Rhoda CROPPER
Feb. 8	Isaac B. SCHOOLFIELD	Polly ATKINSON
Feb. 9	James KNOX	Elizabeth FASSETT
Feb. 12	Kirk GUNBY	Polly MORRIS
Feb. 13	Levin ALLEN	Patience STEVENS
Feb. 19	James FOOKS	Leah DENNIS
March 2	John BENSON	Dolly McNEILL
March 3	Joseph TOWNSEND	Mary TOWNSEND
March 3	Isaac POINTER	Hannah JARMAN
March 4	Levin STEWART	Polly PURNELL
March 5	Joshua STURGIS	Nancy CROPPER
March 8	John WALKER	Caty CROPPER
March 9	George RICHARDSON	Anna PURNELL
March 22	Obed ADDAMS	Ann KNOCK
March 26	John BRADFORD	Rachel JARMAN
April 6	Thomas SLOCOMB	Anne BOWEN
April 6	Stephen PILCHER	Ruthey BLADES
April 6	Zepheniah HOSHIER	Eleanor DENNIS
April 9	Isaac MITCHELL	Eleanor WILLIN
April 9	Henry FOUNTAIN	Betsey BENNETT
April 13	Abisha DAVIS	Patty GRAY
April 20	Isaac WALTER	Betsey GRAY
April 28	Stater TRADER	Sally LONG
May 4	James NICKSON	Polly BRATTEN
May 7	Joshua HOLLOWAY	Elizabeth ADKINS
May 8	William LEWIS	Susanna MARRETT
May 25	Edward BOWEN	Hannah DAVIS
June 4	Littleton ROBINS Jr.	Martha HORSEY
June 9	Samuel R. SMITH	Mary MARSHALL
June 25	Levi PILCHARD	Omi PILCHARD
June 26	William GIVANS	Sophia DALE
July 14	Abraham LITTLETON	Martha TIMMONS
July 17	Coventon BOOTH	Betsy BIRCH
July 17	John DAVIS	Elizabeth FISJAREL
July 19	Selby HUDSON	Peggy DAVIS
July 22	Samuel McMASTER	Sally AYERS
July 27	Thomas WRIGHT	Zebina HICKMAN
July 27	John FARRELL	Lydia QUILLEN
Aug. 3	James TOADVINE	Priscilla AUSTEN
Aug. 5	William HUDSON	Priscilla TOWNSEND
Aug. 6	Walter SIMPSON	Anna B. HANDY
Aug. 9	George HOUSTON	Anna PETTIT
Aug. 11	Fisher TAYLOR	Polly KENNETT

1802

Date	Groom	Bride
Aug. 13	Adam MOOR	Judah SMITH
Aug. 17	John GRAY	Elizabeth PPITTS
Aug. 24	John WEBB	Henrietta HUDSON
Aug. 26	Thomas POWELL	Comfort McCORMICK
Aug. 31	Moses HUDSON	Mary TOWNSEND
Aug. 31	Thomas JONES	Hesse PURNELL
Sept 10	Thomas MARSHALL	Betsey HOLLAND
Sept. 10	Barnaby HENDERSON	Betsey BOWEN
Sept. 15	William FURNIS	Nancy DALE
Sept. 22	Joshua FLEMING	Sally PORTER
Sept. 16	Isaac POYNTER	Polly HADDER
Sept. 25	Wm HAMMOND	Catherine RILEY
Sept. 29	Thomas WINDSOR	Harriett HANDY
Oct. 12	John STEVENS	Betsy M RICHARDSON
Oct. 19	Levi HENDERSON	Betsey HENDERSON
Oct. 21	Curtis HENDERSON	Lydia STEVENSON
Oct. 23	Robert CLUFF	Joanna STURGIS
Nov. 9	John S. MORRIS	Mary JONES
Nov. 12	James TULL	Polly STURGIS
Nov. 16	John JARMAN	Anna DAVIS
Nov. 19	John HUDSON of Sam	Sarah CRAFFORD
Nov. 20	John BENSON	Esther LAYFIELD
Nov. 20	Leonard HUDSON	Leah DENSTON
Nov. 20	Hannan EASHAM	Betsey STURGIS
Nov. 22	Isaac HOUSTON	Mary SCARBOURGH
Nov. 26	George BRATTEN	Betsey Washington SPENCE
Dec. 3	James Walker BAYLY(Perdeau)	Mary LAWS
Dec. 7	Robert F. BELL	Mary BRUMBLY
Dec. 14	Wheelty DENNIS	Nancy BENNETT
Dec. 15	John LOKEY	Hannah RUARK
Dec. 17	James WONNELL	Nancy CAREY
Dec. 21	Robert GIVAN	Sally HANDCOCK
Dec. 21	Hewell Nutter DIXON	Eleanor AUSTIN
Dec. 23	Joseph GILLIS	Maria T. ROBINS
Dec. 24	Eli CAMPBELL	Dolly WINGATE
Dec. 25	Thomas DAVIS	Nancy RIGGS
Dec. 30	John SAVAGE	Comfort KELLAIN
Dec. 31	Charles FOOKS	Mary NOBLE

1803

Date	Groom	Bride
Jan. 3	Daniel JONES	Nancy TOADVINE
Jan. 4	Samuel MILLS	Chole BRADFORD
Jan. 7	William BACON	Tabitha BEAVANS
Jan. 10	John DISHAROON	Elizabeth COVINGTON
Jan. 11	James PITTS	Martha BRATTEN
Jan. 11	Nehemiah CROPPER	Nancy BRITTINGHAM
Jan. 12	Belitha HOOP	Hannah HOPKINS
Jan. 12	William WATTS	Zeoprah PURNELL
Jan. 18	Jno CAUDREY Jr.	Polly OUTTEN

1803
Date	Groom	Bride
Jan. 25	John WILLIAMS	Molly HAMMOND
Jan. 25	Levin HAYMAN	Patty WALSTON
Jan. 25	Josiah COLLINS	Patty BOWEN
Jan. 26	Peter GREW	Hetty MURRAY
Jan. 31	William BOWEN	Zeporah BURBAGE
Feb. 8	William JONES	Nancy AUSTEN
Feb. 11	Belitha CHRISTOPHER	Martha POWELL
Feb. 15	John TAYLOR	Peggy WILLIAMS
Feb. 18	Wm JONES	Catharine SPIEN
Feb. 19	William DALE	Nancy P. PITTS
Feb. 22	Job ALLEN	Betsey (PUDDERY)?
Feb. 26	James JOHNSON	Mary MARTIN
March 9	Henry McJEW(?)	Peggy MORRIS
March 11	Kendall WILLIAMS	Esther BETHARD
March 11	Outten TOADVINE	Rhoda TOADVINE
March 15	Thomas M. CROPPER	Sally RICHARDSON
March 17	Wm POWELL	Sarah WEBB
March 19	Zeno POWELL	Priscilla NEWTON
March 29	Hugh GIMMELL	Jane WILSON
March 30	America RODGERS	Nancy TOWNSEND
April 5	George DAVIS	Sally COLLIER
April 15	Zedikiah BRADFORD	Tabitha BURBAGE
April 19	Levin BRADSHAW	Hannah GRAY
April 19	Matthew DORMAN	Denny TRUITT
	Jesse GUTHERY	Levina DENNIS
April 23	James McFADDEN	Rachel WATERS
April 29	Robert Houston DRYDEN	Priscilla HANDY
May 4	Elijah DORMAN	Elizabeth SHOCKLEY
May 16	Josiah DAVIS	Molly GREEN
May 17	Isaiah TOADVINE	Areada DENNIS
May 25	John T. TAYLOR	Sally VICTOR
June 6	John Kendall Hebrun PERDUE	Sally VANCE
June 7	Henry SHARPLY	Mary CAREY
June 9	Johnson HAYMAN	Esther DIKES
June 11	Elisha PURNELL	Betsey PURNELL
June 15	William COLLIER	Nancy POWELL
June 21	William GIVANS	Mary (?) BOOZEE
June 25	Pierson DICKS	Effie BROWN
June 28	Lemuel PARKER	Levina HILL
July 5	George PERDUE	Elizabeth DIXON
July 12	Kendall MERRELL	Hetty BOWEN
July 15	James FRANKLIN	Nancy FRANKLIN
July 16	William HENDERSON	Peggy BENNETT
July 20	Zadok WHELLER	Zeporah SCHOOLFIELD
July 26	David Long GRAY	Caty PENNAWELL
July 27	Booz ENNIS	Mary MARSHALL
Aug. 2	Wm MARSHALL	Dolly BISHOP
Aug. 13	Wm STAUGHERTY	Attalanta SMACK
Aug. 24	Levin HOLLAND	Amelia DAVIS

1803

Date	Groom	Bride
Aug. 25	Moses HUTT	Rachel BALLARD
Aug. 26	Milby TIMMONS	Sarah JARMAN
Sept. 9	James DALE	Elizabeth GRAVENER
Sept. 9	Belitha BURBAGE	Naomi PEPPPER
Sept. 21	Justus POYNTER	Betsey BAKER
Sept. 30	William MERRELL	Anna HENDERSON
Oct. 5	Elisha JONES	Nancy AYDELOTT
Oct. 13	James H. COLLINS	Elizabeth WONNELL
Oct. 15	Alexander MASSEY	Catherine POWELL
Oct. 26	John P. CHAILLE	Nancy DENNIS
Nov. 15	Wm. MELVIN Junr.	Betsey TOWNSEND
Nov. 19	Sewell DRYDEN	Martha COLLINS
Nov. 24	Peter TARR	Elizabeth TOWNSEND
Nov. 29	Henry DENNIS	Elizabeth SMACK
Nov. 30	John P. MARSHALL	Deborah FISHER
Dec. 2	William BASSETT	Ann Mary ADKINS
Dec. 2	Edward MORRIS	Esther LAYFIELD
Dec. 2	Matthew JONES	Frances DISHAROON
Dec. 2	Thomas PURNELL	Zeporah BRUFF
Dec. 7	John SMITH	Nancy BEAVANS
Dec. 7	Thomas PENNAWELL	Unice HUDSON
Dec. 12	William BOUNDS	Polly BRITTINGHAM
Dec. 13	John JOHNSON	Nancy DENNIS
Dec. 14	Parker SELBY	Attalanta SELBY
Dec. 19	James DISHAROON	Sarah FOOKS
Dec. 20	William WARWICK	Patty OTWELL
Dec. 20	William DRYDEN	Sally BRODWATER
Dec. 23	Thos. LITTLETON	Polly LEWIS
Dec. 23	John JOHNSON	Elizabeth HUDSON
Dec. 24	Elzey SMITH	Holland SMITH
Dec. 27	Eli HOSHIER	Patty SCHOOLFIELD
Dec. 30	Kendall WILLIAMS	Polly GRAY

1804

Date	Groom	Bride
Jan. 3	George WHITE	Sally CONNER
Jan. 4	Stephen FOMMONS	Vine LITTLETON
Jan. 10	Thomas COLLINS	Susanna ROWLEY
Jan. 11	James MITCHELL	Sally DOWNES
Jan. 13	John BRITTINGHAM	Sarah BASSETT
Jan. 13	Edward T. CROPPER	Zeporah RICHARDSON
Jan. 13	Isaac PENNEWELL	Rhoda GAULT
Jan. 17	John HUDSON	Kezzier POWELL
Jan. 17	Thomas FAIR	Catherine PARADISE
Jan. 17	Kellaem LANKFORD	Peggy PURNELL
Jan. 18	William TRUITT	Patty JOHNSON
Jan. 20	Thomas KING	Martha POWELL
Jan. 24	John JONES	Tabitha KILLAEM
Jan. 25	Whittington JONES	Elizabeth GILLETT
Jan. 25	Joseph BISHOP	Attalanta ROBINS

1804

Date	Groom	Bride
Feb. 6	Jacob BOSTON	Nancy LAYFIELD
Feb. 7	James TRAYHEARN	Sally WONNELL
Feb. 10	James FOOKS	Sabra PERDUE
Feb. 10	John DICKERSON	Polly NELSON
Feb..16	Phillip WHITE	Elizabeth DICKERSON
Feb. 18	Wm. A. CAHOON	Nancy BENSON
Feb. 23	Thos. TOWNSEND	Sophia TRUITT
March 7	John MAGEE	Betsey HUDSON
March 12	James BENNETT	Nancy MERRILL
March 13	Smith BREWINGTON	Mary Nutter DIXON
March 17	Charles BENNETT Jr.	Margaret Spence PURNELL
March 18	Handy MILLS	Margaret HARGIS
March 19	Hugh WARD	Atalanta TAYLOR
March 27	Wm BREWINGTON	Bosse ROACH
March 27	Levin Irvin FOUNTAIN	Andesiah Rebia SPENCE
March 28	Michael HUDSON	Polly OUTTEN
March 30	John BULL	Hulldey BLADES
March 31	Henry DENNIS	Rachel DUNCAN
April 4	Thomas Scott WEBB	Catherine SCHOOLFIELD
April 17	John G. JENNOR	Nancy HARRIS
April 18	John HOLLOWAY	Betsey DAVIS
April 28	Jabez STEVENSON	Betsey LANE
April 30	John WATERS	Elizabeth CORBIN
May 15	John CORBIN	Elizabeth TOWNSEND
May 21	Samuel COWLY	Comfort NEWTON
May 23	McKimmey PENNEWELL	Leah SMOCHY
May 26	Thomas BAYLY	Elizabeth WILSON
June 11	Belotha BAYNUM	Nancy PERKINS
June 12	James HALL	Polly PETTIT
June 18	Samuel TINDALL	Polly RICHARDSON
June 26	Selby WARREN	Sarah P. MARSH
June 27	James PARKER	Polly DASHIELL
July 3	John P. CHAILLE	Jane DUNCAN
July 6	Daniel FOOKS	Nancy ROBERTS
July 13	Henry T. BETHARDS	Nancy TARR
July 18	Thomas HALL	Sally BOWEN
July 18	Obadiah LATCHAM	Sarah MIERS
July 20	Wm. ADDAMS	Kittusah MILBOURN
July 30	Stouton RUARK	Molly DRISKELL
Aug. 1	Peter PARIS	Polly TAYLOR
Aug. 1	Parker DUKES	Duny BISHOP
Aug. 21	Walter WARRINGTON	Nancy TRUITT
Sept. 1	Robert HUDSON	Sarah ATKINSON
Sept. 6	William STANDFORD	Elizabeth JESTER
Sept. 13	Daniel JONES	Tabitha SMITH
Sept. 17	Joseph STEVENSON	Sarah JONES
Sept. 20	Noah REGGAN	Andasiah SMACK
Sept. 22	Joshua RICHARDSON	Betsey NICKERSON
Sept. 25	Isaac KNOX	Patty KNOX

1804

Date	Groom	Bride
Sept. 28	James DRYDEN	Sally HOPE
Oct. 1	Parker PEUZEY	Amelia RIGGAN
Oct. 17	Thos. LAYFIELD Jnr.	Priscilla BANKS
Oct. 19	Wm. TUBBS	Polly WARREN
Oct. 30	Cormo G. STEVENSON	Harriet C. HANDY
Nov. 12	John ATKINSON	Sarah DENNIS
Nov. 18	Joseph MILLER	Nancy MILLS
Nov. 20	Henry DAVIS	Nancy BRATTEN
Nov. 27	Isaac HUTSON	Sarah GIVAN
Dec. 1	Jonathan POWELL	Nancy FRANKLIN
Dec. 1	Wm POWELL	Pheuby BEAUCHAMP
Dec. 1	Littlen MUNFORD	Sally RICHARDSON
Dec. 4	Benjamin WHITE	Senah DAVIS
Dec. 11	Robert WARNOCK	Nancy REID
Dec. 12	William HOPKINS	Fanny COLLINS
Dec. 14	Gilly BUSSELLS	Priscilla BRATTEN
Dec. 19	Matthias TAPMAN	Polly TULL
Dec. 20	William TRUITT	Elizabeth GOOTTEE
Dec. 21	Warren JEFFERSON	Saborouh FOOKS

1805

Date	Groom	Bride
Jan. 1	William DAVIS	Sarah CHRISTIE
Jan. 1	William TUNNELL	Lany TARR
Jan. 1	James WARD	Lydia Donny BARNWELL
Jan. 8	Phillip SHORT	Polly STEVENSON
Jan. 8	Cabel JONES	Patty STURGIS
Jan. 9	Levin CONNER	Elizabeth WHITE
Jan. 11	Stephen TOWNSEND	Nancy WONNELL
Jan. 15	Major CLAYWELL	Thamer JONES
Jan. 15	Thomas DAVIS	Nancy TOWNSEND
Jan. 23	George TAYLOR	Nelly COLLINS
Jan. 23	Cornelius DICKERSON	Polly FINNER
Feb. 2	Levi CATHELL	Priscilla DOWNES
Feb. 6	Levi TULL	Sally TAYLOR
Feb. 6	Peter TIMMONS	Sally CAREY
Feb. 8	James BAYNUM	Holland VICTOR
Feb. 12	Samuel WILLIAMS	Ebby MILLS
Feb. 12	Nehemaih TIMMONS	Catharine CAREY
Feb. 13	Schoolfield RODNEY	Betsey PENNEWELL
Feb. 18	Thomas COX	Sally ANDERSON
Feb. 19	Wm. RENNALS	Catharine TRUITT
Feb. 20	Purnell SMACK	Molly FRANKLIN
March 1	Staphen WHITE	Rebecca TILGHMAN
March 1	Jesse DAVIS	Polly POWELL
March 1	William EASHAM	Martha RUARK
March 4	Jonah DAVIS	Sarah MARTIN
March 4	Thomas PATRICK	Betsey DAVIS
March 19	Wm HENDERSON	Catherine HENDERSON
March 20	George WOOLFE	Hetty SELBY

1805

Date	Groom	Bride
March 26	Ephraim DRYDEN	Rebecca HENDERSON
March 28	Stephen WHITE	Polly PATRICK
April 5	James DENNIS	Sarah MADDUX
April 8	Thomas BRITTINGHAM	Margaret MERRILL
April 19	Abraham GIBBS	Betsey TAYLOR
May 25	John HADDER	Hannah GRAY
May 29	John STURGIS	Polly WATERS
June 11	James BUNTING	Kitty HOUSTON
June 11	Edmund REYNOLDS	Nancy BASSETT
June 18	William MILES	Polly JOHNSON
July 3	John WILLIAMS	Comfort STURGIS
July 5	John SEARS	Rebecca TRUITT
July 5	Bassett TIMMONS	Lizy TIMMONS
July 15	Cornelius DICKERSON Jr.	Polly McNEILL
July 20	Milby PURNELL	Sally CAMRON
Aug. 2	John PATTERSON	Sally HENDERSON
Aug. 6	William DAVIS	Polly DUNCAN
Aug. 9	Zadok PURNELL	Catharine SELBY
Aug. 12	Nehemiah TRUITT	Elizabeth SMITH
Aug. 19	Staphen JACKSON	Polly BOSTON
Aug. 23	John BROWN	Catharine CLARKE
Aug. 30	Saml. BANKS	Martha BOSTON
Sept. 5	Levi HOLLAND	Peggy ATKINSON
Sept. 9	William DARBY	Naomi TRONDLE
Sept. 24	Rowland DRISKELL	Jenny AUSTEN
Sept. 25	Jesse JARMAN	Fanny CAMPBELL
Oct. 9	George DICKS	Mary HICKMAN
Oct. 9	Ralph HINMAN	Polly DRYDEN
Oct. 11	Micajah AYERS	Esther DICKERSON
Oct. 28	Micajah BRITTINGHAM	Betsey TAYLOR
Nov. 1	Cord HAZZARD	Polly TAYLOR
Nov. 12	Wm. JOHNSON	Nancy BURROUGHS
Nov. 15	John SMACK	Rebina BOSTON
Nov. 20	The Rev. Charles CUMMIN	Polly R. MORRIS
Nov. 29	Leml. BOWEN	Rhoda PORTER
Dec. 2	Stephen ADKINS	Leah ADKINS
Dec. 2	Parker COLLINS	Nancy SELBY
Dec. 4	John McNEIL	Sarah TOWNSEND
Dec. 10	John C. BACON	Amelia HOUSTON
Dec. 10	James POWELL	Nancy RIGGIN
Dec. 10	Zadok POWELL Jr.	Sarah MASSEY
Dec. 10	Frederick BALL	Harriet BACON
Dec. 14	James RILEY	Martha FRANKLIN
Dec. 14	Joseph JONES	Polly RICHARDS
Dec. 16	Samuel MILLS	Esther AYDELOTT
Dec. 17	Littleton STURGIS	Jane WILSON
Dec. 17	Thomas CAMPBELL	Leah H. CROPPER
Dec. 17	John Fountain ATKINSON	Sarah Lane DIXON
Dec. 18	John JACKSON	Nelly HAMMOND

1805			
Dec. 18		Wm BISHOP	Harriet WRIGHT
Dec. 19		Levin TOWNSEND	Tabitha SAVAGE
Dec. 23		Levi TARR	Polly JARRELL
Dec. 24		Parker DORMAN	Tabitha KELLAEM
Dec. 30		Benjamin DAVIS	Elizabeth REED
Dec. 30		James WHITE	Tenney JUSTICE

1806			
Jan. 7		Kendall PHILLIPS	Sarah HOSHIER
Jan. 8		William W. GRAY	Betsey SCARBOROUGH
Jan. 13		Eli POWELL	Betsey DYMOCK
Jan. 17		Samuel TARR	Polly AYDELOTT
Jan. 18		Jose DAVIS	Patty PARKER
Jan. 21		John PARSONS	Elizabeth DENNIS
Jan. 21		Joseph RICHARD	Sally TILGHMAN
Jan. 23		Joshua PHILLIPS	Ruth HANDCOCK
Jan. 23		Peter HALL	Betsey WILL
Jan. 25		Zadok TAYLOR	Rhoda JONES
Jan. 28		Jonathan COTTINGHAM	Elizabeth DICKERSON
Feb. 5		Major BIRD	Betsey NICHOLS
Feb. 12		Nathan HARMON	Andesiah DAVIS
Feb. 12		Benj. DENNIS	Elizabeth E.Y. PERDUE
Feb. 18		James GUNBY	Nancy ROBERTS
Feb. 19		Thomas GRAY	Charlotte GRAY
Feb. 21		George BREWINGTON	Nancy DASHIELL
Feb. 25		Thomas SNEED	Patty KELLY
Feb. 25		John TAYLOR	Betsey SNEED
March 10		Lemuel HALL	Elizabeth SELBY
March 19		John W. (?)	Henny JOHNSON
March 25		James BROADWATER	Anne TOWNSEND
April 1		Milby DUNCAN	Sally WHITE
April 1		Henry TURNER	Sally AUSTIN
April 8		Jacob ROBERTS	Hatty CAMPBELL
April 15		Handy MERRILL	Rebecca SHEPPAM
April 15		Thomas MADDUX	Ann RUARK
April 22		William ROWND	Uphamy TOWNSEND
April 23		James SNEAD	Lydia BOWEN
May 1		William DARBY	Milly REID
May 6		Thomas DALE	Betsy SMITH
May 6		James KNOX	Priscilla HUDSON
May 7		James MUMFORD	Sally STEVENSON
May 10		Ebenezer WARREN	Peggy TIMMONS
May 20		Elisha DAVIS	Sally LONG
May 24		Levin PURNELL	Elizabeth COLLICK
May 28		Elijah TINDALL	Peggy WILEY
May 29		Samuel TINDALL	Lovy COLLINS
June 2		James FASSETT	Elizabeth FASSETT
June 3		John McCOLLY	Amelia MORRIS
June 3		Richard CULVER	Polly GREEN

1806

Date	Groom	Bride
June 4	Wm. WHEELER	Leah MELVIN
June 12	Levin REGGIN	Hannah STERLING
June 13	William ROWLY	Martha TULL
June 17	Robert KERBY	Betsey FRANKLIN
June 18	John P. MARSHALL	Ann BELL
June 18	Joshua WHITE	Sally TAYLOR
June 20	Seth FOOKS	Polly DAVIS
June 20	James HOLLAND	Elizabeth H. MERRELL
June 21	John STEVENSON	Hetty EVANS
July 1	Jiles JONES	Betsey B. JOHNSON
July 2	Henry R. PRATT	Nancy FASSETT
July 2	Edward JONES	Jenett MOOR
July 22	Selby PARKER	Mary SELBY
July 23	Robert TOWNSEND	Henrietta ROACH
July 25	Henry SELBY	Tabitha OUTTEN
July 29	Caleb POWELL	Patty JONES
Aug. 1	Henry FEDDMAN	Elizabeth KELLAEM
Aug. 2	William POLK	Polly HUBBELL
Aug. 8	Coventon EWELL	Peggy DRYDEN
Aug. 12	Levi DAVIS	Nancy DAVIS
Aug. 13	William BEAVANS	Charlotte TRUITT
Aug. 19	Jonathan GARRISON	Nancy SELBY
Aug. 20	John MARSHALL	Sarah BROADWATER
Aug. 28	John PARKS	Hetty LUCAS
Aug. 30	Henry ROWLY	Catherine PAYNE
Sept. 15	William MUMFORD	Elinor FRANKLIN
Sept. 16	John RANKIN	Elizabeth PURNELL
Sept. 18	John McGRATH	Nelly NEWMAN
Sept. 30	James HOUSTON	Gertrude PARKERT
Oct. 8	Thomas MORRIS	Mary DAVIS
Oct. 8	Joseph YOUNG	Nancy BENSTON
Oct. 8	John HOUSTON	Hulda RICHARDSON
Oct. 10	Hampton LONG	Betsey HODGSON
Oct. 13	Joshua CARY	Martha BETHARDS
Oct. 14	Anderson PATTERSON	Polly MILLS
Oct. 17	William DAVIS	Anna GLASS
Oct. 28	John Henry McNEIL	Nancy DAVIS
Oct. 29	Levin CROPPER	Polly TOWNSEND
Oct. 31	James BRADFORD	Polly SPIRES
Nov. 5	Edwd LAMBDON	Nancy MERRILL
Nov. 5	Eliakem JOHNSON	Nancy TAYLOR
Nov. 5	Levin CROPPER	Catharine PORTER
Nov. 5	John SELBY Jr	Tabitha HENDERSON
Nov. 6	Jesse HUDSON	Rachel PENNEWELL
Nov. 6	George HALL	Bridget HARPER
Nov. 7	William CULLY	Polly STEVENSON
Nov. 18	William HAMMOND	Patey PRICE
Nov. 19	Michael FEDDMAN	Wealthy GILLETT
Nov. 19	William POWELL	Sophia ROBINSON

1806

Nov. 20	Rouse HARRISON	Catharine ROGERS
Nov. 25	John M. BOWHANAN	Mary HARGIS
Nov. 25	Geo. TAYLOR	Wealthy GIBBS
Nov. 25	Thos. LAYFIELD	Polly JACKSON
Nov. 25	Jesse SMITH	Ann CHRISTOPHER
Nov. 27	John CORBIN	Elinor TOWNSEND
Nov. 27	Wm. PILCHARD	Betsey WAGGERMAN
Nov. 28	Abisha HOLLOWAY	Hilda SCHOOLFIELD
Dec. 2	Anania WARREN	Polly FRANKLIN
Dec. 6	Martin RENNELS	Nancy HILL
Dec. 9	Robert TWILLEY	Tabitha DORMAN
Dec. 10	Isaac PHILLIPS	Betsey BRITTINGHAM
Dec. 15	Benjamin BENNETT	Polly ROWLY
Dec. 15	William MURRAY	Comfort Rackliffe DAVIS
Dec. 18	Isaac AYERS	Priscilla STEVENSON
Dec. 19	Josiah CHATHAM	Alice CAUSEY
Dec. 23	Caleb WEEKS	Harrett DUER
Dec. 29	Major MARCINDER	Elizabeth HADDEN
Dec. 30	James (?)	Mary GRAY
Dec. 30	John WILKENSON	Betsey BOWEN

1807

Jan. 7	Josiah BOWEN	Gertrude CROPPER
Jan. 6	Kendall HOLLAND	Martha WILLIAMS
Jan. 10	Nehemiah TINDALL	Nancy TOWNSEND
Jan. 15	William PARKER	Comfort PARKER
Jan. 14	Joseph NICHOLSON	Hannah Cottingham BRITTINGHAM
Jan. 16	James STURGIS	Polly REID
Jan. 16	Patrick CAUSEY	Polly CROPPER
Jan. 16	John HOUSTON	Rachel TUNNELL
Jan. 19	James TULL	Sally MASSEY
Jan. 23	Stephen CHAILLE	Betsey JONES
Jan. 26	Patrick WATERS	Tabitha TRAYHEARN
Jan. 26	Purnell HUDSON	Peggy STURGIS
Jan. 26	Witty BOWEN	Delilah SELBY
Jan. 27	Ebenezer BRATTEN	Comfort BETTS
Jan. 27	William HUBBELL	Deriah L. (?)
Jan. 29	Robert JOHNSON	Polly BRADSHAW
Feb. 3	Purnell BRITTINGHAM	Nancy BISHOP
Feb. 6	Richard STURGIS	Martha TRAYHEARN
Feb. 10	Robert TRUITT	Polly BISHOP
Feb. 13	Ebenezer DRISKELL	Leah SHOCKLEY
Feb. 14	Ananias WARREN	Elizabeth TRUITT
Feb. 14	George TRUITT	Sally TIMMONS
Feb. 17	Major HUDSON	Betsey JOHNSON
Feb. 18	Jesse ENNIS	Sally TRAYHEARN
Feb. 18	John POWELL	Betsey DAVIS
Feb. 18	Willizm RICHARDS	Betsey HOZIER
Feb. 21	John BONAWILL	Nancy HANDCOCK

1807

Date	Groom	Bride
Feb. 24	Josiah HICKMAN	Nancy DUNCAN
Feb. 27	John REDISH	Eleanor DAVIS
March 10	John FISHER	Peggy TAYLOR
March 16	Edward BRIDDELL	Nancy BELL
March 17	Robert McALLEN	Rebecca SCHOOLFIELD
March 18	Coventon ROWLEY	Nancy JONES
March 25	Lowdoin CHRISTOPHER	Frankey BREWINGTON
March 27	Benjamin SHOCKLEY	Sally REDDISH
March 30	John JOHNSON	Elizabeth BENNETT
March 31	Levi POWELL	Sally McALLEN
March 31	Henry BURBAGE	Patty HUDSON
April 1	Ebenezer POWELL	Caty RICHARDS
April 1	Jacob PAYNE	Nancy WAGAMAN
April 8	William COSTON	Polley HALL
	Bable MONGAR	Nancy WILSON
	George JOHNSON	Molly BISHOP
April 13	John TUBBS	Elizabeth BRIMER
April 13	John PREDEAUX	Sally HADDER
April 13	John LAMBERSON	Esther TOWNSEND
April 14	James BANUM	Catharine DAVIS
April	Henry COTTINGHAM	Susanna WHITE
April	John DASHIELL	Euphamy WARD
April 21	Stephen ALLEN	Leah AYDELOTT
April 27	Henry CLUFF	Sally JUSTON
April 27	James BROWN	Sally EVANS
April 28	Elijah BENSTON	Milly WHITE
May 1	John LAMBDON	Sally WARNER
May 13	Thomas P. RACKCLIFFE	Sarah FASSETT
May 14	John TRUITT	Narcesia PURNELL
	Joshua ATKINSON	Nancy LANE
May 19	John H. WINDER	Comfort Q. GORE
May 19	Zadok TOWNSEND	Tabitha DORMAN
May 23	Jesse GRAY	Catherine TUBBS
May 26	Stephen TAYLOR	Nancy STEVENSON
May 28	Thomas BARNES	Sarah ATKINSON
May 28	Mitchell REID	Mary TARR
June 3	Levin POWELL	Nancy RIGGAN
June 10	Isaac LAYFIELD	Rachel BENSTON
June 23	James DRYDEN	Nancy DRYDEN
June 25	Thomas BENSTON	Tabitha BRITTINGHAM
June 25	John McFADDEN	Mary KILLIAM
June 26	John SILVERTHORN	Mary TUNNELL
June 29	Isaac BENSTON	Polly ADAMS
July 7	George PERKINS	Charlotte TIMMONS
July 15	Kendall TUBS	Margaret CAHOON
July 18	Thomas TARR	Polly HADDEN
July 29	Lankford PUZEY	Rose TAYLOR
July 29	John JONES	Betsey SMACK
July 31	William WILLIAMS	Drucilla DUNKIN

1807

Date	Groom	Bride
Aug. 11	Samuel WILLIAMS	Peggy STURGIS
Aug. 14	Matthew JONES	Nancy CATHELL
Aug. 18	John GODFREY	Polly DAVIS
Aug. 20	Jarman TAYLOR	Polly MELVIN
Aug. 21	William NEWTON	Susanna DICKERSON
Aug. 25	William ROWLEY	Esther COLLINS
Aug. 26	James MILLER	Sally FRANKLIN
Sept. 1	Peter SMULLEN	Sally FOOKS
Sept. 2	Stuart WILLIAMSOM	Zepporah P. FASSETT
Sept. 15	Affradazy JOHNSON	Elizabeth HAYMAN
Sept. 15	Isaac Ironshire AYERS	Mary HILL
Sept. 21	Isaac BRIDDLE	Nancy COLLINS
Oct. 14	Silas DAVIS	Sally HENDERSON
Oct. 16	John R. TURNER	Vienna SCARBOROUGH
Oct. 20	John TAYLOR	Polly POWELL
Oct. 21	William MARSHALL	Margaret BURKMASTER
Oct. 23	Isaac COLLINS	Nancy RUARK
Nov. 3	Handy HANDOCK	Polly FURNISS
Nov. 4	Stephen Pope PILCHARD	Sally WATSON
Nov. 5	Thomas BRITTINGHAM	Nancy LONG
Nov. 5	Parker PURNELL	Charlotte DUKES
Nov. 20	William RICHARDSON	Elinor STURGIS
Nov. 24	Hezekiel TAYLOR	Eleanor SMITH
Dec. 5	Joseph SCOTT	Mary GUNBY
Dec. 9	Isaac SELBY	Charlotte JONES
Dec. 16	George BONNAWELL	Betsey PAYNE
Dec. 21	Schoolfield LAMBERSON	Elizabeth GAULT
Dec. 24	Stewart WILLIAMS	Nancy BETHARDS
Dec. 25	William DODD	Catherine TULL
Dec. 26	William GARDNER	Elizabeth WHITE
Dec. 27	Robert STEVENSON	Edy STEVENSON
Dec. 30	Thomas WALKENS	Elipher MASSEY

1808

Date	Groom	Bride
Jan. 4	Isaac JOHNSON	Mary COARD
Jan. 4	Peter EVANS	Elizabeth COARD
Jan. 4	Jacob COFFIN	Peggy TAYLOR
Jan. 5	Isaiah HENDERSON	Susanah COTTINGHAM
Jan. 5	Selby HUDSON	Elizabeth RICHARDSON
Jan. 14	Arraham MOORE	Patty STURGIS
Jan. 15	Joseph MELSON	Rachel FOOKS
Jan. 16	Edward DAVIS	Polly CHRISTIE
Jan. 18	Ayers MASON	Mary AYDELOTT
Jan. 20	John MUMFORD	Patty HADDER
Jan. 21	Purnell JOHNSON	Sally RICHARDSON
Jan. 23	Peter PARKER	Sally JOHNSON
Jan. 25	Benjamin FRANKLIN	Sally POWELL
Jan. 29	Joseph STEVENSON	Mary SMITH
Jan. 30	Severn GUTHERY	Sarah ROWLEY

1808

Jan. 30	Alexander McALLEN	Betty KELLAEM
Feb. 2	James DALE	Mary BAKER
Feb. 2	James RANKIN	Peggy TRUITT
Feb. 4	Luke TOWNSEND	Barshaby BEVANS
Feb. 4	John BREWINGTON	Sally EASHUM
Feb. 12	Elijah TOWNSEND	Susanna PILCHARD
Feb. 16	Zedekiah SMACK	Martha DAVIS
Feb. 16	Parker DUKES	Betsy BENNETT
Feb. 18	Jeremiah MORRIS	Milly FRENEA
Feb. 19	John DUKES	Rebecca TAYLOR
Feb. 19	Schoolfield BRADFORD	Elizabeth DAVIS
Feb. 28	Thomas WHEALTON	Polly GIVANS
March 2	David BANKS	Sarah HOLLAND
March 2	William TOWNSEND	Catherine CAHOON
March 9	John BONNAWELL	Eliza ROBINS
March 11	James TOWNSEND	Esther MERRILL
March 14	Bagwell MASON	Elizabeth TARR
March 16	Levi RICHARDSON	Polly JOHNSON
April 5	John DALE	Nancy POWELL
April 13	Levin WILSON	Lucretia RIGGAN
April 27	William LANE	Elizabeth BEAUCHAMP
April 28	James TRUITT	Andesiah MORRIS
April 28	Caleb MORRIS	Dolly PURNELL
May 2	John CORBIN	Molly CORBIN
May 2	Henry DICKERSON	Nancy BARNES
May 17	Jiles COPES	Matilda REED
May 26	George CHRISTOPHER	Delilah Harriet AUSTEN
June 8	Burton BRADFORD	Charlotte HENDERSON
June 21	James BREVARD	Nancy FASSITT
June 27	Joseph DAVIS	Polly HOLLAND
June 28	George Teackle GREEN	Whealthy TAYLOR
July 5	Moses DAVIS	Hetty MARSH
July 9	Lemuel WATTER	Betsey WILKINS
July 11	Nathaniel WHAYLY	Nancy BRADFORD
July 12	James HAYS	Polly TAYLOR
July 12	John SHELTON	Nancy SMITH
July 26	James JONES	Polly N. JOHNSON
Aug. 1	Jesse CROPPER	Nancy GREEN
Aug. 9	John BRUMBLY	Betsy McGEE
Aug. 10	Collins EASHUM	Molly BEAVANS
Sept. 9	Jonathan CAREY	Rebecca TIMMONS
Sept. 13	Sampson DAVIS	Nancy BOWEN
Sept. 21	Lemuel TOWNSEND	Molly CORBIN
Sept. 21	Lemuel BRITTINGHAM	Henny DIXON
Sept. 22	Evans HUDSON	Nancy RICHARDSON
Sept. 29	Benjamin HAMMOND	Nancy ENNIS
Oct. 3	John EMBERSON	Sarah McNEILL
Oct. 10	Jonathan PARSONS	Betsy PARKER
Oct. 12	Edmund GLADDEN	Betsey WATSON

1808
Oct. 12	Purnell JOHNSON	Sally SHOCKLY
Oct. 17	Samuel JOHNSON	Luritta HUDSON
Oct. 19	John DALE	Nancy GREEN
Oct. 21	William WHITE	Prissy BARNES
Oct. 24	Ezekial RUARK	Sally EASHUM
Oct. 26	Severn FITCHET	Molly SHAVELL
Oct. 29	Jesse MUMFORD	Sarah SHOWELL
Nov. 1	George TRUITT	Martha PURNELL
Nov. 2	James TRUITT	Elizabeth BEAVANS
Nov. 2	John ADKINS	Mary SHOCKLY
Nov. 17	Amos TRUITT	Comfort JOHNSON
Nov. 22	Peter HOLLAND	Nancy JONES
Dec. 2	Josiah HENDERSON	Hannah BENSON
Dec. 5	David CATHELL	Martha HAYMAN
Dec. 6	Elijah C. PERDUE	Alse TOADVINE
Dec. 8	Major SELBY	Hetty COTTINGHAM
Dec. 13	Purnell MASSEY	Nancy HOLLOWAY
Dec. 13	Levi HENDERSON	Jemima KELLIAM
Dec. 13	Elijah M. DALE	Sally PURNELL
Dec. 14	John B. SLEMMONS	Polly WILSON
Dec. 20	Benjamin DENNIS	Priscilla TOWNSEND
Dec. 22	James ARMWOOD	Effy ROBERTS
Dec. 23	Thomas TURNER	Patience HILL
Dec. 23	John ESHAM	Caty MOORE
Dec. 26	Samuel PARSONS	Viny HOSHIER
Dec. 28	James KNOX	Sally HUDSON
Dec. 30	Warrington DAVIS	Letta KILBY

1809
Jan. 3	Henry CLOGG	CADY BEVANS
Jan. 3	Peter ROBERTS	Sally DYER
Jan. 5	William DRYDEN	Nancy NEWTON
Jan. 9	James TOWNSEND	Catherine DAVIS
Jan. 10	Henry BENNETT	Priscilla HOUSTON
Jan. 17	Purnell TAYLOR	Sally SELBY
Jan. 18	William TULL	Sophia HOLLOWAY
Jan. 24	James Walker MELVIN	Esther TAYLOR
Jan. 27	John BRASHIER	Elizabeth SLAUGHTERY
Jan. 28	Joshua CHAPMAN	Rebecca ELLIS
Feb. 8	James PITTS	Nancy F. TINGLE
Feb. 18	James HITCHENS	Nancy POWELL
Feb. 21	Nathan WILLIAMS	Hessey WILKINS
Feb. 21	Arthur McALLEN	Nancy GUNN
March 7	Adam HOLLOWAY	Esther BAKER
March 10	John STEVENS	Nancy VATOPE
March 11	George HALL	Rebecca PORTER
March 16	William MORGAN	Nancy MITCHELL
March 17	Fleety S. HOESKINS	Frances TOWNSEND
March 23	Lemuel HENDERSON	Charlotty PURNELL

1809

Date	Groom	Bride
March 28	Eby WARREN	Nancy BRADORD
April 3	Aaron MEZICK	Sarah DISHAROON
April 4	William BRATTEN	Pattey SMITH
April 5	William HARPER	Sally BISHOP
April 5	Thomas B. ARLINGTON	Elizabeth SIMPSON
April 11	Elijah CHENEY	Anna LEWIS
April 19	Daniel HARMON	Comfort HOLLOCK
April 21	Robert EGNEW	Peggy TOWNSEND
May 2	John HUDSON	Mary BONNAWELL
May 5	John HOOK	Sally GORNELL
May 9	George GIVANS	Nancy JOHNSON
May 17	Seth SMITH	Letty SMITH
May 22	Elijah MASON	Elizabeth HOWARD
May 23	Henry WATTS	Henny MITCHELL
May 24	Perry BECKETS	Caty TEAGUE
June 8	Edward BROUGHTON	Mary R. MILLS
June 17	Zadok TRUITT	Zepporah MORRIS
June 23	John W. B. PARSONS	Nancy NICHOLSON
June 30	William MILLS	Mary HICKMAN
July 6	John DASHIELLS Jr.	Amelia DUNCAN
July 15	George TIMMONS	Hetty BEATHARD
July 16	Thomas DORMAN	Susanah TOWNSEND
July 19	Peter EVANS	Polly PORTER
July 22	James POWELL	Comfort HEATH
July 25	James BUSSELLS	Nancy NEWMAN
Aug. 1	Ephraim DYKES	Betsey DASHIELL
Aug. 1	James LAMBDON	Hetty MERRILL
Aug. 10	John BELL	Polly GIVAN
Aug. 11	John YOUNG	Nancy KILLIAM
Aug. 15	Parker WONNELL	Sarah NEWTON
Aug. 16	Wrixon LINCH	Leah HUDSON
Aug. 21	John LONG	Polly HOPKINS
Sept. 1	Nathaniel BEVANS	Eleanor BRADFORD
Sept. 7	Goldsborough BLADES	Nancy TAYLOR
Sept. 12	Robert JOHNSON	Elizabeth GAULT
Sept. 13	John LOCKMAN	Tabitha JONES
Sept. 19	Isaac BRITTINGHAM	Caty SLAUGHTERY
Sept. 27	William SMITH	Mary MURPHY
Oct. 10	Robert HUDSON	Margaret BRATTEN
Oct. 10	Elias POINTER	Amelia HOPKINS
Oct. 10	Huet N. DIXON	Delila FOOKS
Oct. 12	James RUARK	Sally HUDSON
Oct. 18	George BRITTINGHAM	Elizabeth BRITTINGHAM
Oct. 26	Seth FOOKS	Martha PERDUE
Oct. 26	Robert JOYNES	Polly HEATH
Oct. 26	William SELBY	Leah JOHNSON
Oct. 31	Edward HUDSON	Gertrude HENDERSON
Oct. 31	John NOBLE	Hollday MORRIS
Nov. 1	James SMASHY	Arralanta PENNEWELL

1809
Date	Groom	Bride
Nov. 18	John SHOCKLY	Eleanor DIXON
Nov. 28	Edward DAVIS	Nancy PORTER
Dec. 1	William B. BELL	Mary HORSEY
Dec. 8	Levin TYLOR	Susan WARD
Dec. 9	William WHITE	Henretta RANDALL
Dec. 12	Gedion BENSON	Elizabeth WHITE
Dec. 19	James GRAY	Polly BURROUGHS
Dec. 19	Kendall PATEY	Mary DYERS
Dec. 19	Jacob BOSTON	Narcissa HOPE
Dec. 19	Staphen RILEY	Mary O. PURNELL
Dec. 21	John JONES	Elizabeth JONES
Dec. 29	Josiah POPE	Leah RIGGAN

1810
Date	Groom	Bride
Jan. 1	Willaim BAYNUM	Betsey BRITTINGHAM
Jan. 4	William HANDCOCK	Sally JONES
Jan. 4	George RICHARDSON	Sally BRATTEN
Jan. 5	William JONES	Mary DAVIS
Jan. 17	Abraham MOORE	Sally COTTINGHAM
Jan. 17	William WATERFIELD	Patsey PRICE
Jan. 18	James RIGGAN	Nancy RIGGAN
Jan. 23	Mordica TRUITT	Caty HADDER
Jan. 24	Joseph RICHARDSON	Polly JOHNSON
Jan. 24	Jesse JONES	Rachel CROPPER
Jan. 25	Thomas GORDY	Hetty HEARN
Jan. 30	William PAYNE	Eleanor PAYNE
Jan. 31	Robert WEBB	Hulda BOWIN
Feb. 5	James DEVERIX	Rachel ENNIS
Feb. 12	William LISTER	Elizabeth JOHNSON
Feb. 13	William HENDERSON	Martha ESHAM
Feb. 21	Purnell PENNIWELL	Lovey HUDSON
Feb. 22	Levin BRAISHER	Nancy HITCHEN
Feb. 22	Saml HANDY	Priscilla HANDY
March 1	Thomas WHITE	Eleanor NAIRNE
March 7	William RILEY	Nancy HOLLAND
March 15	William PARKER	Henretta PARKER
March 30	Josiah COLBOURN	Margaret CHAILLE
April 3	Isaac MATTHEWS	Polly HOPKINS
April 4	Dymock MITCHELL	Polly SAVAGE
April 10	John P. SELMAKER	Eleanor MERRILL
April 12	John COLE	Sally COLLIER
April 17	Peter STURGIS	Betsey DUKES
April 24	Levi BALL	Hannah MORRISON
April 26	James HEARN	Ann TOWNSEND
May 1	Peter SCOTT	Mary SAMPSON
May 8	John RICHARDSON	Elizabeth GIVANS
May 10	Johnson HILL	Prisse WILLIS
May 15	Soloman DAVIS	Leah SCOTT
May 15	William F. SELBY	Gertrude HENRY

1810

Date	Groom	Bride
May 22	Moses PURNELL	Charlotte MADDUX
May 23	William MILBOURN	Nancy TREHEARN
May 28	Upshur MASON	Rachel JONES
June 1	Edward GEE	Nancy FLOYED
June 5	James MUMFORD	Peggy TAYLOR
June 5	Levin MILLS	Leah BOSTON
June 7	Zadok HOOK	Mary HOSHIER
June 8	John FLOYD	Betsey STURGIS
June 9	Peter WHITE	Priscilla STURGIS
June 21	James DENNIS	Sally HINDMAN
June 22	Joseph HOLLOWAY	Hetty HOLLOWAY
June 26	West WATSON	Betsey ELLIS
June 30	Isaac P. SMITH	Margaret HANDY
July 2	James GODFREY	Nancy ROAN
July 7	William ATKINSON	Elizabeth DEMIS
July 9	Levin TULL	Susan MAY
July 9	John TOADVINE	Mary HAYMAN
July 12	Jeremiah MEZICK	Peggy GIVANS
July 14	William TOWNSEND	Hannah HUGHES
July 31	Richard FREENA	Peggy E. NELSON
Aug. 2	James BENNETT	Sally MITCHELL
Aug. 10	John JONES	Zepporah DAVIS
Aug. 14	David TRUITT	Rhoda PETTITT
Aug. 17	John HOSHIER	Rachel RICHARD
Aug. 21	David MUMFORD	Molly TRUITT
Aug. 22	William MITCHELL	Peggy HALL
Aug. 22	John SCOTT	Polly BOWEN
Sept 5	Phillip SHORT	Elizabeth PURNELL
Sept. 5	Thomas SELBY	Rachel BRIDDLE
Sept. 11	William CLAYWELL	Sally CLAYWELL
Sept. 11	Turner DAVIS	Milley PURNELL
Sept. 12	Francis ROSSE	Elizabeth WEST
Sept. 14	Joshua LEONARD	Betsey PARKER
Sept. 14	Eleazer JOHNSON	Nancy NOBLE
Sept. 15	John GIBBS	Roasanna NOBLE
Sept. 18	Jesse EVANS	Jane GIBBS
Oct. 2	Saml TWIG	Anna TILGHMAN
Oct. 4	Stephen TIMMONS	Rebecca TIMMONS
Oct. 9	Michael DYKES	Nancy BENSTON
Oct. 11	George CONNER	Sally MERRILL
Oct. 16	Edward BOWLES	Nancy HADDER
Oct. 23	Thomas HARGIS	Elizabeth MILLS
Oct. 23	John SELBY Jr	Priscilla BENNETT
Oct. 26	William BRADFORD	Nelly ADKINS
Nov. 2	Benjamin DENNIS	Elizabeth QUINTON
Nov. 13	William MATTHEWS	Lanta PRUITT
Nov. 20	William HUDSON	Hetty HUDSON
Nov. 21	James HUDSON	Sally TURNER

1810
Nov. 27	Gillitt TAYLOR	Batsy TARR
Nov. 27	Lemuel TIMMONS	Molly SMITH
Nov. 27	Charles DASHIELL	Jane DORMAN
Dec. 1	James MORRIS	Polly POLLITT
Dec. 7	John JONES	Nancy HARGES
Dec. 11	Benjamin BRUMBLY	Sophia PARKER
Dec. 12	Jesse POWELL	Comfort TRUITT
Dec. 12	James BLADES	Hesse MIDDLETON
Dec. 13	Samuel HOWARD	Polly JUSTICE
Dec. 17	Joshua TOWNSEND	Molly SMACK
Dec. 18	Edward BROUGHTON	Sally PARKER
Dec. 18	Robert PITTS	Sally SILVERTHORN
Dec. 19	Puzey REGGAN	Elizabeth CHETTAM
Dec. 25	McKemmy BURBAGE	Molly GRAY
Dec. 25	Frederick CONNER	Anna BEVANS
Dec. 26	Joshua DRYDEN	Anna TOWNSEND
Dec. 27	James DIXON	Hulda HUDSON
Dec. 28	Shadrack BAKER	Leah WHEELER
Dec. 29	Levin M. BENSON	Margaret C. LONG
Dec. 29	Robert LAYFIELD	Jane LAYFIELD

1811
Jan. 1	Elijah ENNIS	Eliza TOADVINE
Jan. 3	William CORBIN	Elizabeth BOZMAN
Jan. 5	William W. BENSON	Gertrude A. HUDSON
Jan. 8	Eyre TRUITT	Sarah WILLIAMS
Jan. 8	Joshua HOLLOWAY	Jane WILDGOOSE
Jan. 8	William REDDISH	Nancy LEVINGSTON
Jan. 8	Charles WARE	Henny WHERLOW
Jan. 8	Robert TRUITT	Polly BENNETT
Jan. 9	George S. GUNBY	Mary King HANDY
Jan. 9	John Selby (of Dan)	Polly SELBY
Jan. 15	James SELBY	Mary COTTINGHAM
Jan. 15	Levin POWELL	Sally TARR
Jan. 28	James Bradford	Sarah H. TARR
Jan. 29	James GRAY	Nancy LEWIS
Jan. 31	Keely BUDD	Peggy WEST
Feb. 4	John RICHARDSON	Betsy SHOCKLY
Feb. 5	Robert BAKER	Hetty LONDON
Feb. 9	Abraham ENOS	Nancy BLAIR
Feb. 13	Asa BELL	Hetty PETTIT
Feb. 16	Daniel FOOKS	Nancy CAREY
Feb. 21	John BELL	Maria TREHEARN
Feb, 21	Purnell TOADVINE	Zepporah FOOKS
Feb. 27	Peter TRUITT	Elizabeth BRADFORD
March 1	Rowland BEVANS Jr. —	Priscilla SELBY
March 5	Lemuel P. SPENCE	Eliza A.A. PREADEAUX
March 8	Robert JOHNSON	Molly JOHNSON
March 9	James KNOX	Chloe MILLS

1811			
March	12	Joshua SHOCKLY	Polly RICHARDSON
March	16	Jesse CROPPER	Sally RILEY
March	18	Darius CRUFF	Charlotte GRAY
April	8	Stephen HARGIS	Nancy MILLS
April	10	Cyrus TREHEARN	Mary GIBBS
April	17	Thomas LINTON	Hannah YOUNG
April	18	Samuel TARR	Nancy JONES
April	25	Alexander LOWE	Nancy DIXON
April	26	Benjamin POWELL	Sarah WARRINGTON
May	4	John TIMMONS	Rebecca FRANKLIN
May	7	John CAMMERON	Ann TINDALL
May	27	William WILLIANS	Sally DUNCAN
May	29	Josiah BRATTEN	Margaret HUDSON
May	29	Peter FRANKLIN	Ann HENRY
May	31	George ROBERTSON	Gede KING
June	11	Jesse DEAR	Euphamy PURNELL
June	13	John BRIDDELL	Sally SHOCKLEY
June	25	Joshua HUDSON	Mary MUMFORD
June	27	John SHOCKLEY	Sally DENNIS
July	8	Jesse POWELL	Elizabeth DORMAN
July	18	Scarborugh TUNNELL	Nancy ROWLEY
Aug.	5	William CLOGG	Nelly SCOTT
Aug.	7	William CROPPER	Elizabeth MACKEY
Aug.	10	Stacey HAILES	Rachel REED
Aug.	13	John DUFFIELD	Sarah HANDY
Aug.	13	William BALL	Sarah STEVENSON
Aug.	14	Benjamin DRISKELL	Sarah ENNIS
Aug.	17	Samuel McMASTER	Ann B. MERRILL
Aug.	20	Thomas WILLIS	Polly POPE
Aug.	28	George DRUMMOND	Sally LILLISTON
Aug.	29	William SEYMOUR	Isabella BOWMAN
Sept.	3	John LINDALL	Sally GRAY
Sept.	3	Charles PARKER	Amelia SELBY
Sept.	5	Francis CHERREX	Polly PRICE
Sept.	10	Major WATERS	Sarah HARMON
Sept.	11	Edward KNOX	Polly TRAYHEARN
Sept.	16	Ceasar MORRIS	Tabitha DUFFEY
Sept.	18	William WHEELER	Nancy MELVIN
Sept.	18	Isaac EVANS	Andasiah FRANKLIN
Sept.	24	George LANDING	Elizabeth TULL
Oct.	8	William WHITTINGHAM	Sarah Catharine WHITE
Oct.	18	John BALL	Leah CAMPBELL
Oct,	21	James POWELL	Mary WONNELL
Oct.	23	Josiah HICKMAN	Henny BOWEN
Oct.	29	James FURNISS	Sarah C. WILLIAMS
Oct.	29	William HILL	Nancy ROCK
Oct.	29	Lambert AYRES	Nancy RICHARDSON
Oct.	29	Parker LUCAS	Hetty MERRILL
Nov.	5	Robert J. HENRY	Mary MITCHELL

1811
Nov. 7	David FARLOW	Elizabeth PARSONS
Nov. 13	Peter JONES	Rosey O. JONES
Nov. 14	John DUREY	Hetty TRUITT
Nov. 19	Ephraim OWENS	Eleanor TOADVINE
Nov. 26	Kendall WEST	Martha MILLER
Nov. 27	Samuel TALBOT	Hetty QUINTON
Nov. 28	Levin MORRIS	Nancy POLLITT
Dec. 7	John PENNEWILL	Ann Mills PAYDEN
Dec. 10	John DENNY	Matilda MARSHALL
Dec. 10	Mitchell GRAY	Sarah DAVIS
Dec. 10	George SELBY	Rosanna BARNES
Dec. 17	William CLARK	Nancy MILLS
Dec. 17	John AYDELOTT	Margaret TARR
Dec. 18	Stephen HILL	Sally STURGIS
Dec. 25	James TRINDELL	Charlotte ESHAM
Dec. 25	Joseph WILKINS	Mary CAREY
Dec. 26	Isaac PORTER	Letitia BISHOP
Dec. 26	Purnell HILL	Nancy MARRETT
Dec. 28	Jacob BELL	Elizabeth BUDD
Dec. 30	William BARRET	Sally FROST
Dec. 30	William CROPPER	Rachel WALLOP

1812
Jan. 3	James PARSONS	Comfort JONES
Jan. 11	William ROWND	Sarah SCHOOLFIELD
Jan. 13	Constant D. STANFORD	Tanpy DISHAROON
Jan. 14	John B. WILLIAMS	Nancy HOLLAND
Jan. 15	Nathan POWDERS	Rachel HARMON
Jan. 15	Joshua GIVANS	Henny DAVIS
Jan. 15	William AYDELOTT	Hetty LINZEY
Jan. 16	Joseph TRUITT	Anna WALSTON
Jan. 21	Joshua PAYNE	Martha AYDELOTT
Jan. 23	Justice SMORHEY?	Polly BURBAGE
Jan. 23	Nathaniel McNATT	Margaret BURBAGE
Jan. 28	Henry GRIFFIN	Polly CAREY
Jan. 29	Thomas CUNNAN	Lydia D. WARD
Jan. 30	James TILGHMAN	Nancy COTTINGHAM
Jan. 30	Hamilton BAYLY	Betsey DRYDEN
Feb. 10	Aaron GORDY	Nelly TOADVINE
Feb. 11	George NELSON	Mary Bell STURGIS
Feb. 12	Ephraim K. WILSON	Ann B. GUNBY
Feb. 22	William DALBY	Betsey STANDFORD
Feb. 24	John ATKINSON	Mary ALLEN
Feb. 24	Charles TARR	Sally SPENCER
Feb. 25	Thomas PURNELL	Mary C. EVANS
Feb. 26	William ROSSE	Nancy BLADES
March 3	Sampson ADKINS	Rachel BASSETT
March 3	Hugh M. STEVENSON	Betsey BRITTINGHAM
March 18	William WELBOURN	Sally DUER

1812

Date	Groom	Bride
March 19	John JOHNSON	Betsey BISHOP
March 23	Jacob EVANS	Catharine BRATTEN
March 24	Levi PORTER	Sarah TAYLOR
March 28	Isaac CANNON	Sally FOOKS
April 1	Frederick CONNER	Mary BEVANS
April 14	John AYDELOTT	Scarbourgh HENDERSON
April 16	William SCHOOLFIELD	Esther TILGHMAN
April 20	Jehu ADKINS	Pressey PARKER
April 21	Charles MASON	Polly WARNER
May 7	Horace M. NEWTON	Tabitha S. WEST
May 29	Benjamin RICHARDS	Martha HOSIER
June 2	William BRITTINGHAM	Nelly PARKER
June 12	James MARNER	Leah HENDERSON
June 27	Azariah PURNELL	Susan PURNELL
June 29	James H. HANDY	Maria A.P. GILLIS
July 9	John CLARK	Henrietta LANKFORD
July 9	Jacob WARD	Alice ROBERTS
July 21	Purnell PORTER	Nancy HAMMOND
July 21	William DAVIS	Mary MORRIS
July 21	Rownds DAVIS	Nancy SMACK
July 29	Henry WHITE	Susan COSTEN
Aug. 9	Matthew MOORE	Andashiah TIMMONS
Sept. 1	Stephen BRITTINGHAM	Hetty POWELL
Sept. 1	Eli BLADES	Sally PILCHARD
Sept. 1	Walty JONES	Martha TRUITT
Sept. 15	Thos PURNELL (Of Thos)	Charlotte COLLINS
Sept. 22	Wm JONES	Anna SELBY
Sept. 23	Elias BROADWATER	Charlotte MERRILL
Sept. 29	Azariah ADKINS	Betsey TOWNSEND
Oct. 3	Samuel ESHAM	Esther FISHER
Oct. 7	Levin WALSTON	Sally B. ADKINS
Oct. 17	William COTTINGHAM	Eleanor TRUITT
Oct. 26	Thomas JONES	Mary TRUITT
Nov. 3	Elijah BUNTING	Sarah JENKINS
Nov. 3	Thomas MELVIN	Sophia WILKINSON
Nov. 12	Peter AYDELOTT	Grace NELSON
Nov. 28	William HENDERSON	Polly TAYLOR
Nov. 31	Isaac S. JOHNSON	Susan COTTINGHAM
Dec. 1	Elijah BURNETT	Catharine DAVIS
Dec. 1	John SELBY Jr.	Ann SMACK
Dec. 5	Charles DASHIELL	Rachel MASON
Dec. 7	George DAVIS	Elizabeth BASSETT
Dec. 8	Thomas COLLINS	Ann SCARBOURGH
Dec. 11	James COLBOURN	Sheda PARSONS
Dec. 11	Abel HARMAN	Mary COLLICK
Dec. 12	Joseph HARPER	Nancy SELBY
Dec. 14	William GIVAN	Mary DARBY
Dec. 21	Isaac TOADVINE	Polly TOADVINE
Dec. 23	John CROPPER	Janette REED

1812
Dec. 24	Elijah WILLIAMS	Polly MELSON
Dec. 29	Samuel TRAHEARN	Nancy GIVANS
Dec. 30	Edward CROPPER	Mary WELDONE

1813
Jan. 6	John STEVEN	Mary D. DIXON
Jan. 6	Robert S. BUNCE	Mary PETTITT
Jan. 6	Isaac AYERS	Hessey ROWLEY
Jan. 11	Wm. McGREGOR	Betsey BRATTEN
Jan. 12	Thos. HOGSHIER	Mary HILL
Jan. 12	Thos JOHNSON	Hetty BRITTINGHAM
Jan. 19	Josiah BRATTEN	Nancy WATERS
Jan. 25	Wm. JONES	Sally HUDSON
Feb. 3	Samuel LUMBER	Nancy BELL
Feb. 10	George LEWIS	Mary HARMAN
Feb. 24	Thos MILBOURN	Margaret Costen TURNER
Feb. 25	John LEWIS	Sally WEBB
Feb. 25	Thomas LANDEN	Rachel Gunby POWELL
Feb. 26	Phillip MORRIS	Mary HALL
March 3	Francis ROSSE	Jane MATTHEWS
March 8	Jonathan POLLITT	Sally LEVINGSTON
March 16	William BEACHBOARD	Hetty BOWEN
March 22	Benjamin TULL	Betsey FLOYD
March 24	William P. CROOPER	Patty BOWEN
April 1	John DRYDEN	Rebecca BENSTON
April 3	Zachariah PEPPER	Anne LAMBERSON
April 5	John MERRILL	Ara HENDERSON
April 6	John MORRIS	Nelly DENNIS
April 13	William CARTER	Sally CAHOON
April 26	Jepthan PILCHARD	Susanna TOWNSEND
April 27	Elihu HOLLOWAY	Patty SELBY
April 28	George BENSON	Betsey PAYNE
April 30	Nehemiah HOLLAND	Mary TOWNSEND
May 6	William HARGIS	Lydia HENDERSON
May 11	Thos. TINDLE	Leah MARNER
May 14	James H. ROWLEY	SARAH DAVIS
May 15	George PARKER	Susanna SAVAGE
May 20	Thomas HARGIS	Peggy MARSHALL
June 2	Wm TINGLE	Eliz RANKIN
June 2	Wm BENSON	Margaret HENDERSON
June 3	John BISHOP	Rhoda HOPKINS
June 10	John SELBY Jr.	Betsey HANDCOCK
June 14	Henry PARKER	Sally JONES
June 15	James DORMAN	Polly TURNER
June 16	David RICHARDSON	Nancy J. WILSON
June 16	Jacob ADAMS	Margaret HANDLEY
June 16	Moses WINGATE	Betsey BRADSHAW
June 19	George STATEN	Sally GIVANS
June 28	John LONG	Nancy PRDEAUX

1813		
June 29	Leml. HOLLOWAY	Nancy HOLLOWAY
July 2	William PATTERSON	Nancy SELBY
July 15	Jeremiah Messick	Sabrough BISHOP
July 20	Zephaniah PARSONS	Rebecca SEARS
July 23	John EVANS	Polly C. McDANIEL
Aug. 2	Robert D. CATLEN	Nelly CAREY
Aug. 4	William W. PORTER	Mary HAMMOND
Aug. 29	Peter CLAYWELL	Peggy MILLS
Aug. 30	John R. PITTS	Julian MITCHELL
Aug. 31	William S. WHITE	Rebecca STEVENSON
Sept. 7	Isaac CLARK	Betsey BENNETT
Sept. 8	Joseph Robertson	Bridget GRAY
Sept. 21	Littleton POPE	Polly NICHOLS
Sept. 22	Thomas R. P. SPENCE	Esther R. PURNELL
Oct. 4	James HOLLAND	Mahela BURBAGE
Oct. 4	John HARLES	Patience SCOTT
Oct. 18	Joseph HOUSTON	Sally REVILL
Oct. 23	Stephen J. LEWIS	Eliza U. FINNEY
Oct. 27	John H. BOWEN	Peggy HILL
Oct. 27	John TRUITT	Henny BRADFORD
Oct. 30	John FASSETT	Elizabeth CUTLER
Nov. 1	Esme M. WALTER	Sarah MARSHALL
Nov. 2	Joshua ROWND	Hannah SHOCKLEY
Nov. 2	Thomas S. FASSETT	Mary S. PURNELL
Nov. 3	Stephen ENNIS	Martha ROBINS
Nov. 11	Powell PATEY	Margaret McGREGOR
Nov. 16	John HEARN	Nancy MORRIS
Nov. 18	Peter JOHNSON	Mary SELBY
Nov. 23	William HOLLAND	Elizabeth McGREGOR
Nov. 25	Francis A. BOYER	Mary DUER
Dec. 3	John DAVIS	Martha TIMMONS
Dec. 3	Thomas WHITE	Polly WALSTON
Dec. 6	THomas GIVAN	Mary JOHNSON
Dec. 14	Lodawick DAVIS	Betsey DAVIS
Dec. 17	Tubman COX	Ann ATKINSON
Dec. 20	Samuel DIXON	Anna DIXON
Dec. 21	Littleton BOWEN	Charlotte HAMMOND
Dec. 21	Adam SCOTT	Nancy Rice WARE
Dec. 21	Laban HUDSON	Peggy TRUITT
Dec. 22	John CATHELL	Nancy JONES
Dec. 22	Joseph ENNIS	Molly GRAY
Dec. 22	Levin O. BURBAGE	Sally CROPPER
Dec. 22	Jesse L. JONES	Milly KELLY
Dec. 23	Barnaba DAVIS	Sarah SCARBOURGH
Dec. 23	Joshua JONES	Andesiah TURNER
Dec. 28	Jacob GIVANS	Priscilla LEWIS
Dec. 29	Joshua JONES	Eleanor AUSTIN

1814

Date	Groom	Bride
Jan. 3	Josiah CAREY	Betsey DALE
Jan. 3	Benjamin H. GORDY	Hetty PARKER
Jan. 4	Caleb H. MASSEY	Euphamy ROSSE
Jan. 6	Robert WILLIAMS	Frances TURLINGTON
Jan. 11	James RAIN	Levicia DAVIS
Jan. 12	John POWELL	Hessey PURNELL
Jan. 17	Stephen HILL	Catharine PILCHER
Jan. 18	Samuel ADKINS	Polly SMACK
Jan. 18	Peter POWELL	Semore TAYLOR
Jan. 18	Nehemiiah REDDEN	Patsey TARR
Jan. 21	Levi REGGAN	Sally SMULLIN
Jan. 25	Stephen TIMMONS	Martha POWELL
Jan. 25	William DRYDEN	Peggy RUARK
Jan. 25	Daniel G. ROBINS	Harriet WEEKS
Jan. 28	David OWENS	Elizabeth COBB
Jan. 31	William EWELL	Maria WISHART
Feb. 1	Nathaniel G. HARMON	Comfort HARMON
Feb. 2	Ebenezer HEARN	Leah BREWINGTON
Feb. 8	Geo JONES	Polly BAYLY
Feb. 10	Robt. RUSSELL	Polly JONES
Feb. 13	Isaac TINDLE	Lancy TURNER
Feb. 21	James SMITH	Hetty DAVIS
Feb. 22	John S. SPENCE	Sarah Maria PURNELL
March 1	John GODFREY	Hetty HOLLOWAY
March 1	Shadrack BAKER	Polly GODFREY
March 5	James BENNETT	Anna SELBY
March 8	John R. ROUND	Sarah McGEE
March 8	John BREWINGTON	Hetty ROACH
March 12	Isaac MITCHELL	Mary BENNETT
March 14	Ezekiel M. JAMES	Charlotte McMASTER
March 14	Joseph McCLAIN	Mary PORTER
March 21	Levin CAREY	Betsey HOLLOWAY
March 22	James JONES	Betsey WATSON
April 1	Thomas WADKINS	Elizabeth TRUITT
April 5	Anania TINMMONS	Denny MUMFORD
April 12	William PURNELL	Amelia PURNELL
April 13	George CAREY	Nancy WILSON
April 19	James MALLETT	Nancy JONES
April 26	Obed BRITTINGHAM	Rebecca PARKER
April 26	James ROACH	Sarah BLACK
May 2	Moses U. JONES	Sarah P. MERRILL
May 13	Peter COLLINS	Mary EASHUM
May 14	Isaac SMITH	Elizabeth BETHARD
May 24	Levin DENSON	Elizabeth DRYDEN
June 3	George HALL	Betsey ALLEN
June 6	James MacLAIN	Hetty DORMAN
June 20	Thomas BRITTINGHAM	Eleanor MERRILL
June 21	Samuel VENSON	Betsey FOOKS
June 21	Benjamin RICHARDSON	Sally JOHNSON

1814

Date	Groom	Bride
July 9	John COLLINS	Nancy GINES
July 19	Isaiah LATCHAM	Hanna TOWNSEND
July 20	John JONES	Nancy BISHOP
Aug. 1	Robert ESHAM	Mary RUARK
Aug. 15	Stephen RUARK	Sally HUDSON
Aug. 17	Joshua DONOHOE	Anna POWELL
Aug. 23	Joshua HOSHIER	Hetty CRIPPEN
Aug. 24	George GREEN	Charlotte TAYLOR
Aug. 27	Nehemiah POLLITT	Sarah SMITH
Sept. 8	Willliam WALEA	Margaret SMITH
Sept. 19	Isaac DICKERSON	Lanta BEVANS
Sept. 22	John STUART	Nancy GODFREY
Sept. 28	Levi ELLISS	Sophia SPENCER
Oct. 6	Daniel FOOKS	Eunice FERMAN
Oct. 19	Henry MATTHEWS	Betsy SCARBOURGH
Oct. 19	Isaac JOHNSON	Nancy KNOX
Oct. 20	Isaac TOWNSEND	Margaret CORBIN
Oct. 21	John RITCHIE	Betsy CONNERLY
Oct. 22	David PENNEWELL	Nancy GARRETSON
Oct. 26	John G. DAVIS	Catharine LONG
Oct. 31	Elijah ELLEGOOD	Polly POLLITT
Nov. 9	James PAYNE	Sarah AYDELOTT
Nov. 17	Stephen TAYLOR	Susan AYDELOTT
Nov. 28	Thomas ATKINSON	Dinah HAMMOND
Nov. 30	Kellaem DYKES	Mary FOOKS
Nov. 30	Edward A. REVILL	Catharine COULBOURN
Dec. 1	John HOOPER	Mary RACKLIFFE
Dec. 6	Stephen HILL	Margaret JOHNSON
Dec. 10	Joseph MILLER	Sarah DUNCAN
Dec. 12	Joseph PORTER	Margaret PORTER
Dec. 12	William S. CORBIN	Ann CORBIN
Dec. 13	John SPENCER	Mary BENNETT
Dec. 16	Severn JOHNSON	Augusta WHITE
Dec. 20	Isaac DERICKSON	Patty DALEY
Dec. 20	Levi CATHELL	Anne JOHNSON
Dec. 20	Henry SILVERTHORN	Tabitha BACON
Dec. 20	Lemuel HADDER	Gertrude HADDER
Dec. 20	John RIAN	Rachell BASSETTE
Dec. 20	Jacob JONES	Lovey MELSON
Dec. 26	Ralph CORBIN	Ann SHOCKLEY
Dec. 29	Robert KNOX	Margaret DOUGLAS

1815

Date	Groom	Bride
Jan. 4	James M. HARGIS	Nancy CONNER
Jan. 4	Johnson GRAY	Anne JOHNSON
Jan. 5	Thomas AYDELOTT	Director MELVIN
Jan. 5	John TEAUGE	Sally BISHOP
Jan. 5	Edward BLAKE	Peggy BLAKE
Jan. 7	James YOUNG	Elizabeth NELSON

1815

Jan. 9	Isaac HOUSTON	Sally JOHNSON
Jan. 10	John WILLIS	Sarah DAVIS
Jan. 13	George SPARKSMAN	Esther ROBERTS
Jan. 18	Esme TAYLOR	Molly JOHNSON
Jan. 18	Riley TRUITT	Betsy LAMBERSON
Jan. 21	Stephen MITCHELL	Polly HAMMONS
Jan. 24	James TULL	Elizabeth HICKMAN
Jan. 25	Robert GRAY	Mary CROPPER
Jan. 26	Edward BLAOKSOME	Rosey LONG
Jan. 31	John MITCHELL	Hetty HILLMAN
Jan. 31	Littleton DENNIS	Polly DENNIS
Feb. 6	Josiah ATKINSON	Nancy BURBAGE
Feb. 7	Isaac BRUMBLY	Rebecca TOWNSEND
Feb. 9	Levin DAVIS	Susan BRITTINGHAM
Feb. 13	William ROGER	Sarah FERRILL
Feb. 14	Ishmeal BAKER	Polly BRADFORD
Feb. 15	Robert DENNIS	Charlotte PENNEWELL
Feb. 16	Micajah ENNIS	Rachel McFADDEN
Feb. 21	Kerdon (?) McDANIEL	Polly DRYDEN
Feb. 21	Samuel BOWLES	Nancy POWELL
Feb. 21	Ephraim TOWNSEND	Rosanna LONG
Feb. 21	John TRUITT	Betsey GRAY
Feb. 23	Caleb MORRIS	Polly HUDSON
Feb. 23	Charles FOOKS	Nancy FOOKS
Feb. 27	Tubman HARRIS	Mary ATKINSON
March 5	John ALLEN	Milly STURGIS
March 8	James FASSITTE	Toy MORRIS
March 15	Samuel TUBBS	Susan BELLEDGE
March 25	John EVANS	Sarah MITCHELL
March 28	Marshall HAMDEN	Betty DAVIS
April 3	Kendall COLLIER	Sally G. JOHNSON
April 3	Isaac BOWER	Polly COLLIER
April 7	James YOUNG	Nancy WARRINGTON
April 8	James W. ELLIOTT	Eleanor STAYTON
April 11	Ephraim SMULLEN	Sally SMULLEN
April 15	William HILL	Rhoda STURGIS
April 17	Burton SHOCKLEY	Leah RUARK
April 17	Thomas TIMMONS	Nancy MILLER
April 18	Jesse BENNETT	Esther ROWLEY
April 19	William Q. DIXON	Maria CONAWAY
April 20	Rowland A. BEAVANS	Leah KILLAM
April 26	George WEST	Priscilla HORNSWAY
May 3	John N. BOWLAND	Susan DIXON
May 4	William BRAXTON	Rhoda COLLICK
May 8	Wm. BRITTINGHAM	Ann TIMMONS
May 9	Jesse BEVANS	Nancy JOYNES
May 9	James STURGIS	Sally TOWNSEND
May 13	Isaac RICHARDS	Molly TRUITT
May 23	Elijah WILLIS	(?) HADDER

1815
May 27	Peter TOWNSEND	Grace TOWNSEND
June 5	John PRICE	Polly WILLIS
June 7	John R. CORD	Comfort FRANKLIN
June 15	Robert H. PURNELL	Sarah FRANKLIN
June 30	Thomas FOX	Elizabeth GRINDLES
July 1	George MALCOMB	Mary RICHARDSON
July 4	Isaac A. DALE	Catharine PITTS
July 11	Peter S. MORRIS	Betsy ROAN
July 15	Roan F. PURNELL	Sarah MILLER
July 18	Isaac RUARK	Nancy MATTHEWS
July 25	Obediah CAREY	Sally ELLIS
July 27	Soloman POWELL	Sally WILLIS
Aug. 8	Thomas DRISKELL	Priscilla TWILLY
Aug. 8	Henry CLOG	Sarah RIGGAN
Aug. 8	William MOORE	Elizabeth COTTINGHAM
Aug. 9	William TOWNSEND	Betsy WILLIAMS
Aug. 12	Stephen SMULLEN	Nelly HERRINGTON
Aug. 15	William PARKER	Ann JOHNSON
Aug. 15	Parker COLLINS	Catharine DUNCAN
Aug. 16	Elijah MASON	Wise STAYTON
Aug. 17	Jethery RICHARDSON	Tabitha LATCHUM
Aug. 22	William BAKER	Nancy BURBAGE
Aug. 22	Henry MEIRS	Sally HARGROVE
Aug. 26	Joseph BUNDICK	Rachel BAKER
Aug. 18	Henry STURGIS	Margaret TILGHMAN
Aug. 29	William WEBB	Nancy HOLLOWAY
Aug. 30	Jacob RIGGIN	Gertrude STEVENSON
Sept. 7	Lemuel SELBY	Betsy B. FLOYD
Sept. 8	Alexander McCOLLOM	Margaret Custis CARLINGTON
Sept. 15	William DORMAN	Jane HOLLOWAY
Sept. 16	William SLAUGHTERY	Catharine Cropper
Sept. 19	Peter McCAULEY	Lotty SELBY
Sept. 20	Wm ROWLEY	Catharine MASSEY
Sept. 20	Henry JARMAN	Nancy HAMMOND
Sept. 23	Eliakim BENNETT	Mary A. MARSH
Sept. 27	John BOWEN	Comfort BOWEN
Sept. 29	Robert STEWART	Betsy BROWN
Oct. 3	Anderson TRUITT	Priscilla PUZEY
Oct. 4	Thomas EVANS	Lotty NICKERSON
Oct. 9	Whittington BOWEN	Elizabeth LUCUS
Oct. 12	James HALL	Betsy DAVIS
Oct. 19	Littleton HUDSON	Grace TOWNSEND
Oct. 24	Benjamin HEARN	Polly KELLEY
Oct. 24	Samuel W. HANDY	Elizabeth H. WILSON
Nov. 1	Levi BISHOP	Priscilla BEVANS
Nov. 2	Levin CONNER	Molly BOWEN
Nov. 7	James MELVIN	Elizabeth LONG
Nov, 8	George KILLEY	Betsey DANIEL
Nov. 9	Peter TOWNSEND	Mary PORTER

1815

Nov. 14	James RIGGAN	Lewis SMULLEN
Nov. 14	Purnell PUZEY	Rebecca PUZEY
Nov. 15	John LONG	Sally L. HENDERSON
Nov. 17	Joseph LEONARD	Polly PARKER
Nov. 22	Jenkins H. BOWEN	Sally T. DAVIS
Nov. 28	Josiah ELLIS	Sally JONES
Dec. 1	Kendall RICHARD	Sally WELDON
Dec. 2	Hugh M. STEVENSON	Martha H. HUDSON
Dec. 5	James TAYLOR	Nancy ELLIS
Dec. 8	Henry SCHOOLFIELD	Molly FASSITT
Dec. 12	James WATSON	Tabitha JONES
Dec. 12	Walter TURNER	Nancy GEE
Dec. 13	John JOHNSON	Anna TARR
Dec. 15	Peter HARGIS	Sarah AYDELOTT
Dec. 15	Stephen WOOLFORD	Eleanor CHRISTOPHER
Dec. 16	George TODD	Eleanor CHRISTOPHER
Dec. 18	Thomas RITCHIE	Sarah BROWN
Dec. 20	THomas EVANS	Hannah EVANS
Dec. 25	William TWIG	Hetty NEWMAN
Dec. 28	Peter ALLEN	Elizabeth ALLEN
Dec. 29	Jenkins ROWNDS	Leah EVANS

1816

Jan. 2	Josiah BRITTINGHAM	Jane BONNAWELL
Jan. 5	Alexander TIMMONS	Sophia TIMMONS
Jan. 9	Ephraim TOWNSEND	Mary STURGIS
Jan. 14	Peter WINBOROUGH	Sally TULL
Jan. 14	William FLETCHER	Margaret GLEN
Jan. 14	Samuel HOSHIER	Nancy BOWEN
Jan. 16	Nathl. E. BROUGHTON	Martha BROUGHTON
Jan. 17	Risdon MUMFORD	Zepporah BOWEN
Jan. 18	Samuel JEFFERSON	Hetty MITCHELL
Jan. 19	James HALL	Hannah HENDERSON
Jan. 20	Joshua LAWS	Jane SHOCKLEY
Jan. 30	James GODFREY	Sarah JOHNSON
Feb. 2	John HOLLOWAY	Elizabeth HICKMAN
Feb. 2	Soloman BUTLER	Elizabeth TAYLOR
Feb. 6	Abel HAMON	Lotty CHERRIX
Feb. 7	Lambert JACKSON	Henrietta COLLINS
Feb. 2	John STURGIS	Mary ROWNDS
Feb. 12	Isaac JARMAN	Rachel LATEN
Feb. 13	Daniel RUARK	Priscilla HUDSON
Feb. 14	Samuel WARRINGTON	Susan PARKER
Feb. 17	George JONES	Leoisa ? SMACK
Feb. 19	Robert J. HENRY	Mary D. HANDY
Feb. 21	Kendall PORTER	Mary GRIFFIN
Feb. 21	Elijah FASSETT	Rachel SELBY
Feb. 22	James DAVIS	Polly BROUGHTON
Feb. 23	George GRAY	Polly DAVIS

1816

Date	Groom	Bride
Feb. 27	Ezekiel WILLIAMS	Martha DAVIS
Feb. 27	Moses PAYNE	Elizabeth BEAUCHAMP
March 5	John BURLINGTON	Sally DINTY
March 12	Major HASTINGS	Betsy GRIFFEN
March 14	Thomas W. BLACKSTONE	Ann P. DIX
March 14	Severn H. DUKES	Mary OUTTEN
March 15	Joshua TULL	Nancy LONG
March 15	Lambert COLLIER	Susan DAVIS
March 15	Thomas MORRIS	Nancy TILGHMAN
March 19	Kendall T. BOWEN	Esther BOWEN
March 19	Jacob HENDERSON	Sally SHEPPERD
March 25	Hillary PITTS	Martha I. GRAY
March 28	Littleton TRUITT	Hulda TURNER
April 1	John RUARK	Caty TARR
April 1	Peter PARSONS	Polly DONAWAY?
April 1	William DRYDEN	Nancy P. TILGHMAN
April 10	Henry KELLY	Zepporah ENNIS
April 16	William PARADISE	Nancy BONNAWELL
April 19	Samuel MORRISON	Peggy TULL
April 22	Thomas GORDY	Ann MADDUX
April 28	William KELLEY	Charlotte HOLSTON
April 29	Benjamin DRISKILL	Rhoda MASSEY
April 29	Ezekiel WILLIAMS	Polly LAWS
May 7	George GLADDEN	Sally HART
May 9	Levin JONES	Betsy TRUITT
May 11	Obed GAULT	Ann BURROUGHS
May 15	John JOHNSON	Sally TARR
May 16	John LAMBERTSON	Eliza TRUITT
May 21	Charles RICHARDSON	Ann CRIPPEN
May 21	Teakle MASON	Nancy TUNNELL
May 30	Levin LAYFIELD	Elizabeth HUDSON
May 30	William E. BRITTINGHAM	Charlotte C. POLK
June 4	Laben BAKER	Sally BURCH
June 7	John AUSTIN	Polly BOTHAM
June 15	Billy F. FARLOW	Sarah FOOKS
June 18	Noah BALL	Charlotte MERRILL
June 28	Mathew PURNELL	Euphamy DUNCAN
June 28	Thomas DAVIS	Peggy FLOYD
June 29	Charels EWELL	Maria EWELL
July 1	Wm MERRILL	Sally MATTHEWS
July 9	Matthew HALES	Mary DUKES
July 25	Littleton COTTINGHAM	Mary E. EASTERLY
Aug. 6	Wm. Thomas BARCRIFT	Luckey KELLY
Aug. 13	James JONES	Rebecca KELLAEM
Aug. 14	George CLAYWELL	Nancy JONES
Aug. 20	Abel BEACH	Catherine BEACH
Sept. 2	James KELLY	Fanny FLETCHER
Sept. 4	William ENNIS	Sophia CLARK
Sept. 4	Elijah DAVIS	Martha GRAY

1816

Date	Groom	Bride
Sept. 5	James CORBIN	Gertrude HUDZON
Sept. 5	Dennis WRIGHT	Nancy GUNTER
Sept. 7	Melvin DUKES	Ede McNEIL
Sept. 10	William JONES	Hetty BRITTINGHAM
Sept. 11	Henry GLADDEN	Polly BUNTING
Sept. 14	William PARKER	Sally TRUITT
Sept. 17	Samuel HARRINGTON	Sally WAINRIGHT
Sept. 24	James PITTS	Sary COVINGTON
Sept. 25	Peter MAWK?	Mary HENDERSON
Sept. 27	Jonathan CHURCH	Euphame Williams
Sept. 28	Gillet WATSON	Priscilla FICKETT
Oct. 1	William B.L. RILEY	Sally FLEMING
Oct. 2	James TAYLOR	Esther DUERY
Oct. 5	Jesse MUMFORD	Levina LATCHAM
Oct..5	Isaac TAYLOR	Nancy TOWNSEND
Oct. 7	Samuel MADDOX	Polly BURD
Oct. 7	George SAMPSON	Rachel HAMMOND
Oct. 7	Levin BRADFORD	Rachel BRADFORD
Oct. 16	William F. RILEY	Martha PURNELL
Oct. 21	James BULL	Polly GRENNEL ?
Oct. 23	Peter DORMAN	Leah JAMES
Oct. 29	Levin RIGGEN	Nancy ROACH
Nov. 9	John LAWS	Nancy BOWNDS
Nov. 11	Nathaniel R. TINGLE	Elizabeth HENRY
Nov. 12	Elijah TIMMONS	Patty TIMMONS
Nov. 12	Peter WHALEY	Elizabeth DAVIS
Nov. 13	Jacob WONNELL	Nancy DICKERSON
Nov. 18	David DAILEY	Sarah EASTERLY
Nov. 20	John P. RULLEDGE	Mary STURGIS
Nov. 22	Elijah ADKINS	Mary ROUNDS
Nov. 25	Charles HENDERSON	Elizabeth DRYDEN
Nov. 30	Samuel R. SMITH	Mary MARTIN
Dec. 2	William BRADFORD	Fanny ADKINS
Dec. 4	Riley JONES	Charlotte HOSIER
Dec. 10	James GRAY	Charlotte SMITH
Dec. 11	Thomas PURNELL	Mary P. MARSHALL
Dec. 12	James PARR	Nancy BUSSELS
Dec. 12	John MUMFORD	Sally PREDUX
Dec. 14	Benjamin BOWEN	Charlotte RICHARDS
Dec. 17	Elijah CAREY	Patty HOLLOWAY
Dec. 17	Mordaca DAVIS	Elizabeth TIMMON
Dec. 18	Joseph HUTCHESON	Mary RICE
Dec. 18	Elijah SHOCKLEY	Mary RICHARDSON
Dec. 19	James BALL	Lydia BALL
Dec. 19	Levin HORSEY	Anny TEAGLE
Dec. 20	John BASSETT	Martha BURBAGE
Dec. 2	Barzella C. ADKINS	Milly PARSONS
Dec. 31	William HOLLAND	Ann BRIDDELL

1817

Date	Groom	Bride
Jan. 2	Isaac EVANS	Mahalia GRAY
Jan. 3	John CLARK	Sally LEWIS
Jan. 6	James DREYDEN	Polly TRUITT
Jan. 6	Richard M. BEATHARD	Anna CAREY
Jan. 6	Mary POWELL	Nancy BAKER
Jan. 6	Isaac SHOCKLEY	Nancy WARREN
Jan. 7	Jess LONG	Elizabeth BENSTON
Jan. 7	Daniel HANDCOCK	Margaret PARKER
Jan. 9	William JONES	Mahala PORTER
Jan. 10	John BISHOP	Dolly MARSHALL
Jan. 13	Covin WATSON	Elizabeth PATY
Jan. 15	Thomas DRYDEN	Milly CLOGG
Jan. 20	Jesse BAKER	Elizabeth BURROWS
Jan. 20	Peter DAVIS	Hetty CROPPER
Jan. 21	Jacob MILBOURN	Frances SPENCER
Jan. 21	Johnson DENNIS	Polly DENNIS
Jan. 24	Henry DUNCAN	Mary HAMMOND
Jan. 25	Peter GRAY	Ann GRAY
Jan. 25	Benjamin HUDSON	Sarah CROPPER
Jan. 28	Joshua JONES	Peggy PREDEAUX
Jan. 28	Wrixham PAYNE	Sally WATSON
Jan. 28	Isaac WEST	Sally TUNNELL
Feb. 3	Purnell BRITTINGHAM	Mary MASEY
Feb. 10	Tubman CHRISTOPHER	Peggy BROWN
Feb. 11	Elisha BOWEN	Mary BOWEN
Feb. 11	Abraham GIBBS	Nancy PRUITT
Feb. 11	John GUTRY	Betsey NELSON
Feb. 13	William YOUNG	Ann COULBOURNE
Feb. 17	Lizor? MARSHALL	Matthew BLAKE
Feb. 18	Levi PORTER	Elizabeth COLLINS
Feb. 19	Robert TOWNSEND	Henrietta DRYDEN
Feb. 19	Peter CLAVILLE	Rodah BOWING
Feb. 20	John D. SMITH	Ann P. HUDSON
Feb. 26	Thomas BOWLEN	Peggy MATTHESS
Feb. 27	James BEEBY	Peggy TAYLOR
Feb. 28	Daniel BATSON	Leah JENKINS
March 5	John SELBY	Martha B. ROBINS
March 5	Henry DENNIS	Mary BLAKE
March 5	Wm BISHOP	Polly RICHARDSON
March 8	John P. MARSHALL	Nancy PURNELL
March 11	Levi PURNELL	Martha McGREGORY
March 14	William COSTON	Elizabeth WILLIS
March 18	John TRUITT	Rodah T. JONES
March 18	Mitchell CHANDLER	Susan BIRD
March 18	John JOHNSON	Nancy STEVENSON
March 18	Jeptha MORRIS	Eliza WHITE
March 18	Levin HENDERSON	Sally TRUITT
March 25	Selby CLAYWELL	Nancy DRYDEN

1817

Date	Groom	Bride
March 28	James TRUITT	Peggy DAVIS
April 1	Isaac TOADVINE	Jane POLLITT
April 1	Samuel BENSON	Mary WHITE
April 8	Edward ROWND	Martha LAWS
April 8	William BEAVANS	Betsey LEWIS
April 16	Seveme WILSON	Milley BUNTING
April 18	Obed BAILEY	Peggy BRANSRUM
April 24	Jethery RICHARDSON	Nancy LATCHUM
April 26	John SILVERTHORN	Levinor SELBY
April 29	Samuel KER	Eliza HANDY
April 29	William BENNETT	Priscilla BENNETT
April 30	Parker DICKERSON	Eliza A. MILES
May 5	Beverly COPES	Margaret BENSON
May 6	William CRAFT	Polly STANDFORD
May 9	Walter SMULLEN	Rachel COLLINS
May 12	Kendall HOLLAND	Elizabeth CROPPER
May 12	James BRITTINGHAM	Sally CUSTON
May 20	Matthias WARREN	Charlotte HICKMAN
May 27	Joshua WHITE	Sarah PARSONS
May 30	Peter DYKES	Molly PRIOR
June 5	Nehemiah STOCKLY	Eliza R. BOISNARD
June 7	John JOSTURE	Tabitha JONES
June 12	Arthur POWELL	Betsey BELL
June 17	Charles CONOLLY	Mary GEORGE
June 23	Ebenezer TAYLOR	Sally TOWNSEND
June 26	Richard E. WELSH	Sarah Jane WILLIAMS
June 28	Littleton TOWNSEND	Andesiah BEAUCHAMP
June 28	Benjamin LEONARD	Mary PARKER
June 28	Joshua BURROUGHS	Hannah WAINWRIGHT
June 30	Jess Heath WENRIGHT	Rosanne Anne Williams BEN
June 30	John WILLIAMS	Margaret WILLIAMS
July 2	John COPES	Sarah PRICE
July 3	Jacob JONES	Sally MADDUX
July 10	Joshua JONES	Elender BOWEN
July 14	Isaac DAVIS	Mary ROUNDS
July 22	William RICHARDS	Henrietta BOWEN
July 23	George SCARBOROUGH	Cassey WEST
July 25	Samuel KANNY	Barshaba BEVANS
Aug. 3	James HENDERSON	Polly WHEELTON
Aug. 4	Joshua DOWNS	Polly DAVIS
Aug. 5	Samuel DORMAN	Elizabeth STATEN
Aug. 9	Littleton FLEMING	Sophia FLOYD
Aug. 11	Henry ADKINS	Ginetta M. DENNIS
Aug. 12	John W. WILLIAMS	Hamutah TOWNSEND
Aug. 13	Thomas BRITTINGHAM	Leah MERRILL
Aug. 18	John TATMAN	Chaney DAVIS
Aug. 21	James SMITH	Martha PETTIT
Sept. 2	Josiah BROTON	Leah B. BEVANS
Sept. 9	James LEWIS	Nelly PENNEWELL

1817

Sept. 9	Joseph F. DARCY	Sarah FRANKLIN
Sept. 10	Thomas GRAY	Clarrecy DAVIS
Sept. 16	Charles TOWNSEND	Elizabeth BAKER
Sept. 18	John WHITE	Sophiah HUDSON
Sept. 18	George WALTON	Bartheba BROWN
Sept. 23	Nehemiah TAYLOR	Elizabeth SPEAKS
Sept. 23	Edmund R. CURTIS	Tabitha T. WISE
Sept. 24	Coulbourn LOUNG	Sally STURGIS
Sept. 27	Zachariah CHAILLE	Ann DORMAN
Oct. 6	James FISHER	Nancy BURCH
Oct. 8	James COLLINS	Nancy TARR
Oct. 27	William BENNETT	Matilda SELBY
Nov. 11	Rackliffe MORRIS	Nancy SHOCKLY
Nov. 12	Josiah JONES	Mary DALE
Nov. 17	David JOHNSON	Nancy Derickson HILL
Nov. 18	James ROBERTS	Elizabeth WINGATE
Nov. 19	Parker BOWEN	Sally TOWNSEND
Nov. 21	James BOTHUM	Polly SHOCKLEY
Dec. 8	Archebald WHITE	Nancy MERRILL
Dec. 8	William SCOTT	Molly POINTER
Dec. 12	Frederick CONNER	Lydia HARGIS
Dec. 13	Henry DAVIS	Polly DICKERSON
Dec. 16	John BULL	Nancy SMITH
Dec. 17	Thomas E. STURGIS	Sarah ROUND
Dec. 19	Thomas BAKER	Pressa FOOKES
Dec. 19	Handy KILPEN	Milly CAREY
Dec. 22	Jonathan Stevens PARSONS	Milly JOHNSON
Dec. 23	Robert LAMBDEN	Sarah TULL
Dec. 23	Elijah DRESKILL	Polly HYLAND
Dec. 23	George HEARN	Martha CATHELL
Dec. 23	William MATTHEWS	Ann HOLLAND
Dec. 24	William PORTER	Elizabeth POWELL
Dec. 30	Samuel T. CAREY	Sarah REDDEN
Dec. 30	James TOWNSEND	Nancy BROWN

1818

Jan. 2	Wm CAUSEY	Nancy LEVINGSTON
Jan. 5	Daniel LAWS	Martha ENNIS
Jan. 6	Thomas QUILLEN	Nancy JONES
Jan. 9	Schoolfield TIMMONS	Patty BEATHARD
Jan. 10	James THORNTON	Lorey BAGWELL(?)
Jan. 17	Robert H. DAVIS	Geturude TINGLE
Jan. 21	James CAMMELL	Manervey STURGIS
Jan. 21	Daniel BEATHARDS	Charlotte BOWEN
Jan. 21	Peter WILLIAMS	Charlotte GRIFFIN
Jan. 21	James RACKLIFFE	Margaretta FASSETT
Jan. 23	Jeremiah CANNON	Eleanor PARKER
Jan. 27	Robert GIVAN	Priscilla COTTINGHAM
Jan. 27	John B.H.W. CLARVOE	Harriet H. HENDERSON

1818
Date	Groom	Bride
Jan. 27	Cove HAZZARD	Mary RANKIN
Jan. 30	Lemuel HENDERSON	Polly Richardson SHALLEY
Feb. 2	Samuel DAVIS	Betsey JOHNSON
Feb. 6	William PARSONS	Mary WHITE
Feb. 9	John BULL	Elizabeth BONNAWELL
Feb. 10	Thomas M. HARGIS	Ann DIXON
Feb. 12	John JACKSON	Patty STURGIS
Feb. 16	William WELBERN	Sally WALLOP
Feb. 17	Wm. M. SCARBOURGH	Eliza Maria READ
Feb. 24	Charles DAVIS	Molly WILLIS
Feb. 24	Bruff BRAUGHTON	Mary WHITE
Feb. 25	Ebenezer HEARN	Margaret STEVENSON
Feb. 25	Warner STATON	Mary GIVAN
Feb. 27	Robert MITCHELL	Mary COLLINS
Feb. 27	George TOWNSEND	Sally TAYLOR
Feb. 28	Teackle A. TRADER	Elizabeth R. HOUSTON
March 6	Robert LAMBDEN	Elizabeth MERRILL
March 10	Joshua REED	Hetty BENNETT
March 13	Levin PAYNE	Elizabeth JONES
March 18	Joshua BRITT	Hessy TOWNSEND
March 20	Joseph SCHOOLFIELD	Mary PATTERSON
April 6	Daniel BENSTON	Eliza POLK
April 7	Isaac TRUITT	Patty JEARMON
April 7	James BRODWATER	Mary CARY
April 13	Curtis DIXON	Mary BREWINGTON
April 23	William REED	Huldah KELLY
April 24	William NUTTER	Phylis DYKES
May 12	Jacob BOSTON	Sally JONES
May 12	John WILLIAMS	Matilda HUDSON
May 25	Levin HOLLOWAY	Mary WILLIAMS
June 2	Thomas SELBY	Elizabeth WATTS
June 3	Elijah POWELL	Henny HILL
June 6	Henry DENNIS	Ann POWELL
June 13	Thomas MATTHEWS	Nancy REGGAN
June 16	Frederick FACK	Rachell BOWEN
June 16	Benjamin OUTTEN	Sally Kelleam SHOCKLEY
June 21	Henry BAKER	Sally KELLY
June 21	John ADKINS	Nancy PARKER
June 25	John FAVOUR	Betsey HEARN
June 25	John LATCHAM	Nancy MELBOURN
July 9	John BISHOP	Elizabeth NICKOLS
July 9	William ELLIS	Johannah MARSHALL
Aug. 9	Jesse BOUDEN	Eleanor REED
Aug. 21	John TOWNSEND	Peggy DALE
Aug. 24	William RADNEY	Anne SMITH
Sept. 3	Isaac BROOKS	Susanna DRYDEN
Sept. 14	Zadok PURNELL	Catharine DERICKSON
Sept. 29	Thomas PURNELL	Rachel FRANKLIN

1818

Date	Groom	Bride
Sept. 31	Ara SPENCE	Anna M. ROBINS
Oct. 1	William H. WEST	Ann C. BANE
Oct. 7	Dempsy HILL	Mary GRAY
Oct. 8	George BENNIT	Uphamy TAYLOR
Oct. 12	Cornelius DICKERSON	Sally HUDSON
Oct. 22	Burton GRAY	Leah SMITH
Oct. 31	John JOHNSON	Sally HERMAN
Nov. 3	William WATSON	Maria BEACHOM
Nov. 3	John SNEED	Elizabeth PILCHARD
Nov. 3	Isaac DRYDEN	Philis JOHNSON
Nov. 7	Charles LITTLETON	Hannah DAVIS
Nov. 10	Robert FRANKLIN	Mary EVANS
Nov. 11	Samuel JOHNSON	Martha P. JONES
Nov. 12	Henry KELLY	Molly HOLSTON
Nov. 14	Stephen PURNELL	Elizabeth P.P. MARSHALL
Nov. 17	David MALONE	Nancy PRUITT
Nov. 23	Soloman VINSON	Grace DISHAROON
Nov. 27	Handy MILES Junr.	Euphamy HARGIS
Nov. 27	John DAVIS	Polly PORTER
Dec. 1	Kendall SCARBOURGH	Tabitha HANDCOCK
Dec. 5	Elijah PARSONS	Elizabeth DYKES
Dec. 5	Samuel ADKINS	Martha BRIDDLE
Dec. 9	Thomas C. JOHNSON	Ann JOHNSON
Dec. 9	George D. SNEED	Mary TARR
Dec. 11	George PARSONS	Hannah HOLLOWAY
Dec. 15	Peter ALEXANDER	Mary ALEXANDER
Dec. 15	Henry HENDERSON	Sally HOUSTON
Dec. 16	Moses CLAVEL	Mary OWENS
Dec. 16	Levin TOWNSEND	Elizabeth PORTER
Dec. 16	John JAMES	Margaret D. DOWNING
Dec. 21	James DISHAROON	Elizabeth (?)
Dec. 22	Samuel ENNIS	Ann MORE
Dec. 22	Isaac WILKERSON	Hetty DAVIS
Dec. 24	Stephen TOADVINE	Jane BROWN
Dec. 26	Joseph LATCHUM	Elizabeth WILLIAMS
Dec. 26	Parker TRADER	Betsy BADGE
Dec. 29	Robert FLEMING	Amelia WILLIAMS
Dec. 31	Colbourn LONG	Mary DAVORIX

1819

Date	Groom	Bride
Jan. 5	Thomas HADDER	Molly ADKINS
Jan. 6	George MERRILL	Nancy DAVIS
Jan. 7	Richard BAKER	Sally BAKER
Jan. 8	William PRUITT	Eleanor REDDEN
Jan. 12	John BURBAGE	Nancy CROPPER
Jan. 12	Milby SMITH	Peggy (?)
Jan. 12	David LONG	Nancy STEVENSON
Jan. 15	William GAULT	Charlotte MORRIS
Jan. 16	Edmond PENDLETON	Exerine HENRY

1819

Date	Groom	Bride
Jan. 19	William STEVENSON	Leah BISHOP
Jan. 21	Milby POWELL	Mary Marshall PURNELL
Jan. 25	William HENDCOCK	Hetty RAIN
	Tully SNEED	Sally RICHARDSON
Feb. 11	Tubman GRAY	Easter GRAY
Feb. 15	Charles KELLEY	Nancy RICHARDSON
Feb. 18	Spencer TODD	Sally NAIRNE
Feb. 23	George VANDUM	Sally MILLS
Feb. 23	Joshua REED	Polly BENNETT
Feb. 24	William McGRAW	Rachel RUARK
Feb. 25	Joseph HICKMAN	Nancy RUSSEL
March 2	Stephen LEWIS	Fanny HADDER
March 3	Richard W. GUEST	Sally ROWLEY
March 9	Thomas SMACK	Elizabeth ADKINS
March 9	Noah HENDERSON	Elizabeth HENDERSON
March 10	John DERICKSON	Polly HICKMAN
March 16	John B, DAVIS	Sarah BRIMER
March 17	Daniel MADDUX	Hetty C. HANDY
March 18	George BISHOP	Zipporah BISHOP
March 20	Charles EWELL	Easter TOWNSEND
March 29	John GLADDEN	Sally BRITTINGHAM
March 31	John ENNALLS	Peggy WILLIAMS
April 13	Haste P. CATHELL	Jane CHRISTOPHER
April 5	Stephen SMULLEN	Charrity TREHEARN
April 12	William PITTS	Gertrude HOUSTON
April 14	Andrew DAVIS	Margret KELLEY
April 20	Benjamin RICHARDSON	Sarah TRUITT
April 21	James WALKER	Sally HARNSBY
May 7	William Parker REED	Anna REED
May 11	William H. EVANS	Martha L. TIMMONS
May 12	William WALTON	Ann S. HOLLAND
May 14	John P. GORDY	Mary DALE
May 15	Peter DAVIS	Tetia MUMFORD
May 31	Samuel ROWLEY	Sally HUDSON
June 1	John E. HAYWARD	Margaret DUER
June 4	John MORRIS	Nancy JONES
June 5	Joseph TULL	Margaret BURNETT
June 14	Nathaniel SMART	Nancy BUNTING
June 14	Elijah LOWS	Hetty SMITH
June 16	Zadok WATSON	Frances REED
June 19	William BEVANS	Mary LANDON
June 22	Lemuel RIGGAN	Nancy RIGGAN
June 23	David GRAY	Nancy ATKINSON
June 24	Cornelius CROPPER	Lybia RUSSEL
June 26	Thomas SAVAGE	Polly HOSHIER
June 30	Isaac H. LAWS	Ann C. RILEY
June 30	Benjamin BARNES	Molly EVANS
July 1	Henry WHITE	Nancy DUER
July 21	James PARSONS	Leasha POLLIT

1819

Date	Groom	Bride
July 23	John PARKER	Martha (?)
July 23	George HUTT	Sally CONNER
Aug. 3	Henry FRANKLIN	Sally A. RANKIN
Aug. 7	William JOHNSON	Delilia BRITTINGHAM
Aug. 21	Jacob RILEY	Eliza HUTT
Aug. 23	Peter P. PARSONS	Gertrude FOOKS
Sept. 2	Handy PHILLIPS	Mary DUBERLEY
Sept. 3	Ephraim TOWNSEND	Mary POWELL
Sept. 6	Henry BENNETT	Ann Maria Parker KELLAM
Sept. 22	William WILKINS	Molly JACKSON
Sept. 24	Isaac BUNTING	Hetty BEVANS
Sept. 29	Thomas EVANS WISE	Maria Amelia FULWELL
Oct. 9	John RICHARDSON	Henny JOHNSON
Oct. 12	John R. PATTERSON	Rebecca WHITE
Oct. 13	Samuel RICHARDSON	Leah HUDSON
Oct. 15	John LEWIS	Sally LEWIS
Oct. 20	Henry L. MILLS	Sarah BULL
Nov. 3	Stephen WALTON	Polly JONES
Nov. 8	James PATTERSON	Rachel STEVENSON
Nov. 11	Littleton TUBBS	Hetty HOSHIER
Nov. 11	John REED	Nancy MARSHALL
Nov. 13	John YOUNG	Betsy MASSEY
Nov. 19	William CORBIN	Esther K. SCARBROUGH
Nov. 23	Elijah HEARN	Sally HEARN
Nov. 24	Thomas SCOTT	Gertrude COLLINS
Nov. 24	Stephen MOORE	Rebecca PARSONS
Nov. 25	Thomas SCOTT	Nancy CHRISTOPHER
Dec. 8	William T. RILEY	July Ann PURNELL
Dec. 8	Soloman ROGERS	Betsey WATERS
Dec. 9	John McFADDEN	Sally HENDERSON
Dec. 11	James SMITH	Polly LAMBERSON
Dec. 14	Elijah PRUITT	Mary POWELL
Dec. 14	Elzey FOZWELL	Leah POLLITT
Dec. 20	William TIRE	Gertrude DAVIS
Dec. 22	Benjamin AYDELOTT	Mary COLLINS
Dec. 22	Josiah DUNCAN	Mary HOLLAND
Dec. 23	Gora TOWNSEND	Polly BLADES
Dec. 28	James (?)	Sarah POLLITT

1820

Date	Groom	Bride
Jan. 3	John HAYS	Dilly MUMFORD
Jan. 5	Henry JARMON	Eliza MILLS
Jan. 6	Joshua BURBAGE	Mahalia DAVIS
Jan. 10	Thomas HUDSON	Elizabeth D. TINGLE
Jan. 11	Jesse WATERS	Nancy BENNETT
Jan. 12	William BUTLER	Nancy HERINGTON
Jan. 14	James DAVIS	Rachel BAKER
Jan. 17	John PURNELL	Nancy PURNELL
Jan. 19	Isaiah LATCHOM	Ellenor BEVANS

1819

Date	Groom	Bride
Jan. 20	Stephen BLADES	Elizabeth DICKERSON
Jan. 21	Henry TRUITT	Mary NICKERSON
Jan. 25	Jacob RIGGAN	Rebecca CATHELL
Feb. 2	Elijah TOADVINE	Esther Politt
Feb. 4	Ayers PARKER	Henrietta WIMBROUGH
Feb. 8	John DENNY	Mary ENNIS
Feb. 9	William W. WEST	Vianna GODWIN
Feb. 9	William PARSONS	Nancy GRIFFIN
Feb. 9	James SELBY	Gertrude STURGIS
Feb. 11	John BOWEN	Eliza CRIPPEN
Feb. 15	Nicholas JONES	Sarah WILLIS
Feb. 19	Edward HAY	Rhoda ROBERTSON
Feb. 22	John ROWLEY	Margaret ALLEN
Feb. 29	Obed JONES	Mary WRIGHT
Feb. 29	John JONES	Sally BURBAGE
March 2	Moses PAYNE	Sarah PAYNE
March 6	Major HUTT	Mary CHURCH
March 7	Joshua TRUITT	Mary REED
March 29	Milby DENSTON	Easther TAYLOR
March 29	James BUTLER	Darkey MORRIS
April 3	Josiah CROPPER	Gertrude DAVIS
April 3	Samuel BAKER	Eunice MITCHELL
April 5	John HOPE	Hellen BURTON
April 13	Thomas CHADWICK	Elizabeth MARRETT
April 17	Samuel BURROUGH	ElizabethH. PITTS
April 20	Riley JONES	Zipporah DAVIS
April 22	David MURRAY	Rachel DALE
May 2	Richard HALL	Levinia HILL
May 9	Jesse G. BURROUGHS	Margaret DUNCAN
May 15	Ebenezer WELDON	Betsey COLLINS
May 22	Joseph GODDEN	Elizabeth P. MERRILL
May 22	John MELBOURNE	Sally D. WHITTINGTON
May 29	Joseph SCHOOLFIELD	Nancy LAMBDEN
June 23	James M. DUNCAN	Martha DAVIS
June 27	Levi WARD	Nancy BEACHBOARD
June 27	Thomas CAREY	Elizabeth MaGRATH
June 28	Peter WEBB	Anny TYRE
June 29	John COULBOURNE	Nancy PITTS
July 5	Rufus K. MITCHELL	Caroline SELBY
July 7	Daniel PARKER	Margaret P. WALLOP
July 18	John GOUTEE	Mary VERDIN
July 18	Charles R. HENRY	Juliana FASSETT
July 25	John POWELL	Henny TRUITT
Aug. 2	Washington TAYLOR	Elizabeth EVANS
Aug. 9	Michael DYKES	Susanna HAYMAN
Aug. 9	Ephraim REECE	Mary DAVIS
Aug. 15	Merrene TAYLOR	Mary BRITTINGHAM
Aug. 17	Benjamin B. HOPKINS	Mary H, GUNBY
Aug. 18	Samuel McGEE	Anna LAWS

1820

April 22	David MURRAY	Rachel DALE
Aug. 22	Elijah CAREY	Sarah DYKES
Aug. 29	Henry WARD	Nancy JONES
Sept. 5	Joshua DAVIS	Gertrude BRATTEN
Sept. 11	Stephen REDDEN	Nancy REDDEN
Sept. 22	Ayers PORTER	Anne TIMMONS
Sept. 23	Levi JONES	Offy TAYLOR
Sept. 26	William BLADES	Charlotte FURNESS
Sept. 27	Peter WHITE	Martha STURGIS
Oct. 2	John HAYS	Molly BRADFORD
Oct. 10	James C. BOWEN	Mary P. BOWEN
Oct. 17	William R. FOOKS	Mary FOOKS
Oct. 18	Gustavus A. WHITE	Rebecca PORTER
Oct. 21	James BALLARD	Milly KERR
Oct. 24	Samuel HITCH	Henrietta BROWN
Oct. 24	Noah TILGHMAN	Henrietta PARSONS
Oct. 25	John BEVANS	Peggy JONES
Oct. 25	William BISHOP	Sally ATKINSON
Oct. 26	Jackson BROWN	Nancy LATCHUM
Oct. 31	James H. MITCHELL	Matilda PARKER
Oct. 31	Kendal LOW	Elizabeth WHITE
Nov. 7	George P. CHANDLER	Julian RILEY
Nov, 8	Benjamin BRUMBLY	Polly WALSTON
Dec. 5	Charles RIDER	Amelia H. PURNELL
Dec. 5	John Westley MELVIN	Sally MATTHEWS
Dec. 5	John DALE	Elizabeth D. JOHNSON
Dec. 7	John KNOX	Mary PIPER
Dec. 8	John CARY	Mary WHITE
Dec. 11	Joshua BRIDDLE	Mary MUMFORD
Dec. 11	James McGREGOR	Hannah DALE
Dec. 12	James DAVIS	Nancy LEWIS
Dec. 13	Milby PENNEWELL	Martha ADKINS
Dec. 14	John STURGIS	Jane STURGIS
Dec. 18	William STEVENS	Sally STURGIS
Dec. 19	Jonathan C. CROPPER	Nancy HALL
Dec. 19	Hancy Miles STURGIS	Catharine HARPER
Dec. 20	Eli CLAYWELL	Mary CLAYWELL
Dec. 20	Thomas HEIGHT(?)	Letta FOOKS
Dec. 25	William BRADFORD	Nancy BRIDDELL
Dec. 27	James HANDY	Betsy BALL
Dec. 27	Isaac WARD	Mary P. NELSON
Dec. 30	William MORRIS	Martha ANDERSON

1821

Jan. 2	John BURBAGE	Nancy GIVANS
Jan. 3	Griffen SAVAGE	Mary GIVANS
Jan. 10	William MORRIS	Nancy HENDERSON
Jan. 15	Isaac WARRINGTON	Leah WEST
Jan. 16	Elijah BRIDDLE	Elizabeth GODFREY

1821

Date	Groom	Bride
Jan. 17	William WILKINS	Caty WILLIS
Jan. 22	Isaac HARRIS	Mary MARSHALL
Jan. 23	William COLLINS	Susan PILCHARD
Jan. 23	David VESTER	Mary HAMMOND
Jan. 27	Peter O. MUMFORD	Elizabeth HECKMAN
Jan. 29	James BRITTINGHAM	Lyda WOUND
Jan. 30	Samuel TAYLOR	Sally TAYLOR
Feb. 1	William H. WHITE	Mary G. DENNIS
Feb. 7	Jenkins WARD	Ann NOBLE
Feb. 8	Peter HUTSON	Elenor STURGIS
Feb. 8	James BRITTINGHAM	Nancy PATTERSON
Feb. 12	Thomas WIMBROUGH	Levica H. PARKER
Feb. 16	Moses PURNELL	Maria BOWEN
Feb. 22	John B. BLAINE	Experance Grant COTTINGHAM
March 2	Powell SMACK	Rebecca CROPPER
March 7	Isaac JONES	Rhodah TURNER
March 10	Peter MASON	Eleanor REDDEN
March 23	Jenkins TOWNSEND	Tabitha SMULLEN
March 23	Elijah SHOCKLEY	Margaret GIVAN
March 23	Peter WILLIAMS	Denny TIMMONS
March 30	William COARD	Fanny GRAY
April 3	Littleton DRYDEN	Eleanor P. JOHNSON
April 5	Peter TRUITT	Nancy ROUND
April 12	William TEAGUE	Nancy KELLY
April 17	Lemuel SHOWELL	Mary R. BRIDEL
April 18	Isaac WALES	Mary WILSON
April 21	James H. COLBOURN	Sally T. OUTTEN
May 8	Jonathan COLLINS	Elizabeth ESHAM
May 8	Isaac CLAYWELL	Mary JONES
May 12	James STEVENS	Priscilla MITCHELL
May 12	Thomas LOKEY	Visa JONES
May 14	Thomas BAKER	Betsy GRAY
May 15	Robert TOWNSEND	Sally RIGGAN
May 24	John FOREMAN	Elizabeth RICHARDS
May 25	Robet F. BOWEN	Andasia EVANS
May 26	Daniel CHERIX	Betsy REID
May 30	Archibald ENNIS	Anna LANKFORD
June 5	John COOPER	Nancy LECATS
June 5	Holland SMACK	Margaret PORTER
June 5	Isaac SMULLEN	Sally SMULLEN
June 8	John HOLLAND	Sally JONES
June 13	Bowdoin ROBINS	Leah HOLLAND
June 20	William BRADFORD	Elizabeth POWELL
June 26	James TILGHMAN	Elizabeth DUKES
July 2	Isaac LAYFIELD	Sarah ADAMS
July 3	Littleton D. BEVANS	Harriett CORBIN
July 10	Samuel LONG	Rachel JONES
July 16	Samuel TAYLOR	Nancy DAVISON
July 18	George CROSDALL	Anamariah HOUSTON

1821

Date	Groom	Bride
July 20	William GIBBS	Mary BEVANS
July 24	William CAREY	Nancy DYKES
July 24	John SAVAGE	Betsey BUNDICK
July 25	Thomas MACKLIN	Zepy POWELL
July 26	Peter MORRIS	Polly BAYLY
July 31	John SMITH	Polly ADKINS
Aug. 1	Moses FLOYD	Lydia WARD
Aug. 2	John P. DUFFIELD	Zepporah BISHOP
Aug. 6	Caleb BELOTE	Mary BELOTE
Aug. 10	Levi CATHELL	Nancy GODFREY
Aug. 14	Sampson SELBY	Sarah BRAZIER
Aug. 15	William G. KILLAEM	Elizabeth D. SELBY
Aug. 15	George MERRILL	Catharine MERRILL
Aug. 22	John DAVIS	Elizabeth JOHNSON
Aug. 27	Melby A. HUDSON	Elizabeth ATKINSON
Aug. 28	Robert POWELL	Elizabeth TAYLOR
Sept. 3	Henry S. HOWARD	Polly DAZEY
Sept. 6	Robert H. JOHNSON	Sally PARKER
Sept. 18	Lemuel TRUITT	PATSEY SMACK
Sept. 20	John BOWDEN	Betsey POWELL
Sept. 22	William POWELL	Nancy WILLIS
Sept. 25	Asa C. COLLINS	Milly DAVIS
Sept. 25	James DERICKSON	Hennerietta W. PURNELL
Oct. 10	Richard SCARBOURGH	Harriet WHITE
Oct. 11	William Hoshier DICKERSON	Susanna BEACHBOARD
Oct. 16	John TILGHMAN	Polly COULBOURN
Oct. 17	Edward TAYLOR	Sally MACKMOTH
Oct. 18	William HUDSON	Mary SELBY
Oct. 23	John HANDCOCK	Wealthy MALLETT
Oct. 24	McKEMMY SMACK	Jane ALLEN
Nov. 13	Bagwell MASON	Ann TOWNSEND
Nov. 14	Branson JAMES	Catharine MERRILL
Nov. 20	Samuel HANDY Jr.	Mary CORBIN
Dec. 1	Robert JONES	Gatty ESHAM
Dec. 4	Joshua DRYDEN	Elizabeth TOWNSEND
Dec. 10	William D. SEYMOUR	Elizabeth C. KERR
Dec. 11	Robert COULBOURN	Elizabeth JONES
Dec. 12	William H. MERRILL	Eliza STEVENSON
Dec. 13	Hezekiah DAVIS	Hetty SMACK
Dec. 14	James MITCHELL	Margaret WYATT
Dec. 15	George VINSON	Elizabeth DRISKILL
Dec. 18	John HARMONSON	Comfort MUMFORD
Dec. 18	Peter TULL	Peggy REDDEN
Dec. 18	Giles JONES	Hetty GIBBS
Dec. 19	William POWELL	Betsey DAVIS
Dec. 20	Henry MUMFORD	Henretta STEVENSON
Dec. 20	Eliu BRIDDLE	Harriet MERRILL
Dec. 26	Thomas MERRELL	Sarah MERRELL
Dec. 26	James Winter BOTTOM	Tabitha WATERS
Dec. 27	Edwin FORMAN	Mary RICHARDS

1822

Date	Groom	Bride
Jan. 2	Jacob DAMNAL(?)	Polly TOWNSEND
Jan. 4	Isaac DENNIS	Sally TIMMONS
Jan. 4	William COLBOURN	Prissey TAYLOR
Jan. 7	Aaron HOLLOWAY	Fanny HOLLOWAY
Jan. 7	John TIMMONS	Kitty Young DALE
Jan. 10	Thomas WEAVER	Margaret MITCHELL
Jan. 16	William HALES	Sally JOHNSON
Jan. 16	James COLLINS	Elizabeth CONNER
Jan. 21	Err GRAY	Matilda HUDSON
Jan. 22	Severn HILL	Rebecca PAYNE
Jan. 22	Sampson MARSHALL	Sally MARSHALL
Jan. 24	William CLARK	Margaret MERRILL
Jan. 26	William WATSTON	Maria WILLIAMS
Jan. 28	Samuel BRITTINGHAM	Elizabeth PATTERSON
Jan. 29	Littleton TRADER	Margaret TULL
Jan. 30	John HOWARD	Charlotte NARS(?)
Feb. 1	Lazarus MADDUX	Elizabeth TOWNSEND
Feb. 2	James PARKER	Harriet ATKINSON
Feb. 5	William DIXON	Sally BOTHAM
Feb. 6	Henry CONOLY	Esther JONES
Feb. 11	Stringer MARSHALL	Rozell WALLOP
Feb. 12	William FRANKLIN Jr.	Elizabeth SCHOOLFIELD
Feb. 12	Samuel E. MOORE	Nancy VANCE
Feb. 12	john TINGLE	Sally M. PURNELL
Feb. 13	Thomas WILLIAMS	Margaret LUKER
Feb. 13	Robert McALLEN	Zepporah ADAMS
Feb. 13	Henry ADAMS	Margaret DAVIS
Feb. 14	Littleton NOCK	Hetty HOLLAND
Feb. 19	Curtis HENDERSON	Jane STURGIS
Feb. 20	Irving SPENCE	Margaret S. ROBINS
Feb. 26	William I. DOWNING	Hannah MELSON
Feb. 26	Isaac BEATHARDS	Darkey MOORE
March 6	Roger TAYLOR	Mary FLOYD
March 11	James COLLINS	Kesiah TIMMONS
March 13	Richard S. TILLMAN	Eliza DUNCAN
March 13	Peter SHOCKLEY	Amelia TAYLOR
March 14	Robert PITTS	Eliza WILLIAMS
March 18	james FOSSEY	Susan SCOTT
March 19	Joshua BOWEN	Nancy TRUITT
March 20	Esme RICHARDSON	Mary STURGIS
March 20	Thomas JONES	Mary TAYLOR
March 27	Henry GRAY	Eliza CROPPER
March 29	Major WHEELER	Eliza G. HUBBELL
April 2	Jesse HICKMAN	Sabrah GRAY
April 9	William DAVIS	Fanny JARMAN
April 18	William TARR	Lotty HUGHS
May 7	Ezekiel COSTON	Henny JONES
May 15	William BASSETT	Nancy SMITH
May 17	Levi ENNIS	Betsey MARRINER

1822

Date	Groom	Bride
May 25	John PRESLEY	Nancy HEARN
May 29	James G. TOWNSEND	Elizabeth RILEY
June 3	James CAMME	Mary PARSONS
June 11	Joel LARKIN	Nancy DAVIS
June 19	Curtis SMULLEN	Priscilla LOEK
June 26	Severn C. PARKER	Catharine G. PURNELL
July 10	John COLLINS	Sally BRADFORD
July 22	Henry BURBAGE	Andesiah DAVIS
July 29	Levi LONG	Eliza RIGGAN
Aug. 1	Andrew B. WYATH	Elizabeth MASON
Aug. 14	David PUZEY	Eleanor RIGGAN
Aug. 21	Gilly SMULLEN	Betsey BUTLER
Aug. 21	Richard SHOCKLEY	Fanny HADDER
Sept. 3	Henry POWELL	Nelly PUZEY
Sept. 3	Moses PAYNE	Eliza PENNEWELL
Sept. 3	Isaac KNOX	Rebecca HILL
Sept. 4	John MERRILL	Mary TAYLOR
Sept. 10	Jesse JUSTICE	Comfort HALES
Sept. 17	Samuel HOLLOWAY	Mehala GODFREY
Sept. 18	Jacob F. JONES	Milly DRYDEN
Sept. 18	William ELLIS	Catherine HADDER
Sept. 24	Noah GORDY	Sarah PARKER
Sept. 25	Isaac HARRIS	Sally LONG
Sept. 26	James H. COLLINS	Betsey JOHNSON
Sept. 28	William LINGER	Sally BRITTINGHAM
Oct. 1	William CLAYWELL	Arrabella ATKINSON
Oct. 7	John DUKES	Nancy JONES
Oct. 8	James WELBOURNE	Clarissa MARSHALL
Oct. 9	John BERRY	Maria HOLLAND
Oct. 15	William BROUGHTON	Zepporah R. TEAGUE
Oct. 20	James NORTHAM	Sally WRIGHT
Oct. 23	Joshua HARMON	Emeline FLOID
Oct. 24	Littleton HARMONSON	Mary JONES
Oct. 30	John MELVIN	Henny HUGHS
Nov. 11	Burton CANNON	Polly R. FOOKS
Nov. 19	Samuel PORTER	Nancy PARKER
Nov. 25	Soloman CAREY	Hetty BELL
Nov. 26	Elisha JONES	Ann JONES
Nov. 26	Isaac BOSTON	Amelia JONES
Nov. 26	William WATTS	Patty WARREN
Nov. 27	William WATERS	Betsy HOUSTON
Nov. 27	William B.S. COTTMAN	Elizabeth G. HANDY
Dec. 3	John STURGIS Jr.	Elizabeth F. TEAGUE
Dec. 4	John CORBIN	Catharine ROWLEY
Dec. 5	Henry TOADVINE	Elizabeth FASSETT
Dec. 5	George RICHARDSON	Nancy HARMAN(?)
Dec. 10	Peter SMITH	Eliza WILLIAMS
Dec. 10	Levin BLADES	Sally REDDEN
Dec. 11	Levin MERRILL	Julian BARRETT

1822
Dec. 12	Nathaniel BENSTON	Margaret LANKFORD
Dec. 12	John W. DENNIS	Nancy M. QUINTON
Dec. 13	Arthur DYKES	Julian FOOKS
Dec. 17	Southy TAYLOR	Wise ALLEN
Dec. 17	Zadok HENRY	Hetty BRIDDLE
Dec. 17	James WATSON	Margaret JONES
Dec. 18	Thomas HENDERSON	Comfort RICHARDSON
Dec. 18	Littleton TOWNSEND	Hetty HUDSON
Dec. 31	William DAVIS	Priscilla SPENCER

1823
Jan. 3	James McGEE	Maria CROPPER
Jan. 4	Peter TRUITT	Katy WILLIAMS
Jan. 6	William Noble SHOCKLEY	Elizabeth LEVINGSTON
Jan. 6	Nathaniel BRATTEN	Betsy HOLLAND
Jan. 7	William FASSETT	Phenettes GRAY
Jan. 8	William FURNISS	Elizabeth TIMMONS
Jan. 10	John THORNTON	Betsey TARR
Jan. 13	John DALE	Margaret BRATTEN
Jan. 14	David BREWINGTON	Peggy TOWNSEND
Jan. 14	Benjamin VINSON	Priscilla MORRIS
Jan. 21	James WARREN	Gertrude WILLIAMS
Jan. 22	James GAULT	Sarah BARCKLEY
Jan. 23	James TAYLOR	Leah COLLINS
Jan. 24	William LAWS	Sally RUSSELL
Jan. 25	John MASSEY	Eliza TAYLOR
Jan. 28	Schoolfield LAMBERSON	Arralanta BOWEN
Jan. 28	David MALONE	Henrietta POLLITT
Jan. 29	Samuel D. HARPER	Elizabeth DALE
Feb. 3	William DRUMMOND	Elizabeth MATTHEWS
Feb. 4	Joseph TULL	Hetty PILCHARD
Feb. 6	James BROWN	Mary FLEMING
Feb. 6	Samuel BURROUGHS	Harriet TOADVINE
Feb. 6	William HENDERSON	Martha BIRCH
Feb. 12	John HOLSTON (of Levin)	Eleanor TOWNSEND
Feb. 17	Elijah PILCHARD	Polly SLOCOMB
Feb. 21	John GILLETT	Elizabeth DAVIS
Feb. 21	Isaac DENNIS	Nancy PARSONS
Feb. 23	Josiah HICKMAN	Mary Mills GUNBY
Feb. 25	John WINSON	Charlotte BURROUGHS
March 5	Peter DAVIS	Martha DALE
March 5	Lemuel TRUITT	Lydia HANDCOCK
March 8	Elijah SHAY	Rebecca NORTHAM
March 11	Robert MALONE	Elizabeth POLLITT
March 11	Isaac GRIFFITH	Rebecca QUILLING
March 12	William HARGIS	Susan BULL
March 20	Eliajh KILBY	Sally TARR
March 20	Henry P. FISHER	Susan CAMPBELL
March 25	Schoolfield RICHARDS	Harriet HOLLAND

1823

Date	Groom	Bride
March 31	Arthur BURROUGHS	Nancy S. CATHELL
April 7	John F. PURNELL	Eliza BOWEN
April 8	Kendal JONES	Mary SMITH
April 15	Edward HAMMOND (of Chs)	Elizabeth VICTOR
April 17	John ANDERSON	Amelia HOUSTON
April 26	Samuel TARR	Rhoda HILL
April 28	George H. DASHIELL	Attlanta FEDDEMAN
April 29	William LAWS	Gertrude DUNCAN
May 2	John AYDELOTT	Sally DAVIS
May 8	Elijah B. POWELL	Elizbeth McDANIEL
May 8	James B. ROBINS	Andasia R. PURNELL
May 12	Charley RUARK	Sally RICHARDSON
May 12	William HUDSON	Margaret BREWINGTON
May 14	Edward D. INGRAHAM	Mary G. WILSON
May 20	Jacob HOLLOWAY	Sally TIMMONS
May 24	Puurnell JOHNSON	Nelly SHOCKLEY
May 30	James DAVIS Jr.	Elizabeth HILL
June 11	William N. PURNELL	Eleanor H. ROBINS
June 12	Joseph HUTCHESON	Sally W. GUNBY
June 16	Samuel CUTLER	Nancy GREY
June 18	John K. CLARK	GATTY DUKES
June 21	John MUMFORD	Mary PERKING
June 23	William LEVINGSTON	Mary SMITH
June 30	Riley JONES	Rachel ELLIS
July 2	Thos R. ROUND	Mary Ann RACKLIFFE
July 8	Charles BENNETT	Mary LENOX
July 10	Joshua CROUCH	Hannah RUKE
July 15	James MILBOURNE	Catharine DICKERSON
July 18	George TODD	Catharine STEVENSON
July 21	James WAIT	Martha NICKERSON
July 28	Isaac BRIDDLE	Fanny FASSETT
July 30	Isaac DONAWAY	Nancy WAIT
Aug. 6	Matthias TAPMAN	Ann PEPPER
Aug. 11	James BURCH	Iza STERRIGE
Aug. 11	Richard BULL	Mary WEST
Aug. 15	Parker COPES	Elizabeth MATTHEWS
Aug. 19	James BLADES	ROSE WEBB
Aug. 27	Isaac DRYDEN	Sarah BARNES
Aug. 30	John L.B. ROBINS	Henrietta SHOWELL
Sept. 1	David MILLS	Maria GASKINS
Sept. 2	Isaac DRYDEN Jr.	Harriet Ann JONES
Sept. 9	Elisha PARSONS	Betsy ROUNDS
Sept. 10	Edward NOCK	Sally M. JOHNSON
Oct. 9	Isaac MITCHELL	Sarah HENRY
Oct. 14	Stephen McKEE	Esther TILGHMAN
Oct.	Lewis JONES	Sally EVANS
Oct. 22	John F. FASSITT	Mary BELL
Oct. 22	Henry J. FRANKLIN Jr.	Mary J. PURNELL
Oct. 24	Esme BAYLY	Nancy TIMMONS

1823

Date	Groom	Bride
Oct. 29	Henry BRATTEN	Eliza MARSHALL
Nov. 1	Levin H. BRITTINGHAM	Harriet LENDZEY
Nov. 1	Alexander McCOLLIER	Tabitha ALLEN
Nov. 3	Isaac MIDDLETON	Muty TOWNSEND
Nov. 4	John E. STEVENSON	Molly HENDERSON
Nov. 11	Josiah BOWEN	Leah GRAY
Nov. 12	Robert RICHARDSON	Betsey TRUITT
Nov. 21	James HOLLAND	Mary JONES
Nov. 26	James G. TOWNSEND	Amelia HAZZARD
Dec. 1	James FARRELL	Sally COBB
Dec. 10	William EVANS	Nancy JOHNSON
Dec. 12	Levin SELBY	Hetty BELL
Dec. 15	Elisha Purnell PARKER	HETTY PARKER
Dec. 15	Milbourne M. DALE	Sarah BRATTEN
Dec. 17	John LAYFIELD	Euphame LAMBERSON
Dec. 18	David BANKS	Ann COLLINS
Dec 23	Samuel PORTER	Charlotte JOHNSON
Dec. 26	Thomas F. MOORE	Eleanor D. HOWARD
Dec. 29	Levin D. HOUSTON	Ann PATTERSON
Dec. 28	Moses RAYNE	Nancy COSTEN
Dec. 31	Josiah BETHARD	Molly PORTER

1824

Date	Groom	Bride
Jan. 5	Ezekiel SMITH	Rachel PARKER
Jan. 5	Daniel MASSEY	Molly Bratten PITTS
Jan. 5	Moses JONES	Maria DRYDEN
Jan. 6	Elijah BAKER	Elizabeth WIATT
Jan. 6	Matthias BEATHARD	Nancy MOORE
Jan. 10	Joseph HOUSTON	Ann LONG
Jan. 14	Isaac ENNIS	Peggy ATKINSON
Jan. 16	Littleton D. TUBBS	Nancy BOWEN
Jan. 20	Levi COLLINS	Elizabeth C. WALSTON
Jan. 20	William W. HANDY	Ann D. AUSTIN
Jan. 28	John CHAPMAN	Mary HILL
Jan. 29	John HOZIER	Elizabeth TURNER
Jan. 29	John WHITE	Charlotte PURNELL
Jan. 30	Thomas SEALES	Arsissy DAVIS
Feb. 2	Hezekiel DORMAN	Maria STURGIS
Feb. 11	Major TARR	Mary RICHARDSON
Feb. 13	Arthur CHERRIX	Nancy TARR
Feb. 16	Elijah PARSONS	Mary ESHAM
Feb. 17	Daniel HANDCOCK	Adaline HUDSON
Feb. 17	Peter TRUITT	Leah BRATTEN
Feb. 23	Meshack MATTHEWS	Ann PORTER
Feb. 26	Elijah MERRILL	Maria McCREADY
March 1	Stephen JONES	Sarah PRUITT
March 2	Whittington HANDCOCK	Sarah Ann GLADDEN
March 3	Samuel J. RODGERS	Ann A. SCARBOROUGH
March 3	Benjamin BEN	Henrietta BURBAGE
March 9	Samuel Tindle JONES	Martha FARRELL

1824

Date	Groom	Bride
March 11	James BOWEN of Salathel	Sally NOCK
March 15	William TRUITT	Ann BENSON
March 17	Soloman COLLINS	Nancy WALSTON
March	Ephraim COLLINS	Agnes BARNES
March 20	Bennet FISH	Mary JONES
March 26	Jones BOUNDS	Mary PUSEY
April 5	David TRUITT	Margaret MILLS
April 7	Ennals CANNON	Pattey BASSETT
April 13	John BAIN	Priscilla TOADVINE
April 17	John HENDERSON	Gattey BLADES
April 19	Levin HOLLAND	Charlotte BOWEN
April 20	Francis A. BOYER	Ann TILGHNAN
April 27	Thomas PEWSEY	Margaret T. HICKMAN
May 1	Purnell SMACK	Huldy WILLIAMS
May 4	David BUNTING	Sally BURCH
May 4	William AYDELOTT	Hetty DAVIS
May 8	John BONNAWEL	Sarah TURLINGTON
May 18	Zadok WILLIS	Mary WILKINGS
May 20	James BUNNITT	Mary WHITTINGTON
May 25	John GODFREY	Huldah JONES
May 28	George JONES	BETSEY WAILES
May 29	William POWELL	Elizabeth BLADES
June 1	James ANDERSON	Ann LAWS
June 2	Josiah ELLIS	Esther PAYNE
June 3	Zadok RICHARDSON	Polly SHOCKLEY
June 18	Lemuel A. HALL	Sarah WHITE
June 25	George M. LEVINGSTON	Sarah JENKINS
June 25	Bowdoin HAMMOND	Catharine HAMMOND
June 25	James TILLMAN	Harriett WHITE
June 30	Francis CHERRIX	Tabby TARR
July 5	Benjamin BARNES	Eleanor POWELL
July 7	Justice Morris BRATTEN	Leah Washington FOUNTAIN
July 7	William H. TILGHMAN	Mary STEVENSON
July 16	Stephen PURNELL	Hannah HENDERSON
July 20	Thomas BOLDS	Louisa JERMAN
July 20	James DRYDEN	Elizabeth HALL
July 21	James R. MERRILL	Elizabeth W. STEVENSON
July 22	John MATTHEWS	Mary TARR
July 23	William RUARK	Priscilla JOHNSON
Aug. 2	James MATTHEWS	Sarah ROWLEY
Aug. 3	James TAYLOR	Eliza GILCHRIST
Aug. 9	Levi MERRILL	Eliza HOUSTON
Aug. 10	William SMITH	Polly NELSON
Aug. 17	James HAMMOND	Charlotte BOWEN
Aug. 24	Kendall TRUITT	Lydia FASSITT
Aug. 26	James DAVIS	Charlotte WILBUR
Aug. 26	William SPENCER	Eliza KELLAIM
Aug. 27	Seth SMITH	Alce PARKER

1824

Date	Groom	Bride
Aug. 27	William WATTS	Mary K. SMACK
Aug. 31	Thomas POWELL	Hetty Matilda TINGLE
Sept. 6	William AUSTIN	Priscilla SHOCKLEY
Sept. 8	George HUDSON	Julia Ann DYMOCK
Sept 10	James MUMFORD	Esther CORBIN
Sept. 11	Ricahard T. TILLMAN	Julia Ann R. SAMPSON
Sept. 15	Zorababel RICHARDSON	Mary Ann CRIPPEN
Sept. 15	Thomas POWELL	Mary PURNELL
Sept. 20	David EVANS (Of Wm)	Molly DAVIS
Sept. 28	Thomas MOORE	Mary O. RILEY
Oct. 6	John ANDERSON	Elizabeth MARSHALL
Oct. 8	John COLEBOURN	Priscilla WARD
Oct. 12	Jenkins WARD	Molly STURGIS
Oct. 20	David BOWEN	Margaret CROPPER
Oct. 22	William GARDNER	Elizabeth BLOXSOM
Oct. 27	James KNOX	Polly JARMAN
Oct. 27	Richard FREENY	Sarah PARKER
Nov. 6	John DRYDEN	Mary CAUSAY
Nov. 15	James WARRINGTON	Molly MURROE
Nov. 17	John COTTINGHAM	Letta NICHOLS
Nov. 19	John DENNIS	Peggy FOOKS
Nov. 23	George FARLOW	Abigale FOOKS
Nov. 24	John GUNBY	Sarah H. WHITINGTON
Nov. 24	Levi NELSON	Charlotte HAZZARD
Dec. 6	Eli DAVIS	Jediah SMITH
Dec. 7	William WHEALTON	Ann Maria DOUGHTY
Dec. 7	Daniel MATTHEWS	Nancy WHITE
Dec. 14	Leonard MORRIS	Lucretia Townsend SHOCKLE
Dec. 17	David DRESKILL	Eliza CATHELL
Dec. 17	Levin F. WHITE	Ann DRESKILL
Dec. 20	Nathaniel NICHOLS	Nancy WILLIAMS
Dec. 20	Thomas LANE	Eleanor Gray FOOKS
Dec. 21	Joshua HAMBLIN	Nancy FARLOW
Dec. 21	Samuel BLADES	Polly REDDEN
Dec. 22	William CAREY	Henrietta TOWNSEND
Dec. 22	Isaac MUMFORD	Eleanor HUDSON
Dec. 27	John DENSTON	Sally FLETCHER
Dec. 28	Elijah SHEPHERD	Dolly TARR
Dec. 29	Peter DICKERSON	Anna B. VICTOR

1825

Date	Groom	Bride
Jan, 5	Laber HILL	Maria BURROUGHS
Jan. 6	Robert CALLENDER	Elizabeth BAYNUM
Jan 7	Elisha POWELL	Martha TINGLE
Jan 7	James MELSON	Elizabeth POLSON
Jan. 10	William GARMON	Elizabeth DEAN
Jan. 10	George S. MERRILL	Charlotte MERRILL
Jan. 11	John CUSTIS	Sally SAVAGE

1825

Date	Groom	Bride
Jan. 11	John CURTIS	Sally SAVAGE
Jan. 11	Samuel ROWLEY	Nancy RICHARDSON
Jan. 12	John COTTINGHAM	Margaret DICKSON
Jan. 13	Daniel BENSTON	Sarah RIGGIN
Jan. 15	William PARSONS	Polly HALL
Jan. 15	William Handy MELVIN	Nancy ROSSE
Jan. 18	John A. PARSONS	Sally JONES
Jan. 18	Washington MARSHALL	Susan SPARROW
Jan. 18	Samuel BENSTON	Matilda HENDERSON
Jan. 18	Elijah MILES	Leah MATTHEWS
Jan. 21	William Henry JONES	Betsey FREEMAN
Jan. 21	John POWELL	Mary McGREGOR
Feb. 8	Samuel LONG	Elizabeth HALL
Feb. 8	Samuel KER	Sally WALLER
Feb. 9	Edmond CROPPER	Comfort BROUGHTON
Feb. 14	John TILGHMAN	Polly TRUITT
Feb. 15	William RICHARDSON	Gertrude P. BEATHARDS
Feb. 16	William BEVANS	Maria MERRILL
Feb. 26	Jacob TAYLOR	Sally BOOTH
Feb. 28	John SHOWELL	Mary DAVIS
March 1	Major GILLETT	Mary Ann EWELL
March 1	James ENNIS	Catharine RUONELLS
March 8	Henry JONES	Elizabeth MELVIN
March 8	Charles GODFREY	Elizabeth HOSHIER
March 9	Soloman SHOCKLEY	Mary Ann SMULLEN
March 10	William TINGLE	Sally Maria WILLIAMSON
March 11	William PURNELL	Juliann DAVIS
March 11	James W. STEVENSON	Elizabeth PATTERSON
March 12	William S. SHOCKLEY	Lovey CAREY
March 16	James MASON	Wealthy HENCOCK
March 22	James WHEALTON	Margaret EWELL
March 29	Peter BEACHBOARD	Mary HARPER
March 29	James MUMFORD	Molly SHOCKLY
March 30	Samuel PATTERSON	Susan LONG
March 30	John H. PRUITT	Sally James JONES
March 30	Joshua W. HITCH	Elizabeth WHITTINGTON
March 31	Walter KELLY	Sally P. ESHAM
April 4	Levin HENDERSON	Esther STEVENSON
April 5	John HALL	Patty DAVIS
April 5	Peter SHOCKLEY	Nancy LOEKEY
April 13	William CORBEN	Sally BACON
April 18	Samuel T. LUCAS	Matilda BIRD
April 18	Curtis BIRD	Mary FISHER
April 18	Joseph DUNNAWAY	Druzilla BAKER
April 19	John SPENCER	Sally SELBY
April 22	William WILLISS	Mary JACKSON
April 26	Peter COSTON	Nancy EVANS
April 27	Benjamin JONES	Caroline PRIOR

1825			
May 3	John GIBBONS	Leah BALL	
May 11	James LILLLISTON	Margaret BELL	
May 13	Littleton JARMAN	Narcissa Ball WILLIAMS	
May 17	Warner BENNETT	Wealthy JONES	
May 17	Charles ATKINSON	Maria LAMBDEN	
May 18	Thomas PURNELL	Mary DAVIS	
May 23	Nixon BEACHARDS	Eliza DAVIS	
May 24	James ROACH	Nancy BREWINGTON	
May 28	Cornelius GODFREY	Elizabeth STURGIS	
June 1	Parker BOWDEN	Anna RUSSELL	
June 8	Henry SMITH	Fanny LANE	
June 8	Levin HOLLAND	Betsey BEATHARDS	
June 14	John W. DOWNING	Matilda CONNER	
June 18	William H. CLAYTON	Hannah JOHNSON	
June 18	Ephraim MATTHEWS	Henny JACKSON	
June 18	Samuel JOHNSON	Mary S. ROBINS	
June 22	James DORETY	Henny WOODEN	
July 13	Edward WARREN	Polly BRADFORD	
July 13	Thomas B. JONES	Ann C. WRIGHT	
July 22	James TAYLOR	Margaret REED	
July 25	Zadok PURNELL Jr.	Jane BOWEN	
July 29	William HADDER	Maria JACKSON	
Aug. 3	John BOSTON	Mary L. BARROTT	
Aug. 10	Henry WHEELER	Harriett LONG	
Aug. 25	George A. COARD	Trafanny G. DIX	
Sept. 21	Noah ADKINS	Fanny BEATHARDS	
Sept. 23	Joshua HUDSON	Molly DUNNAWAY	
Sept. 24	George W. McKNEEL	Nancy BOSTON	
Oct. 11	John SMITH	Catherine BURROUGHS	
Oct. 11	Noah BOWEN	Ann ELIzabeth GRAY	
Oct. 25	Isaac PUZEY	Eleanor BARNES	
Oct. 25	Levin H. JOHNSON	Sally HILL	
Oct. 26	James Thomas JACKSON	Milly ALLEN	
Oct. 31	Isaac E. WEBDELL	Margaret ASKRIDGE	
Nov. 9	Matthias TRUITT	Aralanta DAVIS	
Nov. 14	William MASON	Sally REDDEN	
Nov. 15	William RILEY	Sally RICHARDS	
Nov. 29	Jonathan FOOKS (of E)	Leah FOOKS	
Nov. 30	Milby PURNELL	Hetty CLOGG	
Dec. 2	John GARDNER	Harriett TAYLOR	
Dec. 7	John BYRD	Ann BLOXSOM	
Dec. 8	John HOLLOWAY	Sally BUTLER	
Dec. 10	James HOUSTON	Amelia STEVENSON	
Dec. 13	Handy JACKSON	Mary STURGIS	
Dec. 15	John POWELL	Hetty DEVERIX	
Dec. 15	Peter GODFREY	Mary GODFREY	
Dec. 20	James DICKERSON	Nancy BENNETT	
Dec. 20	Josiah ROCK	Maria L. HOOPER	

1825
Dec.	20	James DRYDEN	Nancy PATTEY
Dec	23	Jesse MUMFORD	Nancy TOWNSEND
Dec.	26	Robert H. ELLEGOOD	Maria PARKER
Dec.	28	John B. CAMERON	Henrietta COWLEY
Dec.	28	Francis D. MILLER	Elizabeth DOWNING
Dec.	29	Belitha GODFREY	Elizabeth CLAYWELL
Dec	31	William BOWEN	Eliza HOSHIER

1826
Jan.	2	John WILLIS	Rebecca BRADFORD
Jan.	3	David G. ODELL	Mary HARRIS
Jan.	3	John DALE	Patty TRUITT
Jan.	3	William WARD	Mary NELSON
Jan.	6	Ananias GARMAN	Patty CAHOON
Jan.	10	Isaac HEARN	Nancy NOBLE
Jan.	10	William LEWIS	Mary BROADWATER
Jan.	17	Jonathan BAKER	Harriett DUNNAWAY
Jan.	23	John WILLETT	Claddy SPYKES
Feb.	3	Jesse BAKER	Rebecca MITCHELL
Feb.	7	Levin SMITH	Mary HENDERSON
Feb.	8	James CAMPBELL	Temperance PARSONS
Feb.	9	Moses GREER	Margaret HALES
Feb.	11	John SMITH	Betsey WILLIAMS
Feb.	13	Joshua COTTINGHAM	Maria WILLIAMS
Feb.	14	Jessie BROUGHTON	Anna BAKER
Feb.	22	George MAGEE	Betsey DALE
Feb.	27	William HAYMAN	Ann CAUSEY
Feb.	27	William FREENEY	Sally NICKERSON
March	1	Turner DAVIS	Mary PARKER
March	1	Levin BAKER	Molly HILL
March	6	William ADAMS	Delila BRADFORD
March	6	William HAMMOND	Nancy JOHNSON
March	7	Zadok HALL	Ronna REDDEN
March	8	Parker WONNELL	Leah Purnell PUZEY
March	8	Lemuel P. SPENCE	Milcah E. FRANKLIN
March	14	Skinner WALLOP	Elizabeth HOLLAND
March	15	Littleton TAYLOR	Tabitha JOHNSON
March	29	Thomas L. DISHAROON	Hetty TEAGUE
March	30	Levin MITCHELL	Ann Maria CORBIN
April	3	John DAVIDSON	Charlotte ANDERSON
April	8	John PARKER	Margaret ESHAM
April	12	James DUNCAN	Sally GARRETSON
April	13	James BENNETT	Milcah COTTINGHAM
April	13	John STURAIS Junr	Fanny DUNCAN
April	19	Allen D. KELLAM	Comfort P. TEAGUE
April	21	James MITCHELL	Harriet ESHAM
April	25	Isaac COVINGTON	Amelia FRANKLIN
May	1	James ANDERSON	Mary MARTIN

1826

May 1	Willaim H. POWELL	Hester Ann CAUSEY
May 2	Joseph H. BENSON	Sally TAYLOR
May 9	William FASSITT	Doretha Esther Waters HENRY
May 10	Moses C. SMITH	Ann HAMMOND
May 15	Peter WARRINGTON	Gatty DEAL
May 17	James CLAYWELL	Hetty PREDEAUX
May 24	William PARSONS	Amelia WHITE
May 24	Benjamin P, AYDELOTT	Nancy RICHARDSON
May 25	Isaac CLAYWELL	Nancy BOWEN
May 29	John JAMBLIN	Jane DALE
May 31	Edward MURRAY	Mary Ann ADAMS
June 1	William COLLINS	Rebecca CAREY
June 3	Samuel LONG	Rachel ESHAM
June 7	Josiah SHOWELL	Hannah DALE
June 12	Walter BROADWATER	Polly BURTON
June 20	Daniel SHARPLEY	Nancy LEWIS
June 21	John S. PURNELL	Margaret C. HENRY
June 21	Jesse ENNIS	Nancy ENNIS
June 23	William McHENRY	Sally LAMBERSON
June 27	James COLLINS	Marandy POWELL
June 27	Wm. DENNIS	Rachel DAVIS
June 29	Samuel TUNNELL	Mary SMITH
June 30	Nathaniel TYSON	Henrietta POWELL
July 10	James STEVENSON	Mary Ann GUNBY
July 11	Stephen McCREADDY	Charlotte BENNETT
July 11	Mathias TAPMAN	Famy LAMBERSON
July 11	William BROUGHTON	Betsy RAIN
July 17	Benjamin AYDELOTT	Elizabeth NELSON
July 22	Robert MITCHELL	Elizabeth Ann COVINGTON
July 26	Zadok STURGIS	Peggy BENNETT
July 26	Elihu PALMER	Elizabeth BRATTEN
July 27	William DAVIS	Mary HENRY
Aug. 11	Wesley GORDY	Nancy McGREGOR
Aug. 14	Augustus W. BAGWELL	Catharine CROPPER
Aug. 15	James DUNCAN	Catharine COLLINS
Aug. 17	Levin DAVIS	Nancy MELVIN
Aug. 23	Benjamin DAVIS	Milcah Ann BEVANS
Aug. 29	Elijah LAWS	Sally GIVANS
Aug. 29	Isaac DAVIS	Susan WEBB
Aug. 31	Asa BOWIN	Leah STINSON
Sept. 6	Joshua W. HITCH	Mary DENNIS
Oct. 3	John PAYNE	Leah PAYNE
Oct. 4	Garritson GORDY	Margaret BURROUGHS
Oct. 9	Levin G. IRVING	Mary HOOPER
Oct. 14	Joseph GIBB	Eliza CROPPER
Oct. 20	Purnell BRITTINGHAM	Esther S. LAMBDEN
Oct. 24	James S. DUNTON	Eliza O. MARSHALL
Oct. 25	Elijah POWELL	Maria Ann HAYMAN

1826
Date	Groom	Bride
Oct. 30	David TRUITT	Mary HILL
Oct. 31	John LOEKEY	Elizabeth JOHNSON
Nov. 8	Thomas WILLIAMS	Mary HENRY
Nov, 11	Levin TOWNSEND	Tracey PUZEY
Nov. 15	Ebenzer MEZICK	Nancy JOHNSON
Nov. 15	John SCHOOLFIELD	Eliza Ann BEAUCHAMP
Nov. 16	James PORTER	Rachell PENNEWELL
Nov. 28	William KELLY	Sally JOHNSON
Nov. 29	Major LOKEY	Nancy TAYLOR
Nov. 30	Shepherd B. FLOYD	Eliza BAYER
Dec. 5	Henry BUTLER	Nancy POWELL
Dec. 7	Nehemiah DORMAN	Eleanor STURGIS
Dec. 8	Peter BLADES	Catherine DUNTON
Dec. 11	Zeno WORRINGTON	Polly DUNCAN
Dec. 12	James DEVORIX	Zilpha CONNER
Dec. 19	Daniel JOHNSON	Catharine COLLINS
Dec. 19	James PAYNTER	Mary Ann SHOWELL
Dec. 19	Rion BRITTINGHAM	Hetty ANDERSON
Dec. 19	Henry M. BASIT	Harriet HALL
Dec. 21	John RICHARDSON	Louisa FRANKLIN
Dec. 25	John O. STURGIS	Eliza NELSON

1827
Date	Groom	Bride
Jan. 2	Purnell T. OUTTEN	Elizabeth NOCK
Jan. 2	George TRUITT	Viny HOLLOWAY
Jan. 11	Isaac STEVENSON	Eleanor Jane POLLETT
Jan. 11	John PILCHARD	Henny WEBB
Jan. 16	William DICKSON	Lucretia TOWNSEND
Jan. 17	John S. PORTER	Ann JOHNSON
Jan. 23	Elijah BRITTINGHAM	Ann COLLOHAM
Jan. 23	Purnell J. BENNETT	Diadanna JONES
Jan. 27	Thomas JAMES	Hetty MILLS
Jan. 29	John C. BREWINGTON	Elizabeth HEARN
Jan. 29	Rowland BEVANS	Mary Ann DUBBER
Jan. 30	William JONES	Jane BOWEN
Jan. 30	Joshua HOSHER	Gatty BOWEN
Feb. 1	Joshua S. A. TRADER	Maranda SMITH
Feb. 7	Stephen HOLLAND	Eliza MARSHALL
Feb. 8	Lemuel SMACK	Mary TULL
Feb. 17	Henry HALL	Sally CORBIN
Feb. 20	William BEACHBOARD	Julianne WARD
Feb. 21	Lutheran M. STURGIS	Rosa BLOXOM
Feb. 25	Samuel WHITE	Sally TAYLOR
Feb. 26	Seth HARRISON	Elizabeth Ann P. MARSHALL
March 1	John STURGIS	Andesiah EVANS
March 5	Joseph HEARN	Sally MELSON
March 6	John C. DERICKSON	Catharine R. BRAVARD
March 7	Brittingham POWELL	Ann BEVANS

1827

Date	Groom	Bride
March 7	Isaac HOLLAND	Elizabeth HAMMOND
March 27	Hewet (?) DICKSON	Sally JOHNSON
April 2	Benjamin H. BYRD	Henrietta FOOKS
April 2	Thomas TIMMONS	Ebbe LYNCH
April 9	George Esme MARSHALL	Elizabeth HAYES
April 10	Elijah TAYLOR	Harriet HENDERSON
April 10	James HOLLAND	Clarissa DICKSON
April 17	Lambert QUILLEN	Rachel DAVIS
April 20	George GERMAN	Leah POWELL
April 21	James BIRCH	Sally COFFIN
April 23	George VANDOME	Martha McNEILLE
April 24	Severn PRUITT	Harriett WHIRLOW
April 26	Ephraim MATTHEWS	Leah DORMAN
May 2	Joseph RICHARDSON	Amelia CONNER
May 3	John CLAYWELL	Henrietta CLAYWELL
May 9	Mitchell HANDCOCK	Susan BLADES
May 14	Ethen LION	Louisa GILLETT
May 16	John SMULLIN	Eliza BUTLER
May 23	John S. STEVENSON	Harriet G. TINGLE
May 24	Edward M. SMITH	Julian M. FARROW
May 29	Parker COPES	Sally PURNELL (of Merrill)
May 31	Jacob GRAY	Elizabeth HALL
June 2	Isaac MATTHEWS	Elizabeth HUDSON
June 2	John GAULT	Rhoda TRUITT
June 2	Arnold PRIOR	Eliza DAVIS
June 19	Isaac S. JOHNSON	Sarah COTTINGHAM
June 20	William MATTHEWS	Leah EWELL
July 5	Thomas DEVORIX	Charlotte STEVENSON
July 7	Shadrack M. AMES	Anna Maria EDMUNDS
July 17	Joseph GRAY	Joicey COLLINS
July 27	John JONES	Maria CLOGG
July 27	Francis MEZICK	Harriett STEVENSON
Aug. 2	William E. BRITTINGHAM	Mary D. STURGIS
Aug. 9	James HALL	Eliza GRAY
Aug. 11	Luther HENMAN	Nancy WHITE
Aug. 16	John RUSSEL	Sally TAYLOR
Aug. 25	Samuel BLOXOM	Elizabeth DOWNING
Aug. 28	Nathaniel TOPPING	Leah RILEY
Sept. 1	William McGRAUGH	Nancy RUARK
Sept. 4	Isaac JONES	Elizabeth HOLLAND
Sept. 15	John MITCHELL	Esther WYATT
Sept. 19	Parker SELBY	Polly ATKINSON
Sept. 25	Azariah BRITTINGHAM	Sarah PARSONS
Sept. 26	Isaac W. DENNIS	Molly TRUITT
Sept. 28	John HOOPER	Mary M. RICHARDSON
Oct. 10	John DUNNAWAY	Charlotte BAKER
Oct. 10	Thomas WATERS	Betsey SELBY
Oct. 10	Samson COULBOURN	Betsey MATTHEWS

1827

Oct. 10	William VERNESTON	Harriet W. BENNETT
Oct. 17	Charles BREWINGTON	Ann PARSONS
Oct. 23	Zebulon G. MUNFORD	Matilda MARRETT
Oct. 23	Henry MEARS	Sarah Ann TAYLOR
Nov. 8	James JONES	Maria DIXON
Nov. 12	John B. PERDUE	Juilan DAVIS
Nov. 20	Ephraim GIVAN	Henrietta BURBAGE
Nov. 26	David HOLLOWAY	Nancy PHILLIPS
Nov. 28	Isaac TIMMONS	Andetiah HOLLOWAY
Dec. 1	John NICKERSON	Elizabeth PARKER
Dec. 6	Syrus LEONARD	Mary JONES
Dec. 11	Noah BENSON	Nancy MERRILL
Dec. 17	Joseph MURRAY	Nancy TAYLOR
Dec. 17	Littleton DUKES	Martha TRUITT
Dec. 18	Jesse WILKERSON	Elizabeth S. MILLS
Dec. 18	James RICHARDSON	Hetty BENSON
Dec. 21	Peter S. JONES	Martha SCOTT
Dec. 24	Soloman SMALL	Sally BIRD
Dec. 24	John PATTERSON	Milcah STEVENSON
Dec. 26	Samuel HOSHIER Junr	Mary GORNWELL
Dec. 27	Wlisha ? WHITETASH ?	Elizabeth M. ATKINSON
Dec. 28	Charles PATTERSON	Mary Ann MERRILL
Dec. 28	Jesse TURNER	Hetty HOLLAND
Dec. 31	Jacob ROGERS	Sarah TAYLOR

1828

Jan. 1	John TAYLOR	Sarah MARSHALL
Jan. 2	Thomas PARADISE	Leah CAREY
Jan. 3	John BOWEN	Elizabeth HOSHIER
Jan. 3	William JOHNSON	Drucilla DUNCAN
Jan. 5	Esekiel HENDERSON	Martha TAYLOR
Jan. 5	James REGGAN	Mary CAMPBELL
Jan. 8	Jesse JARMON	Elizabeth ATKINSON
Jan. 9	Nathaniel P. PARSONS	Nancy DISHAROON
Jan. 15	Zachariah BOWEN	Sarah HOLLAND
Jan. 17	George BAKER	Hetty DALE
Jan. 21	George L. PARSONS	Unice FOOKS
Jan. 22	Theodore MARSH	Hetty BEACHBOARD
Jan, 23	David WALLOP	Mary H. WALLOP
Jan. 23	Nathaniel FITCHET	Susan FITCHET
Jan. 28	Samuel HOSHIER	Nancy HAMMOND
Jan. 29	Levin D. MELSON	Zipporah WILSON
Jan. 29	William C. TRUITT	Sally ROWND
Jan. 29	John M. NELSON	Matila STURGIS
Jan. 30	William WALSTON	Ann REED
Feb. 4	Anranius PENNEWELL	Hetty PENNEWELL
Feb. 4	Samuel C. ABBOTT	Ann SAVAGE
Feb. 12	Samuel TULL	Tabitha TAYLOR

1828

Date	Groom	Bride
Feb. 12	Benjamin KELLY	Sally McFADDEN
Feb. 16	George B. PARSONS	Elizzbeth ADKINS
Feb. 20	Levi BRITTINGHAM	Rosanna CUTTER
Feb. 22	James PORTER	Martha MARSHALL
Feb. 23	Lambert POWELL	Louisa MASSEY
Feb. 27	John H. LIVINGSTON	Mary MITCHELL
Feb. 27	John SPENCER	Mary A. BRATTEN
Feb. 28	Zadok MARSHALL	Zepporah HARRISON
March 3	Nathaniel FISHER	Matilda QUILLEN
March 5	George DYKES	Martha SHOCKLEY
March 7	Zeno WARRINGTON	Eliza HEARN
March 11	Lemuel DENNIS	Margaret JOHNSON
March 12	Thomas JONES	Betsey UNDRILL
March 12	Littleton Z. DENNIS	Elizabeth STURGIS
March 24	Benjamin TOWNSEND	Charlotte MERRILL
March 25	William PRICE	Atty BEACHBOARD
March 25	Cannon FOOKS	Nancy FOOKS
March 29	Ezekiel W. CLOWS	Gatty ANDERSON
April 1	Benjamin DRYDEN	Nancy JOHNSON
April 1	Richard HALL	Elizabeth LAYTON
April 1	Henry JOHNSON	Nancy CAREY
April 7	Hamilton RIGGIN	Nancy STINSON
April 9	George BRATTEN	Gatty TRUITT
April 12	Selby JOHNSON	Hetty SELBY
April 15	Josiah HAYMAN	Rebecca MORRIS
April 17	George WOOTTEN	Elizabeth KING
April 18	Thomas BRADFORD	Elizabeth WRIGHT
April 21	Peter QUILLEN	Sally TIMMONS
April 21	George CORBIN	Maria FIDDEMAN
April 21	Spicer GORDY	Eleanor HASTINGS
April 24	Parker COLLINS	Sally MILBOURNE
April 26	James MERRILL	Nancy COPES
April 29	Eleam EVANS	Charlotte HARRISON
May 1	Thomas TARR	Charlotte WILLIS
May 7	Francis LANE	Sophia POWELL
May 9	Peter ROWNDS	Zillah TOWNSEND
May 21	Lemuel P. SPENCE	Elizabeth B. TRUITT
June 3	William STEVENSON	Hassie WILLIAMS
June 10	John BURNETT	Elizabeth WALES
June 24	Annanias TULL	Getty POWEL
June 25	Robert C. PARKS	Elizabeth BLACKSON
June 28	Levi TARR	Ann TUBBS
July 9	Lemuel COLLINS	Amelia GUNBY
July 16	Major WHEELER	Louisa G. FURNISS
July 23	Smith JOHNSON	Eliza MATTHEWS
July 28	William SHOWELL	Ann BRIDDLE
Aug. 2	Peter SHEILD	Esther OUTTEN
Aug. 12	James PITTS	Gertrude GORMAN

1828
Aug.	19	James TILGHMAN	Nancy RUARK
Aug.	20	Zachariah MARSHALL	Zepporah EVANS
Aug.	26	Mitchell WATSON	Sally DRYDEN
Aug.	26	Samuel SMITH	Elizabeth DAVIS
Aug.	27	George SCOTT	Rosey STEVENSON
Sept.	2	James B. HORSEY	Elizabeth K. STEVENSON
Sept.	9	Levin ENNIS	Sally BROWN
Sept.	23	John HENDERSON	Elizabeth H. HOUSTON
Oct.	6	Kendall JARMON	Adaline WARREN
Oct.	15	Richard BOWEN	Elizabeth CUSTIS
Oct.	15	Tenant BOWEN	Henny H. BOWEN
Oct.	27	Littleton POWELL	Elizabeth JARVIS
Nov.	6	William WILLIAMS	Anna FOOKS
Nov.	7	Joseph DAVIS	Patuna A.W. JOHNSON
Nov.	11	Ara COLLINS	Patty HILL
Nov.	15	Aura BRADFORD	Mary PHILLIPS
Nov.	17	George PARSONS	Nancy GORDY
Nov.	18	James HOUSTON	Andesia S. COLLINS
Nov.	19	Moses PILCHARD	Mary Ann TARR
Nov.	24	Delight RUSSELL	Margaret BAYLY
Nov.	27	William FOOKS	Patty BROWN
Dec.	3	James WILLIAMS	Sally STEVENSON
Dec.	5	Thomas SMITH	Charlotte DALE
Dec.	8	Richard SCARBOROUGH	Ann HUDSON
Dec.	16	Levin HOLLAND	Betsey YOUNG
Dec.	17	Isaac BEATHARDS	Betsy BOWEN
Dec.	19	Uriah FOOKS	Jane JOHNSON
Dec.	20	George JOHNSON	Nancy HUGHES
Dec.	22	William BROUGHTON	Adeline DALE
Dec.	23	Richard TURNELL	Betsy HART
Dec.	23	Annanias JARMAN	Zilla WILLIAMS
Dec.	23	Wriseham PILCHARD	Ann MARSHALL
Dec.	24	Stephen TOWNSEND	Mary F. MILBOURNE
Dec.	24	Thomas GLASS	Elizabeth STEVENSON
Dec.	24	Benjamin T. DALE	Deborah M. MILBOURN
Dec.	29	William T. STEVENSON	Catharine STURGIS

1829
Jan.	2	Thomas POLLETT	Polly DRISKELL
Jan.	2	Eli WHITE	Maria PARKER
Jan.	3	Nathaniel SMART	Susan BUNTING
Jan.	5	John CALLAHAN	Louisa BEVANS
Jan.	6	Nevett SCHOOLFIELD	Charlotte DUNCAN
Jan.	6	James STURGIS	Mary MARSH
Jan.	8	Thomas BOSTON	Rachel CROPPER
Jan.	10	William FIELDS	Nancy TOADVINE
Jan.	13	William B. TILGHMAN	Mary NICHOLS
Jan.	13	Purnell J. JONES	Martha SMITH

1829

Date	Groom	Bride
Jan. 19	Ebenezer B. DAVIS	Molly B. LISTER
Jan. 20	Arthur PRICE	Nancy M. FRANKLIN
Jan. 21	William MARSHALL	Narsissa BOWEN
Jan. 24	John BELL	Nancy HARGIS
Jan. 27	Eliakem JONES	Nancy CRIPPEN
Jan. 29	James M. HOLLAND	Mary Ann JONES
Feb. 3	Soloman CAUSEY	Anna YOUNG
Feb. 4	Joshua BREWINGTON	Eliza JONES
Feb. 4	Thomas DAVIS	Nancy BOWEN
Feb. 10	Lemuel S. TAYLOR	Matilda H. WILLIAMS
Feb. 17	Henry BOSTON	Nancy MORRIS
Feb. 18	John S. EWELL	Elizabeth S. WHITE
March 4	Jacob TAYLOR	Sally COFFIN
March 5	Gilly ENNIS	Mary Ann LeCOMPT
March 7	George HICKMAN	Catharine BARNES
March 10	James HICKMAN	Caty LECATS
March 11	Zadok MILBOURNE	Jane FOOKS
March 17	Edward K. WEATHERLY	Elizabeth PARKER
March 25	William SELBY	Leah GIVAN
March 31	Ayers MASON	Sally HANDCOCK
April 7	Daniel ROWLEY	Sarah Ann RICHARDSON
April 20	John HOLLOWAY	Hety GODFREY
May 5	John CLUFF	Henrietta MADDUX
May 5	Eliakem BENNETT	Altha REDDEN
May 5	William K. KENNEY	Elizabeth CANNON
May 6	Thos HENDERSON	Mary TRUITT
May 12	James MASSEY	Eloza PRIOR
May 21	James W.L. STURGIS	Charlotte SELBY
May 26	Colmore C. HENMAN	Lovey BARNES
May 28	Wreom BLADES	Mary SELBY
June 2	Alfred FURMAN	Charlotte E. COLLINS
June 8	William DRYDEN	Nancy DONOHOE
June 10	Thomas U. HACK	Harriet F. SELBY
June 16	Jehu FOOKS	Hetty NOBLE
June 17	John HENRY	Sarah PARKER
June 18	Ephraim MASSEY	Elizabeth SMYTH
June 25	Thomas LATCHUM	Henny SMITH
June 29	Annanias NICHOLS	Elizabeth CAREY
July 2	Jno B. THOMAS	Catharine S. DUNTON
July 9	Charles C. CARROLL	Anna P. SMITH
July 13	John HUDSON	Maria TINGLE
July 14	Eliajh BRITTINGHAM	Narsissa CALLAHAN
July 14	Major HANDCOCK	Eleanor HANDCOCK
July 14	Joshua DONOHOE	Elenor CORBIN
July 15	James W. DYKES	Catharine A, MERRILL
July 21	William BRIMER	Eliza DAVIS
July 25	Eli COLLINS	Nancy COFFIN
July 27	Lemuel DAVIS	Nancy BAKER

1829

Date	Groom	Bride
July 27	Caleb TIMMONS	Sarah GODFREY
July 28	Samuel WILLIAMS	Leah TAYLOR
July 29	Jesse HAMMOND	Rhoda CLAYWELL
Aug. 18	John FOOKS	Mary Ann WILLIAMS
Aug. 19	Esme P. MORRIS	Mary Ann HILL
Aug. 20	James JONES	Harriet HALES
Aug. 21	Jacob M. ROSS	Sarah Ann TAYLOR
Aug. 24	Thomas PARMER	Nancy BASSITT
Aug. 24	Thomas J. GORDY	Sally E. GORDY
Aug. 25	Levin ENNIS	Causey AILES
Aug. 25	Albert SMACK	Gertrude HOSHIER
Sept. 1	William TULL	Eleanor BEACHBOARD
Sept. 1	Aaron HUDSON	Julian ALLEN
Sept. 2	Walton GRAY	Elizabeth RILEY
Sept. 9	Soloman BRADFORD	Ann BRADFORD
Sept. 16	Samuel L. BRIMER	Ann Eliza BISHOP
Sept. 18	James RAIN	Mary MASSEY
Sept. 22	Zechariah HILL	Margaret AYDELOTT
Sept. 22	John E.H. MARSHALL	Laura Ann HENRY
Sept. 23	John TUBBS	Molly TAYLOR
Sept. 30	Joseph LEONARD	Miracle HOSHIER
Sept. 30	Thomas REED	Elizabeth TAYLOR
Oct. 8	John D. WELBOURN	Zepporah P. MARSHALL
Oct. 12	Henry DUSK	Margaret MUMFORD
Oct. 15	Joshua HOLSTON	Gertrude CLARK
Oct. 21	Sampson COULBOURN	Rhoda ESHAM
Oct. 28	William FASSETT	Julian BRADFORD
Nov. 2	William HARGIS	Nancy BALL
Nov. 3	Stephen ALLEN	Betsey COULBOURN
Nov. 4	Richard HALL	Sarah B. DALE
Nov. 7	William STERLING	Polly BLADES
Nov. 17	Ezeliel BUTLER	Thirzey TRAHEARN
Nov. 19	Annanias JONES	Margaret SMITH
Nov. 21	William SCOTT	Elizabeth CHAILLE
Nov. 23	James A. TINGLE	Sally HUDSON
Nov. 26	William HOLLAND	Mary ROWLEY
Nov	Whittey PUZEY	Mary TOWNSEND
Nov. 30	Elijah ENNIS	Philliss DRISKILL
Dec. 1	Robert FOOKS	Mary DAVIS
Dec. 1	Isaac A. REDDEN	Betsy MASON
Dec. 8	Elijah HOVINGTON	Leah HILMAN
Dec. 11	Ephraim POWELL	Gatty PARKER
Dec. 11	Isaac HUDSON	Patty TRUITT
Dec. 15	William JOHNSON	Mary DAVIS
Dec. 17	John WIMBROUGH	Mahala KELLY
Dec. 18	James CAUSEY	Eleanor FOOKS
Dec. 22	Peter BROWN	Maria SMULLIN
Dec. 22	Thomas DAVIS	Elizabeth MASSEY

1829
Date	Groom	Bride
Dec. 22	Walter SHARPLEY	Matilda DUKES
Dec. 23	William DEVEREN	Ann McFADDEN
Dec. 24	John DEVRIX	Elizabeth McFADDEN
Dec. 26	George L. TREHEARN	Elizabeth A. BEVANS

1830
Date	Groom	Bride
Jan. 4	Benjamin DYKES	Sarah SHOCKLEY
Jan. 6	Southey GORDY	Nancy BREWINGTON
Jan. 6	Merrill DICKERSON	Betsy BURNETT
Jan. 7	William D. DEMPSEY	Ann Mitchell HILL
Jan. 8	John BEVANS	Lydia HENMAN
Jan. 12	Henry B. TAYLOR	Mary WILLIAMS
Jan. 12	Zadok W. BOWEN	Elizabeth P.M. ENNIS
Jan. 12	Purnell TAYLOR	Mary RUARK
Jan. 21	James H. PARRAMORE	Susan M. CURTIS
Jan. 23	Josiah F. CHATTAN	Ana FARREL
Jan. 24	Joseph TRUITT	Henrietta CONALD
Jan. 28	Levi MATTHEWS	Hetty TARR
Feb. 2	Henry BARRETT	Elizabeth Jane HILL
Feb. 2	James HANDCOCK	Elizabeth HUDSON
Feb. 6	Hozey HENRY	Maria ADKINS
Feb. 8	Levi LAMBERSON	Hezey BESEY
Feb. 8	Leonard GORDY	Mary PARKER
Feb. 9	James TARR	Harriet AYDELOTT
Feb. 10	John PENNEWELL	Elizabeth HOLSTON
Feb. 12	Noah WHITE	Sally FOOKS
Feb. 16	Elijah C. SCHOOLFIELD	Harriet MERRILL
Feb. 16	Parker ESHAM	Julian TRAYHEARN
Feb. 16	James ROWLEY	Margaret K. HOUSTON
Feb. 16	Handy BURBAGE	Elizabeth BRATTEN
Feb. 18	Thomas B. FISHER	Sally C. W. ADDISON
Feb. 20	Samuel BURBAGE	Eliza K. JONES
Feb. 23	Joseph DAZEY	Elizabeth TRUITT
Feb. 23	Henry BREWINGTON	Sally MELSON
March 2	Selby RAIN	Hetty Ann TINGLE
March 2	William D. LANDON	Leah Ann TOWNSEND
March 3	James KNOX	Sarah CLAYWELL
March 3	Benjamin HOLTON	Elizabeth SULLIVAN
March 16	Robert ESHAM	Eliza HICKS
March 16	Charles BRITTINGHAM	Nancy ESHAM
March 20	Thomas BRITTINGHAM	Matilda COLLIER
March 23	Southy W. BULL	Ann M. MASON
March 23	Lewis POLLITT	Leah MITCHELL
March 23	William RUARK	Elizabeth LEVINGSTON
March 24	Stewart NELSON	Elizabeth MATTHEWS
March 27	Thomas BARNES	Martha GRAY
March 27	Benjamin FRANKLIN	Rebecca WATTS
March 30	Peter COLLINS	Elinor ESHAM
March 31	Henry W. PETTITT	Sallly HOLSTON

1830

Date	Groom	Bride
April 12	John JACKSON	Sally SMACK
April 17	Henry HOPKINS	Polly FLETCHER
April 27	Henry BROOKSAND	Eliza BROADWATERS
April 27	John LAYFIELD	Susan DRYDEN
May 3	Gillis FIGGS	Mary MADDUX
May 3	James HARRESON	Rosy MARSHALL
May 5	Spicer WHITE	Elizabeth HOPKINS
May 13	William P. BARNES	Rosey Ann MILES
May 19	Isaac LITTLETON	Dolly SMITH
May 25	John TAYLOR	Leah CAREY
May 25	Peter ROWNDS	Nelly GORDY
June 4	John P. MARSHALL	Nancy HUDSON
June 8	Esme P. BOWEN	Mary I. HENDERSON
June 15	Zadok POWELL	Nancy STARLING
June 26	William BOWEN	Sarah COLLINS
June 26	Isaac BAKER	Nancy MASSEY
June 30	Pearce REED	Elizabeth COTTINGHAM
July 9	Gustavus P. PORTER	Henrietta STEVENS
July 14	Robert BOWEN	Rhoda HAMMOND
July 15	Levin LAYTON	Nancy QUILLEN
July 16	John COOPER	Drucilla RUNNELS
July 18	Peter TILGHMAN	Harriet MITCHELL
July 19	Samuel RICHARDSON	Sally LAMDEN
July 20	William RIGGAN	Nancy PUZEY
July 26	William JARMAN	Miranda BRITTINGHAM
July 26	Elijah MELSON	Sophia TOWNSEND
July 26	William P. SMITH	Elizabeth T. HUDSON
July 26	John SAUNDERS	Henrietta R. E. WHITELOCK
July 26	Shepherd PORTER	Eliza STURGIS
July 26	Samuel PARKER	Phebe FOOKS
Aug. 5	James H. REW	Mary Ann WRIGHT
Aug. 7	Elijah MUMFORD	Mary Ann CAREY
Aug. 10	Isaac FEEMAN	Hannah FISHER
Aug. 12	Samuel TATHAM	Sarah Ann NEWBOLDS
Aug. 19	Henry McDANIEL	Nancy COTTINGHAM
Aug. 25	William BASSETT	Elizabeth McNEIL
Aug. 25	Handy WILLIAMS	Leah REED
Sept. 3	Thomas WHEALTON	Hetty VEAZEY
Sept. 22	Nathaniel DOLLY	Elton Gray RILEY
Sept. 23	Henry MASON	Louisa FISHER
Sept. 28	Peter BURBAGE	Anda M. TIMMONS
Sept. 29	Littleton FLEMING	Mary ESHAM
Oct. 2	William CAREY	Gusta BLADES
Oct. 4	John T. LESTER	Lauretta S. TRUITT
Oct. 5	Thomas BELL	Matilda G. DRYDEN
Oct. 6	Nathaniel TYSON	Mary RICKETTS
Oct. 6	John DAVIS	Hetty BOWEN
Oct. 13	Thomas CAREY	Betsy PARSONS

1830
Oct. 18	John A. NELSON	Elizabeth BADGER
Oct. 21	James HENDERSON	Sally BRITTINGHAM
Oct. 27	Stewart BASSETT	Amelia MITCHELL
Oct. 28	Uriah TARR	Elizabeth WHITE
Nov. 4	Robert T. COLLENDAR	Margaret Ann WHITE
Nov. 5	James HUDSON	Nancy MITCHELL
Nov. 8	Joseph ROBINS	Ann Eliza JAMES
Nov. 9	William MUMFORD	Eleanor HOLLAND
Nov. 9	William STEVENS	Elizabeth BROADWATER
Nov. 9	Gilbert HILL	Rachel BAKER
Nov. 15	Ayers G. PARKER	Elizabeth JOHNSON
Dec. 7	Riley COULBOURN	Catharine EVANS
Dec. 7	Samuel A. PAYNE	Polly BONNAWELL
Dec. 7	Elisha PURNELL	Maria BREDELL
Dec. 8	Benjamin HEARN	Polly JACKSON
Dec. 9	James O. SELBY	Sophia A.M. BARNES
Dec. 11	John BLADES	Rachel LANDON
Dec. 14	Isaac SMITH	Sally TREHEARN
Dec. 18	Henry W. JARVIS	Mary Ann RILEY
Dec. 18	Thomas WARREN	Mary WARREN
Dec. 20	James HARMONSON	Mari MONUDER
Dec. 20	Samuel KELLY	Denny NICHOLSON
Dec. 21	Teakle TOWNSEND	Elizabeth T. BEVANS
Dec. 22	Frederick DUKES	Mary RICHARDSON
Dec. 22	Selby BOWEN	Martha TAYLOR
Dec. 22	Isaac JONES	Eliza BONNAWELL
Dec. 29	John DICKERSON	Rebecca BURNETT
Dec. 29	John R. PITTS	Mary Ann E. GRAY
Dec. 29	John CHERRIX	Margaret JOHNSON

1831
Jan. 4	Henry POWELL	Maria TAYLOR
Jan. 5	James BREWINGTON	Elizabeth LAYFIELD
Jan. 4	Willliam NUTTER	Isaac H. ENNIS
Jan. 6	Zadok ALLEN	Hannah ELLIS
Jan. 12	Denwood PILCHARD	Narcissa PAYNE
Jan. 18	Levin CAUSEY	Hetty STINSON
Jan. 18	Daniel BELL	Sally STURGIS
Jan. 18	Samuel TRADER	Milly DAVIS
Jan. 22	Joshua PHILLIPS	Martha KING
Jan. 24	John BUSSELS	Trena GRAY
Jan. 31	Lemuel TAYLOR	Rachel JARMAN
Feb. 12	Isaac DALE	Mary ATKINSON
Feb. 14	James CHERRIX	Henrietta MELVIN
Feb. 15	Walter ROGERS	Sally GODY
Feb. 17	Levi BALL	Henrietta RILEY
Feb. 17	Kendall CROPPER	Mary TRAHEARN
Feb. 21	James TEACHNER	Elizabeth SMITH

1831

Date	Groom	Bride
Feb. 23	Littleton RICHARDSON	Wise SHOCKLEY
Feb. 24	John STURGIS Jr.	Esther TAYLOR
Feb. 28	Charles BUTLER	Maria TWIG
March 7	Elijah TIMMONS	Eleanor BOWDEN
March 7	Kendall TAYLOR	Mary GIVANS
March 15	James MEZICK	Mary BELL
March 16	Littleton CLAYWELL	Drucilla POWELL
March 22	Peter CHAILLE	Nancy BENNETT
March 22	Benjamin DUKES	Elizabeth BISHOP
March 23	Lorenzo LEVINGSTON	Isabella REDDISH
March 29	James CHAPMAN	Nancy ATKINSON
March 30	William PUZEY	Mary RIGGAN
March 30	Richard HALL	Mary JOHNSON
March 31	James A. MASSEY	Ann PARKER
April 5	Nathaniel HENMAN	Sally SHOWELL
April 5	David DAVIDSON	Mary KING
April 6	Josiah BEATHARDS	Matilda MOORE
April 12	Soloman EVANS	Catharine TINGLE
April 13	Seth BRITTINGHAM	Sophia FREEMAN
April 13	Outten ENNIS	Peggy TRUITT
April 14	James YOUNG	Mary Ann WARD
April 28	John DICKERSON	Patty DUKES
May 16	Isaac HOPKINS	Hetty COARD
May 17	Charles ELLIS	Eliza PENNEWELL
May 17	James DAVIS	Ann DUSKY
June 2	George PORTER	Charlotte STURGIS
June 11	Moses CLAYWELL	Sophia BASSETT
June 11	Marten ADKINS	Betsey BASSETT
June 11	Henry MARRELL	Elizabeth AYRES
June 14	Henry POWELL	Elizabeth M.W. HENDERSON
June 15	Thomas D. JOHNSON	Maria DENNIS
June 15	John T. TAYLOR	Hetty C. MADDOX
June 16	William ROCK	Eleanor POWELL
June 24	William SHRIEVES	Louisa BERRY
July 5	George ADDISON	Julian CHAPMAN
July 14	Levin POWELL	Susan ATKINSON
July 19	Matthias TAPMAN	Sally LAMBERSON
July 21	James P. SELBY	Matilda H.M. WALES
July 22	William ROUNDS	Polly BUSSELLS
July 28	John FLOYD	Elizabeth WHEALTON
Aug. 9	Samuel JOHNSON	Elizabeth JONES
Sept. 1	Joseph DAVIS	Drucilla JONES
Sept. 1	John JOHNSON	Rachel UNDERHILL
Sept. 5	Henry SMACK Jr.	Mary SMACK
Sept. 13	William PATTY	Henrietta MATTHEWS
Sept. 13	John H. BENSON	Mary PAYNE
Sept. 23	Jacob SELBY	Wealthy ARMWOOD
Sept. 29	Isaac LEAKEY	Henny WILLIS

1831

Date	Groom	Bride
Oct. 3	Elijah WIMBROUGH	Leah LAYTON
Oct. 4	William HOLLAND	Elizabeth PURNELL
Oct. 12	Thomas ROGERS	Hannah LATCHEM
Oct. 18	John RICHARDSON	Elizabeth BOWDEN
Oct. 19	William TIMMONS	Mary SMACK
Oct. 22	Mitchell HILL	Matilda BENNETT
Nov. 1	Laban HUDSON	Sally MASON
Nov. 8	George LANGSDALE	Mary ROUNDS
Nov. 15	James DAVIS	Leah CATLEN
Nov. 16	Wheatley D. WONNELL	Harriet WHITE
Nov. 19	George N. FOOKS	Margaret DIXON
Nov. 22	Robert DUKES	Mary MADDUX
Nov. 29	David SHARPLEY	Eleanor DUKES
Nov. 29	Benjamin LEVINGSTON	Phebe MITCHELL
Dec. 12	Henry COOPER	Epolita RUNNELLS
Dec. 12	Jacob H. HAYMAN	Mary MELSON
Dec. 14	Thomas BAYLY	Emeline GORDY
Dec. 15	Purnell DEVIRIX	Polly RIGGAN
Dec. 20	Joshua TILGHMAN	Sophia HUSHIER
Dec. 20	James R. S. PURNELL	Mary FRANKLIN
Dec. 20	Joshua BEVANS	Sally TOWNSEND
Dec. 22	John MARSHALL	Ann BUNDICK
Dec. 26	George WALSTON	Elizabeth WINWRIGHT
Dec. 29	James BLADES	Betsey McHENRY
Dec. 29	Francis MURRAY	Wealthy GREER

1832

Date	Groom	Bride
Jan. 3	Lemuel TRUITT	Clarrisa BRATTEN
Jan. 3	Benjamin PARSONS	Nancy HEARN
Jan. 9	Henry BRITTINGHAM	Sarah STURGIS
Jan. 10	Elihu PALMER	Lanta ADKINS
Jan. 10	Samuel HALL	Elizabeth PATEY
Jan. 10	Thomas EVANS	Charlotte RAIN
Jan. 10	Peter PRICE	Catharine BUTLER
Jan. 10	John RIGGAN	Ann JOHNSON
Jan. 13	John HALL	Amalia PURNELL
Jan. 18	Henry TAYLOR	Mary COLLINS
Jan. 30	George W. BENNETT	Elizabeth HUSTON
Jan. 31	Joshua RILEY	Sally TAYLOR
Feb. 1	Denard WILLIAMS	Mary I. FARROW
Feb. 6	Peter SHOCKLEY	Lurenda WIMBOROUGH
Feb. 7	James MELSON	Eliza MILLINER
Feb. 10	Lazarus PRUITT	Elizabeth JONES
Feb. 21	Thomas BURBAGE	Sophia BASSETT
Feb. 29	Steward SHOCKLEY	Mary Ann HENDERSON
Feb. 29	John T. TAYLOR	Sophia Ann McALLEN
March 5	James TUBB	Henrietta PARKER
March 6	Daniel BUTLER	Hetty DYKES

1832

Date	Groom	Bride
March 7	William HALEECH ?	Sally ROBERTSON
March 15	Joseph WAPLES	Amelia WILLIAMS
March 15	Thomas D. HOLLAND	Elizabeth HUDSON
March 15	James STEPHENS	Rachel BELOTE
March 16	Thomas BRITTINGHAM	Ann LAMBDEN
March 26	William WIMBROW	Sarah DIXON
March 26	William ELLENSWORTH	Zipporah EVANS
March 27	Littleton MELVIN	Margaret ENNIS
March 31	John PRUITT	Elizabeth JONES
April 2	Lewis CAUSEY	Sally POWELL
April 2	George A. PARKER	Tabitha Smith NELSON
April 4	James PAYNE	Mary BEVANS
April 10	William LEWIS	Elizabeth COWLEY
April 10	William TULL	Maria RICHARDSON
April 17	Peter RILEY	Welthy TAYLOR
April 18	Joshua SHOCKLEY	Tabitha WHITE
April 29	Abel JONES	Julian McGRATH
May 1	George P. SELBY	Leah ROBINS
May 2	Daniel ARMWOOD	Rebecca PURNELL
May 4	William J. BOSTON	Jane BRITTINGHAM
May 7	Levin HOLSTON	Elizabeth WILDEN
May 7	Leonard GORDY	Julian DAVIS
May 9	George HOSTON	Elizabeth BELL
May 9	John F. TAYLOR	Mary Ann NUTTER
May 17	Littleton POPE	Mary DRYDEN
May 17	Purnell I. BENNETT	Hetty CLAYWELL
May 22	John EVANS	Mary Ann TRADER
May 22	Barnaba STURGIS	Hetty MATTHEWS
May 23	Isaac TAPMAN	Rebecca MASON
May 28	Samuel PARSONS	Charlotte GODFREY
June 1	Hance FOOKS	Julian HOWARD
June 5	Anania JARMAN	Maria WARREN
June 12	Peter RAIN	Emeline WILLIAMS
June 16	William QUINN	Rosey SCHOOLFIELD
June 19	James MUMFORD	Martha DIXON
June 22	Major TOWNSEND	Sarah POWELL
June 27	Stephen POLLITT	Lydia Ann REDDISH
July 3	Robert TOWNSEND	Nancy James WONNELL
July 4	John LAMBERSON	Elizabeth TAPMAN
July 11	Michael MARSHALL	Sarah HENDERSON
July 19	Henry NELSON	Maria DRYDEN
July 21	James FOOKS	Emeline RIGGAN
July 24	James DAVIS	Eliza DAVIS
July 25	Joshua HOLSTON	Nancy PENNEWELL
July 25	Nathan COTTINGHAM	Sally PAINTER
July 31	John CRAWFORD	Mary DISHAROON
Aug. 13	Thomas M. METCALF	Sally G. WARD
Aug. 15	Thomas P. PARKER	Eleanor A. FLEMING

1832
Aug. 15	Thomas KELLAEM	Ann PUZEY
Aug. 28	Isaac HOUSTON	Ann BENNETT
Aug. 29	McKemmy PORTER	Hannah RIGGAN
Aug. 29	Edwae ? TAYLOR	Elizabeth SPEAKS
Aug. 30	Simon MURCHESON	Jane FARROW
Sept. 5	Hosea POTTER	Betsey BEACHBOARD
Sept. 11	Joseph S. COTTMAN	Elizabeth A. DENNIS
Sept. 14	Joseph FISHER	Catharine S. REDDEN
Sept. 18	William HAMMOND	Betsey WILLIAMS
Sept. 22	Elisha PARKER	Eliza PARKER
Sept. 25	Benjamin P. AYDELOTT	Mary RICHARDSON
Sept. 25	Clement I.B. PARKER	Susan Ann BEAUCHAMP
Sept. 25	Thomas WARREN	Maria CROPPER
Oct. 1	Noble CHRISTOPHER	Martha HOUSTON
Oct. 3	Ebenezer WALSTON	Eliza NELSON
Oct. 3	Joseph D. GIVAN	Miranda SMITH
Oct. 9	James EVANS	Eliza BEATHARDS
Oct. 10	Thomas K. DUNTON	Emeline FITCHETT
Oct. 31	Ephraim T. TOWNSEND	Henrietta NELSON
Nov. 5	John TATTMAN	Mary SPALDING
Nov. 7	Stephen GIBBS	Polly YOUNG
Nov.	Thomas BAYLEY	Mary PORTER
	Peter GIVANS	Mary BRADFORD
	John HICKMAN	Eliza HOUSTON
Nov. 20	Robert TOWNSEND	Eliza PRIOR
Nov. 27	Isaac R. JONES	Mary Ann MORRIS
Nov. 29	George TILGHMAN	Lela MASON
Dec. 4	Robert JAMES	Elizabeth LONG
Dec. 10	Schoolfield LAMBERSON	Martha SELBY
Dec. 12	Josiah MARSHALL	Elizabeth ENNIS
Dec. 12	Bowdoin HAMMOND	Henrietta DAVIS
Dec. 13	Joshua HADDOK	Betsey LEAKEY
Dec. 13	William RICHARDSON	Hetty TILGHMAN
Dec. 13	Elijah ESHAM	Hetty BULL
Dec. 17	James FOOKS (of D)	Betsey BASSETT
Dec. 18	McKemmy JARMAN	Rhoda BOWEN
Dec. 18	Littleton BOWEN	Mary PURNELL
Dec. 19	Brinkley ELLIOTT	Catharine JAMES
Dec. 19	Mitchell PENNEWELL	Eliizabeth HUDSON
Dec. 19	Henry JACKSON	Hetty HOLLAND
Dec. 20	David DAVIS	Sarah MILLS
Dec. 22	Peter C. WATTS	Margaret PARKS
Dec. 25	William A. BREWINGTON	Lavica MILLS
Dec. 28	James RALPH	Mary ADKINS
Dec. 29	John REDDEN	Esther REESE
Dec. 31	Lambert WILLIAMS	Maranda DAVIS
Dec. 31	William DISHAROON	Martha GORDY

1833

Date	Groom	Bride
Jan. 1	David PRIOR	Amelia Julian CAREY
Jan. 2	Thomas ESHAM	Sabra CASE
Jan. 8	Nathaniel QUILLEN	Nancy COOPER
Jan. 8	Lemuel WILLIAMS	Elizabeth MORRIS
Jan. 8	John B.A. GILLIS	Ann E. FASSETT
Jan. 12	William SMULLIN	Eliza BROWN
Jan. 14	Benjamin S. MELSON	Eliza FOOKS
Jan. 18	Moses CLAYWELL	Pattey POWELL
Jan. 21	George N. FOOKS	Milly DIXON
Jan. 21	Stephen TIMMONS	Henny BEATHARDS
Jan. 22	Henry BEVANS	Margaret PRUITT
Jan. 22	Zadok SELBY	Mary BENNETT
Jan. 22	Jacob PAYNE	Mary MARSHALL
Jan. 23	James TRUITT	Mary EVANS
Jan. 28	Danl I. HAYMAN	Mary BUSSELS
Jan. 28	Gibson CANNON	Elizabeth STURGIS
Jan. 31	Peter POWELL	Catharine GRAY
Feb. 1	James CROPPER	Ann Elizabeth H. DAVIS
Feb. 4	Peter TARR	Sarah TOWNSEND
Feb. 5	Ebenezer WEBB	Molly WILLIAMS
Feb. 5	William HANDCOCK	Nancy MATTHEWS
Feb. 5	John BRATTEN	Harriet HUDSON
Feb. 11	Merrell D. SMITH	Amelia B. TIMMONS
Feb. 18	Stephen TAYLOR	Mary A. VINCENT
Feb. 20	Ara SPENCE	Priscilla WILSON
Feb. 20	John HAYMAN	Sarah GODFREY
Feb. 23	James HARRISON	Sally TAYLOR
March 5	George TWILLEY	Betsey SHOCKLEY
March 12	John PAYNE	Euphemia MARSHALL
March 20	William WARD	Elizabeth BLADES
March 20	Thomas PARKER	Matilda TRAYHEARN
March 25	Purnell TRUITT	Milly BUTLER
March 26	Joseph GODFREY	Elizabeth GODFREY
April 2	Jonathan FOOKS	Leah JONES
April 3	Nathaniel VEASEY	Nelly PAYNE
April 3	George HANDY	Eliza JONES
April 4	James BRITTINGHAM	Charlotte TAR
April 9	Charles CHATTEM	Henny STEVENSON
April 10	Littleton DEVEREAUS	Susan DORMAN
April 10	James W. BONNEWELL	Sally BANKS
April 16	Griffith JONES	Mary BACON
April 16	Milby HICKMAN	Mary Ann HOLSTON
April 18	James H. COLLINS	Susan PAYNE
April 24	Thomas PALMER	Mary NOCK
May 1	Nehemiah REDDEN	Susan TAYLOR
May 8	James CAREY	Elizabeth BEVANS
May 21	Stephen WARD	Molly PILCHARD
May 22	Levi TULL	Mary JOYNES

1833

May 29	Elihu JONES	Leah GLADDEN
May 28	George WEST	Polly WEST
May 31	Henry FOOKS	Elizabeth Wise WHITE
June 3	Humphrey HUMPHREYS	Elizabeth PARSONS
June 5	John B. CAMERON	Hester A. RICHARDSON
June 5	Peter O. VANCE	Sarah A. ANDERSON
June 15	Bond M. BRAMBLE	Martha NUSMAN
June 18	Naron B. WILLIAMS	Martha TIMMONS
June 18	Joseph SHARPLEY	Sally ADDISON
June 21	Parker SULLIVAN	Sally WEST
June 21	John RICHARDSON	Charlotte JOHNSON
June 25	Robert TAYLOR	Betsey WISE
June 26	William A. PARKER	Juliet L. SCARBORUGH
June 26	Edmund W. UNDERHILL	Mary S. NELSON
July 2	William H. COULBOURN	Mary DUNCAN
July 22	William W. STEVENS	Harriet H. GORDY
July 24	Joshua BOWEN	Sally TEAGUE
Aug. 5	George WAINWRIGHT	Elizabeth S. MACKLIN
Aug. 10	John BINTON	Maria WHEALTON
Aug. 16	John MILLER	Maria LAYFIELD
Aug. 20	Elijah BREDELL	Maia TRUITT
Aug. 21	Sampson SHOCKLEY	Nancy STURGIS
Aug. 22	John DENNIS	Eliza TRADER
Aug. 28	John GUTHRIE	Piercey WILSON
Aug. 28	Thomas N. WILLIAMS	Elizabeth D. HUDSON
Aug. 28	Arthur CHATMAN	Salonia DICKERSON
Sept. 3	Jesse BAKER	Sally DAVIS
Sept. 5	Noah BOWEN	Eliza GRAY
Sept. 10	Zedekiah HAMMOND	Eleanor HAMMOND
Sept. 16	John TINDAL	Emily DAVIS
Sept. 27	William KELLY	Betsey CAREY
Sept. 28	Lewis BLADES	Ann J. RAYFIELD
Oct. 2	Cord H. LISTER	Sally BELL
Oct. 2	John W. SMITH	Charlotte C. WHITTINGTON
Oct. 7	Thomas LAYFIELD	Elizabeth PARKER
Oct. 7	Mordecai HOLLOWAY	Hannah ROUNDS
Oct. 9	James TARR	Eleanor REED
Oct. 14	Jesse P. KING	Mary F. FRANKLIN
Oct. 16	Ezekiel R. BLOXOM	Elizabeth Susan DRUMMOND
Oct. 22	John DUNCAN	Julia A. BOWEN
Oct. 23	Ezeriah HARDIS	Sally AYDELOTTE
Oct. 29	John R. PITTS	Lucretia FASSETT
Oct. 29	Ebenezer WARREN	Patty SMITH
Oct. 30	Preason MASON	Mary WATSON
Nov. 12	William TINDAL	Nancy COLLIER
Nov. 12	Titus POLLITT	Ansy PRICE
Nov. 19	James STURGIS	Margaret BENSON
Nov. 20	John W. MELVIN	Molly HUDSON

1833

Date	Groom	Bride
Nov. 21	Oliver BRODWATER	Maria MARINER
Nov. 27	John TOWNSEND	Elizabeth MORRIS
Nov. 30	Robert HALL	Julian SMITH
Dec. 3	Josiah D. POWELL	Eliza LAMBERSON
Dec. 10	William BASSETT	Isabella BURBAGE
Dec. 10	William NELSON	Hester WHITE
Dec. 10	Laban GUNTER	Isabella CHANDLER
Dec. 17	Luther BLADES	Mary POWELL
Dec. 17	Peter PENNEWELL	Amelia HOLLAND
Dec. 18	Milby GRIFFITH	Margaret MILBOURNE
Dec. 18	Purnell CHERRIX	Mary STURGIS
Dec. 19	John HUDSON	Margaret TARR
Dec. 21	Kendall BRADFORD	Nancy LONG
Dec. 24	Merrill DICKERSON	Mary Ann MARCHANT
Dec. 24	John ENNIS	Ara T. BUNTON
Dec. 25	Benjamin BONNAWELL	Mary HALL
Dec. 26	Henry BLADES	Sally SMITH
Dec. 26	Joseph BOWDOIN	Mary CROPPER
Dec. 27	Major BENSON	Nancy PAYNE
Dec. 31	William MUMFORD	Mary Ann DAVIS

1834

Date	Groom	Bride
Jan. 1	George HUDSON	Caroline HANLY
Jan. 1	Lyban TOWNSEND	Mary E. LONG
Jan. 1	Isaac WEBB	Margaret LANDEN
Jan. 7	Thomas DUKES	Sally E. CLAYWELL
Jan. 8	William POPE	Jane JAMES
Jan. 8	James AYRES	Mary Ann DIRICKSON
Jan. 10	William P. MOORE Jr.	Mary A. SMITH
Jan. 13	Peter MARSHALL	Margaret JOHNSON
Jan. 14	James HENDERSON	Sally GAOTTEN?
Jan. 15	Peter SCARBOROUGH	Mary JOHNSON
Jan. 21	James RICHARDSON	Vicey BOWEN
Jan. 22	Nehemiah REDDEN	Mary JACKSON
Jan. 23	George HUDSON	Mary B. RICHARDSON
Jan. 24	William ATKINSON	Jane SMITH
Jan. 25	Gilbert CARMEAN	Mary Ann WATSON
Jan. 28	John RICHARDSON	Sarah TAYLOR
Feb. 1	George TOWNSEND	Lydia POWELL
Feb. 3	Benjamin HUDSON	Elizabeth D. HUDSON
Feb. 8	Samuel NEWMAN	Hetty RICHARDSON
Feb. 8	James A. WARD	Julia Ann P. JONES
	Benjamin FARLEW	Mary HOLLOWAY
Feb. 11	Hammond REYNOLDS	Holland BUTLER
Feb. 11	Jeptha RICHARDSON	Emeline RUARK
Feb. 11	William SMACK	Nancy TIMMONS
Feb. 12	John Thomas ONLEY	Lovey DARBY
Feb. 13	William JONES	Henny DUKES

1834

Date	Groom	Bride
Feb. 25	Elijah ENNIS	Margaret JONES
Feb. 25	William D. HUDSON	Retta MUMFORD
Feb. 25	James R. POWELL	Matilda Ann FOOKS
March 1	Benjamin MADDOX	Sarah WHITE
March 12	Littleton D. HANDY	Peggy E.P. STRONGER
March 12	William WEBB	Louisa HALL
March 13	Branson CAWLEY	Scarbourgh DAVIS
March 25	Seth SMITH	Elizabeth WILLIAMS
March 25	James MUMFORD	Martha FOOKS
March 27	Hnery SMACK	Louisa FASSITT
March 28	Joshua HOLLOWAY	Mary FARLOW
March 31	John RUSSELL	Elizabeth STURGIS
April 2	Thomas TAYLOR	Mary JOHNSON
April 3	Littleton SMITH	Rosetta BUNTING
April 8	Edwin J.H. BENNETT	Sarah E. BENNETT
April 15	Levin COLLINS	Elizabeth LONG
April 15	Esaw BOSTON	Sarah Ann MARSHALL
April 23	Thomas DRYDEN	Eliza DONOHO
April 23	Jarrell RUARK	Mary BANKS
April 29	Jesse LONG	Mary M. GILLETT
April 29	Stephen B. COLLINS	Leah BOWEN
April 30	William STAYTON	Milcah GASKINS
May 3	George TARR	Hetty POWELL
May 5	James W.T. SMITH	Mary Ann PENNEWELL
May 9	William DICKERSON	Henny A. TRUITT
May 13	Joshua BAKER	Sabra CATTS
May 13	John SEARS	Sarah DIX
May 14	Jesse CROPPER	Eliza HASTING
May 23	William DRYDEN	Nancy VINCENT
May 24	Stephen M. BOWEN	Margaret TARR
June 2	Henry HALL	Amrist NORTHAM
June 2	Daniel J. FOREMAN	Julia Ann DAVIS
June 2	William S. STAKES	Sally WHITE
June 7	William COLLINS	Ann PEACOCK
June 10	William W. DIX	Mary I. BEAVANS
June 10	Peter JOHNSON	Gertrude HANDCOCK
June 12	William BOWEN	Mary HUDSON
June 14	Tubman JONES	Margaret W. JONES
July 2	George BULL	Ann SMACK
July 3	Nevit H. SCHOOLFIELD	Caroline MITCHELL
July 8	Ebenezer QUILLEN	Ann HOLLOWAY
July 9	John CORBIN	Ann WHEALTON
July 22	Henry POWELL	Rebecca POWELL
July 22	Lemuel DUKES	Amelia TOWNSEND
July 28	Leven HAYMAN	Sally WALSTON
July 28	George SMITH	Catharine WESTCOAT
Aug. 6	Levin TOWNSEND	Sarah Amos STURGIS
Aug. 8	William STEWART	Eliza SCARBOROUGH

1834
Aug. 12	Thomas M. HEARN	Nancy JACKSON
Aug. 20	Littleton TAYLOR	Nancy CHERRIX
Aug. 22	William H. WAILES	Sarah A. LEONARD
Aug. 26	William JARMAN	Sally ROUND
Sept. 8	James M. FOOKS	Maria FOOKS
Sept. 6	John HAMMOND	Atta FLEMING
Sept. 8	Thomas BRADFORD	Rachel BRADFORD
Sept. 8	Eli DALE	Hannah TULL
Sept. 9	Whittington JONES	Sally M. PATTERSON
Sept. 9	Levin HAINS	Patsey REDDEN
Sept. 23	Samuel HOUSTON	Elizabeth CHERRIX
Sept. 30	William A. McALLEN	Hannah AYDELOTTE
Oct. 6	William BURBAGE	Milly SELBY
Oct. 7	Ephraim T. TOWNSEND	Margaret NELSON
Oct. 15	John W. CONNER	Elizabeth MILLS
Oct. 20	James RACKLIFFE	Matilda FASSITT
Oct. 21	Littleton FLEMING	Comfort CLAYWELL
Nov. 1	P.W. QUINTON	Charlotte E.M. TOWNSEND
Nov. 3	Isaac H. ENNIS	Elizabeth WILLIAMS
Nov. 4	William BRADFORD	Rachel WEB
Nov. 6	Benjamin BRITTINGHAM	Mina DENNIS
Nov. 14	Ananias W. POWELL	Aralanta S. JOHNSON
Nov. 18	Lambert WILLIAMS	Drucilla JARMAN
Dec. 3	David PRUITT	Margaret H. DICKERSON
Dec. 4	John REED	Mary BETHARDS
Dec. 9	Ananias POWELL	Mary NICHOLS
Dec. 9	John TAYLOR	Augusta BOWEN
Dec. 15	William LAYTON	Amelia LITTLETON
Dec. 17	James BEATHARDS	Martha JARMAN
Dec. 17	George T. MILLS	Elizabeth TOWNSEND
Dec. 19	Elijah WARINGTON	Catharine BRATTEN
Dec. 19	William B. WHITE	Mary Ann HOUSTON
Dec. 20	John DRYDEN	Tabitha HOSHIER
Dec. 22	Joshua JARMAN	Eliza GIVANS
Dec. 26	Ezekiel JONES	Phebe Ann MELSON

1835
Jan. 3	William HASTINGS	Eliza JOHNSON
Jan. 5	William B. TRADER	Mary Ann TWILLY
Jan. 6	Peter RUARK	Elizabeth DOROTHY
Jan. 6	Riley SMACK	Nancy DENNIS
Jan. 6	Elihu JONES	Tabitha Jane PILCHARD
Jan. 6	William FASSETT of Jno.	Elizabeth PITTS
Jan. 6	Seth BRITTINGHAM	Eliza COFFIN
Jan. 7	Robert MILLS	Ann DENNIS
Jan. 13	John HANDCOCK	Sarah HALES
Jan. 14	William JONES	Nancy ALLEN
Jan. 20	James M. DAVIS	Ann Eliza DAVIS

1835

Date	Groom	Bride
Jan. 21	William BROWN	Elizabeth NOCK
Jan. 24	McKemmy SMACKY	Mary DORMAN
Jan. 24	William SELBY	Hetty WHEELER
Jan. 27	Kendal MASSEY Jr.	Julian JONES
Jan. 29	James A. BELL	Charlotte A. SCHURER ?
Feb. 3	Francis FRANKLIN	Mary HILL
Feb. 10	Jesse PURNELL	Elizabeth TEAGUE
Feb. 18	Cannon SHORT	Jane ATKINSON
Feb. 25	Lewis D. HEATH	Emeline SAVAGE
March 2	Littleton TAYLOR	Hester CROPPER
March 9	John B. WARRENGTON	Elizabeth OLIVE
March 10	John JARMAN	Eliza SMACK
March 14	James H. STEVENSON	Julian CRUFF
March 17	Edward TAYLOR	Susan STEVENS
March 17	James LOCKERMAN	Elizabeth JOHNSON
March 24	John P. MARSHALL of Zadok	Sarah G. WILLIAMS
March 31	John E. POWELL	Nancy BRATTEN
April 6	Colomore BUNTING	Elizabeth WILKINSON
April 13	Samuel MELVIN	Elizabeth W. BAYLY
April 20	Isaac MORRIS	Catharine NICKERSON
April 24	William W. LAYFIELD	Maria BRITTINGHAM
April 27	John MERRILL	Shatty MELSON
May 4	William POLLITT	Mary COULBOURNE
May 6	John HOLLOWAY	Mary Ann DALE
May 21	John B. FASSETT	Mary LEWIS
May 26	Edmond ROWLEY	Mary BLAKE
June 6	James LECOMPT	Henrietta TRUITT
June 16	Moses CLAYWELL	Ann JONES
June 20	William FOX	Mary Ann JAMES
June 26	William TAYLOR	Polly LEONARD
June 30	Joshua BOWEN	Margaret KNOX
July 8	William W. JOHNSTON	Resina M. UPSHUR
July 11	George D. ABNER	Susan ROBINS
July 14	Hiram GIVAN	Julian JOHNSON
July 15	Charles PRIOR	Charlotte PARKS
July 23	George C. WATERS	Melinda C. JOYNES
July 24	Thomas NOTTINGHAM	Mary Ann SCOTT
July 29	John Purnell ROBINS	Margaret Ann SPENCE
Aug. 6	Stephen BRADFORD	Margaret MUMFORD
Aug. 10	Armell RICHARDSON	Zippy B. BRITTINGHAM
Aug. 25	Jesse M. JAMIESON	Rebecca TOWNSEND
Aug. 25	James MASON	Tinny JESTER
Aug. 25	Alexander TIMMONS	Dolly BASSETT
Sept. 1	Addison NOTTINGHAM	Lucy JOHNS
Sept. 9	Joshua DRISKILL	Eliza WARD
Sept. 10	James ELLIS	Leah BUTLER
Sept. 15	James W. RUARK	Elizabeth BRUMBLY
Sept. 16	Samuel Q. WHITE	Mahalia GORDY

1835

Date	Groom	Bride
Sept. 29	Samuel BROUGHTON	Drucilla MARSHALL
Oct. 20	Thomas DUKES	Julian CLAYWELL
Oct. 20	John JONES	Elizabeth SELBY
Oct. 21	William R. TRUITT	Sarah HARRIS
Nov. 3	John R. PURNELL	Mary P. MITCHELL
Nov. 7	Lorenzo D. MEARS	Sophia A. KELLAEM
Nov. 11	Cornelius FASSETT	Maria PITTS
Nov. 24	William PATEN Jr.	Nancy PATTERSON
Dec. 1	Thomas W. HARGIS	Ann G. STEVENSON
Dec. 3	Benjamin WHITE	Sarah Ann ADKINS
Dec. 8	Walter TARR	Sarah HILL
Dec. 8	John MORRIS	Jane WILLIAMS
Dec. 12	Elijah HASTING	Hetty BREWINGTON
Dec. 12	William C. LATCHEM	Matilda WILLIAMS
Dec. 14	John DENNIS (of Thos.)	Nancy Eliza Tabitha SMITH
Dec. 15	James R. JACKSON	Mary STURGIS
Dec. 15	James BRODWATER	Henny BLAKE
Dec. 15	Ishmael DAVIS	Sally HAMMOND
Dec. 16	Lemuel HOLLOWAY	Hetty LUCAS
Dec. 18	Eli WHITE	Margaret HENDERSON
Dec. 19	James CALLAWAY	Mary EVANS
Dec. 19	Isaaac DAVIS	Betsey BAKER
Dec. 19	Benjamin D. TINGLE	Mary HOLLAND
Dec. 22	Outten SELBY	Elizabeth AYRES
Dec. 22	James HUGHES	Elizabeth STURGIS
Dec. 28	William T. MADDUX	Elizabeth HOLLAND
Dec. 29	Jesse MUMFORD	Charlott Ann CROPPER
Dec. 29	Tully LITTLETON	Mariah GUNTER
Dec. 30	Lewis SMITH	Charlotte TARR
Dec. 30	James JOHNSON	Sally JOHNSON

1836

Date	Groom	Bride
Jan. 5	Thomas QUILLEN	Rachel A.A. JACKSON
Jan. 7	Thomas CLAYWELL	Comfort E.H. POWELL
Jan. 12	Ananias GRAY	Amelia CLARK
Jan. 16	William BURBAGE	Miranda ADKINS
Jan. 19	Ephraim HUDSON	Sally WARREN
Jan. 19	Peter POWELL	Catharine HUDSON
Feb. 3	Robert NAIRNE	Rebecca M. BAYLY
Feb. 9	William BELL	Mary Grace JOHNSON
Feb. 9	Isaac POINTER	Hetty NEWTON
Feb. 15	George BRUMBLY	Betsey HILL
Feb. 17	John O. SELBY	Catharine R. HUTCHESON
March 8	Edward TOWNSEND	Julian BATTS
March 9	John AYDELOTTE	Nancy MILLS
March 14	Henry BUSTON	Leah ADAMS
March 14	George BOWDUIN	Esther MORRIS
March 18	Thomas D. PARKER	Julia MORRIS

1836

Date	Groom	Bride
March 22	Edward DICKERSON	Hester TRUITT
March 23	Isaac SELBY	Charlotte SLOCOMB
March 25	Samuel SMASHY	Mary GRAY
March 28	John TAYLOR	Louisa PORTER
March 29	John TINDAL	Elizabeth CROPPER
March 30	John W. POWELL	Sarah Ann DAVIS
April 6	George TARR	Henny HALES
April 7	William JARMAN	Leah TIMMONS
April 21	Richard ENNIS	Matilda POWELL
April 25	Samuel T. LANDING	Sally W. BOSTON
April 26	Robert MEARS	Charlotte JAMES
May 3	Levin WALKER	Nancy SHOCKLEY
May 31	William BOWDEN	Maria HOZIOR
June 7	John W. SELBY	Elizabeth Ann TULL
June 11	Joseph BULL	Caroline CLOGG
June 21	Jesse FOOKS	Mary LIVINGSTON
June 22	George LAYFIELD	Hetty MOOR
June 23	Elias PENNYWELL	Exeline HAMMOND
June 24	John JONES	Leah TAYLOR
June 27	Henry PATTERSON	Mary F. SMITH
June	Lemuel WILLIAMS	Nancy HAMMOND
July 2	John WILLIAMS	Rebecca STEVENSON
July 5	John H. MARSHALL	Eliza SHARPLEY
July 14	James POWELL of Solomon	Sarah WARE
July 20	Bayly HICKMAN	Mary Ann PAYNTER
July 20	John TULL	Barsheba KENNY
July 26	William B. FIELD	Mary CROPPER
Aug. 3	Purnell TAYLOR	Rose Anne BUNTING
Aug. 4	John BELL	Elizabeth STEPHENS
Aug. 8	Waters JONES	Elizabeth TRADER
Aug. 24	William LECOMPTE	Rachel MASON
Sept. 7	Henry REED	Lydia TRUITT
Sept. 13	John BLADES	Nancy BRITTINGHAM
Sept. 13	Hiram K. DUNCAN	Catharine TULL
Sept. 27	Thomas TAYLOR	Sarah KING
Sept. 28	Benjamin H. GORDY	Elizabeth JONES
Sept. 28	James H. COLLINS	Comfort RUARK
Oct. 11	Ritcher FOOKS	Eliza W. BROUGHTON
Oct. 18	William T. HOPE	Margaret Jane WATERS
Oct. 18	Elijah KELLY	Hetty Ann BYRD
Oct. 19	Henry SHARPLEY	Sarah WHEALTON
Oct. 24	Edward U. POWELL	Sally B. DRUMIS (?)
Oct. 26	Luther GLADDEN	Margaret LECOMPTE
Nov. 1	Augustus G. GROVE	Julian BACON
Nov. 8	William CLOGG	Nancy LARKIN
Nov. 15	George DYKES	Elizabeth VINCENT
Nov. 16	Moses PILCHARD	Tabitha WINTERBOTTOM
Nov. 28	William HUDSON	Ritta SMITH

1836

Nov. 29	William LEWIS	Ann DENNIS
Nov. 29	William TAYLOR	Margaret TAYLOR
Dec. 6	Edward TRUITT	Eliza BOWEN
Dec. 8	Robert H. POWELL	Maria E. BASSITT
Dec. 13	John Henry DORMAN	Lauretta NICHOLS
Dec. 13	Handy SMACK	Martha Ann MORRIS
Dec. 13	William TUBBS	Ann RUNNELLS
Dec. 16	James LITTLETON	Sarah PARSONS
Dec. 16	Hezekiah MADDUX	Charlotte PARKER
Dec. 16	Joseph COLLINS	Jane PARKER
Dec. 16	Edward M. TRUITT	Ann P. BURROUGHS
Dec. 19	James LANDING	Sally POWELL
Dec. 20	John MATTHEWS	Eliza BRIMER
Dec. 20	John BOWDEN	Jane TARR
Dec. 22	Levi D. TIMMONS	Fanny DUNCAN
Dec. 28	Josiah BOWEN	Charlotte BOWEN
Dec. 30	John WYATT	Sally HAMMOND
Dec. 31	James MASON	Elizabeth BISHOP

1837

Jan. 2	George BUNTICK of Wm	Ann WESSELLS of Isaac
Jan. 6	David I. HAYMAN	Eleanor TOADVINE
Jan. 9	James H. DRAYTON	Nancy D. DOROTHY
Jan. 11	Cave J.W. HACK	Charlotte
Jan. 11	Henry REED	Maria TAYLOR
Jan. 12	William STURGIS	Mary RICHARDSON
Jan. 19	Josiah JOHNSON	Jane CHRISTOPHER
Jan. 21	James ALLEN	Ann W. TATUM
Jan. 23	Peter POWELL	Molly BAKER
Jan. 25	James GIVAN	Priscilla Eleanor PARSONS
Jan. 31	Milton BUSSELLS	Leah JONES
Jan. 31	Joseph Brittingham NICHOLSON	Sarah Ann MILLS
Feb. 2	John F. TRUITT	Charlotte ADKINS
Feb. 3	Henry W. LONG	Julian GRAY
Feb. 4	Shoiles C. TEABRIAN	Maria L. ROCK
Feb. 7	Ephraim WILLIAMS	Charlotte DALE
Feb. 7	John T. MARSHALL	Harriet MACREADY
Feb. 7	John HUDSON	Sophia WATTS
Feb. 13	John WILLIS	Mary Ann QUILLEN
Feb. 14	Purnell W. SHORT	Maria MELSON
Feb. 14	Isaac BRADFORD	Eliza TIMMONS
Feb. 14	Soloman BAKER	Catharine Ann MASSEY
Feb. 15	Barnsbas TAYLOR	Mary JONES
Feb. 17	Peter EAST	Susan W. SCOTT
Feb. 18	James COLLINS	Mary W. DIX
Feb. 25	Joseph H. MILLER	Hannah MITCHELL
Feb. 28	Milby John Slemmone DRYDEN	Eleanor M.R. BENNETT
Feb. 28	Samuel BRITTINGHAM	Elizabeth CALLAHAN

1837

March 12	William DRYDEN	Polly MORRIS
March 21	James M. WILSON	Elizabeth DAVIS
March 25	William FOOKS	Mary Ann BROWN
March 27	Lambert GRIFFIN	Mary COLLINS
March 29	Kendal JARVIS	Elizabeth ANDERSON
April 7	Charles BOWEN	Mahala BRADFORD
April 11	Lorenzo DAVIS	Rachel LUCAS
April 13	Robert CALENDAR	Sarah FREANY
April 18	Thomas MESICK	Jane WHITE
April 26	Zadok PURNELL	Mary H. HAMMOND
May 6	David BOWEN	Mary Ann CROPPER
May 9	Wm. WILLIAMS	May JONES
May 15	Thomas DOUBLIN	Mary JACKSON
May 23	Milby GRIFFIN	Ann HOLLAND
May 23	Babel FOX	Betsey GARRISON
May 27	Joseph SHARPLEY	Rosena MERRILL
May 28	Price COLLINS	Henrietta HUDSON
June 6	Peter BRITTINGHAM	Mary Ann TAYLOR
June 9	Isaac MITCHELL	Nicy ENNIS
June 13	James Fontaine BURKE	Gatty White ADKINS
June 13	James WATERS	Mary SCOTT
June 17	James MELSON	Mary TAYLOR
June 17	Isarael TOWNSEND	Mary BUSTER
June 20	Major REED	Elizabeth TRADER
June 26	Robert WARREN	Mary TIMMONS
June 27	William SNIPE	Hetty GRIFFIN
July 3	William ANDERSON	Eleanor HOOPER
July 3	Peter JOHNSON	Presilla TARR
July 5	Robert NELSON	Zipporah TWINE ?
July 11	John H. BUNTING	Mary SELBY
July 18	George GIVANS	Elizabeth McALLEN
July 19	John GLADDEN	Elizabeth WARD
July 22	John WINBRE	Molina KELLY
July 24	John H. DENNIS	Henny GIVANS
July 29	George BURCH	Eliza Ann SCOTT
Aug. 2	Richard BOWEN	Mary FURKIS
Aug. 5	Nathaniel TOWNSEND	Eliza JACOBS
Aug. 6	Steward RIGGAN	Ann ADISON
Aug. 8	Jas SMULLIN	Ann REDDISH
Aug. 8	Samuel WALTER	Mary BEACH
Aug. 12	William McGRATH	Ellendar CARY
Aug. 12	Elisha JOYNES	Sarah BOGGS
Aug. 26	John MASON	Nancy TILGHMAN
Aug. 26	Henry DRYDEN	Eleanor T. DONAHOE
Sept. 4	Jas N. RUARK	Mary LEAKEY
Sept. 12	John WARD	Hetty DAVIS
Sept. 20	Henry WHITE	Leah Jane McALLEN
Sept. 21	Annanias JARMAN	Euphama WARREN

1837
Sept.	25	Caleb DUNCAN	Charlotte COLLINS
Sept.	25	Leven W. BEAUCHAMP	Margaret HOLLAND
Oct.	4	William BEACHBOARD	Lyda BEVANS
Oct.	12	Billy HAMMOND	Betsy LOKEY
Oct.	15	John W. STEWART	Julia Ann Pitts POWELL
Oct.	18	Morriss H. ADAMS	Elenor WILLIAMS
Oct.	18	Elisha JONES	Jane M. HUDSON
Oct.	20	Charles MASON	Mary BUNDICK
Oct.	22	John MALLETT	Sally MALLETT
Oct.	22	Zeno WARRINGTON	Martha Rounds BRATTEN
Oct.	26	James PHILLIPS	Nancy HANDCOCK
Oct.	29	Peter Thomas ALEXANDER	Henny SHARPLY
Nov.	2	Milby POWELL	Rachel HILL
Nov.	4	James POWELL	Margaret CROPPER
Nov.	11	William W. MUMFORD	May WARREN
Nov.	18	Henry BAYLY	Betsy BULL
Nov.	25	Thomas W. DUNOWAY	May B. TRUITT
Nov.	25	Leml. EVANS	Julian MITCHELL
Nov.	28	Zadok MARSHALL	Cornelia BOWEN
Dec.	6	Belitha HUDSON	Ansley COLLINS
Dec.	12	James BAKER	Julia TRUITT
Dec.	12	John BATEW	Rosana REDDEN
Dec.	13	James COLLINS	Sally HUDSON
Dec.	13	William PARSONS	Elizbth. HEARN
Dec.	15	James BONNEWELL	Elizabeth B. TRUITT
Dec.	16	Elijah CLARK	Elizabeth GRAY
Dec.	18	Samuel COWLEY	Elizabeth HALES
Dec.	19	Ambrose COLLINS	Sarah WHITE
Dec.	20	Benjamin TIMMONS	Charlotte GRIFFIN
Dec.	20	Samuel OWENS	Elizabeth POWDERS
Dec.	20	Handy HEARNE	Elizabeth VIGUS ?
Dec.	21	John HILL	Elizabeth REED
Dec.	21	Teackle W. JACOB	Rachel U. BAYLY
Dec.	26	Levin HENDERSON	Charlotte Jane BOSTON
Dec.	27	Robert DRYDEN	Susan FISHER
Dec.	29	James OLIPHER	Mary BREWINGTON
Dec.	30	Peter W. TARR	Gatty PENNEWELL
Dec.	31	Charles TATHAM	Mary A. MATTHEWS

1838
Jan.	2	James Henry WHITE	Juliet Ann PATTERSON
Jan.	2	William I. PENNEWELL	Mary B. TAYLOR
Jan.	3	James Selby BOWEN	Eliza M. BRATTEN
Jan.	8	Walter RODGERS	Jane HICKMAN
Jan.	8	James MURRAY	Polly ADKISON
Jan.	9	Isaac MILBOURNE	Charlotte JACKSON
Jan.	9	John RAIN	Martha DAVIS
Jan.	9	Thos. WATERS	Eleanor Ann HENDERSON

1838

Jan. 9	John P. MARSHALL	Martha MUMFORD
Jan. 10	Leml. TIMMONS	Matilda TIMMONS
Jan. 12	James P. TRUITT	Eliza RAIN
Jan. 13	Nathaniel BRITTINGHAM	Mary LAWS
Jan. 13	John PHIPPS	Maranda TRUITT
Jan. 15	Henry DENNIS	Mary Ann BASSETT
Jan. 15	Covington ENNIS	Ellanor RICHARDSON
Jan. 15	Henry TULL	Mary DONOHOE
Jan. 21	John BUNTING	Gatty HOLLOWAY
Jan. 23	John T. HILL	Macy WILLISS
Jan. 23	Edward P. PORTER	Mary Ann HOLSTON
Jan. 30	Soloman TULL	Matilda CLAYWELL
Jan. 30	Robert BAKER	Martha W. EVANS
Jan. 31	William NOCK	Ann PRICE
Feb. 1	Patrick W. PARSONS	Julia DOWNING
Feb. 2	Jno. H. LANGSDALE	Elizabeth S. GARRISON
Feb. 6	John JONES	Caroline ELLISS
Feb. 10	Edward THORNTON	Elizabeth ADISON
Feb. 12	Charles DAVIS	Elizabeth HUDSON
Feb. 20	John P. JONES	Ellenor JONES
Feb. 21	Abel WINDER	Mary Ann SCOTT
Feb. 22	Peter OWEN	Sally CHESSER
Feb. 24	James Madison SHOCKLEY	Ellen PARKS
Feb. 28	John GODWIN	Mary TRUITT
March 5	Wm G. LAYFIELD	Martha POWELL
March 6	Thomas BRITTINGHAM	Mary WATERFIELD
March 19	Southy W. BULL	Polly MASON
April 2	William D. PITTS	Erexine S. PURNELL
April 10	Josiah P. COULBOURNE	Leah LEVINGSTON
April 10	Charles A. ORAN	Julia Ann HUDSON
April 17	George R. MURRAY	Eliza A.C. HARRIS
April 28	Jones BOUNDS	Eleanor PUZEY
May 22	William JONES	Luara Ann BOWEN
May 27	Charles TARR	Mary WEBB
May 29	John COLLINS	Harriet CORBIN
May 29	James SMACK	Eleanor BOWEN
May 29	Cyrus WILLIAMS	Ann BRAVARD
May 30	Merrill D. SMITH	Laura Ann DUNCAN
June 2	David JESTER	Nancy CONNER
June 19	John U. DENNIS	Louisa Jane HOLLAND
June 24	Joshua H. LANKFORD	Mary Ann HAYMAN
June 26	William A. HASTINGS	Jane HAMMOND
June 27	William DUBLEY	Henny CHERRIX
July 3	Edward G. JOYNES	Eleanor A.D. RICHARDSON
July 7	John R. PITTS	Ann TAYLOR
July 15	John CAUSEY	Sally HERRINGTON
July 17	John GRAY	Henrietta A. CAREY
July 20	John T. W. RIGGAN	Levina A. MATTHEWS

1838

July 24	Levin HOLSTON	Elizabeth QUILLING
July 31	Josiah MITCHELL	Charlotte RUARK
Aug. 17	David MADDUX	Julia A. PARKER
Aug. 20	Isaac PURNELL	Hetty WILLIAMS
Aug. 26	John BRITTINGHAM	Sarah LAMBDEN
Aug. 28	Thomas G. LANE	Caroline WILLIAMS
Aug. 29	George W. GLADDEN	Milky WILKERSON
Sept. 10	John RIGGAN	Henny CHRISTOPHER
Sept. 16	Major COFFIN	Julia HASTING
Sept. 18	Carey Collier SEARS	Margaret Porter BURNETT
Sept. 20	Thomas TIMMONS	Mary E. SELBY
Oct. 10	Josiah TAYLOR	Ann GODFREY
Oct. 13	Thoregood BELL	Gaty SALSBURY
Oct. 16	Leven B. HOUSTON	Tabitha SILVERTHORN
Oct. 16	Samuel B. TAYLOR	Nancy CLAVELL
Oct. 25	John STURGIS	Elizabeth BLADES
Oct. 27	Puey PUZEY	Mary MADDUX
Oct. 30	Josiah CAUSEY	Sally H. NUTTER
Oct. 30	Phillip WARREN	Adeline TRUITT
Oct. 30	James GREY	Patty DAVIS
Nov. 12	John JONES	Elizabeth DAVIS
Nov. 13	Matthias GODFREY	Elizabeth DONOWAY
Nov. 13	Isaac NICHOLS	Matty PARKER
Nov. 19	James WILLIAMS	Sabra CROPPER
Nov. 20	Daniel CHESSER	Elizabeth MILES
Nov. 24	Lewis E. CARPENTER	Anatha AMES
Nov. 24	Edward C. THOMAS	Sally W. LEWIS
Nov. 26	Peter QUILLING	Martha COOPER
Nov. 26	Tenant BOWER	Nancy CROPPER
Nov. 29	Hillery WARREN	Ann DENNIS
Nov. 30	Kendal MURRAY	Molly GRAY
Dec. 4	Ezekiel HOWARD	Patty HUGHES
Dec. 10	Isaac D. WELBORN	Margaret DOUGHTY
Dec. 10	David PRIOR	Mary LAYFIELD
Dec. 12	Anthony COTTINGHAM	Martha BONNEWELL
Dec. 13	Saml. H. TRUITT	Louisa JOHNSON
Dec. 14	Edward TULL	Sarah Ann JONES
Dec. 17	Levin NICHOLSON	Harriet STEWART
Dec. 17	William BAKER	Rhoda C. DALE
Dec. 17	James T. SYMINGGTON	Nelly A. HANDY
Dec. 19	William SCOTT	Mary E. DAVIS
Dec. 20	John MITCHELL	Ame WILLIS
Dec. 22	Jeptha WEBB	Margaret SCHOOLFIELD
Dec. 24	George HARDIS	Maria TULL
Dec. 26	William TARR	Mary WHEALTON
Dec. 29	William H. BEACH	Ann D. BAYLY
Dec. 31	Cornelius E. BATTHELL	Julia MUMFORD

1839

Date	Groom	Bride
Jan. 1	Henry WEBB	Frankey TARR
Jan. 1	Perry S. RODNEY	Leah COFFIN
Jan. 1	William S. EWELL	Esther BULL
Jan. 2	Jesse WILKINSON	Easther PAYNE
Jan. 2	George S.D. SHIPLEY	Catharine T. BACON
Jan. 5	Revel TWIFORD	Ann BLACKSONE
Jan. 10	Lorenzo D. DAVIS	Eliza TABBS
Jan. 14	William F. BROWN	Harriet A. PARKER
Jan. 14	Luke PENNEWELL	Mary COFFIN
Jan. 15	Samuel CROPPER	Mary HUDSON
Jan. 17	John P. RICHARDSON	Maria DAVIS
Jan. 20	William M. PRUITT	Sally GLADDEN
Jan. 22	Peter TINDALL	Maria JONES
Jan. 23	George BOWDOIN	Caroline WONNELL
Jan. 25	William T. FLEMMING	Mary Elizabeth DICKERSON
Jan. 29	William BEACH	Mary GLASSBY
Jan. 30	Soloman WILKINSON	Maria GLADDEN
Feb. 5	William James BARNES	Mary Elizabeth POWELL
Feb. 6	John BOSTON	Rosanna E. M. WAINWRIGHT
Feb. 11	Zebram MUMFORD	Mary Elizabeth STEELE
Feb. 12	Philip HUDSON	Sophia FISHER
Feb. 14	James HICKMAN	Sally LITTLETON
Feb. 19	Samuel M. MELSON	Esther BOHANNAN
Feb. 20	James COLLINS	Hetty McHENRY
Feb. 22	Custis BULL	Margaret MELSON
Feb. 17	George BRITTINGHAM	Nancy RAIN
March 1	John H. ALLAN	Hester Ann BONNAWELL
March 1	James LONG	Mary HUDSON
March 5	John JONES	Harriet BISHOP
March 6	Benj. BASSITT	Julian BARNES
March 11	Belitha GRIFFIN	Ellener SMACK
March 20	James R. HEARN	Elizabeth LINDZEY
March 20	Bejm HOLSTON	Mary DAVIS
March 25	Roland E. BEVENS	Matilda C. HAYMAN
March 26	John DUKES	Polly AYDELOTTE
March 26	Joshua BOWEN	Hetty PENNEWELL
March 26	Leven HANDY	Betsy COLLINS
April 2	Samuel SMASHEY	Maria DAVIS
April 6	Daniel FOSKEY	Sally MILLS
April 9	Levi FISHER	Sarah COLLINS
April 12	Josiah DAVIS	Sarah LANE
April 16	James BONNAWELL	Harriet WEBB
April 27	John HASTINGS	Margaret LINCH
April 30	John S. MILLS	Mary A. SCOTT
May 7	Benjamin G. HEARN	Eliza WALSTON
May 13	John H. DIXON	Margaret TOWNSEND
May 11	Thomas HALL	Sally DRUMMONED
May 13	Jesse JONES	Sally L. PURNELL

1839

Date	Groom	Bride
May 15	John HUDSON	Sarah M. PEACOCK
May 16	James CANNON	Nancy GODFREY
May 16	Samuel RICHARDSON	Amelia CHAILLE
May 17	James G. BADGER	Charlotte JAMES
May 22	Nehemiah DORMAN	Polly STURGIS
May 28	Peter BURBAGE	Jane GRIFFIN
May 26	Henry ADAMS	Elizabeth DICKERSON
May 29	Rufus MOORE	Mary VADEN
May 29	Abel B. COLONNA	Margaret E.R. POWELL
May 29	Crippen BOOTH	Elizabeth HILL
May 30	Alexander TIMMONS	Nolly WILKINS
June 5	Annanias W. POWELL	Hetty JOHNSON
June 12	Elisha HOLLOWAY	Sally McGEE
June 18	Isaac TOWNSEND	Lydia BEVANS
June 21	Robert BOWMAN	Eliza Ann WRIGHT
July 5	Edward BENSON	Patsy FITCHETT
July 9	James DENNIS	Julia DENNIS
July 18	Charles T. REW	Mary L. NAIRNE
July 30	Jesse TRUITT	Sally SELBY
Aug. 7	Wm BELL	Rebecca WARD
Aug. 20	Moses BOWEN	Sarah MILLS
Aug. 21	Peter SCOTT	Gatty WEBB
Aug. 24	James R. BELL	Maria I. DRUMMOND
Aug. 29	Joshua RUARK	Gatty HOSHIER
Aug. 29	Ephraim STIRGIS	Sarah McALLEN
Sept. 4	William HARPER	Mary TAYLOR
Sept. 4	Geo HUDSON	Mahalae HERRINGTON
Sept. 5	Peter HEARN	Elizabeth MILLS
Sept. 9	William MUMFORD	Catharine PARSONS
Sept. 12	Lophus POWELL	Eliza COTTINGHAM
Sept. 14	Leven HENDERSON	Hetty CHURCH
Sept. 16	Ebe BISHOP	Sarah TULL
Sept. 17	James BRITTINGHAM	Anna McMASTER
Sept. 17	Thomas R. COLLINS	Matilda DOWNING
Sept. 24	James L. VALLANDIGHAN	Mary E. SPENCE
Sept. 30	Elijah PINKETT	Amelia RIDER
Oct. 2	Benjamin JOHNSON	Mary RICHARDSON
Oct. 3	William DICKERTSON	Elizabeth HAMMOND
Oct. 7	Elijah C. SCHOOLFIELD	Irene HENDERSON
Oct. 8	Isaac SELBY	Hetty JONES
Oct. 15	Albert SMACK	Molly KNOX
Oct. 15	George PAYNE	Gatty BOWEN
Oct. 16	McKemmy TIMMONS	Caroline GRIFFIN
Oct. 16	James A. TAYLOR	Charlotte MILBOURNE
Oct. 21	Thomas LITTLETON	Molly LITTLETON
Oct. 22	Levi ROSE	Elizabeth INSLEY
Oct. 22	Peter CHERRIS	Hetty STURGIS
Oct. 23	George M. UPSHUR	Priscilla A. TOWNSEND

1839

Oct. 28	James B. POWELL	Priscilla A. RUARK
Oct. 28	Isaac William HANDY	Mary Jane PURNELL
Nov. 2	Elisha DICKERSON	Mary MUMFORD
Nov. 3	James T. TRUITT	Susan W. HAYWARD
Nov. 3	Ephraim JONES	Mary BOWEN
Nov. 7	Joshua MORRIS	Rachel I. MASSEY
Nov. 7	Obed SHORT	Mary Gatty PITTS
Nov. 11	Marshall SMITH	Sally Ann PERDUE
Nov. 19	James HOUSTON	Elizabeth GRAY
Nov. 19	James MATTHEWS	Mary Ann SHARPLEY
Nov. 20	Henry J. BREWINGTON	Arintha Ann LONG
Nov. 21	George BISHOP	Louisa C. DENNIS
Nov. 26	Severn HILL	Ann PHILIPS
Nov. 30	Elisha COLLINS	Charlotte McCABE
Dec. 3	John BISHOP	Nancy Ann TULL
Dec. 3	Samuel TRAHEARN	Sally C. HAZZARD
Dec. 3	Lewis ROBINS	Susan ROBERTS
Dec. 9	Peter H. COLE	Elizabeth SAVAGE
Dec. 10	Daniel MASON	Patsy WATSON
Dec. 10	Handy HASTINGS	Catharine HICKMAN
Dec. 10	Stephen Decatur BOWDOIN	Mary Ann JONES
Dec. 11	William MILBOURNE	Elizabeth STURGIS
Dec. 14	James MASSEY	Fanny HASTINGS
Dec. 16	William T. COULBOURNE	Henny W. ADKINS
Dec. 16	Robert NELSON	Ann STURGIS
Dec. 16	John T. ADKINS	Leah PARSONS
Dec. 17	James L. WILLIAMS	Sarah FITCHETT
Dec. 17	Jacob WONNELL	Sally RIGGIN
Dec. 17	John TILGHMAN Sr.	Elizabeth TRUITT
Dec. 17	Walter SCOTT	Malinda LONG
Dec. 18	John STURGIS	Charlotte DUNCAN
Dec. 18	Lias BENSTON	Sarah P. MERRILL
Dec. 19	John TAYLOR	Susan MARSHALL
Dec. 21	Joseph QUILLEN	Frances CAUEY
Dec. 23	Littleton T. CLUFF	Nancy SHARPLEY
Dec. 24	George WALLOP	Elizabeth TAYLOR
Dec. 25	Isaac TARR	Charlotte RICHARDS
Dec. 30	James TOWNSEND	Wincy PRUITT

1840

Jan. 3	Thomas ADKINS	Nancy BISHOP
Jan. 6	Handy FOOKS	Mary Ann FOOKS
Jan. 6	Abraham BRUMBLY	Maria POWELL
Jan. 7	Johnson GRAY	Jane SCHOOLFIELD
Jan. 7	James PHILLIPS	Harriet PRUITT
Jan. 9	Lambert JOHNSON	Eliza BUTLER
Jan. 10	Dial WARD	Elizabeth LEWIS
Jan. 11	Kendall TIMMONS	Andy SMACK

1840

Date	Groom	Bride
Jan. 13	Josiah COLLINS	Mary Ann PURNELL
Jan. 13	Kendall SMACK	Elizabeth JARMIN
Jan. 14	Isaac McKABE	Margaret HUDSON
Jan. 15	McKemmy SMACK	Nancy HOWARD
Jan. 18	Jesse SMACK	Charlotte GRIFFIN
Jan. 20	Isaac BUNTING	Nancy GIBBS
Jan. 21	John ROGERS	Sarah Elizabeth DAVIS
Jan. 21	Seth HUDSON	Arenia TRADER
Jan. 21	John F. FLEMMING	Amelia A. HENDERSON
Jan. 31	John KNOCK	Mary WINDER
Feb. 3	John H. HAYMAN	Ann Maria MITCHELL
Feb. 4	George BENNETT	Ann TRADER
Feb. 5	James H. BALL	Elizabeth MELVIN
Feb. 10	Albert SELBY	Margaret JOINS
Feb. 11	Joel WILLIAMS	Mary BEATHARD
Feb. 18	John B. TOADVINE	Elicia Ann TOADVINE
Feb. 18	John P. TAYLOR	Elvira W. HENDERSON
Feb. 19	John DAVIS	Hesse TULL
Feb. 24	John POWELL	Eliza BRADFORD
Feb. 24	William GRIFFEN	Matilda BRITTINGHAM
Feb. 25	Henry MATTHEWS	Elizabeth BOSWELL
Feb. 25	William GUTHRIE	Mary WALKER
Feb. 25	Charles DAVIS	Betsy TARR
Feb. 26	John CARTER	Eliza Jane DASKY
Feb. 26	George HILL	Sally Maria BOWEN
Feb. 27	Thomas PARSONS	Sarah DAVIS
March 2	George W. DRYDEN	Aurelia JOHNSON
March 3	Washington TOMKINS	Sarah Ann KENNARD
March 3	William Shelly MASSEY	Martha HASTING
March 9	Henry W. BRUMBLEY	Matilda CAREY
March 10	Archibald GAULT	Eliza LITTLETON
March 11	Richard HASTINGS	Susan HASTINGS
March 12	Esme WEBB	Drucilla BRADFORS
March 17	Gilley BRADFORD	Mary TUBBS
March 17	Robert H. MARSHALL	Elizabeth LANKFORD
March 21	John NICHOLS	Anna JARMAN
March 21	Nathaniel F. REVELL	Elizabeth COLBOURN
March 24	Levi QUILLEN	Hetty RICHARDSON
March 25	James KING	Elizabeth PRIOR
March 31	George W. RICHARDSON	Rosea Jane TURNER
April 7	Thomas BAKER	Henrietta TYER
April 9	John BLOXOM	Mary JUSTICE
April 14	James P. TRUITT	Elizabeth J. TRUITT
April 21	George ROWND	Sarah TRUITT
April 21	James KNOX	Eliza PENNEWELL
April 27	Samuel McMASTER	Ann E. JOHNSON
April 28	Stephen ROACH	Sarah JONES
May 1	Milby ADKINS	Molly SNEAD

1840

May 7	John P.I. QUILLEN	Ann Maria COFFIN
May 12	John E. SCOTT	Sally BISHOP
May 13	John CATHELL	Mary QUILLEN
May 13	William H. RILEY	Nancy Handy DUFFIELD
May 26	Benjamin HOLLAND	Sarah G.S. PITTS
May 27	Henry RALLION	Charlotte CONNER
May 27	Lemuel PILCHARD	Ara MASON
June 2	John CARSEY	Milly LEWIS
June 9	Revd John D. CURTIS	Sarah Catharine GRAY
June 10	Samuel BOWDOIN	Harriet TINDALL
June 22	Levin W. POWELL	Ann Maria BEVANS
June 27	Isaac KINNIKIN	Betsey POWELL
July 1	William AUSTIN	Jane RICH
July 4	Wesley DIXON	Martha BURBAGE
July 14	William M. OREM	Mary BREWINGTON
July 16	Joshua M. CAREY	Julia A. E. NOCK
July 28	Elisha PARKER	Eliza BAKER
July 30	John A. PARSONS	Hannah BURROUGHS
Aug. 5	James TARR	Margaret RUARK
Aug. 11	William MUMFORD	Mary Margaret MITCHELL
Aug. 11	William HALES	Mary TILGHMAN
Aug. 15	Ephraim WESSELS	Ann LANKFORD
Aug. 18	George F. SMITH	Emily E. SCARBOROUGH
Aug. 20	Purnell TARR	Keturah RUARK
Aug. 26	Isaac SMULLEN	Elizabeth SMULLEN
Aug. 26	Henry REED	Mary STURGIS
Aug. 27	Wm E. TIMMONS	Harriet BURROUGHS
Sept. 5	James CERUTHAS	Rosy LEWIS
Sept. 14	Edward HOLLAND	Clara I. WEST
Sept. 25	Michael M. MOROW	Charlotte M.R. BENNETT
Sept. 25	James FOOKS (of D.)	Huldah PARKER
Sept. 25	Parker ROSS	Ann Byrd STATON
Sept. 26	John R. BULL	Juliet A. CARMINE
Sept. 28	Christopher P. BALL	Elizabeth TINDALL
Oct. 1	James W. L. STURGIS	Martha A. PURNELL
Oct. 3	Thomas W. BALEY	Sarah E. ROBINS
Oct. 9	William B. CORD	Esther EVANS
Oct. 9	Curtis KELLAM	Sarah G. AMES
Oct. 18	Cyrus WILLIAMS	Exerine ADKINS
Oct. 20	John A. PURNELL	Adaliza HENRY
Oct. 20	James BRITTINGHAM	Gatty HOLLOWAY
Nov. 3	John E. BROADWATER	Elizabeth YOUNG
Nov. 3	Benjamin B. FARLOW	Julian McGEE
Nov. 10	Henry STURGIS	Peggy TIMMONS
Nov. 10	John BURBAGE	Matilda WILLIAMS
Nov. 13	William BRITTINGHAM(of Geo)	Ann DAVIS
Nov. 24	George LAYFIELD	Julian ROUND
Dec. 1	William H. ROWLEY	Fidelea S. CAREY

1840
Date	Groom	Bride
Dec. 1	Charles N. HANDY	Elizabeth R. HANDY
Dec. 2	Isaac HARRISON	Elizabeth HARRISON
Dec. 11	Kendall DAVIS	Eliza TRUITT
Dec. 12	John TULL	Hetty KING
Dec. 12	Leven LEWIS	Elizabeth PRESCOT
Dec. 14	James HALL	Elizabeth Ann MERRILL
Dec. 15	Milby PARADISE	Eliza WHEALTON
Dec. 16	Thomas S. TARPIN	Mary E. M. GRAY
Dec. 19	Elijah BRITTINGHAM	Ann DONOWAY
Dec. 21	James L. KELLAM	Sally R. GOFFIGO
Dec. 22	Isaac DALE	Peggy DENNIS
Dec. 22	Peter L. DAVIS	Molly CAREY
Dec. 22	William C. SLOCUMB	Susan AYDELOTTE
Dec. 22	James LILLISTON	Elizabeth HICKMAN
Dec. 23	Leven GRAY	Elizabeth SMACK
Dec. 27	Burton B. TRUITT	Lurany LAWS
Dec. 29	Littleton HALL	Ann YOUNG
Dec. 30	James HARMAN	Milly BASSITT

1841
Date	Groom	Bride
Jan. 1	Sampson BURBAGE	Margaret Ann LAWS
Jan. 4	John LIVINGSTON	Matilda HAYMAN
Jan. 4	Gillis RAIN	Mary BRITTINGHAM
Jan. 5	Curtis W. JACOBS	Mamy A. HOLLAND
Jan. 5	Purnell JACKSON	Levine BEVANS
Jan. 12	Leven DALE	Margaret BRITTINGHAM
Jan. 18	John Byrd RIDER	Hetty A.S. WHALEY
Jan. 19	Samuel DAILY	Mary Jane DISHAROON
Jan. 19	John GUTHREY	Fanny JONES
Jan. 19	Levi BRIMER	Ann RICHARDSON
Jan. 25	George W. DAVIS	Drucilla PAYNE
Jan. 26	George M. DAVIS	Margaret A. MERRILL
Feb. 8	Oliver TILGHMAN	Mary Ann DIXON
Feb. 9	Joseph NICHOLSON	Margaret CLOGG
Feb. 13	David L. ROWLEY	Elizabeth A. COLLINS
Feb. 16	Henry M. STEVENSON	Ann BOSTON
Feb. 16	Levin D. DENNIS	Harriet BEATHARDS
Feb. 22	Caleb T. PARSONS	Mary DAVIS
Feb. 24	James KNOX	Lydia BEACHBOARD
March 8	George N. FOOKS	Esther Ann MURPHY
March 8	Josiah PARSONS	Susan RICHARDSON
March 13	Lewis WHITE	Milly SHOCKLEY
March 20	Joseph GRAY	Kitty Ann WILLIAMS
March 20	Thomas TIMMONS	Nelly BRADFORD
April 6	Major W. JONES	Elizabeth A. POWELL
April 6	Peter HOLLAND	Elizabeth JONES
April 7	Rufus K.M. BAYNUM	Eliza I.M. EVANS
April 7	Richard T. WATERS	Esther A. HOPKINS

1841

April 7	Elisha P. PARKER	Charlotte W. TRADER
April 14	Lambert ADKINS	Clarissa LAWS
April 20	Eliaken JONES	Sarah E. CORBIN
April 20	John E. JARVIS	Margaret FISHER
April 20	Henry GODFREY	Rachel ESHAM
April 27	John HASTINGS	Elizabeth SELBY
April 28	Purnell I. MACLAIN	Elizabeth I. REDDISH
May 4	George TOWNSEND	Esther HOLLAND
May 4	George I. WARNER	Catharine T. DIX
May 12	James BENNETT	Elenor LeKATES
May 13	Leander CLIFTON	Elizabeth PARKER
May 19	Peter HANDCOCK	Mary BISHOP
May 28	James HUGHES	Elizabeth HOPKINS
May 29	John HOWARD	Catharine MERRILL
May 31	Johnson H. DAVIS	Elawiza POWELL
June 1	Thomas PARKER	Elizabeth PALMER
June 1	Daniel HOLLOWAY	Sarah Caroline FOOKS
June 15	William MUMFORD	Jane RICHARDS
June 16	Thomas WILLIAMS	Elizabeth ELLENSWORTH
June 19	Samuel JOHNSON	Hetty MERRILL
June 22	Stephen PAYNE	Ann BENNETT
June 22	Robert JOHNSON	Margaret E.M. HARRISON
June 28	James B. TIMMONS	Mary W. DAVIS
June 30	James H. VINCENT	Sally BUSSELLS
July 12	William G. BETHARD	Eliza M. BROWN
July 14	Robert BAKER	Elizabeth DASEY
July 26	George H. MARTIN	Sally E.S. SMITH
Aug. 3	Benjamin CARMENE	Priscilla Ann FIGGS
Aug. 13	Daniel BUTLEY	Ann STEWART
Aug. 18	Shepherd BUNTIN	Sarah ANN WALKER
Aug. 24	Selby JOHNSON	Nelley TARR
Aug. 28	Samuel MATTHEWS	Phamy BROADWATER
Aug. 30	James L. ROWLEY	Elizabeth WATTS
Sept. 1	Gilly W. JOHNSON	Mary RUSSELL
Sept. 6	Henry Purnell POPE	Priscilla PUZEY
Sept. 10	Michael P. KELLAIM	Ann A. KELLAIM
Sept. 14	Lewis H. MASON	Jane E. CRAIG
Sept. 18	John S.D. HOLLAND	Sally W. WATERS
Sept.	John TWIG	Nancy MALONE
Sept. 27	James RILEY	Jane HANDCOCK
Sept. 29	Richard COLLINS	Sidney WHITE
Oct. 5	Purnell LOW	Susan DYKES
Oct. 9	James HENDERSON	Margaret WATERFIELD
Oct. 12	Hezekiah Gibbs SHOCKLEY	Sally Ann DISHAROON
Oct. 13	Thomas JARMAN	Sally JARMAN
Oct. 16	Levin S. H. SMITH	Milly KING
Oct. 19	Burton BAKER	Druscilla GRAY

1841
Oct.	21	Isaac S. JONES	Margaret JARVIS
Oct.	22	Philip B. TANKARD	Elizabeth V. ROGERS
Oct.	29	Robert TOWNSEND	Maria MATTHEWS
Nov.	9	Charles TOWNSEND	Sarah BEVANS
Nov.	11	Wiilliam KELLY	Elizabeth TRUITT
Nov.	20	Purnell PARSONS	Mary RING
Nov.	23	Samuel J. DAVIS	Nancy VAGON
Nov.	24	Stephen W. ENNIS	Tabitha RICHARDSON
Nov.	27	Ephraim W. PARSONS	Sarah E. LAWS
Nov.	27	Dingley LOKEY	Harriet MORRIS
Nov.	29	Stephen W. MURRAY	Maria MURRAY
Nov.	30	William Chaille MASSEY	Mary TAYLOR
Nov.	30	Revel OUTEN	Emeline PAYNE
Dec.	1	Anelo HARRIS	Harriet BOYER
Dec.	4	Lambert CAMPBELL	Elizabeth MURRAY
Dec.	8	John W. BRADFORD	Nancy NOCK
Dec.	11	Lemuel RIGGAN	Eleanor POWELL
Dec.	11	Lambert WILLIAMS	Emeline SMITH
Dec.	13	Benjamin JOHNSON	Anniss SHOCKLEY
Dec.	14	John B. CHATHAM	Narcissa CAUSEY
Dec.	14	William Henry MILLS	Elenor R. W. HILL
Dec.	14	Jacob RIGGAN	Nancy S. BURROUGHS
Dec.	15	George CURTIS	Louisa ATKINSON
Dec.	15	John Henry TULL	Maria POWELL
Dec.	18	Nathaniel QUILLEN	Sarah Ann JONES
Dec.	21	Peter R. PARSONS	Elizabeth ADKINS
Dec.	22	Gillet NOCK	Mary MARSHALL
Dec.	22	Levin MERRILL	Susan Ann BENSTON
Dec.	23	Winder H. HASTING	Eleanor CLAYWELL
Dec.	25	Gamage(?) EVANS	Elizabeth WARRENTON
Dec.	27	William WILLIAMS	Betsy PRIER
Dec.	28	Joshua HOLLOWAY	Mary HICKMAN
Dec.	31	Jesse ELLIS	Nancy OUTTEN

1842
Jan.	4	Thomas N. WILLIAMS	Harriet HENDERSON
Jan.	4	James H. TWIG	Milley TOWNSEND
Jan.	5	John Francis TOWNSEND	Ann McMaster SMITH
Jan.	5	John MACLIN	Susan LIVINGSTON
Jan.	5	Arthur LATHBURY	Dolly M LATCHUM
Jan.	6	Jonathan LAWS	Juliann FOOKS
Jan.	6	Isaac FARRELL	Elizabeth MUMFORD
Jan.	10	Levin ATKINSON	Comfort E. QUINTON
Jan.	11	William POWELL	Elizabeth POWELL
Jan.	11	Henry T. BURTON	Elizabeth HALL
Jan.	11	John B. MELVIN	Sarah Ann JONES
Jan.	12	Benjamin RIGGAN	Elizabeth H. WEST
Jan.	12	Peter PRICE	Priscilla DYES

1842

Date	Groom	Bride
Jan. 19	George P. FRANKLIN	Laura Ann PORTER
Jan. 24	Thomas B. MELVIN	Ann BLADES
Jan. 24	John D. MILLS	Elizabeth AYDELOTTE
Jan. 24	John MURRAY	Sarah PARSONS
Jan. 25	Seth M. WHALEY	Mary Ann MUMFORD
Jan. 25	Thomas RICHARDSON	Mary Purnell PUZEY
Jan. 25	Stephen FISHER	Jane DAVIS
Jan. 26	John WILLIAMS	Maria WEBB
Jan. 27	Doctor Hillary PITTS	Mary WILLIAMS
Feb. 1	James E. DAVIS	Elizabeth JOHNSON
Feb. 1	Edward H. WHITE	Priscilla W. HANDY
Feb. 2	Michael JESTER	Sally SCARBOROUGH
Feb. 7	George PRUITT	Susan C. JOHNSON
Feb. 8	Gilly C. SHORT	Priscilla F.B. MELSON
Feb. 9	Lodwick F. DAVIS	Vicy Quinton LITTLETON
Feb. 14	Arthur W. HILL	Eleanor DERICKSON
Feb. 15	Elijah L. PERDUE	Henrietta COULBOURNE
Feb. 17	John HICKMAN	Ann HOLSTON
Feb. 17	Perry RODNEY	Ransey MASSEY
Feb. 21	James BOWEN	Mary SHADRICK
Feb. 21	James JONES	Harriet DICKS
Feb. 22	James M. HOLLAND	Margaret Jane WARREN
Feb. 22	Renattus HEARN	Mary BRATTEN
Feb. 23	William TWILLEY	Mary Ann WHITE
Feb. 23	Isaac R. WILLETT	Drusilla HOLLAND
Feb. 27	William BENSON	Mary DRYDEN
March 8	Robert FLEMMING	Sally TRUITT
March 9	Peter TRUITT	Emeline HOUSTON
March 15	Levi D. HARVEY	Sarah Elizabeth GRAVENER
March 16	John GLADDEN	Harriet PHILLIPS
March 16	John Hiram POWELL	Eliza M. DUNCAN
March 26	Littleton SMITH	Pamelia HOBBS
March 29	George HUDSON	Susan BIRCH
March 30	Seth W. LATCHUM	Elizabeth LYNCH
April 2	James B. WRIGHT	Demirah B. HICKMAN
April 12	James P. KNOX	Caroline PENNEWELL
April 19	Henry I. ROWLEY	Sally T. SAVAGE
April 21	Ebenezer H. FOOKS	Rebecca CATHELL
April 22	John WOOLRIDGE	Sarah POWELL
April 23	Phillip RODNEY	Catharine CATHELL
May 11	John TINGLE	Mary BOWEN
May 19	William HAILES	Nancy MUMFORD
May 31	Parker BOWEN	Mary J. BOWEN
June 1	Peter BEACHBOARD	Margaret WEBB
June 1	Stewart NELSON	Mary Jane McCREADY
June 4	Isaiah M. TOADVINE	Nancy M. LAYFIELD
June 8	John PRICE	Martha HUDSON
June 21	Henry DENNIS	Esther TRUITT

1842

Date	Groom	Bride
June 21	John FLOYD	Mary BRITTINGHAM
June 28	Rixom PILCHARD	Emeline BENSTON
July 12	Joshua WORKMAN	Ann CLAYWELL
July 18	John T. JOHNSON	Margaret S. FISHER
July 19	Severn I. HILL	Sally A. SCOTT
July 27	William MILES	Hetty FISHER
July 30	Elijah M. DENNIS	Mary DENNIS
Aug. 4	Abner MARTON	Margaaret Ann WILLIAMS
Aug. 4	Vaughan SMITH	Mary E. SHEPHERD
Aug. 10	Anthony B. FIELDS	Ann M. CAREY
Aug. 15	Joshua G. STEWART	Tabitha H. RAYFIELD
Aug. 30	Richard R. KELLY	Elizabeth A.W. TRADER
Sept. 8	Laurance BATES	Eliza BAYLEY
Sept. 27	William A. CALHOON	Mary POWELL
Oct. 3	Joseph BUNTING	Kitty MAGEE
Oct. 4	Joseph McENTASH	Margaret POWELL
Oct. 4	Southy WARRINGTON	Ann MASON
Oct. 12	John DUKES	Hannah PORTER
Oct. 13	Joseph J.G. DICKERSON	Maria Jane MATTHEWS
Oct. 18	Archibald BODILY	Catharine DONOWAY
Oct. 19	Arthur D. McKEEL	Miss Sally R. ELLIOTT
Oct. 20	John KELPIN	Sarah HALL
Oct. 24	Wm S. ATKINS	Martha DAVIS
Oct. 24	Thomas DOUBERY?	Mary WILLIS
Oct. 26	Henry HOLLOWAY	Elizabeth SNEAD
Nov. 1	Elijah MADDUX	Mary A.F. SCHOOLFIELD
Nov. 7	Bayard RIGGAN	Eleanor POLLITT
Nov. 8	Joseph LEONARD	Eliza WHITE
Nov. 8	Jacob H. JONES	Rachel BISHOP
Nov. 8	Daniel P. RUSSELL	Elizabeth MEZICK
Nov. 10	James DUKES	Mary BENSON
Nov. 15	Daniel F. MELSON	Hetty Jane PARKER
Nov. 16	Levin DUNTON	Eliza POWELL
Nov. 16	William DAYZY	Julian DAVIDSON
Nov. 16	John I. WIMBROW	Elizabeth LEWIS
Dec. 3	David RICHARDSON	Auganett BENNETT
Dec. 6	William TIMMONS	Hetty TOWNSEND
Dec. 6	Elijah MURRAY	Sarah PARSONS
Dec. 7	John TAYLOR	Mary SAVAGE
Dec. 8	Stephen HOPKINS	Ann MELSON
Dec. 10	Bowman BLACKSTON	Kessy PALSBURG
Dec. 12	Elzey TIMMONS	Ann TRUITT
Dec. 17	Henry JONES	Hetty Ann S. COULBOURN
Dec. 20	William J. WIMBROW	Caroline HOWARD
Dec. 20	Outten TULL	Harriet GLADDING
Dec. 21	George SCOTT	Nancy DRYDEN
Dec. 22	Thomas DUKES	Nancy DUKES
Dec. 28	George T. BUNDICK	Sarah H. HICKMAN
Dec. 29	John L. HUDSON	Hetty MATTHEWS

1843

Jan. 2	James BULL	Sally MIERS
Jan. 4	Littleton RICHARDSON	Harriet SCARBOROUGH
Jan. 4	James ENNIS	Milly ENNIS
Jan. 4	Henry DENNIS	Elizabeth SMACK
Jan. 4	William W. HAYMAN	Anna Maria MALONE
Jan. 4	Edward HICKMAN	Mary Ann SELBY
Jan. 10	Robert C. HARRISON	Catharine McNEILE
Jan. 10	William ROSS	Mary LAMDEN
Jan. 11	Henry COLLINS	Nancy OUTTEN
Jan. 11	John JOHNSON	Eleanor RIGGIN
Jan. 14	John D. WELBOURNE	Mary B. MELVIN
Jan. 16	James CLOGG	Elizabeth MOORE
Jan. 16	Arthur H. TRAHEARN	Sarah E. McALLEN
Jan. 24	Thomas ATKINSON	Mary DUKES
Jan. 24	Stepphen BLADES	Ara PILCHARD
Jan. 24	James B. COLLINS	Margaret TIMMONS
Jan. 31	Burton GORDY	Sarah Jane TRADER
Jan. 31	Jesse L. LONG	Elizabeth L. HEARN
Jan. 31	John W. ROWLEY	Eliza B. WELBOURNE
Jan. 31	Robert P. LONG	Mary Ann BISHOP
Feb. 7	Alfred H. BENSON	Ann TAPMAN
Feb. 7	Josiah BROWN	Mary W. PUZEY
Feb. 20	George MITCHELL	Susan RADDISH
Feb. 21	William RICHARDSON	Sally DORMAN
Feb. 28	Wrixon BURNETT	Edith STURGIS
March 3	Peter BOWEN	Leah WILKINS
March 6	Leonard C. MILLS	Hetty Ann GORDY
March 14	John P. SURMAN	Elizabeth M. STATON
March 14	Handy H. LITTLETON	Sarah Jane DIXON
March 14	Levin WARNER Jr.	Araianta HANDCOCK
March 18	Stephen REDDEN	Elizabeth PARADISE
March 18	William STANFORD	Sally M. HOLLAND
March 18	William TWIFORD	Margaret M. WATERS
March 28	Whittington JONES	Anna R. GRAY
March 28	William CLARK	Martha QUILLEN
March 28	Henry DRYDEN	Nancy ROSS
March 29	Henry SMACK	Nancy JONES
April 12	Smith K. MARTIN	Louisa A. BADGER
May 10	James G. SMITH	Elizabeth S. BURTON
June 1	James K. WALKER	Margaret S. WATSON
June 1	John K. WESTCOUT	Elizabeth Sarah BEACH
June 13	Isaac Thomas BUNTING	Mary E. GORDY
June 17	Charles DAVIS	Emeline KELLY
July 11	John H. POOL	Milly HALL
July 20	Samuel T. TRADER	Ann M. TOWNSEND
July 26	William J.S. CLARK	Amanda C. CLARVOE
Aug. 2	Thomas REED	Clarissa HOLLAND
Aig. 1	William HUIT	Euphemia HARMAN

1843

Date	Groom	Bride
Aug. 17	John RUARK	Mary Ann NICHOLSON
Aug. 28	James PAYNE	Sally JONES
Aug. 29	William D. COLLIER	Sarah M. HARRISON
Aug. 29	Levin CROPPER	Gatty TULL
Oct. 2	Milby ADKINS	Mary HAILES
Oct. 3	Oliver KITCHEN	Jane THOMAS
Oct. 10	William Q. PUZEY	Mary PUZEY
Oct. 11	Stephen PILCHARD	Susan BRITTINGHAM
Oct. 19	Thomas L.B. ROBERTS	Elizabeth S. MATTHEWS
Oct. 30	Cathell HUMPHREYS	Isabella HUSTON
Oct. 31	John S. MILLS	Amelia El BACON
Nov. 1	Samuel R. SHIELDS	Margaret P. BAYLY
Nov. 3	John HAMBLIN	Mary Ann CAREY
Nov. 7	William T.J. PURNELL	Elizabeth B.C. COTTMAN
Nov. 7	John W. DENNIS	Mary Ann DENNIS
Nov. 18	William B. JACOBS	Sarah W. LAWS
Nov. 20	Giles JONES	Clarissa AYDELOTTE
Nov. 21	James I. BENSTON	Catharine MEARS
Nov. 21	Elijah S. MADDUX	Louisa HALL
Dec. 5	David H. GRAY	Mary Elizabeth CLAYTON
Dec. 6	George JONES	Margaret ONLEY
Dec. 7	William P. PITTS	Ann Maria BOYER
Dec. 8	John W. WEST	Eleanor S. MELSON
Dec. 11	George H. BRITTINGHAM	Catharine DAVIS
Dec. 11	James JONES	Nancy BUNDICK
Dec. 11	John HOLLAND	Mary FASSITT
Dec. 12	Daniel B. SHORT	Matilda G. MELSON
Dec. 12	John H. GORDY	Charlotte PARKER
Dec. 12	Joel COFFIN	Maria POWELL
Dec. 13	Stephen PURNELL	Mary Jane LAWS
Dec. 18	William WATSON	Mary AYDELOTTE
Dec. 18	Thomas EWELL	Susan WALKER
Dec. 19	Sampson PARKER	Sally LEWIS
Dec. 19	James DALE	Elizabeth BRUMBLY
Dec. 19	Rufus K.M. BAYMUM	Ann C. BOWEN
Dec. 19	John REEDE	Elizabeth TULL

1844

Date	Groom	Bride
Jan. 1	James M. CATHELL	Mary E. MESSICK
Jan. 2	Edward R. SCOTT	Aralanta PENNEWELL
Jan. 9	Elias TAYLOR	Elizabeth WATSON
Jan. 17	Joseph McGEE	Mary E.A. DISHAROON
Jan. 18	William MARSHALL	Nancy DIXON
Jan. 23	Kendall B. DAVIS	Mary Jane JONES
Jan. 24	John L. TURPIN	Henrietta C. PITTS
Jan. 24	James S. JONES	Emily WALES
Feb. 6	Stephen TARR	Nancy MILBOURNE
Feb. 12	Uriah FOOKS	Emeline JOHNSON

1844

Date	Groom	Bride
Feb. 12	Levin GODFREY	Eliza VICKERS
Feb. 13	Isaac HOLLAND	Mary Ann BLADES
Feb. 14	William ENNIS	Nancy MARSH
Feb. 19	John POWELL	Mary Jane WALSTON
Feb. 20	Peter FURBUSH	Sarah M.O. FRANKLIN
Feb. 21	James M. WATERS	Emeline CLAYWELL
Feb. 26	James DAVIS	Alexine BAKER
March 2	Oliver BLADES	Emeline TAPMAN
March 5	Johnson H. DAVIS	Matilda LITTLETON
March 14	William W. SCOTT	Elizabeth M. SCOTT
March 19	William J. SCOTT	Elizabeth C. BOSTON
March 19	William C. FLOID	Margaret HUDSON
March 26	Kendall V. WEST	Nancy E. TIMMONS
April 1	Levin W. PARKER	Mary E. BREWINGTON
April 2	Thomas ONLY	Sally DAVIS
April 3	Samuel TAYLOR	Maria SHOCKLEY
April 9	Edward T. RIGGIN	Margaret A. PATTERSON
April 16	Willliam BENSON	Euphemia OUTTEN
April 16	John T. HAMMONDS	Isabel C. BOWEN
April 22	Noah BRUMBLY	Hester E. HOLDER
April 29	Kendall COLLINS	Maria CATHELL
June 3	Jesse LONG	Sally DAVY
June 5	James HOLSTON	Elizabeth MILBOURNE
June 11	William H. JONES	Mary P. BOSTON
June 11	Elisha TAYLOR	Sophia Ann Elizabeth HICKMAN
June 19	Edward J. WAINWRIGHT	Olivia RIGGAN
June 19	George BAKER	Elizabeth BAKER
June 21	John A. BUNDICK	Elizabeth B. PARKS
June 25	Peter OUTTEN	Sally GOOTY
July 9	William RALEIGH	Tabitha W. SAVAGE
July 10	Littleton DUKES	Elizabeth RICHARDSON
July 16	William LECOMPT	Sally WELDON
July 23	Robert DRYDEN	Elizabeth LATCHUM
July 30	George W. STATON	Elizabeth Ann MITCHELL
July 31	Richard WILLIAMS	Mary BEAUCHAMP
Aug. 6	Richard ROSSE	Mahala TULL
Aug. 6	John B. BAKER	Hetty B. WHARTON
Aug. 20	William T. PURNELL	Henrietta SPENCE
Aug. 20	Samuel J. CONNER	Emeline M. CARSLEY ?
Aug. 25	Thomas SCOTT	Mary DUNCAN
Aug. 28	James ADKINS	Elizabeth ADKINS
Sept. 4	Sewell T. TAYLOR	Margaret E. MILBOURNE
Sept. 11	Hamilton B. ESHAM	Sarah DICKERSON
Sept. 17	John W. DENNIS	Elizabeth J.S. WHITE
Sept. 18	Isaac BUTLER	Emeline POPE
Sept. 18	Henry REEDE	Catharine JOHNSON
Oct. 3	Samuel P. FISHER	Mary C. SMITH
Oct. 9	Henry D. TINGLE	Mary S. PURNELL

1844
Date	Groom	Bride
Oct. 10	Robert M. BAKER	Jane W. PORTER
Oct. 10	John P. TAYLOR	Emely JAMES
Oct. 22	Purnell PUZEY	Mary Ann DRYDEN
Oct. 30	Ephraim H. PUZEY	Mary Ann TOWNSEND
Nov. 4	Handy BOWEN	Martha COLLINS
Nov. 5	Benjamin B. JOHNSON	Catharine MORRIS
Nov. 16	Stephen D. TIMMONS	Mary GRIFFIN
Nov. 19	Zadok O. SELBY	Sarah Ann ROWLEY
Nov. 19	Samuel DENSTON	Mary Ann POWELL
Dec. 7	Powell DOWNAY	Nancy COFFIN
Dec. 9	Thomas DAVIS	Elizabeth BRITTINGHAM
Dec. 10	George TRAHEARN	Mary WARD
Dec. 10	William COULBOURNE	Elizabeth TARR
Dec. 16	William SHOCKLEY	Harriet BLADES
Dec. 16	William HUDSON	Ann Maria RYON
Dec. 16	Edward TOWNSEND	Patty TAYLOR
Dec. 17	William JONES	Mary S. COULBOURNE
Dec. 17	Lambert HASTEN	July WAIGHT
Dec. 17	William SHORT	Martha C. QUILLING
Dec. 18	Major HANDCOCK	Tabitha TULL
Dec. 18	John C. HALL	Mary C. FASSITT
Dec. 19	Samuel LAMBERSON	Sally COLLINS
Dec. 19	Rufus MURRAY	Ann DAVIS
Dec. 23	William BRATTEN	Mary Ann MATTHEWS
Dec. 24	Robert POWELL	Elizabeth WONNELL
Dec. 24	Thomas TOWNSEND	Mary STEWART
Dec. 28	Peter POWELL	Nancy LEWIS

1845
Date	Groom	Bride
Jan. 6	James R.E. EVANS	Ann Maria PENNEWELL
Jan. 6	Isaac COFFIN	Amanda S. DAVIS
Jan. 6	Samuel POWELL	Ann FEDDEMAN
Jan. 7	David GAULT	Charlotte LITTLETON
Jan. 7	John PARADISE	Amelia MASON
Jan. 9	William NOCK	Comfort WALLOP
Jan. 13	Peter DAVIS	Dorcas Ann MOORE
Jan. 14	Elijah RYON	Alexine HUDSON
Jan. 15	William C. HUDSON	Mary J. JONES
Jan. 21	Joshua HASTINGS	Elizabeth L. FARRELL
Jan. 21	Levin J. JONES	Sally TAYLOR
Jan. 21	Thomas ROGERS	Mary BISHOP
Jan. 28	William DUNCAN	Martha WILLIAMS
Jan. 29	Rufus TRADER	Nancy DENNIS
Feb. 8	James M. DRYDEN	Tabitha J. BEVANS
Feb. 10	James MADDUX	Sally M.J. GAULT
Feb. 10	Rufus W. MITCHELL	Gatty F. DENNIS
Feb. 11	Henry POPE	Sally ELLIS
Feb. 11	William S. HUDSON	Julia A. POWELL

1845

Date	Groom	Bride
Feb. 11	Isreal TOWNSEND	Sally TOWNSEND
Feb. 12	Thomas H. JONES	Mary A. SELBY
Feb. 12	James H. TAYLOR	Eliza SOMERS
Feb. 17	Minos TRUITT	Elizabeth TWILLY
Feb. 18	James NOCK	Rachel HINMAN
Feb. 25	Rufus L. ABBOTT	Ann MEZICK
Feb. 25	Jesse LEKIERTZ	Eliza JOHNSON
Feb. 26	William Roger ADAMS	Elizabeth BREWINGTON
March 3	William ADKINS	Betsy McGEE
March 6	James REED	Molly EVANS
March 10	Abel James BIRD	Sarah Ann MEARS
March 12	William PAYNE	Hannah TAYLOR
March 18	James HUSK	Leah STEVENS
March 22	Henry T. JOHNSON	Sarah DAVIS
March 31	Seth HUDSON	Milcah COTTINGHAM
April 2	John BARNES	Matilda TWIGG
April 12	Thomas H. HOPPER	Lucretia B. WALES
April 15	Levin PUZEY	Susan POLK
April 15	William Levinas EVANS	Elizabeth QUILLEN
April 29	Levin	Priscilla LOKEY
May 3	Elijah KNOCK	Zipporah STURGIS
May 17	Josiah SELBY	Dolly Ann BISHOP
May 21	Rixon PAYNE	Elizabeth JONES
May 27	Henry MILBOURNE	Esther SCOTT
June 3	William SCHOOLFIELD	Margaret Ann REDDEN
June 5	Thomas J. BLAIN	Sarah BARNETT
June 6	Calvin H. SAVAGE	Esther R. FITCHET
June 9	Augusten L. SHERWOOD	Julietta S. KELLAM
June 10	Ezekiel WIMBROW	Sally WATSON
June 17	George MATTHIS	Sarah PRUITT
June 18	William Thomas CLARK	Sarah GOODNY
June 24	William ENNIS	Priscilla EVANS
July 1	Joshua H. TAYLOR	Mary Jane DRYDEN
July 8	John DICKERSON	Leah PRUITT
July 8	Samuel TAYLOR	Merridy HUDSON
July 23	Stephen PUZEY	Matilda PUZEY
Aug. 1	George BENNETT	Charlotte BRITTINGHAM
Aug. 4	Edward FAREBROTHERS	Maria CONNER
Aug. 6	William GOOTON	Margaret Ann KNOCK
Aug. 20	William T. POWELL	Mary A. E. COLLIER
Aug. 28	Edward H. BOWEN	Ann HAYWARD
Sept. 3	Burton JONES	Mary Ann HAILES
Sept. 15	James BOWEN	Mary A. HUDSON
Sept. 15	Joshua COLLIER	Eliza MOORE
Sept. 19	Asa WENELLS	Elvisa THORNTON
Oct. 1	Benjamin BOWEN	Henny COULBOURNE
Oct. 3	John J. BLOXOM	Miss Mary YOUNG
Oct. 6	William MASON	Matilda ELLIS

1845

Date	Groom	Bride
Oct. 13	Lemuel S. PRUITT	Rebecca E. HAYMAN
Oct. 14	Francis POWELL	Elizabeth STUART
Oct. 14	John REED	Mary DAVIS
Oct. 21	Annanias GRAY	Sarah DAVIS
Oct. 21	John C. DOLLOY	Mary A. SAUNDERS
Oct. 28	Jesse JARMAN	Elizabeth TIMMONS
Oct. 29	Nathaniel BTITTINGHAM	Tabitha JONES
Nov. 4	Esme JONES	Mary Eleanor MORRIS
Nov. 11	William FOLIO	Mary Polly TURNER
Nov. 18	Irving Spence LITTLETON	Margaret DIXON
Nov. 21	Levin MILLS	Mary GOUTY
Nov. 25	Josiah H. CAREY	Priscilla A. SHOCKLEY
Nov. 25	James HENDERSON	Alexene DAVIS
Dec. 6	William SMITH	Ann Maria CLAYWELL
Dec. 8	William TIMMONS	Martha BEATHARDS
Dec. 8	Joshua McBRIETY	Mary Ann MADDUX
Dec. 9	John S. MERRILL	Emeline C. BOSTON
Dec. 9	Josiah MUMFORD	Mary MURRAY
Dec. 11	Henry DAVIS	Clarissa BAYLEY
Dec. 16	Robert J. HENRY	Esther H. PURNELL
Dec. 16	James TIMMONS	Eleanor HADDEN
Dec. 17	Thomas WHITE	Mary Elizabeth HUDSON
Dec. 17	Bassitt RAYN	Julia A.D. DAVIS
Dec. 23	William TULL	Nancy HANDCOCK
Dec. 23	Edward HOLLAND	Nancy EVANS
Dec. 26	Job JARMAN	Andy WEBB
Dec. 26	George GIBBS	Elizabeth TOWNSEND
Dec. 30	Wilson P. MASON	Martha E.A. DUKES

1846

Date	Groom	Bride
Jan. 5	Samuel M. HINMAN	Margaret Ann CLARK
Jan. 6	David BLADES	Mary BLADES
Jan. 6	Isaac D. CAREY	Sarah HASTINGS
Jan. 7	James TIMMONS	Mary TARR
Jan. 9	Laban HUDSON	Margaret ENNIS
Jan. 10	George TEAUGE	Zila Ann PAYNE
Jan. 12	Elijah M. GORDY	Martha E. SHEPPARD
Jan. 19	Thomas LAMBDEN	Catharine BRITTINGHAM
Jan. 19	Sampson HAMMOND	Letty TOWNSEND
Jan. 20	Edward T. CONNER	Margaret A. RIGGIN
Jan. 20	Wheatly J. ATKINSON	Jane HENDERSON
Jan. 26	Joseph GODFREY	Maria H. MASSEY
Jan. 27	Joseph LYNCH	Elizabeth TAYLOR
Jan. 27	Sampson S. DAVIS	Phebe TRUITT
Jan. 28	Joseph I. ENNIS	Ann M. RICHARDSON
Jan. 29	Edward BOWEN	Leah JONES
Jan. 31	William H. MELSON	Mahala MADDUX
Feb. 2	William J. HOLLAND	Aralanta PHILLIPS

1846

Date	Groom	Bride
Feb. 2	John Hill PURNELL	Emeline PORTER
Feb. 2	William H. HOLLAND	Elenor RICHARDSON
Feb. 14	William T. MITCHELL	Elizabeth SELBY
Feb. 17	Victor BELL	Emeline LAMBDEN
Feb. 20	Henry T. BRICKHOUSE	Sarah PUZEY
Feb. 24	Kendall BOWEN	Mary C. TAYLOR
Feb. 25	Charles ATKINSON	Mary Elizabeth MATTHEWS
Feb. 26	David MILLS	Nelly PARKER
March 2	William W. SANDERS	Marand HOULT
March 3	James B. WRIGHT	Margaret A. HOPE
March 9	Levin DENSTON	Lydia TOWNSEND
March 10	Ara STURGIS	Elizabeth WARD
March 16	Isaac BEATHARDS	Leah JARMAN
March 18	William JONES	Margaret PRIOR
March 18	Elihu J. PUSEY	Margaret J. SHEPHERD
March 18	Enock MULLENER	Mary TRADER
March 19	John CHERRICKS	Mary PHILLIPS
March 21	Mordecai DONOWAY	Shada Ann LONG
March 23	George W. CUTLER	Mary Ann ROBERTS
March 23	Adam P. BEATHARDS	Mary ADKINS
March 30	William J. WHAYLAND	Jane DISHAROON
March 31	Zadok COLLIER	Jane E. PATEY
April 13	Lemuel D. WILSON	Adeline F. CARSLEY
April 14	Edward F. JOHNSON	Aurena BRITTINGHAM
April 20	Peter CHERRICKS	Leah BOWDOIN
April 23	James E. SMITH	Sophia CAUSEY
April 29	James T. PALMORE	Elizabeth B. CROPPER
May 2	Jonathan CAREY	Leah Elizabeth DALE
May 5	Lambert C. POWELL	Margaret LEWIS
May 5	David B. PARSONS	Nelly ENNIS
May 5	James L. HENDERSON	Mary Ann PILCHARD
May 5	Peter CLAYWELL	Nancy PARADISE
May 7	John SNEAD	Charlotte SHARPLEY
May 19	Augustine W. TAYLOR	Julia Ann BENNETT
May 21	Zadok CARTER	Mary RUSSELL
May 23	Henry H. HASTED	Mary E. HENDERSON
May 26	Allen Bowie HOWARD	Anne Maria SPENCE
June 1	John PAYTON	Henrietta CLUGG
June 15	Jacob PARKER	Andy ADKINS
June 17	John T. HUDSON	Sarah Ann ARDIS
June 18	James ALLEN	Sarah SCOTT
June 20	David DAVIDSON	Martha DONOWAY
June 24	Jesse S. JONES	Sally A. ROWLEY
July 11	Peter SMITH	Matilda WILKINS
July 11	John Williams ENNALLS	Ellen A. MERRILL
July 13	Thomas J. WATSON	Ann BEACHAMP
July 15	Major HILL	Amanda WATSON
July 21	James TAYLOR	Mary Ann BRITTINGHAM

1846

Date	Groom	Bride
July 23	James EVANS	Mary HOLLOWAY
July 24	Littleton DENNIS	Elizabeth U. DENNIS
Aug. 9	John P. WALKER	Lucinda PARKER
Aug. 12	James B. HAMBLIN	Mary C. DENNIS
Aug. 14	John CHERICKS	Tabby HOPKINS
Sept. 2	Dr. John G. SAVAGE	Mary Catharine ROWLEY
Oct. 12	Richard B. DRUMMOND	Eliza A. CROSWELL
Oct. 12	Thomas I. GRINNALDS	Elizabeth B. CLAYTON
Oct. 20	William DAVIS	Milly CARSLEY
Oct. 23	Jacob PAYNE	Catharine J. RICHARDSON
Oct. 27	Thomas KELLY	Ann Maria TARR
Oct. 27	Thomas B. BRITTINGHAM	Mary A.E. BRITTINGHAM
Oct. 27	Jesse POWELL	Henrietta SCHOOLFIELD
Oct. 28	Thomas B. JONES	Mrs Nancy ROWLEY
Oct. 28	Jocob COURDRY	Elenor BREWINGTON
Oct. 29	Stephen R. HAMMOND	Mary POWELL
Nov. 3	Thomas N. PITTS	Mary E. GRAY
Nov. 9	Thomas R. FLETCHER	Elizabeth HENMAN
Nov. 9	John F. WILLIAMS	Hester A. BISHOP
Nov. 9	George CROPPER	Elizabeth A. CROPPER
Nov. 10	Hiram B. DUNCAN	Sally M. MASSEY
Nov. 11	Richard HUDSON	Mary J. ROGERS
Nov. 17	Wilson McNEILL	Mary BISHOP
Nov. 17	James BONNEWELL	Mary DRYDEN
Nov. 21	James BAKER	Ann W. FARRELL
Nov. 25	Benjamin MORRIS	Drucilla JOHNSON
Nov. 25	John GLADDEN	Betsy RICHARDSON
Nov. 28	John B. PARSONS	Sabra FOSKEY
Nov. 30	William A. MILLS	Margaret A. CURMEAN
Dec. 1	Thomas REED	Matilda ELLIS
Dec. 8	Theodore BREWINGTON	Sarah Ann PARKER
Dec. 8	William MEGRATH	Emeline CAUSEY
Dec. 8	Henry T. COSTON	Mary Ann JONES
Dec. 9	James B. BISHOP	Jane ATKINSON
Dec. 12	John A. EDWARDS	Margaret S. BURTIN
Dec. 14	John H. BURNETT	Alexene B. BENSTON
Dec. 14	Nathan G. WEST	Mary E.L. NELSON
Dec. 15	George W. McALLEN	Eleanor BOUNDS
Dec. 15	James H. HADDOCK	Mary A. STURGIS
Dec. 15	Levin M. DASHIELL	Amelia A. NOBLE
Dec. 15	Annanias F. HUDSON	Jane E. CAREY
Dec. 21	James D. PUZEY	Nancy COLLINS
Dec. 22	William H. BRITTINGHAM	Ann WHITE
Dec. 22	James MITCHELL	Ann WILLIAMS
Dec. 23	Elijah KELLY	Elizabeth JOHNSON
Dec. 30	John J. JONES	Margaret RICHARDSON

1847

Date	Groom	Bride
Jan. 2	Andrew J. KEENRIGHT	Anna M.S. HICKMAN
Jan. 5	Isaac H. PARKER	Maria MEER
Jan. 5	Thomas PORTER	Elizabeth STURGIS
Jan. 5	Peter J. GILLISPEC	Susan MEDCALF
Jan. 5	Phillip MARSH	Eleanor W. PAYNE
Jan. 5	William S. LUCAS	Elizabeth Jane BUNDICK
Jan. 5	Alfred LINCH	Sarah J. BISHOP
Jan. 6	Benjamin T. RICHARDSON	Maria HOLLAND
Jan. 7	Thomas H. DENNIS	Alexene H. FLEMMING
Jan. 9	John DENNIS	Elizabeth ADKINS
Jan. 11	Benjamin BASSITT	Sally Mary HARMON
Jan. 16	Henry Thomas MERRILL	Caroline P. PATTERSON
Jan. 18	James P. DRYDEN	Frances A. SHOCKLEY
Jan. 19	William OUTTEN	Mary Ann TULL
Jan. 20	Caleb TRUITT	Henny DENNIS
Jan. 23	Thomas TAYLOR	Patsey CHESER
Jan. 25	Joshua CAREY	Mary DORMAN
Jan. 25	William DIXON	Mary SHOCKLEY
Jan. 26	William EVANS	Hester Ann WALTERS
Feb. 1	William GAULT	Mary Ann POWELL
Feb. 1	Josiah M. POLLITT	Rebecca A. HAYMAN
Feb. 1	George T. TRUITT	Lauretta S. POWELL
Feb. 1	Henry TULL	Harriet TRADER
Feb. 2	Esau BOSTON	Maria A. MELVIN
Feb. 6	Josiah COLLINS	Nancy DAUGHTERS
Feb. 9	James W. BISHOP	Miss Rossetta BEVANS
Feb. 13	Benjamin COLLUNOR	Mary D. POWELL
Feb. 13	Francis KELLAM	Frances E. SCHIRER
Feb. 13	David S. DRUMMOND	Lavina C. SLOCUM
Feb. 13	William COLLINS	Harriet Ann COLLICK
Feb. 15	William E. HALL	Sarah T. HILL
Feb. 19	Ebenezer DYKES	Ann Maria DIXON
Feb. 20	Littleton B. DAVIS	Mary A. SAVAGE
Feb. 23	Benjamin J. RICHARDSON	Mary T. BULL
Feb. 23	Peter TINEL	Zeporah PENEWELL
March 2	Robert TWILLY	Esther HEARN
March 2	Eliphalet C. STUDLEY	Elizabeth BOWDEN
March 9	John R. DOWNING	Rebecca PARKER
March 9	Henry HAISTING	Julia Ann COLLINS
March 15	James J. MORE	Eleanor C. McA. DRYDEN
March 15	John L. HEARN	Sally E. ATKINSON
March 16	Erastus B. BAYLY	Sally EWELL
March 17	Robert AGNEW	Elizabeth CAREY
March 17	Benjamin HUDSON	Mary DUKES
March 30	Levin JONES	Elizabeth W. PUSEY
April 1	Daniel KELLY	Sally MACKLIN
April 5	John THOMAS	Emeline W. POOL
April 6	Alison A. SHOCKLEY	Mary HARINGTON
April 13	William MILBOURNE	Sarah TAPMAN

1847

Date	Groom	Bride
April 17	William BAKER	Charlotte SCHOOLFIELD
April 20	John STEWART	Eleanor MADDUX
April 27	Benjamin COOPER	Margaret HICKMAN
April 28	Zadok Henry BRITTINGHAM	Anda Rebecca SMITH
May 4	John GUNBY	Elizabeth BAKER
May 12	James BRITT	Betsey PUSEY
May 18	Joshua JOHNSON	Sally WEST
May 19	John GIBBS	Margaret HOLLAND
May 25	James SCOTT	Susan HOLLMAN
May 25	John S. RICHARDSON	Mary JONES
May 26	James F. LOREMAN	Arena CALAWAY
June 2	Isaac HUDSON	Betsy MORRIS
June 2	Thomas W. HARGIS	Margaret W. FETCHER
June 5	William LEWIS	Mary J. RICHARDSON
June 8	Isaac T. HUGHES	Elizabeth A. BURNETT
June 15	William VEASEY	Sally E. BRITTINGHAM
June 29	Joseph LARKINS	Ann Maria POLLITT
June 30	James A. BRINDLE	Ann C. PARKER
July 6	William ROBERTSON	Susan MITCHELL
July 14	George H. BENNETT	Andasia RICHARDSON
July 20	Joshua C. JOHNSON	Virginia A. COTTINGHAM
July 22	Thomas N. QUILLON	Mary C. BOWEN
July 26	Richard BLOXSOM	Patience JONES
July 29	John D. HEATH	Margaret AMES
July 31	William T. MITCHELL	Sarah H. GIBBONS
Aug. 6	Jeremiah TAYLOR	Hester Ann SHOWARD
Aug. 7	Peter BLADES	Jane HINMAN
Aug. 10	William DICKERSON	Elizabeth PAYNE
Aug. 12	William MARSHALL	Mary POWDERS
Aug. 18	John CLAYWELL	Priscilla STURGIS
Aug. 24	Henry P. LEWIS	Sally BETHARDS
Aug. 24	George BOWEN	Sally TURPIN
Aug. 24	John MORRIS	Hannah SHOCKLEY
Aug. 25	John H. WHEALTON	Elizabeth Ann EVANS
Aug. 27	Albert Henry WARREN	Mary Ann COOPER
Sept. 8	Henry RICHARDSON	Mary JOHNSON
Sept. 14	James HANNON	Hetty SMACK
Sept. 14	James Henry WILSON	Priscilla A. GODFREY
Sept. 29	William SELBY	Maria McFADDEN
Oct. 4	John Smith MELVIN	Sarah G. WILLACE
Oct. 4	Edward D. NEILL	Nancy HALL
Oct. 5	Benjamin PARKER	Mary J.H.H. WEST
Oct. 5	William B. LITTLETON	Sarah J. LITTLETON
Oct. 12	William SHOCKLEY	Henrietta TOWNSEND *Henerici*
Oct. 12	James RICHARDSON	Catharine HENDERSON
Oct. 18	Edward Twiford AYERS	Sarah Frances PUSEY
Oct. 19	Thomas DUKES	Sally LING
Oct. 21	T.C.B. HOWARD	Louise SPENCE

1847
Oct. 23	James DASEY	Nancy HOLLOWAY
Nov. 1	John D. POWELL	Sarah M. ENNIS
Nov. 2	Leonard MORRIS	Sally Ann RICHARDSON
Nov. 2	Robert TWIFORD	Tabitha W. DIX
Nov. 3	Edward MASON	Elizabeth DICKERSOPN
Nov. 8	Barthelamew MATTHEWS	Sally MATTHEWS
Nov. 9	Josiah H. SMITH	Eliza LITTLETON
Nov. 9	Joshua BISHOP	Charlotte MURRAY
Nov. 9	Samuel BALL	Polly DUKES
Nov. 15	John STURGIS	Jane DENNIS
Nov. 16	William H. JONES	Harriet WARRINGTON
Nov. 18	James BOWEN of Josiah	Charlotte BOWEN
Nov. 22	Teackle ELLIOTT	Lavina C. GARROSON
Nov. 23	David PRUITT	Prisy NEWTON
Nov. 23	McKemmy HOLLOWAY	Phrenette WARREN
Nov. 25	Thomas COLLINS	Mary Elizabeth PURNELL
Nov. 27	Dr. George TYLER	Mary A. ADAIR
Nov. 30	Renattus HEARN	Sarah WHITE
Dec. 6	William CLOGG	Mary A. DENSTON
Dec. 6	James RICHARDSON	Mary Ann BRIMER
Dec. 6	Peter STURGIS	Ann ELLIS
Dec. 6	Thomas L. HARRIS	Mary I. DERICKSON
Dec. 8	Francis BOWEN	Mary Ann SCARBOROUGH
Dec. 11	James Colbourne KELLY	Emeline JOHNSON
Dec. 14	William CROPPER	Comfort COLLIER
Dec. 14	John W. AYDELOTTE	Drucilla PAYNE
Dec. 14	Sampson ADKINS	Hildah SHOCKLEY
Dec. 14	Theodore HAYMAN	Matilda MORRIS
Dec. 14	Nathaniel POWELL	Margaert WINDER
Dec. 20	Thomas McGRATH	Polly TOADVINE
Dec. 20	Benjamin HENDERSON	Jane DAVIS
Dec. 21	James McGREGOR	Mary HUDSON
Dec. 21	Lemuel BAKER	Mary WILKERSON
Dec. 23	David WEBB	Hester REDDEN
Dec. 23	Henry B. PENNEWELL	Mary Ellen PRIOR
Dec. 25	Robert PRUITT	Sarah RUSE
Dec. 27	Thomas DYKES	Elizabeth DENSTON
Dec. 30	Elijah BAKER	Sally RAIN

1848
Jan. 3	Edward NOCK	Mary GROTEN
Jan. 3	Phillip POWELL	Mary LITTLETON
Jan. 10	James ASHBY	Jane GARRISON
Jan. 12	William PRUITT	Sarah STURGIS
Jan. 15	James B. TIMMONS	Rachel R. DIRICKSON
Jan. 17	William W. DRUMMOND	Rebecca CORBIN
Jan. 21	Thomas HARGIS	Mary FOSQUE
Jan. 24	George T. EVANS	Mary A. E. WALTERS

1848

Date	Groom	Bride
Jan. 26	Thomas GRAY	Susan I. TURPIN
Jan. 28	Albert BAKER	Clarissa DONOWAY
Feb. 1	Thomas GODFREY	Julina LOKEY
Feb. 1	John R. ADKINS	Leah ADKINS
Feb. 3	Rufus M. TRUITT	Joice P. BURROUGHS
Feb. 4	James HENDERSON	Dorinthy AMES
Feb. 7	Wilson MUMFORD	Mary BOWDEN
Feb. 7	John ADKINS	Maria NICHOLS
Feb. 9	Samuel M. RILEY	Mary Jane BETHARDS
Feb. 9	Alfred James RUNNELS	Mary A. WILLIAMS
Feb. 15	William W. SELBY	Patsy CORD
Feb. 16	Joshua SHOCKLEY	Mary M. CLAYWELL
Feb. 17	William J. BROWN	Mary E. GORDY
Feb. 22	James A. DAVIS	Mary WARD
Feb. 22	George W. HAMMOND	Mary Eliza WILLIS
Feb. 29	Zadok P. HENRY	Sally M. PURNELL
Feb. 29	James JONES	Eliza Ann STEVENS
March 2	Elijah KELLY	Elizabeth GLADDEN
March 6	Charles WRIGHT	Margaret A. GRAY
March 13	Henry W. HITCH	Matilda M. DENSTON
March 20	Nehemiah W. NOCK	Mary R. WALLOP
March 21	Ralph ROSS	Keasey MITCHELL
March 21	Gilbert L. BOWEN	Margaret BISHOP
March 25	John K. MASSEY	Gertrude GORDY
March 31	Levin Henry TOWNSEND	Mary Ellen ENNIS
April 1	James S. SMACK	Margaret BRADFORD
April 10	Sampson DENNIS	Mary BOUNDS
April 20	William LAYTON	Mary E. SCOTT
April 25	John POWELL	Margaret KELLY
April 25	Henry COSTON	Susan POWELL
May 2	James W. HAYMAN	Emeline E. PARKER
May 2	John ALLEN	Elizabeth J. RUSSELL
May 2	Edward SCARBOROUGH	Jane BOWEN
May 2	Soloman POWELL	Elizabeth BOWDEN
May 11	William W. POOL	Elizabeth E. MILLS
May 13	George MUMFORD	Mary ENNIS
May 22	George Bowman MARINER	Elizabeth TAYLOR
May 23	James LAYFIELD	Sally LOKEY
May 24	William H. McDANIEL	Mary H. COLLINS
May 24	Thomas T. TAYLOR	Angelina WATERS
May 25	George R. CURTIS	Ellen DORSEY
June 1	Thomas J. BURROUGHS	Elizabeth HOLLAND
June 5	Joseph F. HENDERSON	Margaret M. JONES
June 7	Levin I. DERICKSON	Sarah E. FOREMAN
June 7	Levin B. McALLEN	Caroline P. NELSON
June 13	William C. MITCHELL	Martha E. CAREY
June 13	Sydnum LONG	Margaret A. BAKER
June 20	John ROBERSON	Sarah TULL

1848

Date	Groom	Bride
July 17	Edward E. DAVIS	Eliza S. HEARN
July 18	James CHAPMAN	Mary E. STURGIS
July 18	Luther T. HOOLE	Sarah F. JOHNSON
July 19	James TULL	Amanda WATSON
July 25	Edward T. PITTS	Mary W. DENNIS
Aug. 28	Jacob WARNER	Siner HICKMAN
Aug. 29	Revell REW	Jane BULL
Aug. 31	Thomas B. ROBERTSON	Elizabeth W, BENNETT
Sept. 5	Zadok HALL	Araminta BEACHBOARD
Sept. 18	Nathaniel W. WYATT	Margaret E. BRICKHOUSE
Sept. 18	Joseph S. CAREY	Hetty Ann HAMBLIN
Sept. 19	William H. MASSEY	Mary G. CALLANHAN
Sept. 23	James A. HUDSON	Elizabeth WHITE
Oct. 6	Annanias W. POWELL	Sarah M. TINGLE
Oct. 9	Charles Parker TURNER	Mary G. TOWNSEND
Oct. 10	John DAVIS	Elizabeth POWELL
Oct. 13	Elijah BRITTINGHAM	Mary E. PRUITT
Oct. 17	Mordecal DAVIS	Jane E. BAKER
Oct. 28	James TAYLOR	Anna BAKER
Oct. 31	Curtis S. CONOWAY	Sarah H.T. SMITH
Oct. 31	Zadok HOLSTON	Margaret BOWEN
Nov. 3	David COFFIN	Maria WIATT
Nov. 6	Warrer HASTINGS	Elizabeth VINCENT
Nov. 9	Jackson WARD	Margaret NOTTINGHAM
Nov. 13	Levin MARRILL	Elizabeth Leah HOWARD
Nov. 15	Henry REED	Elizabeth TURNER
Nov, 21	William BRITTINGHAM	Harriet WALKER
Nov. 21	Levin H. HARGIS	Susan H. GODWIN
Nov. 25	John H. DORMAN	Sally TARR
Nov. 27	James S. PARSONS	Gidy SMITH
Nov. 28	William DONOWAY	Jeanetta HALL
Nov. 28	Robert H. POWELL	Ann HOLLAND
Nov. 29	Thomas M.P.S. WHITE	Susan MILLS
Nov, 30	Thomas J. MILLS	Sally O. CAREY
Dec. 2	Jonathan F. BAKER	Lovey MURRAY
Dec. 5	Purnell JOHNSON	Maria Ann PARKER
Dec. 6	Michael WHEALTON	Eliza REED
Dec. 6	Robert S. TODD	Ann E. MADDUX
Dec. 8	George W. HUDSON	Mary Jane HUDSON
Dec. 11	James McFADDEN	Sarah Ann TARR
Dec. 11	Richard HASTINGS	Adaline COLLYER
Dec. 12	James R. GORDY	Eliza PARKER
Dec. 12	Josiah H. WARREN	Pierce Ann DALE
Dec. 12	Albert BAYLEY	Elizabeth GAULT
Dec. 12	Peter J. BENNETT	Mary A. JONES
Dec. 13	John W. CLARK	Mary A. P. TAYLOR
Dec. 18	John WILLIAMS	Leah C. LAWS
Dec. 18	James W. BREWINGTON	Margaret C. MITCHELL

1848

Date	Groom	Bride
Dec. 19	George R. FARLOW	Clarissa PARKER
Dec. 19	William ARDIS	Rosena PORTER
Dec. 19	Milby R. HUDSON	Margaret WHITE
Dec. 19	William BRITTINGHAM	Harriet Jane HUDSON
Dec. 19	Samuel H. TRUITT	Mary J. CLAYUWELL
Dec. 19	Henry CHERIX	Tabitha CHERIX
Dec. 19	James DAY	Mary HUDSON
Dec. 26	Nathaniel BAKER	Elizabeth DONOWAY
Dec. 28	Thomas J. MORRIS	Elizabeth TILGHMAN
Dec. 19	Levi CALLOWAY	Mary HOPKINS
Dec. 30	William H. SINGLETON	Mary E. S. DIX
Dec. 30	John R. HILL	Louisa A. CALENDER

1849

Date	Groom	Bride
Jan. 1	Thomas STURGIS	Julia Ann CAREY
Jan. 2	Benjamin DENSTON	Mary Ann JOHNSON
Jan. 2	Robert WARREN	Martha DAVIS
Jan. 3	Robert Henry EASHAM	Emeline ELLIS
Jan. 6	Joshua REED	Mary WILLIS
Jan. 9	William JONES	Phebe Ann PHILIPS
Jan. 9	Major T. HALL	Julia A JONES
Jan. 9	William R. POWELL	Indiana M. WEST
Jan. 15	James BRATTEN	Mary PARSONS
Jan. 16	George P. FRANKLIN	Jane FRANKLIN
Jan. 19	Billy H. FARLOW	Tabitha PARKER
Jan. 23	William H. MATTHEWS	Sally COLBOURNE
Jan. 23	Charles GEWELL	Susan NELSON
Jan. 24	Philip MARSH	Sally CAYVILLE
Jan. 25	Albert KNOX	Mary BENSON
Jan. 30	Minos WYATT	Hetty BOWEN
Jan. 30	Henry T. ONLEY	Sally E. TRUITT
Jan. 31	William BOSTON	Charlotte Ann DAVIS
Feb. 7	John H. DIX	Ann ATKINSON
Feb. 12	Henry DONOWAY	Elizabeth DAVIS
Feb. 12	James H. BUSSELLS	Sarah A. POLLITT
Feb. 13	Lemuel BRITTINGHAM	Charlotte PRUITT
Feb. 15	J.H. TARR	Sallie E. ROCK
Feb. 20	Henry J.B. SMITH	Sarah H. WEST
Feb. 26	George T. BATCHEL	Lucretia BUNDICK
Feb. 26	James W. DOWNING	Sarah C. SMITH
Feb. 27	John B. TIMMONS	Ann Maria JARMAN
Feb. 28	Joshua STURGIS	Mary REDDISH
Feb. 28	Noah BRATTEN	Ann Maria SPENCER
March 1	John S. MATTHEWS	Catharine EVANS
March 7	Edward B. FASSITT	Mary J. DAVIDSON
March 8	Lein L. CORE	Mary A. HICKMAN
March 17	Gilbert RAIN	Elizabeth TRUITT
March 19	Henry BEESON	Mary BUDD

1849

Date	Groom	Bride
March 19	Henry F. BRINKLY	Adaline W. HORSEY
March 23	William TAYLOR	Mary DYKES
April 3	John SEARS	Catharine ESHAM
April 16	John S. TIMMONS	Mary E. WHALEY
April 17	George HILL	Elizabeth HANDCOCK
April 24	Zacheus BOWEN	Elizabeth W. CONNER
May 14	Isaac M. BOWEN	Ann M. BRADFORD
May 17	John PETIT	Ann Maria JOHNSON
May 29	John J. COLBOURNE	Sarah E. TILGHMAN
June 5	Lorenzo D. DAVIS	Mary Ann QUILLEN
June 6	John H. PURNELL	Bettie SPENCE
June 6	Thomas I. RICHARDSON	Juliana CROPPER
June 7	William KELLY	Rebecca BOWDEN
June 13	William H. PURNELL	Margaret N. MARTIN
June 18	Samuel C. SMITH	Henrietta H. DOWNING
June 18	Sampson PARKER	Hannah PARSONS
July 6	John LAMBERSON	Hetty COLLINS
July 10	Hilliary R. PITTS	Rebecca A. BOWEN
July 16	Theodore PARKER	Nancy RILEY
July 17	John P. DENNIS	Mary PERDUE
July 31	Charles H. BOWEN	Ellen J. PURNELL
Aug. 6	James A. PARSONS	Susan MILLS
Aug. 23	Elijah NOCK	Hetty BENNETT
Sept. 5	Levin WHITE	Charlotte WHITE
Sept. 13	Alfred L. ROBERTSON	Emeline S. ANDERSON
Sept. 18	William I. TOWNSEND	Martha A. BETHARDS
Oct. 4	William DICKERSON	Ann Z. SMACK
Oct. 7	George E. BOWEN	Ann M. PURNELL
Oct. 15	Thomas W. KILMAN	Caroline F. CROCKETT
Oct. 20	Jonathan S. FARLOW	Maria B. GORDY
Oct. 20	Daniel J. FARLOW	Mary E. GORDY
Oct. 23	Thomas DENNIS	Nancy CAREY
Oct. 23	John W. CLARK	Margaret WATTS
Nov. 5	William S. MOORE	Mary Ann JENKINS
Nov. 12	Hiram PHILLIPS	Leah TAYLOR
Nov. 12	George W. FASSITT	Mary S. WEST
Nov. 13	Joseph G. B. WHITE	Lavinia A. WEST
Nov. 14	Benjamin F. AYDELOTTE	Harriet H. HARGIS
Nov. 15	Joseph BAKER	Louisa DONOWAY
Nov. 19	Balitha GODFREY	Sopha Ann GODFREY
Nov. 19	Henry COOPER	Sally WARRINGTON
Nov. 19	John R. TRADER	Sally BEVANS
Nov. 20	Benjamin M. HAMBLIN	Nancy PALMER
Nov. 27	Eli PARSONS	Hetty BAKER
Dec. 6	George JONES	Julia Ann LAMBERSON
Dec. 11	William RICHARDS	Elizabeth COLBOURNE
Dec. 12	Irving T. MATTHEWS	Sarah H. HUDSON
Dec. 13	Josiah HAMMOND	Jane Elizabeth TUBBS

1949

Dec. 17	Lemuel H. PERDUE	Henrietta DENNIS
Dec. 17	Joshua R. PARKER	Gatty M. FARLOW
Dec. 18	Peter T. PARSONS	Gatty M. WALSTON
Dec. 18	Sampson SHOCKLEY	Milly HADDOCK
Dec. 21	Robert PERKINS	Julia BOWEN
Dec. 22	Bartine T. McCABE	Hetty D. MURRAY
Dec. 24	Ar CHERRIX	Mary Ann HOLLAND
Dec. 24	James GODFREY	Susan GODFREY
Dec. 25	John I. PAYNE	Mary Ann HANCOCK
Dec. 27	John H. LANKFORD	Nancy WALKER

1850

Jan. 1	John WILLIAMS	Emily CAMPBELL
Jan. 5	William BODLEY	Elizabeth RYON
Jan. 5	Jocob W. CANNON	Cornelia S. EVANS
Jan. 8	Thomas STURGIS	Elizabeth I. TILGHMAN
Jan. 8	Major HASTINGS	Elizabeth MASSEY
Jan. 12	I. S. HOUGHTON	Laura C. WHITE
Jan. 12	Jesse JONES	Sally M. CLAYWELL
Jan. 14	Sylvester H. DAVIS	Harriet Z. NELSON
Jan. 15	William S. JOHNSON	Elizabeth N. JOHNSON
Jan. 16	Thomas CONOWAY	Sarah WARD
Jan. 16	Zadok H. RICHARDSON	Elizabeth S. DEVERIX
Jan. 17	George W. VANDUM	Ann MURREY
Jan. 19	Benjamin L. POLLITT	Elenor L. HAYMAN
Jan. 21	John M. PATTEY	Mary Jane GORDY
Jan. 22	Joshua H. STURGIS	Harriet E. MITCHELL
Jan. 28	Nathaniel HENMAN	Gatty ENNIS
Jan. 28	Henry R. AYERS	Elizabeth HOLLAND
Jan. 28	John McNAMARA	Ann M. JONES
Feb. 5	James WARRINGTON	Ann BOWEN
Feb. 5	Dr William S. HORSEY	Sally W. CUSTIS
Feb. 5	William LYNCH	Emeline PARSONS
Feb. 6	Edward H. JONES	Mary JARMON
Feb. 8	William James MERRILL	Margaret Frances AYDELOTTE
Feb. 11	Elijah PARSONS	Maranda C. GORDY
Feb. 11	Thomas BENSON	Amanda C. HENDERSON
Feb. 11	William J. LONG	Martha A. JONES
Feb. 12	James BOWDEN	Patty HUDSON
Feb. 13	Elijah C.T. WILSON	Sarah E. McCREADY
Feb. 14	Samuel P. WIMBROW	Julia Ann GORDY
Feb. 14	Modica J. POWELL	Elizabeth A. DAVIS
Feb. 16	Lemuel A. HALE	Jane E. HUDSON
Feb. 20	James M. POWELL	Leah Jane TULL
Feb. 21	William DOUGHERTY	Priscilla CANFIELD
Feb. 22	Samuel HOLLOWAY	Sally PALMER
Feb. 23	Thomas SMITH	Elizabeth BURBAGE
Feb. 25	Peter TILGHMAN	Margaret WHITE

1850

Date	Groom	Bride
Feb. 26	John HAYMAN	Ann DYKES
Feb. 26	William MUMFORD	Mary E.D. NEWTON
Feb. 26	Isaac B. LANDING	Susan ELLIS
Feb. 26	Elijah NOCK	Isabella GRIFFIN
Feb. 28	John P. JOHNSON	Mary G. PARSONS
March 2	Charles H. NIBBLET	Lucinda ADKINS
March 7	Littleton S. JOHNSON	Elmira PITTS
March 7	Thomas BRITTINGHAM	Susan J. BRITTINGHAM
March 9	Noah J. TILGHMAN	Henny COLBOURNE
March 9	Thoeogood S. TAYLOR	Emeline T. WESSELLS
March 13	Erastus PILCHARD	Mary RATLIDGE
March 25	Wilmor S. RICHARDSON	Emma E. STEWART
March 26	Cannon WELLS	Sally MITCHELL
April 1	Walter P. SNOW	Ann Jane WILSON
April 13	Zedekiah TRUITT	Gatty E. LAWS
April 13	Isaiah CAMPBELL	Esther HICKMAN
April 15	Benjamin HOLLAND	Elizabeth DAVIS
April 17	George B. HARRIS	Elizabeth SHIELD
April 22	Jacob PARKER	Emeline SMITH
April 22	Samuel SLOCOMB	Elizabeth MASON
April 23	Charles W. BISHOP	Mary CLAYVELL
April 30	Benjamin T. AYDELOTT	Sarah PAYNE
April 30	Samuel H. PAYNE	Ann J. HANCOCK
May 4	Joshua MITCHELL	Susan TOWNSEND
May 18	samuel J. LAMBDON	Sally A. MERRILL
May 25	Joshua TOWNSEND	Sarah E. DALE
June 3	William S. LEWIS	Emeline BLADES
June 5	Jacob STURGIS	Mary E. BRATTEN
June 10	Selby DYKES	Elizabeth BLADES
June 10	Isaac W.K. HANDY	Sarah S. MARTIN
June 11	Nathan MILBOURNE	Harriet EVANS
June 11	John WHITE	Sally PARSONS
June 12	Zadok T. MILBOURNE	Priscilla H.H. TRUITT
June 13	Levin LAMBDEN	Leah BOSTON
June 13	William H. BAYNE	Elizabeth H.P. BRITTINGHAM
June 17	Lawrenson HASTINGS	Sally ENNIS
June 18	William J. RIGGIN	Catharine M. JOHNSON
June 18	Cornelius WIDGEON	Hetty M. PHILLIPS
June 20	Soloman M. WILKERSON	Mary M. DENNIS
June 24	Milburn BEACHAMP	Ann M. VANDAUM
June 25	George T. HOLLAND	Mary M. HALL
June 28	Edward PORTER	Margaret LOKEY
July 4	William HOPE	Sally WRIGHT
July 16	Josiah HUDSON	Eliza AINSON
Aug. 2	William BURBAGE	Margaret Ann JARMAN
Aug. 20	Lemuel S. TRUITT	Elizabeth C. HICKMAN
Aug. 22	Robert STURGIS	Ary Catharine LATCHUM
Aug. 22	George C. BOWEN	Hetty FASSITT
Sept. 10	James T. SMACK	Sarah M. HENDERSON

1850

Date	Groom	Bride
Sept. 12	John C. NOCK	Maria DRYDEN
Sept. 12	David B. VESSELS	Nancy AYERS
Oct. 3	John KELLY	Elizabeth HOSIER
Oct. 7	Jenkins GAULT	Julia HARRISON
Oct. 16	Selby P. TRUITT	Henrietta RICHARDS
Oct. 22	James D. STURGIS	Sarah A. STEVENSON
Oct. 22	Peter GIVINS	Martha J. QUILLEN
Oct. 22	John READ	Elizabeth A. DAVIS
Oct. 26	George W. TODD	Fanny HOOPER
Oct. 29	John J. EVANS	Mary H, MITCHELL
Nov. 6	James H. BULL	Mary Ann ROSS
Nov. 11	William H.S. MERRILL	Mary W. HARGIS
Nov. 12	Burton C. MELSON	Priscilla E. FARLOW
Nov. 13	James HOLLAND	Charlotte MUMFORD
Mov. 23	McKimma B. HOLLOWAY	Nancy A. DOWNING
Nov. 25	Nathaniel TYSON	Charlotte REVELL
Nov. 25	Brinkley A. HEARN	Sarah Ann PERDUE
Nov. 26	Littleton J.M. DUER	Matilda C. TAYLOR
Nov. 26	John T. PHILLIPS	Martha BOWEN
Dec. 3	Robert M. BAYLY	Mary E. SHOCKLEY
Dec. 5	Hiram D. PARKER	Mahala E. FARLOW
Dec. 5	William H. ROWLEY	Mary C. SELBY
Dec. 9	William F. EVANS	Sally A.W. GORDY
Dec. 10	Ephraim K.W. BRITTINGHAM	Elizabeth S. PARSONS
Dec. 10	Edward HALL	Sarah PARSONS
Dec. 10	Thomas PARKER	Ann G. ADKINS
Dec. 12	Samuel S. LIVINGSTON	Rebecca A. MATTHEWS
Dec. 12	Asa GRAY	Elizabeth GAULT
Dec. 16	Peter A. WIMBROUGH	Zilpha A. MORRIS
Dec. 16	Josiah WILLIAMS	Nancy GRIFFIN
Dec. 17	Silas TRUITT	Ritta TRUITT
Dec. 17	Arch J. BAKER	Rhoda DONAWAY
Dec. 17	Purnell J. JONES	Esther A.R. CLAYWELL
Dec. 17	Samuel J. LITTLETON	Adeline GRAY
Dec. 18	William S. QUILLEN	Mary Ann TYSON
Dec. 23	Robert L. BOWEN	Catharine CLAYWILL
Dec. 24	John L. BEACHBOARD	Hester CONOWAY
Dec. 25	Hamilton RIGGAN	Louisa TWIG
Dec. 25	William H. HOLLAND	Zipporah BRATTEN
Dec. 30	Lemuel D. WILSON	Sally R. CARSLEY
Dec. 30	William ENNIS	Elizabeth DAVIS
Dec. 31	Samuel JOHNSON	Elizabeth LYNCH

1851

Date	Groom	Bride
Jan. 1	Samuel MELVIN	Sally BELL
Jan. 2	William L. NIBBLET	Henrietta AUSTEN
Jan. 2	John ESHAM	Sarah Ann McGEE
Jan. 6	Soloman TULL	Sally JOHNSON

1851			
Jan. 6	Robert T. STATON	Charlotte E. DISHAROON
Jan. 14	Alfred W. CANNON	Elizabeth HALEY
Jan. 14	James H. COLLINS	Louisa DRYDEN
Jan. 14	William S. BRATTEN	Mary H. SMITH
Jan. 21	Alexander MELONE	Elizabeth CAREY
Jan. 22	Theodore W. WILLIAMS	Mary Ann TRUITT
Jan. 25	Billy F. FARLOW Jr.	Elizabeth HEARN
Jan. 28	Joshua J. WARD	Sally E. MORRIS
Jan. 28	Charles COLLINS	Hetty BISHOP
Jan. 28	James GAFFORD	Rebecca POWELL
Feb. 4	John WILKERSON	Rhoda BAKER
Feb. 5	Adam PARSONS	Margaret E. RILEY
Feb. 7	Thomas H. PARKER	Martha Ann GIVANS
Feb. 7	William BOWDIN	Margaret JONES
Feb. 7	Parker JESTER	Mary CARPENTER
Feb. 12	William T. PEARSON	Margaret S. HYSELUP
Feb. 14	Philip W. HALL	Mary A. McGRIGOR
Feb. 18	Thomas W. DAVIS	Hetty M. HUDSON
Feb. 18	James JOHNSON	Margaret B. MARSHALL
Feb. 18	Charles RICHASON	Julia WARRINGTON
Feb. 19	Robert CROPPER	Eleanor PRUITT
Feb. 22	Littleton BIRCH	Rosa TURNER
Feb. 25	Stephen T. DYKES	Nancy C. PEPPER
Feb. 25	John H. HUDSON	Keturah E. BISHOP
March 3	William W. SELBY	Mary P. BARNES
March 4	Jesse DRYDEN	Lavisa HUDSON
March 11	Edward BISHOP	Elizabeth COLLINS
March 11	Samuel MALLET	Isabella COLLINS
March 11	Soloman BEATHARDS	Susan J. SHOCKLEY
March 13	Zirobabel C. MASON	Hester Ann MEARS
March 18	Zadok S. LEWIS	Gatty TRUITT
March 18	James H. KNOX	Sarah SMITH
March 19	Levi ADAMS	Mary A.M. HOPKINS
March 25	Jesse HOLLAND	Sarah PARSONS
April 1	James BEACHAM	Hetty TULL
April 1	Henry J. DENNIS	Sarah TRUITT
April 7	William W. MUMFORD	Martha A.W. HAMMOND
April 8	William H. TWIG	Julia A. WATSON
April 9	Samuel H.T. TILGHMAN	Hetty A. JONES
April 15	William PARSONS	Hetty BEACHAMP
April 15	John H. YOUNG	Maria FAIRBROTHERS
April 22	Charles H. FASSITT	Mary M. JONES
April 30	Gilly W. FIGGS	Elizabeth DICKERSON
April 30	Littleton P. MITCHELL	Harriet CLAYWELLE
May 6	James FASSITT	Jane TIMMONS
May 6	James HUGHES	Eliza JOHNSON
May 6	Benjamin JOHNSON	Comfort PRUITT
May 7	William S. RISLEY	Rebecca BOWDOIN

1851

Date	Groom	Bride
May 14	John McMASTER	Elizabeth C. STEVENSON
May 26	John D. WILLIAMS	Mary E. JONES
June 3	John TARR	Sarah WATSON
June 4	William BAKER	Mary JARMAN
June 4	Peter W. JOHNSON	Sally BLADES
June 11	Edward SCARBOROUGH	Matilda COLLINS
June 17	Henry JONES	Louisa ALLEN
June 23	James D. RILEY	Hannah W. BETHARDS
June 24	William BETHARDS	Mary Ann BURBAGE
June 26	Henry TAYLOR	Louisa TEAGUE
June 28	Kendall T. BOWEN	Henrietta PARSONS
July 17	Hugh S. POWELL	Catharine WISE
July 24	Charles TATHAM	Mary A. WALLOP
July 25	William H. WEST	Sarah E. WALLOP
July 26	John CURTIS	Sally LANDING
July 28	Hiram D. PARSONS	Miranda F. PERDUE
July 30	George W. PATTERSON	Caroline TRADER
Aug. 1	Littleton PAYNE	Hetty ELLIS
Aug. 7	William T. HOLLAND	Mary A. JENKINS
Aug. 19	Albertus CLARK	Mary E. REVEL
Aug. 25	Lemuel D. HICKMAN	Zipporah C. DAVIS
Aug. 27	Major CLAYWELL	Aralanta P. NOCK
Sept. 2	John R. LYNCH	Margaret A. JONES
Sept. 2	Henry J. WILSON	Leah JONES
Sept. 10	William BOYD	Jane MEZICK
Sept. 16	James MUMFORD	Elizabeth McLANE
Sept. 16	John D. SHOWELL	Mary C. DUNCAN
Sept. 17	John JOHNSON	Sarah A. JONES
Sept. 22	Henry CHESSER	Mary A. TAYLOR
Sept. 26	Richard B. WINDER	Sally M. CUSTIS
Sept. 27	James M. DICKERSON	Henrietta LOKEY
Oct. 1	Levi NELSON	Ann Elizabeth DIXON
Oct. 7	Edward Teagle LING	Hester Ann TAYLOR
Oct. 8	George T. BRATTEN	Augusta C. RICHARDSON
Oct. 14	Revel OUTTEN	Wealthy J. MASON
Oct. 14	Hezekiah JONES	Amanda W. HANCOCK
Oct. 17	Jonathan POLLITT	Maria JONES
Oct. 21	Daniel F. PARSONS	Elizabeth A. PARSONS
Oct. 22	Henry CAREY	Elizabeth DENNIS
Oct. 25	John F. PARSONS	Elizabeth A. DAVIS
Oct. 28	George W. DAVIS	Lovey B. HUDSON
Oct. 30	Levie D. DIX	Margaret E. DARBY
Nov. 3	John B. TOADVINE	Sally J. DRYDEN
Nov. 5	James CLAYWELL	Polly CLAYVILL
Nov. 10	William T. CULENA	Chatlotte A. WINDER
Nov. 17	Isaac H. HASTINGS	Henrietta GORDY
Nov. 18	William R. TUBBS	Martha T. WILLIAMS
Nov. 24	Mordica G. PARSONS	Eliza J. BUTLER

1851

Nov. 26	Samuel P. TRUITT	Eliza M. TRUITT
Nov. 29	Willliam P. DORMAN	Sally E. PERDUE
Dec. 2	Richard CROPPER	Emeline DAZEY
Dec. 5	William T. DARSON	Mary A. ROUNDS
Dec. 6	John S. GORDY	Amelia E. FOOKS
Dec. 9	Robert J. LAMBDEN	Charlotte ROSS
Dec. 10	Ananias PETTIT	Elizabeth DEVEREUX
Dec. 13	Stephen P. MOORE	Sally L. TRUITT
Dec. 13	Thomas KING	Sarah HUDSON
Dec. 16	Uriah E. FOOKS	Hetty FOOKS
Dec. 16	William GRAY	Maria COLLYER
Dec. 16	Henry Emerson DENNIS	Catharine T. ROBERTS
Dec. 17	Richard L. PARSONS	Hannah E. FARLOW
Dec. 22	Peter TRUITT	Sally J. BRITTINGHAM
Dec. 24	Levin J.M.P. BRODWATER	Amanda P. BEVANS
Dec. 25	George CAMPBELL	Lydia MURRAY
Dec. 27	William POWELL (of Elisha)	Sarah M. TAYLOR

1852

Jan. 1	William H. BACON	Mary E. POWELL
Jan. 3	Elijah KELLY	Eliza HANCOCK
Jan. 3	John L.R.B. CAREY	Ann COLLINS
Jan. 5	John PARMER	Zipporah HUDSON
Jan. 6	Joseph R. ELLIS	Sinah E. POPE
Jan. 6	James P. DRISKILL	Mary A. SHOCKLEY
Jan. 7	James S. TAYLOR	Elizabeth BOSTON
Jan. 9	Gilliss J. DAUGHTERS	Mary A. MOORE
Jan. 10	John D. TRUITT	Nevey P. DONNEY
Jan. 10	Charles COLLINS	Jane COOPER
Jan. 13	Jesse B. TRUITT	Erixene MOORE
Jan. 13	Jesse WORKMAN	Hetty TAYLOR
Jan. 13	William C. HILL	Margaret T. HUDSON
Jan. 15	Thomas POULSON	Mary E. BIRD
Jan. 16	Jerome B. HALL	Julia C. MERRILL
Jan. 17	James H. TRADER	Elizabeth BENNETT
Jan. 20	Walter H. HICKMAN	Eleanor HILL
Jan. 21	John G. HUTCHESON	Sally Maria PURNELL
Jan. 24	Peter MASON	Priscilla PATTERSON
Jan. 24	Benjamin JACKSON	Sarah Ann SAYERS
Jan. 26	Walter TURNER	Hester SNEED
Jan. 26	William H. CAREY	Charlotte E. BUSSELS
Jan. 27	David A. HOLLOWAY	Louisa E. HUDSON
Jan. 27	Francis O. HAYMAN	Henrietta F. BROWN
Feb. 3	Isaac DAVIS	Elizabeth JOYNES
Feb. 3	James LOKEY	Elizabeth J. ENNIS
Feb. 3	Nathaniel SELBY	Catherine A. NICKOLS
Feb. 3	Phillip NICKOLS	Matilda R. DIRICKSON
Feb. 9	George W. HANCOCK	Ann E. BONNEWELL

1852

Date	Groom	Bride
Feb. 9	James C. CORDRY	Sally Ann HAYMAN
Feb. 10	Theodore CAREY	Sally PENNEWELL
Feb. 10	John H. DUER	Mary Ann MADDUX
Feb. 10	Davis KELLY	Martha DYKES
Feb. 10	James WONNELL	Mary Ann BOUNDS
Feb. 17	Samuel M. MILLS	Leah Jane CAMPBELL
Feb. 17	Edward HUBBELL	Elizabeth H. ENNIS
Feb. 21	John G. PERDUE	Mary Eliazbeth ELLIS
Feb. 23	James TOADVINE	Rachel J. McGRATH
Feb. 23	Gillis BUSSELS	Charlotte CAREY
Feb. 23	John W. FIDDEMAN	Hester AYDELOTTE
Feb. 24	Benjamin G. FARLOW	Jane EVANS
Feb. 25	Handy PHILLIPS	Anniss CAREY
Feb. 28	James PARKER	Mary RAYPHIELD
March 2	William G. GORDY	Sarah C. GORDY
March 2	Annanias RODNEY	Fanny QUILLEN
March 6	Thomas PRIOR	Elizabeth A. WARD
March 15	John P.W. GAULT	Hester E. HOLLAND
March 17	Thomas J. LATCHUM	Nancy PHILLIPS
March 18	James H. SHOCKLEY	Phillip J. JOHNSON
March 22	Samuel BENSON	Priscilla COTTINGHAM
March 23	Josiah BOSTON	Rachel Jane GRAY
March 29	George JOHNSON	Polly KELLY
March 30	William BRADFORD	Martha BRADFORD
March 30	Peter WILKERSON	Harriet BRIMER
April 6	George T. JONES	Cora MILBY
April 9	Alfred B. RIGGIN	Eliza S. BYRD
April 13	Minos B. BROWN	Elizabeth JACKSON
April 24	Dewit C. FOOKS	Mary FOOKS
April 26	James F. WILLIAMS	Henrietta PARKER
April 27	Levin TULL	Charlotte BEAVANS
April 27	Thomas PRUITT	Sally ALLEN
April 30	George TARR	Margaret POWELL
May 8	George P. CAMPBELL	Margaret A.M. FIGGS
May 12	John H. THORNTON	Margaret CLAYWELL
May 12	David PETIT	Hetty NOCK
May 14	John E. STEVENSON	Matilda TAYLOR
May 18	Jacob M. HOLLOWAY	Zilla M. WARREN
May 18	William L. BLADES	Emerst W. PILCHARD
May 24	Robert PERKINS	Leah BOSTON
May 26	Stephen TIMMONS	Hannah ADKINS
May 29	Henry DYKES	Charlotte Jane POPE
June 2	Harry TOADVINE	Mary E. POLLITT
June 8	William LATHBURY	Elizabeth HUDSON
June 8	Collymore TAYLOR	Rosae A. TRADER
June 16	Jacob POWELL	Elizabeth SMACK
July 13	Isaac D. JONES	Mary K. MARTIN
Aug. 3	Benjamin BRITTINGHAM	Sally J. BENSON

1852

Aug. 12	John M. PURNELL	Sarah A. LEONARD
Aug. 16	Archibald BODLY	Eliza TOWNSEND
Aug. 24	William S. BENSTON	Henrietta B. HIGGIN
Aug. 28	Samson TOWNSEND	Jane HUDSON
Aug. 31	Hugh KER	Annie YERBY
Sept. 11	Gideon MASON	Maria ELLIS
Sept. 17	Charles P. BUCKHOUSE	Margaret I. CUTLER
Oct. 6	Johnson H. DAVIS	Jane M. BURBAGE
Oct. 13	John E. SPENCER	Elizabeth W. BRATTEN
Oct. 25	Lewis S. CONAWAY	Mary Jane WARD
Oct. 26	David GAULT	Mary Elizabeth BAILEY
Oct. 28	West WATSON	Susan TAYLOR
Nov. 2	John J. LAMBERSON	Amanda HOLLAND
Nov. 3	George C. PURNELL	Elizabeth STEVENSON
Nov. 6	William GOOTEE	Harriet WATSON
Nov. 9	Charles T. DAVIS	Mary P. PRUITT
Nov. 17	William PENNEWELL	Sally SHOCKLEY
Nov. 17	James E. STURGIS	Julia Ann PARSONS
Nov. 23	Charles BELSATE	Elizabeth HARMAN
Nov. 27	Isaac DOWNS	Matilda A. HASTINGS
Nov. 30	Thomas JONES	Cordella HANCOCK
Dec. 6	Jenkins GAULT	Eliza A. LANE
Dec. 7	Winder PEPPER	Mary TAYLOR
Dec. 7	Hamilton BUTLER	Charlotte TIMMONS
Dec. 7	Phillip HUDSON	Matilda FISHER
Dec. 8	Thomas LITTLETON (of E)	Sarah J. LITTLETON
Dec. 9	Silas W. DAVIS	Sally Jones (of Isaac)
Dec. 11	Irving FOOKS	Charlotte J. COLBOURNE
Dec. 11	Daniel J. STATON	Liticia Ann FOOKS
Dec. 13	Hiram W. HEARN	Irena F. HEARN
Dec. 14	Thomas W. BROWN	Elizabeth A. MORRIS
Dec. 15	William VINCENT	Olivia FEDDEMAN
Dec. 16	James HALL	Priscilla BRUMBLY
Dec. 16	Richard HALL	Polly BAKER
Dec. 20	Eliajh James TRUITT	Lucretia L. MORRIS
Dec. 21	William J. TUBBS	Margaret TOWNSEND
Dec. 21	Joseph J. ENNIS	Emma E. COLLINS
Dec. 21	George BRITTINGHAM	Sarah SMITH
Dec. 21	James H. QUILLEN	Matilda A. HASTY
Dec. 22	Isaac R. POWELL	Mary A. BOWEN
Dec. 23	Jonathan S. FARLOW	Martha J. HAYMAN
Dec. 23	Edward CLAYWELL	Martha HAMMOND
Dec. 29	Edward TIMMONS	Oma DICKERSON

1853

Jan. 1	Thomas L.	Louisa S. TURLINGTON
Jan. 3	Alfred D. MERRILL	Harriet Jane LAMBDEN
Jan. 5	Wrixam TAYLOR	Sally EWELL

1853

Date	Groom	Bride
Jan. 7	Levin JONES	Louisa HANCOCK
Jan. 8	Severan P. MILES	Harriet BEASLY
Jan. 10	Joshua ENNIS	Elizabeth KELLY
Jan. 10	James WARD	Mary Ann TULL
Jan. 11	James GUTHERY	Sally SMACK
Jan. 11	Joshua PHILLIPS	Fanny Caroline BAYLY
Jan. 11	William JOHNSON	Mary SCARBOROUGH
Jan. 12	John T. ADKINS	Mary E. WILLIAMS
Jan. 12	John H. TRUITT	Polly ROWLEY
Jan. 15	Michael J. HASTINGS	Elizabeth S. LAYFIELD
Jan. 17	William W. MUMFORD	Mary A. LANE
Jan. 18	Benjamin BISHOP	Matilda MACKLIN
Jan. 18	John BRADFORD	Mary HADDOCK
Jan. 18	Minos LITTLETON	Martha WARREN
Jan. 19	Ephraim K. WILSON	Mary Ann DICKERSON
Jan. 25	John PARSONS	Mary Jane PALMER
Jan. 26	Isaac FLEMMING	Rebecca PUSEY
Jan. 27	John H. CAREY	Sarah M. BRUMBLEY
Jan. 31	Urbin J. WHITE	Rosetta BISHOP
Feb. 1	William T. GRIFFIN	Mary Ann WEBB
Feb. 1	Avera BRADFORD	Mary TAYLOR
Feb. 4	Edward M. TRUITT	Nancy E. TRADER
Feb. 8	Littleton P. FRANKLIN	Sarah E. CHANEY
Feb. 8	John SHANAMAN	Margaret STURGES
Feb. 15	Elisha RION	Jennetta McCOLUM
Feb. 18	Isaac J. TRUITT	Jane B. BRITTINGHAM
Feb. 22	Robert TOWNSEND	Margaret G. PORTER
March 1	Irving SPENCE	Harriet Mary HAYWARD
March 8	Kendal W.S. HASTINGS	Ann Maria PARSONS
March 8	John S. LANKFORD	Elizabeth HALL
March 15	George ENNIS	Mary PHILLIPS
March 21	Isaac KNOX	Mary M. GIVAN
March 29	William S. BUTLER	Mary E. POPE
March 29	John P. JOHNSON	Elizabeth GRAY
March 31	Daniel F. MELSON	Sarah E. WHITE
April 5	John H. POOL	Julia A. WILLIS
April 5	Lewis S. BARNES	Margaret M. THAMS
April 12	Arthur W. TAYLOR	Margaret Ellen BOWEN
April 20	Peter D. COTTINGHAM	Elizabeth S. PARKER
April 21	Henry GRAY	Nancy WEIGHT
April 28	James B. ROBINS	Elizabeth HAYWARD
April 30	William H. WEST	Henrietta Virginia PANAMORE
May 3	Anthony BROWN	Mary Elizabeth MALONE
May 3	William GUTHERY	Sarah A. JONES
May 14	Gibbs SHOCKLEY	Martha SHOCKLEY
May 19	Michael J. STURGIS	Esther J. HOUSTON
May 30	William T.G. POLK	Mary HENRY
June 1	William BOSTON	Harriet DUNCAN

1853

Date	Groom	Bride
June 2	William TIMMONS	Mary Ann SMACK
June 4	Obediah H. MORRISON	Emma CLARKE
June 6	Gillett P. BRITTINGHAM	Clarrissa E. BAKER
June 7	Peter RAIN	Leah BETHARDS
June 16	Henry POWELL	Fanny ADKINS
June 27	William D. CROPPER	Rebecca W. TULL
July 11	Robert E. BAKER	Sally A. TYRE
July 12	Zechariah BOWEN	Ellen POWELL
July 14	William J. HOLLAND	Sally E. TULL
July 23	Colmore G.D. BAYNE	Sally A. HARRIS
July 27	Peter C. BLADES	Nancy E. WEST
Aug. 2	Peter C. CORBIN	Rosa YOUNG
Aug. 2	George KELLY	Martha Ann HENDERSON
Aug. 8	Elijah NICHOLSON	Sarah LITTLETON
Aug. 10	Willliam M. ROSS	Sally TAYLOR
Aug. 18	William D. DAVIS	Sarah PETIT
Aug. 23	John T. REED	Martha S. DAVIS
Sept. 3	David HILL	Mary RICHARDSON
Sept. 12	Stephen D. HADDER	Sarah Jane BEACHAMP
Sept. 14	Levin P. CORBIN	Harriet A. AYDELOTTE
Sept. 17	Rufus K.M. BAYNUM	Lydia Jane ABBOTT
Sept. 20	Robert I. SILVERTHORN	Eliza CORBIN
Sept. 21	William R. MUMFORD	Sally Ann CHERICKS
Oct. 4	James DYKES	Anne Maria HASTINGS
Oct. 4	Benjamin DENNIS	Milly J. DENNIS
Oct. 4	William P. SMITH	Sarah JACKSON
Oct. 4	John S. PAYNE	Nancy W. PAYNE
Oct. 5	James RUARK	Gatty FARLOW
Oct. 10	Edwin DIXON	Priscilla KNOX
Oct. 18	Frederick HAUBERT	Mary E. BRIDELL
Oct. 24	William N. HASTINGS	Margaret E. ELLIOTT
Oct. 25	Jonathan DENNIS	Maria C. DAVIS
Oct. 26	John W. SILVERTHORN	Amelia A. TOWNSEND
Nov. 1	Littleton Q. DENNIS	Martha E. DENNIS
Nov. 1	John HENDERSON	Catharine HENDERSON
Nov. 14	Thomas PENN	Charlotte A. BRUMBLY
Nov. 14	Isaac MALLETT	Sarah COLLINS
Nov. 17	Alfred BRATTEN	Milly LITTLETON
Nov. 17	Curtis DIXON	Hetty RICHARDSON
Nov. 22	John V. DENNIS	Hester C. TIMMONS
Nov. 22	Dr. Edward W. MARSHALL	Levenia L. SHEPARD
Nov. 23	John J. HILL	Charlotte A. DEVEREUX
Nov, 24	Charles KELLY	Mary C. PRUITT
Nov. 26	Nathan T. ADKINS	Sarah REDDISH
Nov. 28	Levin W. BEACHAMP	Sarah L. HOLLAND
Nov. 28	Teagle H. TAYLOR	Sarah F. NORTHAM
Nov. 29	Sewell A. BYRD	Ellen J.S. JAMES
Nov. 29	Benjamin H. GORDY	Charlotte E.B. DENNIS

1853

Nov. 29		John COLLINS	Zipporah C. POWELL
Nov. 30		Samuel H. TRUITT	Amelia E. MILLS
Dec. 2		Salathiel BAKER	Mary E. LAYTON
Dec. 6		Noah GIVAN	Eliza A. CAMPBELL
Dec. 6		Samuel MELVIN	Jane BLADES
Dec. 7		Samuel T. WILLIAMS	Ann Elizabeth FOOKS
Dec. 12		Noah J. TILGHMAN	Mary E. WHITE
Dec. 12		Albert WARREN	Mary E. RAIN
Dec. 12		Wiliam L. SHOCKLEY	Drucilla WILLIAMS
Dec. 15		Albert NOCK	Mary R. NOCK
Dec. 15		John RICHARDSON	Elizabeth ENNIS
Dec. 15		Elijah P. COLBURN	Gatty J. JONES
Dec. 20		William T. HEARN	Anna H. HENDERSON
Dec. 20		George W. SHOCKLEY	Sophia A. HOSIER
Dec. 20		Edward W. STEVENSON	Sarah M. COTTINGHAM
Dec. 21		Robert J. POWELL	Aralanta C. STURGIS
Dec. 27		George W. RITCHIE	Mary S. KELLY
Dec. 27		Albert J. CHERRIX	Margaret POPE
Dec. 27		John Thomas FISHER	Hester Ann BLOXSOM
Dec. 28		Daniel ADKINS	Hetty Ann DENNIS
Dec. 28		Edward H. BELL	Mary E. STURGIS
Dec. 28		Zadok BOWEN	Martha FRANKLIN
Dec. 31		Daniel JONES	Charlotte BOWEN

1854

Jan. 2		Ebenezer BREWINGTON	Martha SHOCKLEY
Jan. 3		Ayers G. PARKER	Hester MIDDLETON
Jan. 3		James E. HANCOCK	Martha W. JONES
Jan. 3		Leonard W. HANCOCK	Sarah E. TRADER
Jan. 3		Nathan MITCHELL	Ann MILVEN
Jan. 4		James Thomas DUFFY	Mary Ann NOCK
Jan. 4		John E. BRITTINGHAM	Mary HENDERSON
Jan. 4		Stockely TAYLOR	Charlotte PURNELL
Jan. 5		Emory A. PUSEY	Amelia A. DUKES
Jan. 6		George W. HAMBLIN	Mary PALMER
Jan. 10		George H. WARD	Mary J. TRUITT
Jan. 10		William S. BISHOP	Louisa GRAY
Jan. 10		John H. ELLISS	Mary SELBY
Jan. 17		Benjamin B. BASSITT	Jane E. SMACK
Jan. 17		Isaac LEWIS	Patty BRADFORD
Jan. 18		Uriah CHARION	Mary BOWEN
Jan. 24		William LYNCH	Lavinia WELLS
Jan. 24		John F. DICKERSON	Mary FIGGS
Jan. 30		John ROYALL	Caroline ACKWORTH
Jan. 31		John NOCK	Elizabeth PILCHARD
Jan. 31		Littleton POPE	Alley MADDOX
Feb. 1		John T. HAYMAN	Levema E. FIGGS
Feb. 6		Moses N. WINBROW	Laura J. WARD
Feb. 6		Samuel ELLIS	Frances LANDING
Feb. 7		John H. CROSWELL	Arinthia E.S. JOHNSON

1854

Date	Groom	Bride
Feb. 14	Thomas JONES	Sarah E. TRUITT
Feb. 14	Colmore G. TAYLOR	Elizabeth D. CORBIN
Feb. 14	Parker BOWEN	Sally A. JOHNSON
Feb. 21	William BROWN	Rebecca SMULLIN (alias Besy)
Feb. 22	James TRUITT	Elizabeth COLLINS
Feb. 22	Winder PEPPER	Lydia TAYLOR
Feb. 23	Stephen T. BLADES	Jane E.A.B. DICKERSON
Feb. 27	Isaac A. WEBB	Elizabeth A. JONES
Feb. 28	John H. HOWARD	Comfort A. SELBY
Feb. 28	Edward T. PRUITT	Sally E.H. NELSON
March 1	Jesse DAVIS	Jane GRAY
March 7	John W. JONES	Virginia M. SAVAGE
March 7	John T. HICKMAN	Elizabeth SCHARBOURGH
March 7	Benjamin DAVIS	Harriet BEVANS
March 8	Isaac MORRISS	Nancy CAREY
March 8	John B. TWIGG	Jane H. TOWNSEND
March 18	William CARMEAN	Eliza A. WARD
March 18	John J. PARSONS	Milly Ann PARKER
March 28	Elijah MADDUX	Nancy RUARK
March 29	John JONES	Elizabeth PRUITT
March 29	William A. WAPLES	Harriet F. HARRIS
March 31	Leonard BEACHAMP	Nancy C. CAREY
April 11	James MILLS	Hester WILLIAMS
April 18	Samuel J. YOUNG	Margaret ENNIS
April 19	Seth W. TYER	Sarah A MORRIS
April 19	Isaac DISHAROON	Hannah G. PARSONS
April 19	James RICHARDSON	Nicy JOHNSON
April 22	Clement C. HEARN	Irena HEARN
April 25	Charles P. COLLINS	Jane ROGERS
May 2	John T. LANKFORD	Leah E. BOSTON
May 16	Isaac B. PHILIP	Hester A.H.J.P.DENNIS
May 16	Sylvester J. ANNIS	Rebecca TAYLOR
May 17	Selby BRADFORD	Julia Ann KELLY
May 24	William R. MORRISS	Mary E. MADDOCKS
May 24	George E. CROSWELL	Matilda S. TAYLOR
May 31	Washington J. BOUNDS	Sally E. TAYLOR
June 6	Joseph WESCOAT	Elizabeth B. EDMONDS
June 13	Lorenzo POWELL	Hester BRAZIER
June 20	Thorogood MASON	Elizabeth HICKMAN
June 28	John TAYLOR	Sally JONES
June 28	James BLADES	Elizabeth DRYDEN
June 29	Isaac B. PURNELL	Mary A. MARSHALL
July 4	Thomas DICKERSON	Sally E. RICHARDSON
July 11	Elijah CAREY	Margaret FITACHETT
July 22	Henry BIRCH	Rosannah CLARKE
July 24	William M. FEDDEMAN	Catharine J. FEDDEMAN
July 25	Thompson SMACK	Mary C. PRUITT
July 28	Richard NIBLET	Mary BROWN

1854

Date	Groom	Bride
July 31	James WELLS	Mary PARSONS
Aug. 7	William ENNIS	Sarah HICKMAN
Aug. 9	Littleton REED	Mary SAVAGE
Aug. 14	George CATHELL	Mary J. CAREY
Aug. 15	Joseph ELLIOTT	Sally JOHNSON
Aug. 15	John A. RAYNE	Mary A. GODFREY
Aug. 15	James N. JONES	Sarah A. JONES
Aug. 16	Johnson DENNIS	Jane SHOCKLEY
Aug. 26	Josiah ADKINS	Maria McGEE
Aug. 28	Benton C. GRAVENOR	Joyce B. DAVIS
Aug. 29	Benjamin D. PAYNE	Elizabeth ARDIS
Aug. 30	Elijah SHEPPARD	Sally CURTIS
Aug. 30	James HARMON	Hester BLACK
Sept. 12	William A. ROWLEY	Charlotte MASON
Sept. 12	Thomas WARD	Martha A. SHEPHERD
Sept. 14	Joseph J. ENNIS	Susan A. BOWEN
Sept. 26	Nathaniel WILKERSON	Mary Ann GODFREY
Oct. 3	William P. HARPER	Ann M. WHITE
Oct. 7	James H. PARKER	Charlotte A. CULVER
Oct. 9	Samuel TAYLOR	Elizabeth HENDERSON
Oct. 10	Samuel J. LAMBDEN	Mary E. MERRILL
Oct. 16	Covington TAYLOR	Bridget HALL
Oct. 17	Levin POWELL	Mary MUMFORD
Oct. 17	James BOWEN of K	Margaret J. HOLLAND
Oct. 18	Alfred T. JONES	Mary E. MUMFORD
Oct. 19	Purnell PUSEY	Ellenor CANTWELL
Oct. 24	Azariah ARDIS	Sally BURNETT
Oct. 30	William L. LAWS	Margaret A. FOOKS
Oct. 31	Thomas DEVEREUX	Mary JOHNSON
Oct. 31	Samuel J. TOWNSEND	Emaline PETITT
Nov. 8	Thomas MUMFORD	Elizabeth READ
Nov. 14	Robert T. WIMBROW	Mary Ann McGEE
Nov. 14	John SHEPHERD	Hester HOLLAND
Nov. 15	James LEWIS	Claissa LITTLETON
Nov. 15	Henry C. JONES	Ann C. HENDMAN
Nov. 16	Daniel D. ROUNDS	Rachel HEARN
Nov. 21	Hyram BAILY	Jane SMITH
Nov. 22	Lewis SMITH	Sarah E. AYERS
Nov. 22	John P. PARKER	Margaret MEARS
Nov. 22	James W. BIRCH	Elizabeth WIDGEON
Nov. 23	Littleton TATMAN	Mary H. BONNAWELL
Nov. 27	William TRUITT	Esther PERKINS
Nov. 29	William J,T. NOCK	Mary Ann DRYDEN
Nov. 30	Lambert G. PERDUE	Hannah E. TRUITT
Dec. 2	Henry TAPMAN	Matilda MARSHALL
Dec. 5	David BOWEN	Jane L. BOWEN
Dec. 6	Lemuel PURNELL	Ann M. ENNIS
Dec. 8	Irving S. LITTLETON	Jane PURNELL

1854			
Dec. 8		Charles TAYLOR	Esther E. NOCK
Dec. 9		William H. JARMAN	Jane WARREN
Dec. 9		Edwin G. HARRISON	Mary A. BRITTINGHAM
Dec. 11		Kendal J. PATEY	Maria E. COOPER
Dec. 12		Elijah NICHOLSON	Eliza MORRIS
Dec. 12		Levin TRADER	Eliza ARDIS
Dec. 12		George HALL	Peggy SAVAGE
Dec. 12		Josephus H. NELSON	Julia A. FARLOW
Dec. 14		Uriah SHOCKLEY	Julia A. TILGHMAN
Dec. 14		George W. HEARN	Lavinia E.B. GORDY
Dec. 14		Jeremiah PASTERFIELD	Helena W. HOLLAND
Dec. 16		David JOHNSON	Sarah QUILLIN
Dec. 18		Littleton J. STURGIS	Sarah M. POWELL
Dec. 18		Wiliam J. GODFREY	Mary A. MORRIS
Dec. 20		Ebenzer WEST	Drucilla TAYLOR
Dec. 23		Stephen A. REDDEN	Sarah W. DUKES
Dec. 25		Nelson HALL	Susan A. HALL
Dec. 28		John EVANS	Susan BUNDICK
1855			
Jan. 1		Edward REVEL	Julia KELLY
Jan. 2		George W. LANK	Rhoda TRUITT
Jan. 2		Stephen REDDEN	Ellen PILCHARD
Jan. 2		Archibald ANNIS	Mary Ann BLOXSOM
Jan. 3		Thomas BLOXOM	Phebe BULL
Jan. 5		William S MOORE	Amelia J. MOORE
Jan 5		George W. GORDY	Sarah E. COULBOURNE
Jan. 9		William T. WEST	Lavinia E.B. GORDY
Jan. 9		Henry LAMBERSON	Hester TOWNSEND
Jan. 11		Charles PARKER Jr.	Ellen A. MATTHEWS
Jan. 16		Wesley PENEWELL	Mary A. JARMAN
Jan. 17		Jesse DRYDEN	Charlotte WATERS
Jan. 22		Wiliam PAYDON	Hetty SELBY
Jan. 22		McKimma TIMMONS	Zilla WILLIS
Jan. 23		James MADDUX	Marthenia PUSEY
Jan. 25		John WARREN	Martha A. JARMAN
Jan. 29		Edward LITTLETON	Annis SHOCKLEY
Jan. 30		George J. ELLIS	Mary E.W. LANDING
Jan. 30		Ayers MASON	Sally DUKES
Jan. 30		James S. JONES	Elizabeth A. SELBY
Feb. 1		Littleton R. PURNELL	Ellen W. WILSON
Feb. 3		William RODGERS	Jane FISHER
Feb. 5		William BRITTINGHAM	Eliza DUNCAN
Feb. 6		John R.P. HENDERSON	Margaret HICKMAN
Feb, 8		David BRIDDLE	Sally A. PALMER
Feb. 13		Kendal D. TAYLOR	Mary E. JARVIS
Feb. 13		Samuel C.S. DAVIs	Nancy T. RILEY
Feb. 21		Wiliam BRITTINGHAM	Eliza HALL

1855

Date	Groom	Bride
Feb. 22	Thomas MALLET	Priscillla POWELL
Feb. 27	Gideon TULL	Harriet ARDIS
Feb. 27	John DISHAROON	Leah A. DIXON
March 6	Zacheus BOWEN	Emily WILLIAMS
March 8	John B. NOCK	Sarah CAREY
March 12	John B. TOADVINE	Elizabeth A. BROWN
March 18	George ROUNDS	Mary C. BRIDDEL
March 22	James EWELL	Julia Ann JESTER
March 26	William J. POWELL	Mary E. LAYFIELD
March 27	Samuel TRADER	Elizabeth BYRD
March 27	Harry JARVIS	Mary E. TIMMONS
April 3	William JUSTICE	Tuphany POULSON
April 16	Samuel CROPPER	Lettitia DAVIS
April 19	Henry H. HAMBLIN	Rachel W. LEWIS
April 21	John KNAPP	Ann HALL
April 24	William HUDSON of L.	Jane H. BLADES
April 24	George BRUMBLY	Jane DRYDEN
April 25	Samuel H. JARMAN	Sallie M. RICHARDSON
April 25	James M. POWELL	Rachel M. SOMERS
May 8	Selby P. TRUITT	Amelia E. TIMMONS
May 9	William H. PAYNE	Julia Ann TAYLOR
May 18	Isaac DAVIS	Jane ENNIS
May 21	William J. BELOATE ?	Rosean BACON
May 21	John S. ROBINS	Fanny J. WALLACE
May 23	John H. TILGHMAN	Sally M. DAVIS
May 30	Joseph B, COX	Margaret D. POWELL
June 12	Edward SMULLEN	Henrietta BROWN
June 12	Isaac HANDCOCK	Mary A. OUTTEN
June 23	James CURTIS	Sarah BERRY
June 23	Josiah H. WARREN	Elizabeth LAWS
June 23	Elisha M. COLLINS Jr.	Sarah C. SELBY
July 10	William TURNER	Fanny M. PATTEY
July 16	Ayers TATHAM	Sarah Ann TAYLOR
July 25	Edward G. TOWNSEND	Catharine VICKERS
July 31	Thomas F. STEVENSON	Rose TRUITT
Aug. 7	William C. RICHARDSON	Mary A. CURTIS
Aug. 9	Nathaniel NICHOLS	Maranda COLLINS
Aug. 15	James M. DENNIS	Henrietta PERDUE
Aug. 16	John RUARK	Mary A. DYKES
Aug. 28	Irving MASON	Lavina HANDCOCK
Sept. 1	Daniel BOWDEN	Mary WATSON
Sept. 1	Isaac J.S. EDWARDS	Elizabeth A.B. POULSON
Sept. 4	Henry Long MERRILL	Hester Ann HOWARD
Sept. 4	Edward JONES	Margaret TWIFORD
Sept. 8	Francis LANE	Mary J. STEVENS
Sept. 11	James B. HAMBLIN	Elexine DUSKY
Sept. 13	James H. PRUITT	Elizabeth DUKES
Sept. 13	Cannon SHORT	Mary DICKERSON

1855

Date	Groom	Bride
Sept. 13	George W. HEARN	Sophia Elizabeth JORDAN
Oct. 2	Wiliam K. BRUMBLY	Leah Ann DIXON
Oct. 6	Milby GRIFFIN	Maria MOORE
Oct. 9	Thomas LITTLETON	Elizabeth PENEWILL
Oct. 9	James CAREY	Sarah FASSITT
Oct. 10	Lemuel J. DUNCAN	Charlotte A. TIMMONS
Oct. 10	Peter PARKER	Mary LYNCH
Oct. 13	John FOOKS	Matty FOOKS
Oct. 13	Joshua M. BEATHARDS	Martha C. ADKINS
Oct. 13	Joshua J. HOLLOWAY	Ritta Emeline BEATHARDS
Oct. 16	George W. DAVIDSON	Jane GAULT
Oct. 16	George C. OWENS	Margaret E. JOHNSON
Oct. 22	Abraham W. CRAMMER	Amelia A. BOSTON
Oct. 22	Thomas TOWNSEND	Sally E. COULBOURNE
Oct. 23	George TULL	Mary E. FLOYD
Oct. 23	Wiliam CHAPMAN	Mary S. ARDIS
Oct. 23	George D.H. COLONA	Adaline MELVIN
Oct. 25	Samuel L. WEBSTER	Priscilla A. SHEPPARD
Oct. 27	Isaac JESTER	Margaret BOWDEN
Oct. 29	Lemuel H. PERDUE	Mary CAREY
Oct. 30	George WAINWRIGHT	Elizabeth C. REYNOLDS
Nov. 6	Joshua J. HAMBLIN	Mary C. TRUITT
Nov. 6	Salathiel BAKER	Nancy BEAUCHAMP
Nov. 9	Isaac CAMPBELL	Mary Ann BIRCH
Nov. 12	Severn SAVAGE	Priscilla HALL
Nov. 12	William H. RICHARDSON	Mary H. MOORE
Nov. 12	William T. DISHAROON	Henrietta A. BAILEY
Nov. 12	Josiah TAYLOR	Charlotte TARR
Nov. 15	George W. SHOCKLEY	Charlott DAVIS
Nov. 17	Levin W. GORDY	Mary Jane DENNIS
Nov. 20	Kendal PARADISE	Ann DAVIS
Nov. 21	Joshua H. STURGIS	Emily THOMAS
Nov. 27	Zadok PURNELL	Andy FRANKLIN
Dec. 4	Seth WYATT	Mary E. HAMBLIN
Dec. 5	Lemuel J.S. DENNIS	Julia J. DENNIS
Dec. 5	William T. TRUITT	Mary A. POWELL
Dec. 11	James ARDIS	Eliza ALEXANDER
Dec. 11	Zadok P. TOWNSEND	Maria J. TEAGUE
Dec. 11	George I. MILES	Emily A.G. WATTS
Dec. 11	Benjamin W. FARLOW	Mary A.S. WHITE
Dec. 11	Elijah AYDELOTTE	Amelia CLAYVILLE
Dec. 11	John F. JONES	Eliza J. BOWEN
Dec. 11	George H. BLOXOM	Sally A. FLOYD
Dec. 15	Ephraim D. BRITTINGHAM	Martha J. WILLIAMS
Dec. 15	William H. JARMAN	Caroline COARD
Dec. 17	Samuel WALKER	Maria Ann SHREAVES
Dec. 17	Peter HANCOCK	Laura Ann REDDEN
Dec. 18	James P. RAYNE	Elizabeth A. DUKES

1855

Date	Groom	Bride
Dec. 18	James R. TUBBS	Elizabeth WILLIAMS
Dec. 18	Noah TILGHMAN	Louisa MATTHEWS
Dec. 18	William J. HALES	Mary POWELL
Dec. 18	Thomas POWELL	Mary Ann Elizabeth ROSE
Dec. 18	Levin A. MERRILL	Mary M. HARRIS
Dec. 20	Samuel J. WHITE	Lovey D. REW
Dec. 22	William POWELL	Sally GRIFFIN
Dec. 24	Minos F. PARKER	Charlotte BRITTINGHAM
Dec. 24	Joshua J. VINCENT	Mary TILGHMAN
Dec. 25	James S. TARR	Margaret J. RUARK
Dec. 25	Samuel F. JONES	Priscilla CHANLER
Dec. 25	Milby GRAY	Sarah PHILIPS
Dec. 25	James DRYDEN	Ann GRAY
Dec. 31	Josiah C. COLLINS	Mary Jane RILEY

1856

Date	Groom	Bride
Jan. 3	Theodore W. WILLIAMS	Rosa F.D. TRUITT
Jan. 7	William T. WIMBROW	Gatty MORRIS
Jan. 8	James HANCOCK	Louisa CALLAHAN
Jan. 11	Thomas GROLTON	Harriet J. FISHER
Jan. 14	Stephen E. MASON	Nancy N. WATERS
Jan. 14	George W.P. SMITH	Elmira C. PURNELL
Jan. 15	Levin BUTLER	Priscilla TOWNSEND
Jan. 15	John R. TAYLOR	Martha E. KELLAM
Jan. 16	Charles TARR	Margaret Ann HUDSON
Jan. 18	Kellam DYKES	Mary Ellen DIXON
Jan. 18	Samuel J. MUMFORD	Sarah E. HENDERSON
Jan. 21	Edward PAYNE	Elizabeth LONG
Jan. 22	John H. BUTLER	Elizabeth MADDUX
Jan. 22	John S. DAVIS	Mary FREEMAN
Jan. 30	Francis H. DENNIS	Mary A. PETTIT
Jan. 30	Mephibosbeth C. WEBB	Sally A. WEST
Feb. 1	James H. FARLOW	Margaret E. WEST
Feb. 4	Charles D. JOHNSON	Leah J. TILGHMAN
Feb. 5	William C. HUDSON	Susan P. NOCK
Feb. 5	Merrill CAMPBELL	Nancy COLLINS
Feb. 12	Robert GODFREY	Mary E. WIMBROW
Feb. 12	Samuel R. ENNIS	Charlotte A. QUILLEN
Feb. 19	Isaac T. VICKERS	Laura A. W. NELSON
Feb. 23	Richard HUDSON	Sally A. FASSITT
Feb. 25	William RICHARDSON	Caroline WARD
Feb. 27	Thomas J. LAYTON	Maria B. TRUITT
March 1	Benjamin T. RICHARDSON	Elizabeth A. RIGGIN
March 4	William PARSONS (of Sam)	Mary FOSKEY
March 4	Irving HITCH	Sarah Eleanor TAYLOR
March 5	John S.S. DRYDEN	Charlotte E. BOSTON
March 5	Francis A. MERRITT	Rosa J. YOUNG
March 5	Thomas ROWLEY	Leah W. HUDSON

1856

Date	Groom	Bride
March 5	George E. POWELL	Jane DISHAROON
March 5	George H. ANDERSON	Mary E. DYKES
March 17	Samuel J. GODFREY	Rachel RION
March 24	John E. LEWIS	Margaret S. TOWNSEND
March 24	Soloman BUNTING	Mary E. THORNTON
March 26	Francis HARMONSON	Mary SAYES
March 29	Robert J. BAKER	Nancy C. HUDSON
April 1	Edward GRIFFIN	Mary JACKSON
April 2	Isaac BOSTON	Jane BLADES
April 8	William POWELL	Elizabeth DRYDEN
April 9	James E. WIMBROUGH	Mary E. CROPPER
April 9	Seth LATCHUM	Ann TAYLOR
April 26	John W. JOHNSON	Margaret Ann BRITTINGHAM
April 28	Irving RIGGIN	Harriet HAYMAN
April 28	Warner W. HENDERSON	Drucilla MATTHEWS
May 5	William JONES	Hessie DAVIS
May 6	Donard PILCHARD	Rosa VEASEY
May 6	William REDDEN	Ellen VEASEY
May 10	Isaac H. HEARN	Mary H. HAYMAN
May 18	Benjamin W. NELSON	Nancy S. EVANS
May 21	John W. BLADES	Mary Jane DAVIS
May 26	Isaac HANCOCK	Drucilla A. PRUITT
May 26	Thomas MASON	Harriet A. MASON
May 27	Garrison DENNIS	Charlotte DENNIS
May 27	James PENNEWILL	Margaret WALKER
May 28	William JONES	Elizabeth SHOCKLEY
May 30	James T. MAPP	Betsy WILLIS
May 31	William S. ADKINS	Mary E. BOWEN
June 3	Ezekiel HENDERSON	Sally HASTINGS
June 9	Wessley BROADWATER	Eliza GIBBONS
June 13	David B. FARLOW	Mary M. MILBOURNE
June 14	Woodstone BRIMER	Serena Jane TAYLOR
June 14	Hillary P. QUILLEN	Jane E. JONES
June 18	Thomas BONAWELL	Margaret GIBBONS
July 2	John W. SELBY	Catharine J. PAYNE
July 5	Thomas DAVIS	Louisa MASSEY
July 5	Elijah H. BRITTINGHAM	Henny A. TYER
July 16	William W. MATTHEWS	Sally E. BLADES
July 20	Joshua SMACK	Sally WILKINS
July 20	Samuel KELLY	Alley W. RIGGIN
July 31	Albert LITTLETON	Nancy A. DENNIS
July 31	William DAVIS	Mary OWENS
Aug. 26	Theodore CAREY	Jane LEWIS
Aug. 26	Walter CAREY	Clarissa HAMBLIN
Aug. 26	William J.S. CLARKE	Elizabeth Ann HARGIS
Aug. 27	Mitchel MASON	Drucilla HUDSON
Aug. 30	Josiah T. SELBY	Julia HAMBLIN
Sept. 2	William PORTER	Sally HANDCOCK

1856

Date	Groom	Bride
Sept. 5	Charles PARSONS	Jane BRATTEN
Sept. 9	Edgar SMACK	Hannah HUDSON
Sept. 16	Oliver I. WHELTON	Margaret TULL
Sept. 19	Elijah WAINWRIGHT	Nancy J. REYNOLDS
Sept. 19	Leonard B. SAVAGE	Mary S. TURNER
Sept. 27	Seth SMITH	Julia C.C. SMITH
Oct. 1	George K. JACKSON	Ansaline HILL
Oct. 3	Harvey BUNTING	Hester EVANS
Oct. 7	James H. FARLOW	Sarah A. FARLOW
Oct. 7	Thomas H. BLADES	Priscilla S. PENNEWELL
Oct. 7	J.W. WESSELLS	Cordelia TAYLOR
Oct. 8	Isaac DAVIS	Elizabeth SELBY
Oct. 11	Thomas BIRTCH	Martha BOWENN
Oct. 16	Robert H. POWELL	Mary E. BOWEN
Oct. 27	Sandy POWELL	Sarah Ellen TULL
Oct. 28	Levin H. MERRILL	Esther A. BROUGHTON
Oct. 29	Samuel D. MELVIN	Elizabeth J. BROUGHTON
Nov. 3	Henry P. JACKSON	Eliza BOSTON
Nov. 3	Isaac N. VEASEY	Barsheba J. BEVANS
Nov. 4	Houten Jas. HAMAN	Eliza J. PARSONS
Nov. 10	Isaac T. HEARN	Isabella GORDY
Nov. 10	George W. GLADDING	Sally STOCKLEY
Nov. 10	Alford BLOXOM	Emma A.V. ADAMS
Nov. 11	George S. MAY	Easther STURGIS
Nov. 18	John D. Arey DIDIEY	Priscilla A. MUMFORD
Nov. 19	Alfred WINGATE	Lydia Ann DOUGHERTY
Nov. 20	William AGNEW	Leah PETTIT
Nov. 24	John MURRAY	Margaret ESHAM
Nov. 24	Thomas E. MARSHALL	Sally R. HALL
Nov. 25	John FARREL	Ellen A. BOWEN
Nov. 25	Peter LIVINGSTON	Sarah A. DIXON
Dec. 3	John W. McKEE	Emmeline KELLY
Dec. 3	George GIBBS	Charlotte TULL
Dec. 3	John McHENRY	Martha MASON
Dec. 8	Isaac DENNIS	Henrietta WIMBROUGH
Dec. 10	Henry SHOCKLEY	Tabitha KELLEY
Dec. 13	Joshua COLBOURN	Ann M. POWELL
Dec. 16	William J. DAVIS	Mary J. SAVAGE
Dec. 16	Thomas MARSH	Sally BOSTON
Dec. 16	John S. DUSKEY	Elizabeth CAMPBELL
Dec. 16	Moses PAYNE	Ellen A. MASSON
Dec. 16	William H. BRATTEN	Mary A. PAYNE
Dec. 16	O. Wilson JONES	A. Amanda HARRIS
Dec. 17	James S. DUFFEY	Atty M. SHOCKLEY
Dec. 20	John HUGHES	Nancy BISHOP
Dec. 20	William PRUITT	Caroline GIBBS
Dec. 22	William T. CORD	Leah Ann ELLIOTT
Dec. 22	John Skinner TAYLOR	Mahala TOWNSEND

1856
Dec. 23	William HADOCK	Sarah KELLEY
Dec. 24	James DUNTON	Adline PAYNE
Dec. 24	Levin P. CARMINE	Julia A. CLAYVILLE
Dec. 27	John H. WILLIAMS	Sally WIGGEN
Dec. 29	William ELLIS	Eliza TRULOVE
Dec. 29	Thomas T. FRAZIER	Julia C. CATHELL
Dec. 30	John H. CALLAHAN	Elizabeth J. PRUITT

1857
Jan. 1	Isaac BEACUCHUM	Oma DONAWAY
Jan. 2	Richard HICKMAN	Sarah A. JUSTICE
Jan. 6	John SLOCUM	A. (?) Jane MASON
Jan. 6	James H. SHOCKLEY	Gertrude J. PERDUE
Jan. 7	William PARKER	Rebecca WYATT
Jan. 8	Peter T. HARRIS	Martha J. MORRIS
Jan. 13	Purnell PUSEY	Martha BUTLER
Jan. 13	Washington MITCHELL	Charlotte E. SMACK
Jan. 16	Leonard J. TIMMONS	Sarah G. HOLLOWAY
Jan. 20	Daniel H. MILLS	Elanor DRYDEN
Jan. 21	Noah PENAWELLL	Adline JONES
Jan. 26	Minos FIGGS	Rodah COULBORN
Jan. 27	John WILLIS	Nancy TOWNSEND
Jan. 28	Isaac M. BROWN	Levinia A.M. MIDLETON
Feb. 2	James HOLSTON	Jane RATLIGE
Feb. 3	William TAYLOR	Jane CHERRIX
Feb. 3	John HOWARD	Elizabeth SELBY
Feb. 9	William S. DICKINSON	Cynthia M. PRIMROSE
Feb. 9	James H. TRUITT	Elizabeth HALL
Feb. 11	Albert P. ELLIS	Martha Ann ELLIS
Feb. 16	Dewit C. FOOKS	Mary Ann SHOCKLEY
Feb. 19	William HATHAWAY	Louisa MARRINER
Feb. 20	William L. LAW	Eliza COLLINS
Feb. 21	Joseph W. MATTHEWS	Sallie A. TUNNEL
Feb. 23	Robert W. POWELL	Mary J. STURGIS
Feb. 24	George W. TILGHMAN	Hanah E. TILGHMAN
Feb. 24	John H. DAVIS	Elizabeth TARR
Feb. 25	George HILL	Tabitha HOLLAND
March 2	John GOOTEE	Mary G. HANCOCK
March 3	James TRADER	Rachel POWELL
March 12	Caleb TRUITT	Nancy Carolin PARSONS
March 20	William J. FISH	Joanna J. JONES
March 23	Edward J. LANKFORD	Nancy MEZICK
March 30	Seth H. BRITTINGHAM	Leah LEWIS
March 31	Josiah M. ADKINS	Mary PARSONS
April 1	Levi C. PARSONS	Elizabeth TARR
April 6	Isaac J. HOLLAND	Isabel WILLIAMS
April 14	Peter S. PANAWELL	Mary S. BAKER
April 21	Seymour CHRISTIAN	Sarah A.C. CORE

1857

Date	Groom	Bride
April 27	Edwin C.P. DICKERSON	Virginia TINGLE
April 28	John BRADFORD	Sally SMACK
May 4	Elijah C. SCOTT	Mary J. TILGHMAN
May 4	John M. DENNIS	Emmie S. SAVAGE
May 11	William J. LONG	Cordelia W. LANDING
May 13	William J. BYRD	Sarah A. HENRY
May 18	Ebenezer GRAY	Sally Mary R. JACKSON
June 3	Henry L. PILCHARD	Sally A. BOSTON
June 4	William K. ROLEY	Mary P. HUDSON
June 9	Albert HARLEY	Josephine A. AMES
June 9	John EVANS	Mary DAVIS
June 9	Edgar H. JARVIS	Sallie M. TRUITT
June 17	Joseph E. RICHARDSON	Mary Ann PENNEWELL
June 23	Thomas B. GORDY	Amelia E. GORDY
June 23	James H. LANDING	Sarah E. BONNEWELL
June 23	Daniel J. WILLIAMS	Sallie W. TRUITT
June 23	Joseph S. JOHNSON	Margaret D. CAREY
June 27	Wiliam S.T. BELOTE	Charlotte WARD
July 4	Isaac TIMMONS	Elizabeth HOLSTON
July 7	Joseph WARTERS	Levina JACKSON
July 25	Cornelius T. TAYLOR	Mary E. MILLIR
July 29	Irving W. MERRILL	Olivia A. SELBY
Aug. 6	John W. WATSON	Mary Ann COLE
Aug. 11	Lodawick F. DAVIS	Lydia M.A. FARREL
Aug. 18	Jehue WHITE	Martha E.J. TRUITT
Aug. 22	James W. EVANS	Maria J. WEST
Aug. 22	John S. RICHARDSON	Mary E. HADDER
Aug. 28	Archibald GAULT	Mary Ann TILGHMAN
Sept. 18	Benjamin WATSON	Martha Ann BANJER
Sept. 22	Samuel H.T. TILGHMAN	Martha E. BAILEY
Sept 28	Littleton T. CLARKE	Amaret J. TRADER
Oct. 12	John Edward DYKES	Jane WARD
Oct. 12	James REED	Sally E. WHITE
Oct. 13	Daniel TILGHMAN	Sarah E. PARSONS
Oct. 15	Lemuel W. BOWDEN	Henny M.H. TUBBS
Oct. 19	John Warner WILKINS	Margaret COLLINS
Oct. 27	William M. SCHOOLFIELD	Emma BARNES
Nov 2	George FOOKS	Mary LAYFIELD
Nov. 7	Sheppard GRAY	Mary BELL
Nov. 7	Isaac W. SMACK	Rebecca GRIFFIN
Nov. 9	Denard HENDERSON	Charlott A. WILLIAMS
Nov. 10	William G. MADDUX	Eleanor R. HEARN
Nov. 16	James H. JONES	Elizabeth A. WARD
	Robert Asbury PURDEU	Ann Maria FIGS
	Josiah McGRATH	Elinora C. ROBERTSON
	Thomas F. PHILLIPS	Amelia H. CORBIN
Nov. 30	Samuel R. TRADER	Mary E. ARDIS
Nov. 30	Martin SHARPLEY	Sally RALLION

1857

Date	Groom	Bride
Dec. 1	Thomas JACKSON	Matilda COLLINS
Dec. 3	Josiah J. CAREY	Susan COLLINS
Dec. 8	John T. GORDY	Laura A. PARSONS
Dec. 8	Joshua OWENS	Hulda Ann ELLIOTT
Dec. 11	Lambert W. PARSONS	Henrietta PARSONS
Dec. 14	James A. POLLITT	Mahala BUSSELLS
Dec. 14	Daniel H. DENNIS	Mary E. FARLOW
Dec. 16	John P.P. GILLIS	Hettie A. S. RIDER
Dec. 17	Soloman CHARNICK	Sarah Ann KILLMAN (VA.)
Dec. 18	Geore C. OWINS	Catharine E. GROTON (VA.)
Dec. 22	Isaac H. RICHARDSON	Sally E. CAMERRON
Dec. 22	Henry CAREY	Sarah OWENS
Dec. 22	Thomas D. PURNELL	Julianna GRAY
Dec. 23	Major M.C. PHILLIPS	Caroline COULBURN
Dec. 23	Major REID	Margaret Jane HENDERSON
Dec. 23	Joshua T. BRIDELL	Mary I. GILLS
Dec. 23	Samuel DAILY	Elinor DYKES
Dec. 24	Lambert SMACK	Harriet WILSON
Dec. 26	Jonathan DENNIS	Sarah Ann BRITTINGHAM
Dec. 29	John SMACK	Martha SMACK

1858

Date	Groom	Bride
Jan. 4	James H. TRADER	Martha A. COLLINS
Jan. 5	William J.C. McKEE	Rachael COLBOURN
Jan. 6	John ELLIOTT	Ellen BRUMB
Jan. 12	Stanton HOLLOWAY	Gatty Elizabeth PARSONS
Jan. 12	John Cooper	Sally PATEY
Jan. 12	William C. JOHNSON	Martha A. SHARPLEY
Jan. 12	Seth M. WHALEY	Ritta M. TAYLOR
Jan. 13	Samuel HOLLAND	Catharine BOWDOIN
Jan. 14	Edward I. MARINER	Sarah E. DUKES
Jan. 19	Stephen T. MASON	Eleaner A. HUDSON
Jan. 21	William C. RIGGIN	Marcellena J. HOUSTON
Jan. 25	Wesley DIXON	Mary A. GRIFFIN
Jan. 26	Saml. M.H. DRYDEN	Ann Mariah BOWEN
Jan. 26	Francis MORRIS	Jane BENSON
Jan. 28	Handy J. TRUITT	Charlotte M. LAWS
Feb. 2	Handy HAYMAN	Betsy CAREY
Feb. 10	Robert H. TWIG	Amanda H. CAUSEY
Feb. 10	Isaac W. BURBAGE	Hetty HOLLAND
Feb. 15	George W. McKEE	Sophia Jane TILGHMAN
Feb. 16	Samuel H. PAYNE	Althea J. PILCHARD
Feb. 17	William C. COLEBURN	Sally ROSSE
Feb. 17	Jesse TAYLOR	Hannah COFFIN
Feb. 20	John SHARPLY	Susan PAYNE
Feb. 22	James E. CAREY	Amelia E. SHOCKLEY
Feb. 27	Hezekiah JONES	July Ann MASON
March 1	Lambert WILKINS	Alexine BRADFORD

1858

Date	Groom	Bride
March 2	Stewart SHEPERD	Sally Ann HENDERSON
March 2	James LIVINGSTON	Elizabeth PRIOR
March 6	Oliver J. BUNTING	Ann Eliza CUTLER
March 10	Levin P. CORBIN	Margaret E. DENNIS
March 15	James H. DRYDEN	Tabitha E. HEARN
March 15	Noble DRYDEN	Sally TATMAN
March 16	John ADKINS	Laura HOLLAND
March 17	David J.P. TRUITT	Martha Ellen BEVANS
March 22	George S. MERRILL	Louisa F. GUNBY
March 23	William GRAVENOR	Maranda MIDDLETON
March 27	Thomas H. VINCENT	Carolin H. TOADVINE
March 29	Samuel G. DAVIS	Elizabeth WHEALTON
March 30	James LAWS	Sallie M. FOOKS
March 30	James TARR	Elizabeth MARSHALL
April 3	Robert LILLISTON	Mary GASKINS
April 13	Stephen R. GRAY	Sarah HOLSTON
April 14	James RILEY	Ann HILL
April 15	Charles E. MESSICK	Anna MARSHALL
April 20	Severn TAYLOR	Sarah MATTHEWS
April 27	James S. DALE	Levinia BATTELL
May 1	Richard STANFORTH	Martha W. ROBERTSON
May 5	George BOWDOIN	Ann CLAYVILLE
May 5	William CORDRY	Mary P. PORTER
May 7	Elijah REGISTER	Cornelia JARVIS
May 11	Charles W. TRUITT	Sally Elizabeth LEWIS
May 20	Handy SMACK	Jane DAVIS
May 26	Edward B. ADKINS	Mary E. BRITTINGHAM
June 3	Smith W. FLOYD	Mary W. STURGIS
June 3	Augustine C. TAYLOR	Elizabeth M. HINMAN
June 7	Major TOWNSEND	Fanny SMACK
June 8	Jesse HUDSON	Miranda WILLIS
June 8	Hiram LEWIS	Harriet LITTLETON
June 9	Henry QUILLIN	Margaret JOHNSON
June 26	Thomas POWELL	Hester N. COFFIN
June 28	William TAYLOR	Jane SELBY
July 1	Isaac W. DRYDEN	Elmira W. MESSICK
July 3	Joshua J. FREENY	Mary Ann PARSONS
July 22	Thomas E. MARTIN	Sarah W. BIXBY
July 22	Henry A. AYRES	Anne C. COLBURN
July 22	James H. McGRATH	Lydia A. PUSEY
July 28	John CHONNICKS	Caroline HOLLAND
Aug. 5	Mitchell T. SCARBOROUGH	Mary H. YOUNG
Aug. 6	Edmund B. COLONA	Lucitta PARADIS
Aug. 16	Wm C. COLLONA	Roburtta H. CAREY
Aug. 18	William TULL	Catharine SAVAGE
Aug. 19	David PETTIT	Ann E. JONES
Aug. 31	Littleton TRADER	Mary Ime BRADFORD
Sept. 13	Ev. T. GRAY	Leah JARMAN

1858

Date	Groom	Bride
Sept. 14	Samuel J. MUMFORD	Eliza O.P. BRATTON
Sept. 30	Ira BOWDOIN	Mary Ann DAISEY
Oct. 5	Zachias M. BOWEN	Georgiana TARR
Oct. 7	John LITTLETON	Elizabeth WIMBRO
Oct. 12	James MITCHELL	Margaret PURNELL
Oct. 19	Samuel WARRINGTON	Sally GRAY
Oct. 19	Wm. H. HOLLOWAY	Mary Elizabeth HASTINGS
Nov. 1	William P. HEARN	Lavinia A. PARKER
Nov. 2	William L. PENNEWILL	Lydia Ann SULLIVAN
Nov. 4	Levin T. TOWNSEND	Laura SMITH
Nov. 4	John BYRD	Mary K. SAVAGE
Nov. 5	Andrew CRISP	Julia YOUNG
Nov. 15	John H. ELLIS	Amelia A. RICHARDSON
Nov. 16	James P. CROPPER	Sally Mary QUILLEN
Nov. 18	William T. LEWIS	Elizabeth W. BELL
Nov. 22	Thomas MUMFORD	Aralanta TURNER
Nov. 25	Joshua JOHNSON	Mary E.L. JOHNSON
Nov. 26	George R. FARLOW (of Geo	Hester A. PARSONS
Nov. 30	Littleton T.C. DAVIS	Esther J. TULL
Dec. 1	Thomas TAYLOR	Sarah E. CAUSEY
Dec. 4	John W. FREENEY	Laura Ann FREENEY
Dec. 7	James M. BRATTEN	Hetty A. TURNER
Dec. 7	Peter WHALEY	Catharine TIMMONS
Dec. 7	Severn J.M. PRUITT	Nancy CLAYVILL
Dec. 13	Minos HAMMOND	Mahala WYATT
Dec. 13	Peter J. HOLLAND	Rosa MASON
Dec. 14	Matthias HALES	Eliza BAILEY
Dec. 14	James WILKERSON	Alexene H. BOWEN
Dec. 14	Littleton J. JONES	Mary A. CONNER
Dec. 15	Peter BAKER	Nancy BAKER
Dec. 15	A. Francis CLARK	Margaret A. McALLEN
Dec. 16	John H. ONLEY	Mary Anne COLE
Dec. 20	Soloman WARNER	Arintha D. CORBIN
Dec. 21	James McGREGGER	Mary E. POWELL
Dec. 21	William ANDERSON	Henrietta PAYTON
Dec. 21	Edward O. CLAYVELL	Sallie L. BOWEN
Dec. 21	Benjamin JONES	Hariet HANDCOCK
Dec. 22	Zadok G.W. PURNELL	Mariah C. WHALEY
Dec. 22	Luther WARD	Elizabeth MASON
Dec. 22	Thomas RION	Catharine BLADES
Dec. 25	Samuel SULLIVAN	Mary Jane FREENEY
Dec. 28	Edward MALLETT	Priscilla MALLETT
Dec. 30	James E. JONES	Henrietta CROPPER

1859

Date	Groom	Bride
Jan. 4	William P. SELBY	Mary A. SELBY
Jan. 4	Thomas SMACK	Ellen BOWEN
Jan. 4	William SHAY	Ann Maria COLBOURNE

1859

Date	Groom	Bride
Jan. 4	John S. HICKMAN	Mary E. BOSTON
Jan. 4	Stephen M. GODFREY	Nancy PARSONS
Jan. 11	Esma DAVIS	Ellen CLAYVELL
Jan. 11	Francis HICKMAN	Indiana EVANS
Jan. 11	George CONNER	Pamela SELBY
Jan. 12	William C. SCOTT	Sarah BOWDEN
Jan. 17	William POWELL	Relbaca RILEY
Jan. 18	John HALES	Henrietta HOSIER
Jan. 25	William SHARPLEY	Sarah E. PAYTON
Jan. 26	Emory E. BELL	Henrietta M. TAYLOR
Jan. 31	George W. DIXON	Elizabeth HEARN
Feb. 1	Samuel H. FOOKS	Matilda A. PARKER
Feb. 2	Littleton B. DAVIS	Hester A. MEARS
Feb. 8	Levin DISHAROON	Ellen HALES
Feb, 8	Job JARMAN	Sally TYRE
Feb. 8	Rounds T. PAYNE	Elizabeth C. HANDCOCK
Feb. 9	George K. TRUITT	Sally A. HAMMOND
Feb. 15	Joseph S.B. HALL	Mary C.W. LEWIS
Feb. 15	George W. BISHOP	Cora A. LINDSEY
Feb. 19	Burton JONES	Hetty WELLS
Feb. 22	Garrison S. ADKINS	Melinda T. TRUITT
Feb. 22	Thomas S. LINDSEY	Mary T. COLLINS
Feb. 23	George TARR	Margaret CONNOWAY
Feb. 24	William H. PAYNE	Andasia R. BENNETT
Feb. 26	Aquilla E. HINMAN	Mary E. BROWN
Feb. 27	George W. DOUGHTY	Margaret S. BYRD
March 2	William T. POWLSON	Mary Ann DARBY
March 3	Henry S.C. TRUITT	Sarah E. HITCHINGS
March 5	Henry J.P. DICKINSON	Emily F. LAMDEN
March 12	Avery JESSTER	Eliza BLOXSOM
March 23	John E. HANDCOCK	Mary DEVENX?
March 26	James H. LYNCH	Mary Jane HOLLOWAY
April 4	Benjamin S. PARSONS	Jane COLLINS
April 12	John W. PAYNE	Esther J. PAYNE
April 14	George BRUMBLY	Leah A. HAYMAN
April 21	Francis A. WHITE	Eliza HICKMAN
April 26	Samuel BAKER	Jane BOWEN
April 27	George M. UPSHUR	Sophia H. BOYER
May 2	Thomas DENNIS	Ann M. SMACK
May 3	Christopher C. LLOYD	Mary A.C. McMASTER
May 3	Henry B. JOHNSON	Elizabeth G. HENRY
May 5	Nicholas B. JENKINS	Emily D. MUMFORD
May 9	Levin B. PRICE	Mary I. TURNER
May 18	John J. HILL	Esther H. TAYLOR
May 23	Denard W. JOHNSON	Elizabeth M. PURNELL
May 24	James LEWIS	Sarah LEWIS
May 24	James TRUITT	Elen BUNDICK
May 30	Sylvester J. MARSHALL	Mary F. BYRD

1859

Date	Groom	Bride
June 6	John S. MERRILL	Harriet E. TAYLOR
June 15	Minos H.F. POWELL	Eliza J. LITTLETON
June 19	James A. WINDER	Mary D. HOLT
June 20	George W. CATHELL	Sarah M. BIRCH
June 23	Alfred PINCHIN	Esther SMITH
July 8	Wilson P. MASON	Mary H. DAVIS
July 18	Marshall SMITH	Laura A. HALL
July 21	Zadok O. SELBY	Sally E. MATTHEWS
Aug. 1	Albert W. SHOCKLEY	Ann M. TOWNSEND
Aug. 9	John C. KELLY	Jane HASTING
Aug. 19	James H. GLADDEN	Mary I. BURTON
Aug. 22	William E. BRIMER	Nancy C. JONES
Sept. 3	Robert W. BAILEY	Martha SMITH
Sept. 5	John W.A. TOWNSEND	Elizabeth BURBAGE
Sept. 7	Levin CROPPER	Elizabeth A. RODNEY
Sept. 6	Joshua TOWNSEND	Rebecca WHEALTON
Sept. 19	William J. JONES	Mary E. COFFIN
Sept. 20	Gilbert T.J. ENNIS	Ursula C. DISHAROON
Sept. 22	Isaac A. CONNOWAY	Rosa BOWDEN
Sept. 27	John T. LANK	Eliza BRADFORD
Oct. 3	Levi James CATHELL	Rosa F. JONES
Oct. 4	James A. MELVIN	Elizabeth T. MORRIS
Oct. 11	John REDDEN	Sally A. TARR
Oct. 17	John A. SMITH	Mary C. DORMAN
Oct. 19	William J. TOWNSEND	Eleanor A. PUSEY
Oct. 25	Peter CHERIX	Mary Martha BRITTINGHAM
Oct. 31	Isaac B. CONNER	Elizabeth W. SPENCER
Nov. 8	James T. SMULLEN	Henrietta TAYLOR
Nov. 9	Levin J.M.P. BROADWATER	Olivia H.D. VINCENT
Nov. 14	Ebenezer GRAVENOR	Matilda EVANS
Nov. 15	William I. ROUNDS	Mary A. TRUITT
Nov. 21	Allison T. ROUNDS	Margaret H. PARKER
Nov. 22	Asberry KELLEY	Mary P. ESHAM
Nov. 23	William T. BOWEN	Catharine WIMBRO
Nov. 28	Jesse H. TURNER	Mary C. GRIFFIN
Nov. 29	Nathaniel S. SMITH	Sallie P. JUSTICE
Nov. 30	John E. HAYWARD	Sarah H. CURTIS
Nov. 30	Theadore D. MORRIS	Mary E. WARD
Nov. 30	Lemuel I. TIMMONS	Zipporah BISHOP
Dec. 5	John H. DAVIS	Mary E. QUILLEN
Dec. 5	William D. MACKEY	Laura PITTS
Dec. 6	Harley M. BOSTON	Mary Jane BECKETT
Dec. 6	Littleton D. DAVIS	Charlotte I. PAYNE
Dec. 6	William DYKES	Mary DYKES
Dec. 6	James COTTINGHAM	Matilda J. DEVERUX
Dec. 8	John H. MADDUX	Matilda FURNACE
Dec. 8	Edward A. RICHARDSON	Mary A. BRATTEN
Dec. 12	Daniel J.A. PARSONS	Mariah ADKINS

1859
Dec. 13	Robert W. COLONA	Anne B. PAYTON
Dec. 13	John T.P. MOORE	Sarah BISHOP
Dec. 15	Francis WEST	Henrietta V.C. WEST
Dec. 17	William THORNTON	Emiline CHRISTOPHER
Dec. 17	George M. RICHARDSON	Caroline L. HASTING
Dec. 19	Alfred L. TILGHMAN	Hetty I. COLBOURNE
Dec. 19	John CAREY	Harriet J. TIMMONS
Dec. 20	William W. REESE	Esther B. SAVAGE
Dec. 20	Ira PAYNE	Emma CHAPMAN
Dec. 21	Zadok HOLSTON	Sally C. BOWEN
Dec. 21	Isaac BETTS	Catharine WYATT
Dec. 28	Henry B. HENDERSON	Ursula B. HORSEY
Dec. 30	Thomas O. DONOWAY	Martha E. GODFREY

1860
Jan. 3	Samuel M. GODFREY	Mary E. FARLOW
Jan. 3	John FISHER	Mary E. GRAY
Jan. 3	Robert H. GILLETT	Harriet HENRY
Jan. 4	John P. BISHOP	Wealthy SELBY
Jan. 4	Rider ADKINS	Mariah WILLIAMS
Jan. 9	John H. PRUITT	Barshaba B. BEVANS
Jan. 10	Minos WEBB	Hetty BRADFORD
Jan. 11	Levin ADKINS	Henny CAREY
Jan. 11	Parker D. TRADER	Julia A. BOSTON
Jan. 12	Hugh I. KING	Ann M. COLLINS
Jan. 19	Benjamin T. FIGGS	Mary GODFREY
Jan. 21	John J. TUNNELL	Sinah WARNER
Jan. 21	Oliver H. TAYLOR	Mary KELLY
Jan. 23	James D. BYRD	Sally BYRD
Jan. 24	William H. DENNIS	Mary A. E. HOLLOWAY
Jan. 25	Joseph L. STATON	Louisa TILGHMAN
Jan. 26	Noah BAILEY	Mary J. PHIPPIN
Jan. 26	Washington CHESSER	Caroline MASSEY
Jan. 30	Henry H. HUSTED	Mary WHITE
Jan. 31	John BRUMBLY	Elizabeth CHATHAM
Jan. 31	John R. PURNELL	Emma C. DIRICKSON
Jan. 31	Joshua CHAPMAN	Mary F. PAYTON
Feb. 13	William J. DAVIS	Maria E. PARKER
Feb. 14	Thomas MUMFORD	Mary H. POWELL
Feb. 14	Levin H. CONNER	Sally E. POWELL
Feb. 14	Tomothy RAINE	Laura A.S. WILLIAMS
Feb. 21	Leonard W. HANCOCK	Esther A. KING
Feb. 21	Sydney HANCOCK	Sally JONES
Feb. 23	Elisha DAVIS	Sarah C.M. GRAY
Feb. 24	E. W. EVANS	Anna BISHOP
Feb. 28	William HAMMOND	Ann MARSHALL
Feb. 28	James B.W. PURDUE	Sarah C. PHILLIPS
March 1	Benjamin C. STINGER	Sarah Jane DOWNING

1860

Date	Groom	Bride
March 2	Adam P. BETHARDS	Isabella BURBAGE
March 3	Joshua HOSIER	Rachel RUARK
March 7	Cannon SHORT	Leah J. CAUSEY
March 7	Isaiah POWELL	Susan BIRCH
March 7	Isaac G. PENNEWILL	Nancy E. LEWIS
March 14	Joshua R. BEVANS	Erexine M. STURGIS
March 14	Elijah B. CAREY	Cornelia HUDSON
March 19	William FLEETWOOD	Elizabeth SMITH
March 19	James M. DICKERSON	Drucilla RUARK
March 20	Stephen P. DAVIS	Elizabeth Ann SHOCKLEY
March 20	Amos PETERSON	Mahala A. GRIFFIN
March 24	Alfred L.S. MORAND	Elizabeth LEWIS
March 27	Sampson BURBAGE	Margaret Ann BURBAGE
March 27	Charly H. GODFREY	Julian MASSEY
April 3	Elisha McCABE	Sarah C. MURRAY
April 6	James LEWIS	Sarah DAVIS
April 10	William H. JARMAN	Mary Ann TIMMONS
April 14	Wilson DAVIS	Martha Ann BRITTINGHAM
April 16	Levi TAYLOR	Laura A. POWELL
April 16	James T. DICKINSON	Lizzie H. SAVAGE
April 17	Edward HAMMOND	Rebecca HOSIER
April 17	William H.J. BENNETT	Rosa S. JONES
April 26	James H. SELBY	Mary P. PARKER
May 1	Isaac W. SMITH	Isabella TRUITT
May 4	Joseph S.C. ALLEN	Ann E. BREWINGTON
May 8	John H. CAREY	Mary J. LITTLETON
May 8	Andrew DORFUER	Mary Ann MUMFORD
May 22	Stephen TAYLOR	Matilda WHITNEY
May 23	Thomas GIBBS	Henrietta WILLIAMS
May 28	William T. LAMBERSON	Mary E. REED
May 31	James P. SELBY	Margaret P. ROWLEY
June 5	Charly RICHARDSON	Nelley RILEY
June 7	John PINKETT	Hester HUSTON
June 13	Peter TINDLE	Mary GAULT
June 13	John MATTHEWS	Eliza Jane COLLINS
June 26	Levin W. FIGGS	Hetty M.E. FIGGS
June 26	Edward J.C. BRITTINGHAM	Mary J. BRITTINGHAM
July 2	William P. JONES	Margaret R. CONNAWAY
July 2	Stephen J. BLADES	Mary A.E. MARCHANT
July 2	Randall SMULLEN	Adeline RUARK
July 13	Asa SELBY	Elizabeth DAVIS
July 23	Edward J. BALL	Harriet A. TREHEARNE
July 30	James SELBY	Sarah COLLYER
July 31	James T. NOCK	Drucilla DRYDEN
July 31	Joshua HUDSON	Leah JESTER
Aug. 13	William H. BRITTINGHAM	Mary E. LEWIS
Aug. 14	Dowe MISTER	Susan AYERS
Aug. 29	Josiah H. BAILEY	Mary G. ADKINS

1860

Date	Groom	Bride
Sept. 3	Isaac J. LEWIS	Martha C. LITTLETON
Sept. 4	Willliam H. ROSS	Dolly A. RIGGIN
Sept. 6	Henry S. NELSON	Elizabeth A. R. TOWNSEND
Sept. 11	William S.C. POLK	Margaret POWELL
Sept. 12	Willimore F. TARR	Rosetta POWELL
Sept. 17	Lorenzo D. SHOCKLEY	Elizabeth J. LOKEY
Sept. 19	William TAYLOR	Sally Ann MILES
Sept. 20	Gilly BRADFORD	Sally E. ELLIS
Sept. 24	William J. GRAY	Mary A. DICKERSON
Sept 24	John J. FISHER	Mary J. FISHER
Sept. 26	Parker J. HICKMAN	Mary A. HICKMAN
Sept. 27	William L.P. BOWEN	Sally L. MASSEY
Oct. 2	Kendal TRUITT	Martha E. DICKERSON
Oct. 2	Joseph W. HEARN	Elizabeth MILLER
Oct. 9	Littleton JUSTICE	Mary MISTER
Oct. 9	James MORRIS	Mary M. ADKINS
Oct. 10	James MALLETT	Ann Maria HUDSON
Oct. 23	Jacob U. MILLS	Hester J. MADDUX
Oct. 24	Eyedlite HUDSON	Purdy LYNCH
Oct. 25	John NICHOLSON	Leah J. ELLIS
Oct. 25	Joseph COFFIN	Ellen EVANS
Oct. 25	Francis J. ROSS	Sarah M. POWELL
Nov. 1	Hamilton VICKERS	Laura J. BOWEN
Nov. 2	Alfred H. BENSON	Leah BOSTON
Nov. 9	Henry P. LEWIS	Gatty J. WHITE
Nov. 12	Daniel L. FLEMMING	Emma S. FARROW
Nov. 15	John F. PUSEY	Mary Ellen DUKES
Nov. 16	William HOLLAND	Mary JOHNSON
Nov. 20	Elisha HALL	Sarah STURGIS
Nov. 20	Levi T. ELLIOTT	Amelia A. FREENY
Nov. 20	William T. BOWEN	Mary A. BAKER
Nov. 20	Edward K. B. LANKFORD	Olivia E. ADREAN ?
Nov. 26	John S. PARKER	Matilda E. BRITTINGHAM
Dec. 5	George W. PORTER	Tabitha BLADES
Dec. 10	William J. FITCHETT	Georgianna WIDGEON
Dec. 13	Valentine DENNIS	Sally BECKETT
Dec. 17	Uriah BUTLER	Esther EWELL
Dec. 18	Thomas BRATTEN	Elizabeth TRUITT
Dec. 18	James REDDEN	Elizabeth MITCHELL
Dec. 18	Stephen SCOTT	Elizabeth PURNELL
Dec. 19	Elijah M. POWELL	Rosa M. HOLLAND
Dec. 19	Samuel REED	Sally M. MASSEY
Dec. 20	Leonard JARMAN	Mary Jane LEWIS
Dec. 22	Mitchell WATSON	Rosetta PILCHARD
Dec. 25	Hiram WEBB	Hetty GIBBS
Dec. 25	William TARR	Harriet STURGIS

1861

Date	Groom	Bride
Jan. 1	Levi D. GORDY	Clarissa TRUITT
Jan. 1	James JARMAN	Priscilla DENNIS
Jan. 2	John W. SELBY	Mary Priscilla TAYLOR
Jan. 2	George POWELL	Elizabeth BOWEN
Jan. 2	Elijah FREENY	Maria Ellen FOOKS
Jan. 3	Henry CLAYVELL	Mary Esther STURGIS
Jan. 7	Stephen HILL	Elizabeth TAYLOR
Jan. 7	William T. BOSTON	Leah E. PAYNE
Jan. 7	Elzy LEONARD	Sally A. LEONARD
Jan. 8	William T. DAVIS	Clarinda F. HAMMOND
Jan. 8	William H. WILSON	Leah M. PUSEY
Jan. 8	Josiah AYDELOTTE	Elizabeth MADLOCK
Jan. 14	George W. LAYFIELD	Laura A. COLLINS
Jan. 15	Thorogood TAYLOR	Sallie BURTON
Jan. 15	Hillary BAILEY	Mary E. PARSONS
Jan. 16	Zadok RICHARDSON	Cordella HOLSTON
Jan. 21	William WYATT	Mary BAKER
Jan. 22	Moses WARD	Sally JOHNSON
Jan. 22	Allison GRAVENOR	Martha H. PURNELL
Jan. 22	Peram E. JONES	Eliza M. TULL
Jan. 23	Ara PENNEVILLE	Mary Ann RICHARDSON
Jan. 23	Levin T. PUSEY	Sarah E. MARSHALL
Jan. 23	George MALLET	Catharine CHERICKS
Jan. 29	Thomas MASON	Louisa BOWDON
Jan. 29	James RILEY	Sarah M. HOLSTON
Feb. 1	William J. ADAMS	Elizabeth WALKER
Feb. 1	Jonithan G. BEACH	Mary E. GORDY
Feb. 5	Elijah AYDELOTT	Aralanta CLAYVELL
Feb. 9	John W. LAWS	Jane MESSICK
Feb. 9	William E. CRISP	Martha DRYDEN
Feb. 9	John W. WINDER	Mary F. TAYLOR
Feb. 11	John TATMAN	Elizabeth PILCHARD
Feb. 11	Wolsy B. HOPKINS	Eliza A. DALE
Feb. 12	Moses U. JONES	Henrietta DAVIS
Feb. 12	George W. GORDY	Mary A. PUSEY
Feb. 12	Joseph CAREY	Julia C. HAMBLIN
Feb. 12	Thomas P. ROUNDS	Catharine BISHOP
Feb. 19	John M. JONES	Ellen A. STURGIS
Feb. 26	John BURK	Louisa MADDUX
Feb. 26	John SMITH	Elizabeth POWELL
Feb. 26	George BISHOP	Mary HASTINGS
Feb. 26	Joshua T. GODFREY	Louesa ENNIS
March 5	Frederic J. DUKES	Martha C. JONES
March 6	Jesse HOVINGTON	Hester E. PARKER
March 8	Samuel BAKER	Matilda ENNIS
March 18	Thomas C. MORRIS	Elizie A. FOOKS
March 26	Ebenezer DRISKELL	Julia C. BAKER
March 28	William H. JONES	Elizabeth PARSONS

1861

Date	Groom	Bride
April 3	Henry C. LINDSEY	Amanda TOWNSEND
April 9	Ephraim W. BRITTINGHAM	Emiline E. TURNER
April 18	Charles TARR	Mary BLADES
April 23	Daniel J. BETHARDS	Miranda LITTLETON
April 23	Francis J. PURNELL	Sarah A. TAYLOR
May 1	John Handy BURBAGE	Nancy PAYNE
May 4	George HILL	Sally W. BISHOP
May 9	Albert J. MERRILL	Virginia A. QUINN
May 13	Francis Marion SLEMONS	Martha A.E. MORRIS
May 14	Edward WHITE	Mary BURBAGE
May 14	Thomas DUBERLY	Hetty JACKSON
May 14	Rowland F. BEVANS	Sallie E. POWELL
May 14	Robert MUMFORD	Elizabeth HOLLOWAY
May 14	John HARTHWAY	Sarah Ann KELPIN
May 17	Alfred LEWIS	Rebecca A. ADAMS
May 29	Joseph RICHARDSON	Mary Ann DEVEREUX
June 1	James BIRK	Aurelia W. WHITE
June 3	Luke LEWIS	Elizabeth LEWIS
June 8	Henry W. CLAYVILLE	Mary TURNTON
June 12	William H. ELLIS	Mary J. ADKINS
June 19	George W. STATON	Mary E. BRITTINGHAM
June 19	John OWENS	Elizabeth ELLIOTT
July 3	Jesse HOLLAND	Eliza A. GAULT
July 8	William B. TIMMONS	Elizabeth POWELL
Aug. 13	Benjamin T. JOHNSON	Margaret W. TRUITT
Aug. 20	Benjamin G. SPENCER	Henrietta S. BARNES
Sept. 2	Thomas WHITE	Louisa FOOKS
Sept. 3	Edward BRITTINGHAM	Louisa HARDISH
Sept. 24	Uriah OWENS	Susan C. BRIDDELL
Oct. 1	Robert W. ELLIS	Mary Elizabeth PARSONS
Oct. 8	Daniel HOLLOWAY	Margaret E. LAW
Oct. 10	Samuel M. HUDSON	Mary E. HUDSON
Oct. 12	Jonathan FAULKNER	Alberta H. HALL
Oct. 16	William C. BRATTEN	Priscilla A. HUDSON
Oct. 21	William BENSON	Elizabeth SNEAD
Oct. 23	John O. PALMER	Mary Ann WARREN
Oct. 28	Emerson G. POLK	Addie O. DRYDEN
Oct. 30	James T.H. SPENCER	Anna M. BARNES
Nov. 4	Edward C.H. ADKINS	Mary H. BAILEY
Nov. 12	Samuel T. SCHOOLFIELD	Mary S. BARNES
Nov. 12	Joshua R. BEVANS	Emily R. TOWNSEND
Nov. 19	Isaac LAMBERSON	Elizabeth TOWNSEND
Nov, 19	Levin HILL	Mary HOWARD
Nov. 19	Burton JONES	Sarah A, MELVIN
Nov. 25	Lemuel SHOWELL	Annie B. JACOBS
Nov. 26	James RUARK	Emeline JOHNSON
Nov. 27	Levin J. MOORE	Mary C. HAMMOND
Dec. 3	John T. FINNEY	Bettie A. KELLAM

1861

Date	Groom	Bride
Dec. 3	James C. MAPP	Saphronia A. MEARS
Dec. 3	William C. BONNEWILL	Amelia P. HANDCOCK
Dec. 3	Henry H. MERRILL	Anne PRINROSE
Dec. 3	Joshua MORRIS	Drucilla GODFREY
Dec. 3	Allen D. SPENCER	Sarah P. KING
Dec. 3	Zadok P. HENRY Jr.	Elizabeth DIRICKSON
Dec. 4	Charles A. HURLEY	Harriet CROPPER
Dec. 9	George H. RIGGIN	Emily F. HAYMAN
Dec. 9	John POWELL	Hettie H. WILLIAMS
Dec. 9	William S. FITCHETT	Sophia CAREY
Dec. 10	Thomas ADKINS	Eliza E. MORRIS
Dec. 10	Jonhn T. COLLINS	Amelia A.E. LAMBERSON
Dec. 10	Joshua HALL	Martha WHITTINGTON
Dec. 10	Sealamore BLACKSON	Jemina ADAMS
Dec. 11	Alfred J. TAYLOR	Hetty C. PARKS
Dec. 12	John B. WILLIAMS	Laura S. FITCHET
Dec. 16	Franklin STEVENSON	Alexine MILLER
Dec. 17	Wrixham E. PILCHARD	Emma C. JONES
Dec. 17	Elijah R. FIGGS	Mary E. POWELL
Dec. 18	William G. NICHOLSON	Rachel C. WILKINS
Dec. 18	Miles TULL	Ann HUDSON
Dec. 20	John K. POWELL	Martha E. LITTLETON
Dec. 23	David H. STRAUGHN	Mary Q. GLADDEN
Dec. 23	William J. LEWIS	Margaret HINDMAN
Dec. 24	Soloman TULL	Mary POPE
Dec. 25	John FISHER	Jane GRAY
Dec. 25	Daniel BETTS	Sarah C. BETTS
Dec. 26	Elias PETTIT	Sally JOHNSON

1862

Date	Groom	Bride
Jan. 4	Daniel E. HASTINGS	Amelia H. PARSONS
Jan. 7	Levin PARSONS	Sarah Jane PRIOR
Jan. 8	John FREEMAN	Eliza BRITTINGHAM
Jan. 8	Francis L. JARMAN	Charlotte Ann JACKSON
Jan. 11	John H. SMITH	Mary C. BRITTINGHAM
Jan. 11	John M. RAYNE	Rosina Andasia JARMAN
Jan. 13	John H. McNAMAR	Mary A. HARRIS
Jan. 15	George I. TRUITT	Clarasa M. LEWIS
Jan. 15	Charles W.B. MARSHALL	Georgianna C. PURNELL
Jan. 15	George PRIOR	Mary W. TOWNSEND
Jan. 15	John W. PAYTON	Mary E. HOLLAND
Jan. 16	John W. TURLINGTON	Amanda O. FEDDEMAN
Jan. 20	John P. QUILLIN	Sarah E. TAYLOR
Jan. 21	Littleton S. HENDERSON	Amelia A. STEPHENS
Jan. 22	Stephen P. TIMMONS	Martha E. BETHARDS
Jan. 22	William P. PRIOR	Sally A. MADDUX
Jan. 22	Elijah POWELL	Drucilla W. HUDSON
Jan. 22	Lemuel E. TRUITT	Sarah L. DAVIS

1862

Date	Groom	Bride
Jan. 23	Jesse BOWDEN	Irena HUDSON
Jan. 25	Geogre B. TAYLOR	Pattie A. DUNTON
Jan. 28	William WARRINGTON	Emily A. POWELL
Jan. 30	George SHARPLEY	Maria SMACK
Jan. 31	Alfred TRADER	Mary Ann BAILEY
Feb. 3	James CAUSEY	Harriet W. LOKEY
Feb. 3	James PORTER	Margaret DAVIS
Feb. 3	William H. MARSHALL	Margaret J. ROSS
Feb. 3	Samuel J. MASSEY	Hetty L. LYNCH
Feb. 4	William MATTHEWS	Catharine J. HOSIER
Feb. 4	John T. TIMMONS	Martha WILKINS
Feb. 5	Levin T.A. POWELL	Sophia E. CAUSEY
Feb. 10	Peter McCAIN	Sarah E. FISHER
Feb. 11	Selby BRADFORD	Jane WILKINS
Feb. 15	John H. PARKER	Matilda RIGGIN
Feb. 15	George W. CONKLIN	Josephine E.B. EWELL
Feb. 17	William H.H. COPES	Sallie A. CUTLER
Feb. 18	Zadok RICHARDSON	Adaliza HOLSTON
Feb. 20	Samuel C. BUNTING	Mary H. TRADER
Feb. 25	George W. WALKER	Maggie E. WEST
Feb. 25	Lemuel P. COLLINS	Sallie E. PURNELL
Feb. 28	Joseph J. DEVERAUX	Henrietta B. BEVANS
March 10	George W. PARSONS	Theodosia CAUSEY
March 19	Esma P. SMULLEN	Rhoda J. ESHAM
March 24	Levin S. HENDERSON	Emily Frances HOWARD
March 26	Dr. Hillary R. PITTS	Mary Ann COLLINS
March 30	George BAKER	Henrietta COSTON
April 9	John P. PUSEY	Nancy COLBOURNE
April 22	Quinton SHOCKLEY	Sally E. PARKER
April 22	Avary ROBINSON	Nancy RICHARDSON
May 10	John S. PRUITT	Mary Ann CLAYVILLE
May 20	Joseph BOWEN	Martha Jane DALE
May 30	Purnell B. CAREY	Tabitha WHITE
June 2	James A. VENABLES	Mary E. LEONARD
June 10	John H. KELLEY	Milly ADKINS
June 11	James W. RIDER	Margaret A. MUMFORD
June 11	John E. MASON	Levina H. JONES
June 24	William H. DENNIS	Mary WHEALTON
June 26	James P. SELBY	Esther J. MILLER
June 30	Lambert J. QUILLEN	Sarah E. LEKITTS
July 30	Samuel GALE	Harriet Hester LAMBDEN
July 21	William L. SMITH	Margaret A. DENNIS
July 21	Jehu PARSONS	Sally M. BOWEN
July 22	George LAYFIELD	Maria J. HASTINGS
July 23	Dr James B. B. PURNELL	Elizabeth K. AYRES
July 28	George PRUITT	Sarah C. BAKER
July 29	William BRITTINGHAM	Amanda BRITTINGHAM
July 29	Henry R. CLAYTON	Sallie M. REID

1862

Date	Groom	Bride
Aug. 1	Edward M. GUNTER	Malissa J. JOHNSON
Aug. 2	John Thomas RICHARDSON	Mary Ann TAYLOR
Aug. 12	Jesse P. WILKERSON	Emily S. ARDIS
Aug. 13	John TRADER	Eliza MARSHALL
Aug. 27	William A. DAVIS	Sallie TRUITT
Sept. 9	Thomas Z. JOHNSON	Elizabeth M. BEYER
Sept. 16	William M. BROADWATER	Margaret A. HUSTON
Sept. 18	Michael M. BRADY	Mary G. WHEALTON
Sept. 25	Francis BLADES	Cora Ann HUDSON
Sept. 19	Stephen GOSWELLING	Hester Jane HUDSON
Oct. 1	Samuel T.P. PORTER	Eliza BENSON
Oct. 2	George C. CLAYVILLE	Mary E. HOLLAND
Oct. 2	Victor A. MAPP	Maggie DUNTON
Oct. 2	William T. MAPP	Annie S. ?
Oct. 2	Frederic FLOYD	Indiana F. MAPP
Oct. 6	Levin D. MADDUX	Leah Ann ELZEY
Oct. 8	Jesse GRAY	Leah J. DENNIS
Oct. 14	William C. PRUITT	Louesa G. BRIDDELL
Oct. 15	William H. BRIDDELL	Mary Priscilla NELSON
Oct. 16	George W. BROWN	Margaret J. HOLLAND
Oct. 20	James RICHARDSON	Hulda ELLIOTT
Oct. 23	Benjamin FOOKS	Mary E. CAUSEY
Oct. 29	George SMACK	Ibba Jane SHOCKLEY
Oct. 29	Arthur T. MEARS	Mary E. McMATH
Oct. 29	Wm. E. MAPP	Catharine S. AMES
Nov. 3	James H. DORMAN	Amelia SELBY
Nov. 3	Stephen McDANIEL	Mary BRITTINGHAM
Nov. 4	Josephus CHATHAM	Drucilla MESSICK
Nov. 6	James TINDALL	Susan Ann LEWIS
Nov. 18	John S. DRISCAL	Mary Jane DENNIS
Nov. 18	William J. STURGIS	Henrietta TARR
Nov. 20	Joseph L. MILLS	Marietta DICKINSON
Nov. 22	John B. COLLINS	Amanda J.R. SMITH
Nov. 24	Josiah ADKINS	Eliza A. LEWIS
Nov. 24	Joseph J. LEWIS	Eliza E. DAVIS
Dec. 3	John H. CONNELLEY	Rebecca E.C. ADKINS
Dec. 4	Soloman P. EWELL	Laura C. TAYLOR
Dec. 8	Kibble J. BROWN	Matilda SMITH
Dec. 8	Henry MORRIS	Leah Jane POLLITT
Dec. 9	Frederic Edward WARD	Rachell E. MINSON
Dec. 9	Joseph Thomas PALMER	Martha Jane LAYFIELD
Dec. 15	John J. EVANS	Margaret Ellen DAVIS
Dec. 15	Chalres W. PARKER	Fanny H. SMITH
Dec. 16	John J. BOUNDS	Tricy Eleanor TOWNSEND
Dec. 16	Elijah W. MORRIS	Fane FOOKS
Dec. 17	John W. HYSLOP	Molly C. COLONA
Dec. 17	Jesse A. BENSON	Mary J. COARD
Dec. 18	Henry E. BYRD	Martha J. MATTHEWS

1862			
Dec. 22		William WATSON	Mary Eliazabeth TRADER
Dec. 23		William PILCHARD	Sally MASON
Dec. 24		Samuel MILBOURNE	Aurena PILCHARD
Dec. 24		William B.L. BRITTINGHAM	Caroline TOWNSEND
Dec. 26		Henry J. WHEATLEY	Sarah Elizabeth LONG
Dec. 27		John E. JOHNSON	Mary E. MAPP
Dec. 29		Stephen R. HAYMAN	Louisa D. PUSEY
Dec. 29		Littleton T. DRYDEN	Charlotte E. BOWEN
Dec. 30		James BURBAGE	Milly BURBAGE
Dec. 30		John W.H. NOCK	Mary A. FISHER
1863			
Jan. 6		Milbourne S. LEWIS	Drucilla TOWNSEND
Jan. 6		Joseph H. HEBARD	Hester J. WEST
Jan. 7		William H. ADKINS	Amelia Jane WEBB
Jan. 9		Riley J. SHOCKLEY	Henny M. ELLIS
Jan. 10		Ebenezer WHITE	Mary Jane MILLS
Jan. 14		John B. RICHARDS	Sarah Elizabeth WILLIAMS
Jan. 14		James S. WILLIAMS	Margaret Ann DAVIDSON
Jan. 20		James H. PORTER	Laura A. HANCOCK
Jan. 20		Ebenezer DENNIS	Nancy D. FARLOW
Jan. 20		Stringer HOLLAND	Hetty GRAY
Jan. 20		George T. COLLINS	Salley E. POWELL
Jan. 22		John W. BOWEN	Elizabeth BISHOP
Jan. 24		Thomas H. WHITE	Margaret E. SEARS
Jan. 26		Levin W. PARKER	Eliza E. OLIPHANT
Jan. 27		Edward T. STANT	Augenotte SILVERTHORN
Jan. 27		Josiah TOWNSEND	Lucretia REDISH
Jan. 27		John J. TAYLOR	Ellen PRICE
Jan. 29		Thomas S. TOWNSEND	Elizabeth PENNEWILL
Feb. 2		Prieson P. TOWNSEND	Narcissa PUSEY
Feb. 3		George GUTHERY	Ann Maria WHITE
Feb. 3		Andrew HANDCOCK	Jane YOUNG
Feb. 7		Joshua T. BUTLER	Elizabeth BRITTINGHAM
Feb. 9		James A. PHILLIPS	Emma V. PARSONS
Feb. 12		James CARTER	Sarah DORMAN
Feb. 12		George W. SMITH	Sibbil S. HOPE
Feb. 13		Lemuel D. GORDY	Mary C. SMITH
Feb. 17		Elisha T. BUNTING	Nancy C. SELBY
Feb. 18		Levin SCOTT	Sally Ann BRITTINGHAM
Feb. 24		Seth CAUSEY	Mary E. LEONARD
March 2		Dugal S. BURTON	Rachel A. DUNCAN
March 12		George BLOXOM	Nancy BULL
March 16		Peter BONAWELL	Drucilla MILES
March 17		Stephen HADDER	Rebecca REED
March 18		Alfred FLEMMING	Mary Ann BUTLER
March 24		Benjamin WARD	Olevia REDDEN
March 24		Samuel J. PAYNE	Laura BURBAGE

1863

Date	Groom	Bride
March 24	George H. EVANS	Mary E. DRYDEN
March 24	Severn BRITTINGHAM	Elizabeth S. DOUGHTY
March 31	Francis J. BARNES	Sarah E. A. MERRILL
April 10	Willliam TAYLOR	Lavinia JARMAN
April 13	Joshua J. DAVIS	Mary E. SHOCKLEY
April 20	John REDDISH	Sally A. STATEN
April 30	James T. NOCK	Mary MARSHALL
May 4	William S. MATTHEWS	Sarah S. BERRY
May 5	David W. GAULT	Sally Mary BAKER
May 11	Lambert SMULLEN	Elizabeth CAUSEY
May 19	Stephen WILKERSON	Ann BALL
May 21	Levin S. JAMES	Maggie S. DUNTON
May 29	William JESTER	Emily WATSON
May 30	John O. MILLS	Mary Ann SELBY
June 1	Minos B. WEST	Hetty Ann RUARK
June 4	Edward L. PARRAMORE	Harriet E.P. SMITH
June 8	Samuel RUARK	Mary Ann TIMMONS
June 30	William H. COLBOURNE	Margaret J. GORDY
July 1	James DAVIS	Mary HUDSON
July 1	George J. NORTHAM	Mary Ann NOCK
July 14	James A. SMITH	Ella E. KELLAM
July 21	Thomas E. WILLIAMS	Mary C. MADDUX
Aug. 8	Sidney J. BISHOP	Maria Gracia W. TUERO
Aug. 11	Josiah TOWNSEND	Mary Jane VANDOM
Aug. 17	William JONES	Priscilla DRYDEN
Aug. 21	Henry Emerson DENNIS	Alexine N. BRICKHOUSE
Aug. 21	Willliam B. MORRIS	Sarah C. LITTLETON
Aug. 31	Levi M. LAMBERSON	Catharine A. BLADES
Sept. 1	George E. BRITTINGHAM	Hester A. TIMMONS
Sept. 1	Arthur J. TURLINGTON	Charlotte E. FIELDS
Sept. 1	Thomas PETIT	Louellen CARMINE
Sept. 3	William B. BRATTEN	Martha J. PARKER
Sept. 8	Covington WINGATE	Sally ELLIOTT
Sept. 16	Robert PITTS	Julia A.P. MASSEY
Sept. 18	James J. BARRETT	Catharine CARROLL
Sept. 28	Joseph W. MEARS	Sarah E. BULL
Sept. 29	Joseph WALLER	Leah Jane NICHOLS
Sept. 30	Joseph H. TOWNSEND	Comfort J. COWLEY
Oct. 3	Peter H. DONAWAY	Mary WELLS
Oct. 8	Lemuel CLARKE	Mary Elizabeth DAVIS
Oct. 8	Abselon PHIPPS	Emma BOWDEN
Oct. 15	Purnell F. OUTEN	Martha E. WALKER
Oct. 20	Jacob STEVENSON	Grace YOUNG
Oct. 28	Rufus J.M. DENNIS	Sally A. SELBY
Oct. 28	James W. EDMONDS	Mollie A.B. ASHBEY
Oct. 31	Charley GUTHERY	Hannah RUARK
Nov. 2	Albert S. STEVENS	Mary E. TRUITT
Nov. 10	William T. BULLIN	Sarah V. DRYDEN

1863		
Nov. 10	Robert J. SILVERTHORN	Mary J. FIELDS
Nov. 13	Washington MATTHEWS	Caroline HARMAN
Nov. 14	John WARD	Julia BISHOP
Nov. 16	Milbourn A. LAYTON	Charlotte E. LEWIS
Nov. 23	Albert I. BRITTINGHAM	Lizzie Ayres COFFIN
Nov. 24	John J. PALMER	Mary E. SAVAGE
Nov. 25	Hiram W. FARLOW	Theodosia BRITTINGHAM
Nov. 30	Levin H. DAVIS	Martha A. PARSONS
Dec. 2	Jeromiah MARSHALL	Maria A. CROCKETT
Dec. 2	William J. BALL	Elizabeth A. LIVINGSTON
Dec. 2	John R. HALL	Emily D. CAREY
Dec. 2	Edwin F. CAUSEY	Margaret D. COX
Dec. 2	William W. QUINN	Mary C. CLARKE
Dec. 10	Garrett W. CLIFTON	Lizzie A. LAWS
Dec. 12	Peter LIVINGSTON	Louisa K. DIXON
Dec. 12	Isaac HADDOC	Emeline SMACK
Dec. 14	James P. BURROUGHS	Delilah A. PURNELL
Dec. 15	Samuel HOUSTON	Eleanor CROPPER
Dec. 15	Henry H. HAMBLIN	Jane CAMPBELL
Dec. 15	Joshua E. CAREY	Julia A. FASSITT
Dec. 16	Rowland J. EVANS	Amanda P. CAUSEY
Dec. 16	Isaac I. FREEMAN	Nancy C. QUILLEN
Dec. 17	Benj. F. NOTTINGHAM	Sophia S. THOMAS
Dec. 18	Warren I. HASTY	Charlotte A. PARKER
Dec. 21	John HADDOCK	Jane SMACK
Dec. 22	Danl W. COLBOURNE	Mahala E. FIGGS
Dec. 22	Tingle HAMBLIN	Sarah M. TAYLOR
Dec. 22	Samuel KELLY	Sarah Annn GORE
Dec. 22	Thomas PILCHARD	Elizabeth HANCOCK
Dec. 28	Joshua W. HASTY	Mary E. MASSEY
Dec. 28	Samuel J. COWLEY	Margaret D. LEWIS
Dec. 30	Geo W. FOOKS	Mary W. LAYFIELD
Dec. 30	John H. STEVENSON	Annie H.L. COTTINGHAM

1864		
Jan. 4	Humphrey SMULLEN	Sally SMULLEN
Jan. 4	Samuel WARD	Elizabeth TAYLOR
Jan. 4	Benj F. HOLADAY	Susan G. TRADER
Jan. 5	Washington TINDAL	Charlotte A. THOMAS
Jan. 6	Peter TARR	Sally MASON
Jan. 9	Jesse J. FIGGS	Martha PARSONS
Jan. 11	Major J. WATSON	Mary E. WILKERSON
Jan. 12	Isaac YOUNG	Sallie M. EWELL
Jan. 12	Sophrius BLADES	Cora Ann NICHOLS
Jan. 12	Jenkins TIMMONS	Rachel Ann JARMAN
Jan. 12	Benjamin D. SMITH	Mary J. W. PARKER
Jan. 12	Major C. WILLIAMS	Maria E. PARKER
Jan. 12	Purnell M. PENNEWILL	Hetty Amelia JACKSON

1864

Date	Groom	Bride
Jan. 13	Wm H. LEWIS	Mary W. LANKFORD
Jan. 15	Isaac T. DRYDEN	Cordelia E. ANDERSON
Jan. 18	Francis E. FISHER	Ann Mariah FREEMAN
Jan. 19	James HOLDZKOM	Emma R. COLLINS
Jan. 19	Thomas N. W. CANNON	Mary H. BOWEN
Jan. 19	James W.M.W. RICHARDSON	Mary Elizabeth SCOTT
Jan. 19	Thomas P. HANCOCK	Mary A. TRUITT
Jan. 25	John KELLY	Gertrude RUARK
Jan. 26	George PRUITT	Emma RITCHIE
Jan. 26	Samuel H. ADAMS	Sallie H. DRYDEN
Feb. 1	James L. WILKINS	Julia J. PARSONS
Feb. 2	John W. PARSONS	Mary J. HASTINGS
Feb. 2	Lemuel DAVIS	Rhoda LEWIS
Feb. 4	George PARSONS	Susan E. JOHNSON
Feb. 8	John H. DRYDEN	Mary O. BOSTON
Feb. 13	William DOWNS	Mary H. EVANS
Feb. 13	J.W. H. TAYLOR	Mary A. HOPKINS
Feb. 13	William H. WALTERS	Emily E. COLBOURN
Feb. 16	Thomas BOSTON	Sallie A. SCHOOLFIELD
Feb. 16	Joseph QUILLEN	Sarah POWELL
Feb. 16	Edward J. QUILLIN	Emeline RODNEY
Feb. 16	James H. VINCENT	Sarah E. TULL
Feb. 22	William BAILEY	Margaret BRATTEN
Feb. 23	George L. PARSONS	Gertrude E. DENNIS
Feb. 27	James BRUMBLY	Mary E. LIVINGSTON
Feb. 29	Raymond LEWIS	Sarah SCOTT
Feb. 29	Edward LOW	Clara MESSICK
March 1	Levi J. BRIMER	Rachael A. RICHARDSON
March 2	Hiram J. AKE	Mary G. HOLLOWAY
March 7	William L. TAYLOR	Mary E. FASSITT
March 8	Hugh S. STEVENSON	Jane C. BAILEY
March 11	Rufus T. SMITH	Charlotte E. BRITTINGHAM
March 12	Francis P. JONES	Edith E. LIVINGSTON
March 14	Francis A. HAYMAN	Mary E. BROWN
March 14	Charles CLARKE	Sarah TIMMONS
March 15	Thomas H. KELLY	Martha J. RICHARDSON
March 17	Albert G. MARSHALL	Julia T. FOOKS
March 22	Samuel CHAPMAN	Jane PAYTON
March 28	Thomas J. TREHEARN	Harriet A. ATKINSON
March 28	Webster M. STRAYER	Martha A. BEVANS
April 1	Southey J. TAYLOR	Sarah COVINGTON
April 4	Cyrus NEAL	Mary HENDERSON
April 4	Caleb WYATT	Ellen DENNIS
April 6	Geo W. ESHAM	A.E. CHATHAM
April 18	James T. BOWEN	Laura A. POWELL
April 20	Moses J. HUDSON	Emma JONES
April 20	Sydney LANE	Cathareine POWELL
April 21	Wm W. THORINGTON	Susan A. CONAWAY

1864

Date	Groom	Bride
April 26	Wm B. COLGAN	Mary C. PARKER
April 28	William WEST	Priscilla A. TRUITT
April 28	William GILROY	Mary Elizabeth BIRCH
April 30	Israel TOWNSEND	Rebecca C. TRACY
May 24	William DENNIS	Sophia ADKINS
June 9	Louis POLLITT	Mary A. TAYLOR
June 21	William CROPPER	Sarah JONES
July 1	Joshua J. HOLLOWAY	Phoebe E. LAYFIELD
July 5	Severn F. WILLIAMS	Emily H. TURPIN
July 6	Charles P. MUMFORD	Ellen GODFREY
July 12	Thomas H. RICHIE	Octava WARD
July 26	Brinkley F. ELLIOTT	Elizabeth J. HASTINGS
July 28	Samuel D. MELVIN	Sarah V. AYDELOTT
Aug. 1	Ephraim W. DENNIS	Elizabeth Ann PARSONS
Aug. 2	Edward H. LAMBDEN	Virginia BOHM
Aug. 12	Joseph E. BROADWATER	Elizabeth W. TAYLOR
Aug. 15	James H. PARSONS	Mary A. PENNEWILL
Aug. 16	Albert BOWEN	Ann Maria DAVIS
Aug. 22	Peter W. HANCOCK	Letitia J. REDDEN
Aug. 23	Joseph HASTINGS	Harriet E. HALL
Aug. 24	Levin TOWNSEND	Maria C. HAYMAN
Aug. 25	Alexander MALONE	Catharine POLLET
Aug. 26	Samuel J. REGISTER	Ellen A.R. JARVIS
Aug. 29	Mardecal J. POWELL	Sarah C. EVANS
Aug. 31	Stephen D. BOWDEN	Ann Maria SHOCKLEY
Sept. 5	James B. ROBINS	Ellen A. PURNELL
Sept. 8	John CLARK	Jane JONES
Sept. 14	Edward J. DAVIS	Minerva G. DAVIS
Sept. 28	Samuel E. ADKINS	Clarissa J. MORRIS
Oct. 1	William FOOKS	Elizabeth J. DRYDEN
Oct. 3	James W. HOLLAND	Sarah PARSONS
Oct. 3	William BLOODGOOD	Ida SLOCOMB
Oct. 6	John T. SHARPLEY	Elizabeth PAYNE
Oct. 11	James LITTLETON	Clarissa PARSONS
Oct. 15	James B. MIDDLETON	Hetty C. DAVIS
Oct. 18	Brinkley A. HEARN	Eliza J. WILLIAMS
Oct. 18	George R. DALLY	Maria E. BELOTE
Oct. 31	Noah R. ADKINS	Sarah E. HASTINGS
Nov. 10	James H. DISHAROON	Rena HASTINGS
Nov. 10	Edward TAYLOR	Harriet J. TULL
Nov. 22	Wm L. BROWN	Elizabeth BETTS
Nov. 23	James T. TULL	Margaret E. RIGGIN
Nov. 24	Thomas BOWEN	Cornelia JARMAN
Nov. 26	Peter WATSON	Mary E. TAYLOR
Nov. 29	Alexander LORD	Mary C. PARKER
Nov. 29	James DISHAROON	Rebecca E. BRITTINGHAM
Nov. 29	Leonard J. BLADES	Mary A. V. LANDING
Dec. 3	David S. LEWIS	Mary E. GORDY

1864			
Dec. 7		James S. PRIMROSE	Amelia STEVENSON
Dec. 7		Levin J. FEDDEMAN	C.C. JONES
Dec. 7		Asa TAYLOR	Rosa A. JUSTICE
Dec. 10		John W. MESSICK	Josephine HUGHES
Dec. 12		James DURHAM	Mary W. SWIFT
Dec. 12		Wm MASSEY	Sarah BRITTINGHAM
Dec. 12		Benj. DAVIS	Sarah J. TARR
Dec. 15		Martin KELLY	Elizabeth W. GIBB
Dec. 19		Levin TULL	Sarah Jane GODFREY
Dec. 20		Elisha Q. HOLLOWAY	Sarah J. P. HOLLOWAY
Dec. 20		Perry W. COLBOURNE	Laura A. GORDY
Dec. 21		William C. DIXON	Sally E. TWILLEY
Dec. 27		William TRADER	Lauretta PARADISE
Dec. 27		Peter T. PILCHARD	Dolly A. ROSS
Dec. 28		Marcellus PRUITT	Amelia BLADES

1865			
Jan. 3		Wm J. SHOCKLEY	Mary E. SERMAN
Jan. 3		Lemuel TIMMONS	Bettie HASTINGS
Jan. 4		Joshua M. CAREY	Adelia K. POWELL
Jan. 4		Levin J. BAKER	Hester FREEMAN
Jan. 4		Henry E. DAVIS	Elizabeth DENNIS
Jan. 5		Daniel H. HAYMAN	Mary KAYLOT
Jan. 9		Perry R. POLLITT	Levey A. JONES
Jan. 10		Charles J. DAVIS	Ellen R. HAMMOND
Jan. 10		Polk DONAWAY	Ellen ENNIS
Jan. 10		William F. WARD	Sarah E. H. WIMBROUGH
Jan 11		Hiram J. DENNIS	Matilda M. LITTLETON
Jan. 11		James TULL	Mary CHERRIX
Jan. 11		John H. CLARKE	Harriet Anna WILLIAMS
Jan. 12		John PHIPS	Zelpha A. WIMBROUGH
Jan. 12		Abner MARTIN	Mary PILCHARD
Jan. 16		Joel COFFIN	Charlotte Ellen REED
Jan. 17		Wm D. KNOX	Sally SCARBOROUGH
Jan. 17		Minos B. WATSON	Mary E. BETTS
Jan. 18		William J. RUARK	Margaret SHOCKLEY
Jan. 18		William J. POPE	Margaret D. BUTLER
Jan. 24		Elijah J. BRITTINGHAM	Elizabeth TIMMONS
Jan. 25		Levin LYNCH	Sarah A. COFFIN
Jan. 26		Selby P. TRUITT	Annie M. RAYNE
Jan. 31		William McGRATH	Maria POWELL
Jan. 31		James E. CROPPER	Amelia A. NICHOLSON
Feb. 1		John CORBIN	Elizabeth J. BRIMER
Feb. 1		John J. DUFFY	Mary E. HANCOCK
Feb. 1		John J. BEACHBOARD	Rosa BARNES
Feb. 6		John POLLITT	Margaret A. PARSONS
Feb. 6		John H. DAVIS	Mary Ann CATHELL
Feb. 8		James E. ANDERTON	Joanna PARKER

1865		
Feb. 13	James B. RODNEY	Aralanta BIRCH
Feb. 13	Edward POWELL	Donna ENNIS
Feb. 14	Zadock P. ROBERTSON	Susan Jane COLONNA
Feb. 17	William H. STURGIS	Elizabeth A. GUNTER
Feb. 21	Marcellus SMALL	Sally BYRD
Feb. 22	John RITCHER	Clarissa YOUNG
Feb. 28	Lambert A. HALL	Oma DUNAWAY
Feb. 28	William T. HOWARD	Henrietta RIGGEN
March 1	W.S. MILLS	Martha A. GODWIN
March 1	Josiah SMITH	Nancy LITTLETON
March 4	J.W. CHARLTON	May C. FARROW
March 6	James L. CAMPBELL	Charlotte PARSONS
March 6	Orlando G. MILLS	Olevia E. GORDY
March 6	James JONES	Ann JOHNSON
March	John E. EVANS	Sarah M. BRATTEN
March 9	J.C. CAUSEY	Careline DEVEREUS
March 14	Wm S. HAMBLIN	Sarah E. DAVIS
March 17	John W. PARKER	Priscilla J. MITCHELL
March 20	Tennart BOWEN	Ritta LYNCH
March 21	Ebenezer W. TURNER	Mary E. DYKES
March 27	John N. HENMAN	Martha J. BURBAGE
March 28	Major S.J. DAWSON	Ellen R. STURGIS
March 28	Thomas A. WINDSOR	Elizabeth LAMBDEN
March 29	William FISHER	Nancy GRAY
March 29	Elijah B. MEARS	Elizabeth M. PARKS
April 4	King V. WHITE	Lidie C. BURBAGE
April 4	Elisha GRAVENER	Mary Ann BAKER
April 6	Wm J. AYRES	Sarah F. ROSS
April 10	Robert H. LAYFIELD	Mary E. DENNIS
April 12	Isaac W. TOWNSEND	Cordelia M. CLAYVILLE
April 12	Joshua WATERS	Georgianna BRUMLY
April 18	Charles S. WHEALTON	Tabitha BACON
May 1	Lemuel JONES	Narissa TRUITT
May 2	George F. WARD	Bettie E. P. BLOXOM
May 13	Colmar TAYLOR	Sarah Ann GILLETT
May 17	Thomas M. MUMFORD	Frances Catherine NICHOLSON
May 18	George JARVIS	Anna MUMFORD
May 23	John BISHOP	Sally Ann PITTS
May 23	George W. CORBIN	Missouri TAYLOR
May 30	William Johnson (Of Saml)	Sarah W. JONES
June 2	Oliver BLAKE	Sarah Ann WHITTINGTON
June 12	John W. STATON	Mary Margareta PITTS
June 20	James DORMAN	Mary E. BUTLER
June 27	Zadok P. DUFFY	Matilda RICHARDSON

INDEX

ABBOTT
Elizabeth 9
Lydia Jane 125
Ruffus L. 105
Samuel C. 66

ABNER
George D. 83

ACWORTH
Caroline 126

ADAIR
Mary 111

ADAMS
Emma A.V. 134
Henry 53, 92
Jacob 33
Jemina 147
Leah 84
Levi 119
Mary Ann 63
Morriss 88
Polly 22
Rebecca A. 149
Samuel H. 153
Sarah 51
William 62
William J. 145
William Roger 105
Zeporah 53

ADDAMS
Obed 12
Wm. 16

ADDISON
George 74
Sally 79
Sally C. W. 71

ADISON
Ann 87
Elizabeth 89

ADKINS
Andy 107
Ann G. 118
Ann Mary 15
Azarkiah 32
Barzella C. 41
Charlotte 86
Daniel 126
David 5
Edward B. 138
Edward C.H. 146
Elijah 41
Eliza 10
Elizabeth 12, 47, 67
98, 103, 109
Erexine 95
Fanny 41, 125
Garrison S. 140
Gatty White 87
Hannah 122
Hannah Jenkins 3
Henry 43
Henry W. 93
James 103
Jehu 32
John 25, 45, 112, 138
John R. 112
John T. 93, 124
Josiah 128, 149
Josiah M. 135
Lambert 97
Lanta 75
Leah 18, 112
Levin 142
Lucinda 117
Maria 71
Mariah 141
Marten 74
Martha 50
Martha C. 131
Mary 77, 107
Mary G. 143
Mary J. 146
Mary M. 144
Milby 94, 102

ADKINS con't
Milly 148
Miranda 84
Molly 46
Nathan T. 125
Nelly 28
Noah 61
Noah R. 154
Polly 52
Priscilla 8
Rachel 2
Rebecca E.C. 149
Rider 142
Sally B. 32
Sampson 31, 111
Samuel 35, 46
Samuel E. 154
Sarah Ann 84
Sophia 154
Stephen 18
Thomas 93, 147
William 105
William H. 150
William S. 133

ADKISON
Polly 88

ADREON
Olevia E. 144

AGNEW
Robert 109
William 134

AILES
Causey 70

AINSON
Eliza 117

AKE
Hiram J. 153

ALEXANDER
Eliza 131
Mary 4, 46
Peter 46
Peter Thomas 88

ALLAN
John H.   91

ALLEN
Anna   7
Betsey   35
Elizabeth   39
James   86, 107
Jane   52
Job   14
John   2, 37, 112
Joseph S.C.   143
Julian   70
Levin   12
Louisa   120
Margaret   49
Mary   31
Milly   61
Nancy   82
Peggy   3
Peter   39
Sally   122
Stephen   22, 70
Tabitha   8, 57
Wise   55
Zadok   73

AMES
Anatha   90
Catharine   149
Dorinthy   112
Josephine A.   136
Margaret   110
Sarah G.   95
Shadrack M.   65

ANDERSON
Charlotte   62
Cordelia E.   153
Elizabeth   87
Emeline S.   115
Gatty   67
George H.   133
Hetty   64
James   58, 62
John   56, 59
Martha   50
Nancy   8

ANDERSON Con't
Sally   9, 9, 17
Sarah A.   79
Stephen   6
William   87, 139

ANDERTON
James E.   155

ANGAVINE
James   10

ANNIS
Archibald   129
Sylvester J.   127

ARDIS
Azariah   128
Eliza   129
Elizabeth   128
Emily S.   149
Harriet   130
James   131
Mary E.   136
Mary S.   131
Sarah Ann   107
William   114

ARLINGTON
Thomas B.   26

ARMSTRONG
Nancy   5

ARMWOOD
Daniel   76
James   9, 25
Wealthy   74

ASHBEY
Mollie A.B.   151

ASHBY
James   111

ASKRIDGE
Margaret   61

ATKINS
Wm S.   100

ATKINSON
Angelo   1
Ann   34, 114
Arrabella   54
Charles   61, 107
Elizabeth   52, 66
Elizabeth M   66
Harriet   53
Harriet A.   153
Jane   83, 108
John   17, 31
John Fountain   18
Joshua   22
Josiah   37
Levin   98
Louisa   98
Mary   2, 37, 73
Mary J.   2
Milby   9
Nancy   47, 74
Peggy   18, 57
Polly   12, 65
Sally   50
Sally E.   109
Sarah   16, 22
Susan   74
Thomas   36, 101
Whealty J.   106
William   28, 80

AUSTEN
Deliah Harriet   24
Jenny   18
Nancy   14
Priscilla   12
Henrietta   118

AUSTIN
Ann D.   57
Eleanor   13, 34
Hetty   6
John   40
Sally   19
William   59, 95

AYDELOTT
Benjamin 48, 63
Benjamin P. 63, 77
Benjamin T. 117
Elijah 145
Esther 18
Harriet 71
John 31, 32, 56
Leah 22
Margaret 70
Martha 31
Mary 23
Nancy 15
Peggy 1
Peter 32
Polly 19
Sarah 36, 38
Sarah V. 154
Susan 36
Thomas 36
William 31, 58

AYDELOTTE
Benjamin F. 115
Clarissa 102
Elijah 131
Elizabeth 99
Hannah 4, 82
Harriet A 125
Hester 122
John 84
John W. 111
Josiah 145
Margaret Frances 116
Mary 102
Polly 91
Sally 79
Susan 96

AYERS
Edward Twiford 110
Elizabeth K. 148
Henry A. 138
Henry R. 116
Nancy 118
Sarah E. 128
Susan 143
Wm J. 156

AYRES
Elizabeth 74, 84
Isaac 21, 33
Isaac Ironshire 23
James 80
Lambert 30
Micajah 18
Sally 12

BACON
Amelia El 102
Anthony 10
Catharine T. 91
Harriet 18
John C. 18
Julian 85
Mary 78
Rosean 130
Sally 60
Tabitha 36, 156
William 13
William H. 121

BADGE
Betsy 46

BADGER
Elizabeth 73
James G. 92
Louisa A. 101

BAGWELL
Augustus W. 63
Lorey 44

BAILEY
Eliza 139
Henrietta 131
Hillary 145
Jane C. 153
Josiah H. 143
Martha E. 136
Mary Ann 147
Mary Elizabeth 123
Mary H. 146
Obed 43
Noah 142
Robert W. 141
William 153

BAILY
Hyram 128
Nancy 5

BAIN
John 58

BAKER
Albert 112
Alexine 103
Anna 62, 113
Arch J. 118
Archibald 7
Betsey 15, 84
Burton 97
Charlotte 65
Clarrissa E. 125
Druzilla 60
Elijah 57, 111
Eliza 95
Elizabeth 44, 103, 110
Esther 25
George 66, 103, 147
Henry 44, 45
Hetty 115
Isaac 72
Ishmeal 37
Jane E. 113
James 88, 108
Jesse 42, 62, 79
John B. 103
Jonathan 9, 62
Jonathan F. 113
Joseph 115
Joshua 81
Julia C. 145
Laban 40
Lemuel 111
Levin 62, 155
Margaret A. 112
Mary 24, 145
Mary A. 144
Mary Ann 156
Mary S. 135
Molly 7, 86
Nancy 42, 69, 139
Nathaniel 114
Patty 3
Peter 139
Polly 123

BAKER Con't
Rachel 38,48,73
Rhoda 119
Richard 46
Robert 29,89,97
Robert E. 125
Robert J. 133
Robert M. 104
Salathiel 126,131
Sally 46
Sally Mary 151
Samuel 49,140,145
Sarah C. 147
Shadrack 29,35
Solomon 86
Thomas 51,94
William 1,38,90
 110,120

BALEY
Thomas W. 95

BALL
Ann 151
Betsy 50
Christopher P. 95
Edward J. 143
Frederick 18
James 41
James H. 94
John 30
Leah 61
Levi 27,73
Lydia 41
Nancy 70
Noah 40
Samuel 111
William 30
William J. 152

BALLARD
James 50
Rachel 15

BANE
Ann C. 46

BANJER
Martha Ann 136

BANKS
David 24,56
Mary 81
Priscilla 17
Sally 78
Samuel 18

BANUM
James 22

BARCKLEY
Sarah 55

BARCRIFT
William Thomas 40

BARN
Patzy 6

BARNES
Agnes 58
Anna M. 146
Benjamin 47,58
Catharine 69
Eleanor 61
Emma 136
Francis J. 151
Henrietta S. 146
John 105
Julian 91
Lewis S. 124
Lovey 69
Mary P. 119
Mary S. 146
Nancy 24
Prissey 25
Rosa 155
Rosanna 31
Sarah 57
Sophia A.M. 73
Thomas 22,71
William James 91
William P. 72

BARNETT
Sarah 105

BARNWELL
Lydia Donny 17

BARRET
William 31

BARRETT
Henry 71
James 8
James J. 151
Julian 54

BARROTT
Mary L. 61

BASIT
Henry M. 64

BASSETT
Betsey 74,77
Dolly 83
Elizabeth 32
John 41
Mary Ann 89
Molly 11
Nancy 18
Patty 58
Rachel 31
Sarah 11,15
Sophia 12,74,75
Stewart 73
William 15,53,72
 80,

BASSETTE
Rachell 36

BASSITT
Benj. 91
Benjamin 109
Benjamin B. 126
Maria E. 86
Milly 96
Nancy 70

BATES
Laurence 100

BATSON
Daniel 42

BATTELL
Cornelius E. 90
Levinia 138

BATTS
Julian 84
Rebecca 9

BAYER
Eliza 64

BAYLEY
Albert 113
Clarissa 106
Eliza 100
Thomas 77

BAYLY
Ann D. 90
Elizabeth 83
Erastus B. 109
Esme 57
Fanny Caroline 124
Hamilton 31
Henry 88
Margaret 68
Margaret P. 102
Polly 35, 52
Rachel U. 88
Rebecca M. 84
Robert M. 118
Thomas 16, 75

BAYNE
Colmore G. D. 125
William H. 117

BAYNUM
Belitha 16
Elizabeth 59
James 17
Rufus 96, 102, 125
William 1, 27

BEACH
Abel 40
Catharine 40
Elizabeth Sarah 101
Jonithan G. 145
Mary 87
William 91
William H. 90

BEACHAM
James 119

BEACHARDS
Nixon 61

BEACHBOARD
Aramintal 113
Atty 67
Betsey 77
Eleanor 70
Hetty 66
John J. 155
John L. 118
Josa 2
Lydia 96
Nancy 48
Peter 60, 99
Susannah 52
William 33, 64, 88

BEACHAMP
Ann 107
Hetty 119
Leonard 127
Levin W. 125
Milburn 117
Sarah Jane 125

BEACHOM
Maria 46

BEACUCHUM
Isaac 135

BEASLY
Harriet 124

BEASY
Hezey 71

BEATHARD
Hetty 26
Mary 94
Matthias 57
Patty 44
Richard M 42

BEATHARDS
Adam P 107
Betsey 61
Daniel 44
Eliza 77
Fanny 61
Gertrude P. 60
Harriet 96
Henny 78
Isaac 5, 53, 68, 107
James 82
Joshua M. 131
Josiah 74
Martha 106
Nancy 24
Ritta Emeline 131
Soloman 119

BEAUCHAMP
Andasiah 43
Eliza Ann 64
Elizabeth 24, 40
Leven W. 88
Mary 103
Nancy 131
Pheuby 17
Susan Ann 77

BEAVANS
Charlotte 122
James 7
John 8
Mary 32
Mills 6
Rowland A. 37
William 43

BEAVENS
Elizabeth   25
Mary I.   81
Molly   24
Nancy   15
Tabitha   13
William   20

BECKET
Perry   26

BECKETT
Mary Jane   141
Sally   144

BEEBY
James   42

BEESON
Henry   114

BELL
Ann   20
Asa   29
Betsey   43
Daniel   73
Edward H.   126
Elizabeth   76
Elizabeth W. 139
Emory E.   140
George   10
Hetty   54, 57
Jacob   31
James A.   83
James R.   92
John   26, 29, 69, 85
Margaret   61
Mary   57, 74, 136
Nancy   6, 22, 33
Polly   10
Robert F.   13
Sally   79, 118
Sally Kendall 10
Thomas   72
Thorogood   90
Victor   107
William   3, 84
William B.   27
Wm   92

BELLEDGE
Susan   37

BELOATE
William J.   130

BELOTE
Caleb   52
Maria E.   154
Mary   52
Rachel   76
William S.T. 136

BELSATE
Charles   123

BEN
Benjamin   57

BENNETT
Andasis R.   140
Ann   77, 97
Auganett   100
Benjamin   21
Betsey   12, 34
Betsy   24
Charles   11, 57
Charles Jr. 16
Charlotte   63
Charlotte M.R. 95
Dolly   3
Edwin J.H.   81
Eleanor M.R. 86
Eliakim   38, 69
Elizabeth   22, 121
Elizabeth W. 113
George   94, 105
George H.   110
George W.   75
Harriet W.   66
Hetty   45, 115
James   16, 28, 35, 62, 97
Jesse   37
Julia Ann   107
Mary   35, 36, 78
Matilda   75
Nancy   13, 48, 61, 74
Peggy   14, 63

BENNETT Con't
Peter J.   113
Polly   29, 47
Priscilla   28, 43
Purnell I.   76
Purnell J.   64
Rosanna Adam Williams
             43
Sarah   9
Sarah E.   81
Scarbourgh   10
Warner   61
William   43, 44
William H.J. 143
William Purnell 8

BENNIT
George   46

BENSON
Alfred H.   101, 144
Ann   58
Edward   92
Eliza   149
Esther   2
Gedion   27
Hannah   25
Hetty   66
Jane   137
Jesse A.   149
John   9, 12, 13
John H.   74
Joseph H.   63
Levin M.   29
Luretta   9
Major   80
Margaret   43, 79
Mary   100, 114
Nancy   16
Noah   66
Sally J.   122
Samuel   43, 122
Thomas   116
William   99, 103, 146
William W.   146
Wm   33

BENSTON
Alexine B. 108
Daniel 45,60
Elijah 22
Elizabeth 42
Emeline 100
Isaac 22
James I. 102
Lias 93
Nancy 20,28
Nathaniel 55
Rachel 22
Rebecca 33
Samuel 60
Sarah 5
Susan Ann 98
Thomas 22
William S. 123

BENTEW
John 88

BERNARD
Barneby 64

BERRY
John 54
Louisa 74
Sarah 25 130
Sarah S 151

BETHARD
Elizabeth 35
Esther 14
Josiah 56
William G. 97

BETHARDS
Adam P. 143
Daniel J. 146
Elizabeth 1
Hannah W. 120
Henry T 16
Leah 125
Martha 20
Martha A. 115
Martha E. 147

BETHARDS Con't
Mary 20
Mary Jane 112
Nancy 23
Sally 104
William 120

BETTS
Comfort 21
Daniel 147
Elizabeth 154
Isaac 142
Mary E. 155
Sarah 147

BEVANS
Amanda P. 121
Ann 64
Anna 29
Anna Maria 95
Barshabe 24,43,142
Barshaba J. 134
Cady 25
Elizabeth 78
Elizabeth A. 71
Elizabeth T. 73
Elleanor 48
Harriet 127
Henrietta B. 147
Henry 78
Hetty 48
Jesse 37
John 50,71
Joshua 75
Joshua R 143,146
Lanta 36
Leah B. 43
Levine 96
Littleton D. 51
Louisa 68
Lydia 88,92
Martha A. 153
Martha Ellen 138
Mary 52,76
Milcah Ann 63
Nathaniel 26
Priscilla 38

BEVANS Con't
Rosetta 109
Rowland 64
Rowland F. 146
Rowland Jr. 29
Sally 115
Sarah 98
Tabitha 104
William 47,60

BEVENS
Roland E. 91

BEYER
Elizabeth M. 149

BINTON
John 78

BIRCH
Aralanta 156
Betsey 12
Hannah 3
Henry 127
James 65
James W. 128
Littleton 119
Martha 55
Mary Ann 131
Mary Elizabeth 154
Sarah M. 141
Susan 99, 143

BIRD
Abel James 105
Curtis 60
Major 19
Margaret 10
Mary E. 121
Matilda 50
Sally 66
Susan 42
Thomas 4

BIRK
James 146

BIRTCH
Thomas 134

BISHOP
Anna 10,142
Ann Eliza 70
Benjamin 124
Betsey 3,4,32
Catharine 145
Charles W. 117
Dolly 14
Dolly Ann 105
Duny 16
Ebe 92
Edward 119
Elizabeth 74,86,150
George 47,67,93,145
George W. 140
Harriet 91
Hester A. 108
Hetty 10,119
James B. 108
James W. 109
John 10,33,42,45
    93,156
John P. 142
Joseph 15
Josiah 111
Julia 152
Keturah 119
Leah 47
Levi 38
Lititia 31
Margaret 112
Mary 97,104,108
Mary Ann 101
Molly 22
Monze 11
Nancy 3,21,36,93
    134
Nath 5
Polly 21
Rachel 100
Rosetta 124
Sabrough 34
Sally 4,26,36,95
Sally W. 146
Samuel 2
Sarah 142
Sarah J. 109

BISHOP Con't
Sidney J. 151
William 50
William S. 126
Wm 42
Wm. Jr. 19
Zepporah 52
Zipporah 47,141

BITTS
John 4

BIXBY
Sarah W. 138

BLACK
Amy 9
Hester 128
Sarah 35

BLACKSOME
Edward 37

BLACKSON
Elizabeth 67
Sealamore 147

BLACKSTON
Bowman 100

BLACKSTONE
Ann 91
Thomas W. 40

BLADES
Amelia 155
Ann 99
Benjamin 11
Catharine 139
Catharine A. 151
Comfort 7
David 106
Eli 32
Elizabeth 6,58,78,
    90,117
Emeline 117
Francis 149

BLADES Con't
Gattey 58
Goldsborough 26
Gusta 72
Handy 7
Harriet 104
Henry 80
Huldey 16
James 5,29,57,75
    127
Jane 126,133
Jane H. 130
John 73,85
John W. 133
Leah 11
Leonard J. 154
Levin 54
Lewis 79
Luther 80
Mary 146,106
Mary Ann 103
Nancy 31
Oliver 103
Peter 64,110
Peter C. 125
Polly 48, 70
Ruthey 12
Sally 120
Sally E. 133
Samuel 2,59
Sophius 152
Stephen 49,101
Stephen J. 143
Stephen T. 127
Susan 65
Tabitha 144
Thomas H. 134
William 50
William L. 122
Wreom 69

BLAIN
John 51
Thomas J 105

BLAIR
Nancy 29
Robert 9

BLAKE	BOHM	BOOZEE
Edward 36	Virginia 154	Mary 14
Henny 84		
Mary 83	BOISNARD	BOSTON
Matthew 42	Eliza R. 43	Amelia 131
Oliver 156		Ann 96
Peggy 36	BOLDS	Charlotte E. 132
	Thomas 58	Charlotte Jane 88
BLEZARD		Eliza 134
John 6	BOLING	Elizabeth 121
	Sarah 6	Elizabeth C. 103
BLOODGOOD		Elizabeth C. 106
William 154	BONAWELL	Esau 81,109
	Peter 150	Harley M. 141
BLOXOM	Thomas 133	Henry 69,84
Alfred 134		Isaac 54,133
Bettie E.P. 156	BONAWILL	Jacob 16,27,
George 150	John 21	45
George H. 131		John 61,91
John J. 105	BONNAWELL	Josiah 122
Thomas 129	Benjamin 80	Julia A. 142
	Edward 6	Leah 28,117,122
BLOXSOM	Eliza 73	144
Ann 61	Elizabeth 45	Leah E. 127
Eliza 140	George 23	Mary E. 140
Elizabeth 59	Hester Ann 91	Mary O. 153
Ezekiel 79	James 91	Mary P. 103
Hester Ann 126	Jane 39	Nancy 61
John 94	John 24,58	Polly 18
Mary Ann 129	Mary 26	Rebina 18
Richard 110	Mary H. 128	Sally 134
Rosa 64	Nancy 40	Sally A. 136
Samuel 65		Sally W. 85
	BONNEWELL	Saml 11
BODILY	Ann E. 121	Thomas 68,153
Archibald 100	James 88,108	William 114,124
	James W. 78	William J. 76
BODLEY	Martha 90	William T. 145
William 116	Polly 73	
	Sarah E. 136	BOSWELL
BODLY		Elizabeth 94
Archibald 123	BONNEWILL	
	William C. 147	BOTHAM
BOGGS		John 5
Sarah 87	BOOTH	Polly 40
	Coventon 12	Sally 53
BOHANNAN	Crippen 92	
Esther 91	Sally 59	BOTHUM
		James 44

BOTTOM
James Winter 52

BOUDEN
Jesse 45

BOUNDS
Eleanor 108
John 9
John J. 149
Jones 58,89
Mary 112
Mary Ann 122
Washington J. 127
William 15

BOWDEN
Daniel 130
Eleanor 74
Elizabeth 75,109,112
Emma 151
James 116
Jesse 148
John 52, 86
Lemuel W. 136
Margaret 131
Mary 112
Parker 61
Rebecca 115
Rosa 141
Sarah 140
Stephen D. 154
William 85

BOWNDS
Nancy 41

BOWDIN
William 119

BOWDOIN
Catharine 137
George 84,91,138
Ira 139
Joseph 80
Leah 107
Samuel 95
Stephen Decatur 93

BOWDON
Louisa 145

BOWEN
Albert 154
Alexene H. 139
Amelia 4
Ann 12,116
Ann C. 102
Ann Mariah 137
Arrlanta 55
Augusta 82
Benjamin 41, 105
Betsey 13,21,68
Charles 87
Charles H. 115
Charlotte 44,58,58
86,111,126
Charlotte E. 150
Comfort 38
Cornelia 88
David 59,89,128
Dolly 3
Edward 12, 106
Edward H. 105
Eleanor 89
Elender 43
Elisha 42
Eliza 56,86
Eliza J. 131
Elizabeth 145
Ellen 139
Ellen A. 134
Esme P. 72
Esther 40
Francis 111
Gatty 64,92
George 110
George C. 117
George E. 115
Gilbert L. 112
Handy 104
Henny 30
Henny H. 68
Henrietta 43
Hetty 14,33,72,
114
Isaac 37
Isaac M. 115

BOWEN Con't
Isabel 103
James 10,99,105
James C. 50
James of Joshia 111
James of K. 128
James of Salathel
58
James Selby 88
James T. 153
Jane 61,64,112,140
Jane L. 128
Jenkins H. 39
John 5,38,49,66
John H. 34
John W. 150
Joseph 148
Joshua 53,79,83,91
Josiah 21,57,86
Julia 116
Julia A. 79
Kendall 107
Kendall T. 40,115
Laura Ann 89
Laura J. 144
Leah 81
Lemuel 18
Littleton 34,77
Lydia 20
Margaret 113
Margaret Ellen 124
Maria 51
Martha 118,134
Mary 3,42,93,99,126
Mary A. 123
Mary C. 110
Mary E 133,134
Mary H. 153
Mary J. 99
Mary P. 50
Milby 11
Molly 92
Moses 92
Nancy 24,39,57,63,69
Narcissus 69
Noah 61,79
Parker 44,99,127
Patty 14, 33
Peter 101

BOWEN Con't
Polly 28
Rachell 45
Rebecca A. 115
Rhoda 2,77
Richard 68,87
Riley 10
Robert 72
Robert F. 51
Robert L. 118
Sally 4,8,16,66
Sally C. 142
Sally L. 139
Sally M. 147
Sally Maria 94
Selby 73
Stephen M. 81
Susan A. 128
Tenant 68
Tennart 156
Thomas 154
Vicey 80
Whittington 38
Whitty 21
William 14,62,72,81
William L. P. 144
William T. 141,144
Zachariah 66,12
Zacheus 115,130
Zachias
Zacheus 115,130
Zadok 126
Zadok W. 71
Zepporah 39

BOWER
Tenant 90

BOWHANNAN
John 21

BOWIN
Asa 63
Hulda 27

BOWING
Rodah 42

BOWLAND
John N. 37

BOWLEN
Thomas 42

BOWLES
Edward 28
Nancy 11
Samuel 37

BOWMAN
Isabelle 30
Robert 92

BOYD
William 120

BOYER
Ann Maria 102
Francis A. 58
Harriet 98
Sophia 140

BOZMAN
Elizabeth 29

BRADFORD
Ann 57,70
Ann M. 115
Annania 2
Alexine 137
Aura 68
Avera 124
Burton 24
Chole 13
Delila 62
Drucilla 94
Eleanor 26
Eliza 94, 141
Elizabeth 29
Gilley 94
Gilly 144
Henny 34
Hetty 142
Isaac 86
James 20,29

BRADFORD Con't
John 12,124,136
John W. 98
Julian 70
Kendall 11,80
Levin 41
Mahala 87
Margaret 112
Martha 122
Mary 77
Mary Ime 138
Molly 50
Nancy 24,26
Nelly 96
Patty 126
Polly 37,61
Rachel 41,82
Rebecca 62
Sally 8,11,54
Schoolfield 24
Selby 127,147
Soloman 70
Stephen 83
Thomas 67,82
William 28,41,50,
         51,82,122
Zedikiah 14

BRADSHAW
Betsey 33
Levin 14
Polly 21

BRADY
Michael 149

BRAMBLE
Bond M. 79

BRANSRUM
Peggy 43

BRAISHER
John 25
Levin 27

BRASON
George T. 47

BRATTEN
Alfred 125
Betsey 33
Catherine 5,32,82
Clarissa 75
Ebenezer 21
Eliza M 88
Eliza O.P. 139
Elizabeth 63,71
Elizabeth W. 123
George 13,67
George T. 120
Gertrude 50
Henry 57
James 114
James M. 139
Jane 134
John 1,5,78
Josiah 30,33
Justice Morris 58
Leah 57
Margaret 26,55,153
Martha 13
Martha Rounds 88
Mary 99
Mary A. 67,141
Mary E. 117
Nancy 17,83
Nathaniel 55
Noah 114
Polly 11,12
Priscilla 17
Rhoda 3
Sally 6,27
Sarah 8,56,156
Thomas 144
William 26,104
William B. 151
William C. 146
William H. 134
William S. 119
Zipporah 118

BRAUGHTON
Bruff 45

BRAVARD
Ann 89
Anna 8
Catherine R. 64

BRAXTON
William 37

BRAZIER
Hester 127
Sarah 52

BREVARD
James 24

BREDELL
Elijah 79
Maria 73

BREWINGTON
Ann E. 143
Charles 66
David 55
Ebenezer 126
Elenor 108
Elizabeth 105
Frankey 22
George 19
Henry 71
Henry J. 93
Hetty 84
James 73
James W. 113
John 24,35
John C. 64
Joshua 69
Leah 35
Margaret 56
Martha 11
Mary 45,95,88
Mary E. 103
Nancy 4,61,71
Smith 16
Theodore 108
William A. 77
Wm 16

BRICKHOUSE
Alexine 151
Henry T. 107
Margaret E. 113

BRIDDEL
Mary C. 130

BRIDDELL
Ann 41
Edward 22
John 30
Louesa 149
Nancy 50
Susan C. 146
William H. 149

BRIDDLE
Ann 67
David 129
Elijah 50
Eliu 52
Hetty 55
Isaac 23,57
Joshua 50
Leah 8
Martha 46
Rachel 28

BRIDEL
Mary R. 51

BRIDELL
Joshua T. 137
Mary E. 125

BRIMER
Eliza 86
Elizabeth 22
Elizabeth J. 155
Harriet 122
Levi 96
Levi J. 153
Mary Ann 111
Samuel L. 70
Sarah 47
William 69
William E. 141
Woodstone 133

BRINDLE
James A. 110

BRINKLY
Henry 115

BRION
Hanson 3

BRITT
James 110
Joshua 45

BRITTINGHAM
Albert I. 152
Amanda 147
Aralanta 1
Aurena 107
Azariah 65
Benjamin 82, 122
Betsey 21, 27, 31
Catharine 106
Charles 71
Charlotte 105, 132
Charlotte E. 153
Delila 48
Edward 146
Edward J.C. 143
Elijah 64, 69, 96, 113
Elijah H. 133
Elijah J. 155
Eliza 147
Elizabeth 26, 104, 153
Elizabeth H.P. 117
Ephraim D. 131
Ephraim K.W. 118
Ephraim W. 146
George 26, 91, 123
George E. 151
George H. 102
Gillett P. 125
Hannah Cottingham 21
Henry 75
Hetty 33, 41
Isaac 2, 26
James 43, 51, 78
   92, 95

BRITTINGHAM Con't
Jane 76
Jane B. 124
John 15, 90
John E. 126
Josiah 39
Lamuel 24
Lemuel 114
Levi 67
Levin H. 57
Margaret 96
Margaret Ann 133
Maria 83
Martha Ann 143
Mary 49, 96, 100, 149
Mary A. 129
Mary A.E. 108
Mary Ann 107
Mary C. 147
Mary E. 138, 146
Mary J. 143
Mary Martha 141
Matilda 94
Matilda E. 144
Micajah 18
Miranda 72
Nancy 1, 5, 13, 85
Nathaniel 89, 106
Nathl. 11
Obed 35
Peggy 10
Peter 87
Polly 15
Purnell 21, 42, 63
Rebecca 154
Rion 64
Sally 47, 54, 73
Sally Ann 150
Sally E. 110
Sally J. 121
Samuel 53, 86
Sarah 155
Sarah Ann 137
Seth 74, 82
Seth H. 135
Severn 151
Stephen 32

BRITTINGHAM Con't
Susan 37, 102
Susan J. 117
Tabitha 22
Theodosia 152
Thomas 18, 23, 35, 43
   71, 76, 89, 117
Thomas B. 108
William 32, 113, 114, 129
   129, 147
William B.L. 150
William E. 40, 65
William of Geo 95
William H. 108, 143
Wm 2, 37
Zadok Henry 110
Zippy B. 83

BROADWATER
Elias 32
Eliza 72
Elizabeth 73
Joseph E. 154
Mary 62
Phamy 97
Walter 63
Wessley 133
William M. 149

BRODWATER
James 45, 84
Levin J.M.P. 121, 141
Oliver 79
Sally 15
Sarah 20

BRODWATTER
James 19

BROOKS
Isaac 45

BROOKSAND
Henry 72

BROTHERY
Sarah 5

BROTON
Josiah 43

BROUGHTON
Comfort 60
Edward 26,29
Eliza 85
Elizabeth J. 134
Esther A. 134
Jesse 62
Martha 40
Nathl E. 40
Polly 39
Samuel 84
William 54,63,68,

BROWN
Anthony 124
Barheba 44
Betsey 38
Effie 14
Eliza 78
Eliza M. 97
Elizabeth A. 130
George W. 149
Henrietta 50,121,130
Hesse 1
Isaac M. 135
Jackson 50
James 22,55
Jane 46
John 18
Josiah 101
Kibble 149
Mary 127
Mary Ann 87
Mary E. 140,153
Minos 122
Nancy 6,44
Patty 68
Peggy 42
Peter 70
Sally 68
Sarah 39

BROWN Con't
Thomas W. 123
William 3,83,127
William F. 91
William J. 112
Wm L. 154

BRUFF
Zeporah 15

BRUINGTON
John 40

BRUMB
Ellen 137

BRUMBLY
Abraham 93
Benjamin 29,50
Charlotte A. 125
Elizabeth 83.102
George 84,130,140
Georgianna 156
Isaac 37
James 153
John 24,142
Lucretia 2
Mary 13
Noah 103
Priscilla 123
William K. 131

BRUMLEY
Henry W. 94
Jabez 2
Sarah M. 124

BRUMLY
Tabitha 3

BUCKHOUSE
Charles P. 123

BUDD
Elizabeth 31
Keely 29
Mary 114

BULL
Betsy 88
Curtis 91
Esther 91
George 81
Hetty 77
James 41,101
James H. 118
Jane 113
John 16,45,44
John R. 95
Joseph 85
Mary T. 109
Nancy 150
Phebe 129
Richard 57
Sarah E. 48.151
Southy W. 71,89
Susan 55

BULLIN
William T 151

BUNCE
Robert S. 33

BUNDICK
Ann 75
Betsey 52
Elen 140
Elizabeth Jane 109
George T. 100
John A. 103
Joseph 38
Lucretia 114
Mary 88
Nancy 102
Susan 129

BUNNITT
James 38

BUNTICK
George of William
  86

BUNTIN
Sheppard 97

BUNTING
Colomore 83
David 58
Elijah 32
Elisha T. 150
Harvey 134
Isaac 48,94
Isaac Thomas 101
James 18
John 89
John H. 87
Joseph 100
Milley 43
Nancy 47
Oliver J. 132
Polly 41
Rosa Anne 85
Rosetta 81
Samuel C. 147
Soloman 133
Susan 68

BUNTON
Ara T. 80

BURBAGE
Belitha 15
Dolly 31
Edward 1
Eleanor 6
Elizabeth 2,116,141
Handy 71
Henrietta 57,66
Henry 22,54
Isaac W. 137
Isabella 80,143
James 150
Jane M. 123
John 46,50,95
John Handy 146
Joshua 48
Laura 150
Leah 6
Levin O. 34
Lidie 156
Mahala 34
Margaret Ann 143

BURBAGE Con't
Margaret 31
Martha 41,95
Martha J. 156
Mary 146
Mary Ann 120
McKemmy 29
Milly 150
Nancy 37,38
Peter 72,92
Polly 9
Rhoda 4
Sally 49
Sampson 15,96,143
Samuel 71
Tabitha 14
Thomas 75
William 82,84,117
Zeporah 14

BURCH
George 87
James 57
Nancy 44
Sally 40,58

BURD
Polly 41

BURK
John 145

BURKE
James Fontaine 87

BURKMASTER
Margaret 23

BURNETT
Betsey 71
Elijah 32
Elizabeth A 110
John 67
John H. 108
Margaret 47
Margaret Porter 90
Rachel 6

BURNETT Con't
Rebecca 73
Sally 10,128
Wrixom 101

BURROUGHS
Ann 40
Ann P. 86
Arthur 56
Catharine 61
Charlotte 55
Hannah 95
Harriet 95
James P.. 152
Jesse G 49
Joice P. 112
Joshua 43
Margaret 63
Maria 59
Nancy 18
Nancy S. 98
Polly 27
Samuel 49,55
Thomas J. 112

BURROWS
Elizabeth 42

BURTIN
Margaret S. 108

BURTON
Dugal S. 150
Elizabeth S. 101
Helen 49
Henry T. 98
Mary I. 141
Polly 63
Sallie 145

BUSSELLS
Gilly 17
James 26
James H. 114
Mahala 137
Milton 86
Polly 74
Sally 97

BUSSELS
Charlotte E. 121
Gillis 122
John 73
Mary 78
Nancy 41

BUSTER
Mary 87

BUTLER
Betsey 54
Catharine 75
Charles 74
Daniel 75
Eliza 65, 93
Eliza J. 120
Ezekial 70
Hamilton 123
Henry 64
Holland 80
Isaac 103
James 49
John H. 132
Joshua T. 150
Leah 83
Levin 132
Margaret D. 155
Martha 135
Mary Ann 150
Mary E. 156
Milly 78
Rosanna 1
Sally 61
Samuel 8
Soloman 39
Uriah 144
William 48
William S. 124

BUTLEY
Daniel 97

BYRD
Benjamin H. 65
Eliza S. 122
Elizabeth 130
Henry E. 149

BYRD Con't
Hetty Anne 85
James D. 142
John 61, 139
Margaret S. 140
Mary F. 140
Sally 142, 156
Sewell A. 125
William J. 136

CAHOON
Catharine 24
Margaret 22
Nancy 6
Patty 62
Sally 33
Wm. A. 16

CALAWAY
Arena 110

CALHOON
Thomas 1
William A. 100

CALLAHAN
Elizabeth 86
John 68
John H. 135
Joseph 9
Louisa 132
Mary G. 113
Narcissa 69

CALLAWAY
James 84
Levi 114

CALENDAR
Louisa A. 114
Robert 87

CALLENDAR
Robert 59

CALLOHAM
Ann 63

CAMME
James 54

CAMMELL
John 44

CAMERON
John B. 62, 79

CAMERRON
John 30
Sally E. 137

CAMPBELL
Eli 13
Eliza A. 126
Elizabeth 134
Emily 116
Fanny 18
George 121
George P. 122
Hatty 19
Isaac 131
Isaiah 117
James 62
James L. 156
Jane 152
Lambert 98
Leah 30
Leah Jane 122
Mary 66
Merrill 132
Susan 55
Thomas 18
William 11

CAMRON
Sally 18
John 10

CANFIELD
Priscilla 16

CANNON
Alfred 119
Burton 54
Elizabeth 69
Ennals 58

CANNON Con't
Gibson 78
Isaac 32
Jacob W. 116
James 92
Jeremiah 44
Thomas N.W. 153

CANTWELL
Elleanor 128

CAREY
Amelia Julian 78
Anna 42
Anniss 122
Ann M. 100
Betsey 1,79,137
Catharine 17
Charlotte 122
Elijah 41,50,127
Elijah B. 143
Elisha 11
Elizabeth 3,69,109
             119
Emily D. 152
Fidelea 95
George 35
Henrietta A. 89
Henny 142
Henry 120,137
Isaac D. 106
James 78, 131
James E. 137
Jane E. 108
John 142
John H. 124,143
John L.R.B. 121
Jonathan 24, 107
Joseph 145
Joseph S. 113
Joshua 109
Joshua E. 152
Joshua M 95,155
Josiah 35,106
Josiah J. 137
Julia Ann 114
Leah 66,72

CAREY Con't
Levin 35
Lovey 60
Margaret D. 136
Martha E. 112
Mary 7,14,31,131
Mary Ann 72,102
Mary J. 128
Matilda 94
Milly 44
Molly 96
Moses 11
Nancy 13,29,67,
       115,127
Nancy C. 127
Nelly 34
Obediah 38
Polly 31
Purnell B. 148
Rebecca 63
Roburtta 138
Sally 17
Sally Q 113
Samuel T. 44
Sarah 130
Soloman 54
Sophia 147
Theodore 122,133
Thomas 49, 72
Walter 133
William 52,59,72
William H. 121

CARLINGTON
Margaret Curtis 38

CARMEAN
Beauchamp 11
Gilbert 80
William 127

CARMENE
Benjamin 97

CARMINE
Juliet A. 95
Levin P. 135
Louellen 151

CARPENTER
Lewis E. 90
Mary 119

CARROLL
Catharine 151
Charles C. 69

CARSEY
John 95

CARSLEY
Adeline F. 107
Emeline M. 103
Milly 108
Sally R. 118

CARTER
James 150
John 94
William 33
Zadok 107

CAREY
Ellender 87
John 50
Joshua 20
Mary 45

CASE
Sabra 78

CATHELL
Betsey 11
Bridget 1
Catharine 99
David 25
Eliza 59
George 128
George W. 141
Haste P. 47
James M. 102
John 3,34.95
Julia C. 135
Levi 17,36,52
Levi James 141
Maria 103
Martha 44

CATHELL Con't
Maria   103
Martha   44
Mary Ann   155
Nancy   23
Nancy S.   56
Rebecca   49, 99

CATLEN
Leah   75
Robert D.   34

CATTS
Sabra   81

CAUDREY
John Jr.   13

CAUDRY
Polly   5
William   4

CAUEY
Frances   93

CAUSAY
Mary   59

CAUSEY
Alice   21
Amanda H.   137
Amanda P.   152
Ann   62
Edwin F.   152
Elizabeth C. 151
Emeline   108
Hester Ann 63
James   148
James S.   70
J.C.   156
John   89
Josiah   90
Leah J.   143
Levin   73

CAUSEY Con't
Lewis   76
Mary E.   149
Naricissa   98
Patrick   21
Sarah E.   139
Seth   150
Soloman   69
Sophia   107, 148
Theodosia   148
Wm   44

CAWLEY
Branson   81

CAYVILLE
Sally   114

CERUTHAS
James   95

CHADWICK
Thomas   49

CHAILLE
Amelia   5, 92
Elizabeth   70
Dolly   7
Henrietta Done 10
John P.   15, 16
Margaret   27
Peter   74
Sally   9
Stephen   21
Zachariah   44

CHANDLER
George P.   50
Isabella   80
Mitchell   42

CHANEY
Sarah E.   124

CHANLER
Priscilla   132

CHAPMAN
Emma   142
James   74, 113
John   57
Joshua   25, 142
Julian   74
Samuel   153
William   131

CHARION
Uriah   126

CHARLTON
J.W.   156

CHARNICK
Solomon   137

CHATHAM
A. E.   153
Elizabeth   142
John B.   98
Josephus   149
Josiah   21

CHATMAN
Arthur   79

CHATTAN
Josiah F.   71

CHATTEM
Charles   78

CHENEY
Elijah   26

CHERICKS
Catharine   145
John   108
Sally Ann   125

CHERIX	CHRISTIAN	CLARK Con't
Daniel 51	Seymour 135	William J.S. 101
Henry 114		William Thomas 105
Peter 141	CHRISTIE	
Tabitha 114	Elizabeth 1	CLARKE
	Nancy 11	Catharine 19
CHERREX	Polly 23	Charles 153
Francis 30	Sarah 17	Emma 125
		Esau 119
CHERRICKS	CHRISTOPHER	John H. 155
John 107	Ann 21	Lemuel 151
Peter 107	Belitha 14	Littleton T. 136
	Ebben 6	Mary C. 152
CHERRIS	Eleanor 39, 39	Roseannah 127
Peter 92	Eli 2	William J.S. 133
	Elijah 8	
CHERRIX	Emiline 142	CLARVOE
Albert J. 126	George 8, 24	Amanda C 101
A.R. 116	Henny 90	John B.H.W. 45
Arthur 57	Jane 86	
Elizabeth 82	Lowdoin 22	CLAVEL
Francis 58	Mary 10	Moses 46
Henny 89	Nancy 47, 48	
James 73	Noble 77	CLAVELL
Jane 135	Polly 9	Nancy 90
John 73	Tubman 42	
Lotty 39		CLAVILLE
Mary 155	CHURCH	Peter 42
Nancy 82	Hetty 92	Selby 42
Purnell 80	Jonathan 41	
	Mary 49	CLAYTON
CHESER		Elizabeth 108
Patsey 109	CLARK	Henry R. 148
	A Francis 139	Mary Elizabeth 102
CHESSER	Albertus 120	William 61
Daniel 90	Amelia 84	
Henry 120	Elijah 39, 88	CLAYVELL
Sally 89	Gertrude 70	Aralanta 145
Washington 142	Isaac 34	Edward Q. 139
	John 32, 42, 154	Ellen 140
CHETTAM	John K. 56	Henry 145
Elizabeth 29	John W. 113, 115	Mary 117
	Margaret Ann 106	
CHONNICK	Richard 6	CLAYVILL
John 138	Sophia 40	Nancy 139
	William 9, 53, 101	Polly 120

CLAYVILLE
Amelia   131
Ann   138
Cordelia M 156
George C.   149
Henry W.   146
Julia A.   135
Mary Ann   148
William   2

CLAYWELE
Rhoda   7

CLAYWELL
Ann   100
Ann Maria   106
Comfort   82
Edward   123
Eleanor   98
Eli   50
Elizabeth   62
Emeline   103
Esther A.R. 118
George   40
Henrietta   65
Hetty   76
Isaac   51, 63
James   63, 120
John   65, 110
Julian   84
Littleton   74
Major   17, 120
Margaret   122
Mary   50
Mary J.   114
Mary M.   112
Matilda   89
Moses   74, 78, 83
Peter   34, 107
Rhoda   70
Sally   28
Sally E.   80
Sally M.   116
Sarah   71
Selby   42
Thomas   84
William   28, 54

CLAYWELLE
Harriet   119

CLAYWILL
Catharine   118

CLIFTON
Garrett W. 152
Leander   97

CLOG
Henry   38
John   10
Sarah   11

CLOGG
Caroline   85
Henry   25
Hetty   61
James   101
Margaret   96
Maria   65
Milly   42
William   30, 85, 111

CLOWS
Ezekiel W. 67

CLUFF
Henry   22
John   69
Littleton   93
Robert   13

CLUGG
Henrietta   107

COARD
Caroline   131
Elizabeth   23
George A.   61
Hetty   74
Mary   23
Mary J.   149
Nancy   9
William   51

COBB
Elizabeth   35
Sally   57

COFFIN
Ann Maria   95
David   113
Eliza   82
Hannah   137
Hester N.   138
Isaac   104
Jacob   23
Joel   102, 155
Joseph   144
Leah   91
Lizzie Ayres 152
Major   90
Mary   91
Mary E.   141
Nancy   69, 104
Sally   65, 69
Sarah   155

COLBOURN
Elizabeth   94
Emily E.   153
James   32
James H.   51
Joshua   134
Josiah   27
Rachael   137
William   52

COLBOURNE
Ann Maria   139
Charlotte J. 123
Daniel W.   152
Elizabeth   115
Henny   117
Hetty I.   142
John J.   115
Nancy   148
Perry W.   155
Sally   114
William   151

COLBURN
Ann C.   138
Elijah P.   126

COLE
John 27
Mary Ann 136
Mary Anne 139
Peter H.   93

COLEBURN
William C.   137

COLEBOURN
Elijah 6
John 59
Nancy 5

COLIBOURN
Betsey   5

COLGAN
Wm B.   154

COLLENDER
Robert 73

COLLICK
Elizabeth 19
Harriet Ann   109
Levin William 9
Mary   32
Rhoda   37

COLLIER
Comfort 111
Joshua   105
Kendall   37
Lambert   40
Layfield 4
Mary A.E.   105
Matilda   71
Nancy   79
Polly 37

COLLIER Con't
Sally 14,27
William 14
William D.   102
Zadok   107

COLLINS
Ambrose   88
Andesia S. 68
Ann   56,121
Ann M.   142
Ansley   88
Ara   68
Asa C.   52
Belitha   8
Betsey   49
Betsy   91
Catharine 63,64
Charles 119,121
Charles P.   127
Charlotte 32,88
Charlotte E. 69
Eli   69
Elisha 93
Elisha M. Jr 130
Eliza   135
Eliza Jane   143
Elizabeth 42, 119,127
Elizabeth A. 96
Emma E.   123
Emma R.   153
Ephraim 58
Esther   23
Fanny   17
George T.   150
Gertrude 48
Henrietta 39
Henry 101
Hetty   115
Isaac 5.23
Isabella 119
James 3,7,11,44 53
   53,63,86,86,88,91
James B.   101

COLLINS Con't
James H. 15,54,78
    85,119
Jane   140
John . 9,36,54,
    89,126
John B.   149
John T.   147
Joicey   65
Jonathan   51
Joseph   86
Josiah 14,84,94
    109
Josiah C.   132
Julia Ann   109
Kendall   103
Laura A.   145
Leah   55
Lemuel   67
Lemuel P.   148
Levi   57
Levin   81
Lovey   19
Maranda   130
Margaret 136
Martha 15,104,137
Mary 8,45,48,75,88
Mary Ann   148
Mary H.   112
Mary T.   140
Matilda 120,137
Nancy 23,108,132
Nelly 17
Parker 19,38,67
Peggy   7
Peter 35,71
Polly   8
Price   87
Rachel   43
Richard   97
Sally   104
Sarah 72,91,125
Sidney F.   126
Soloman 58
Stephen B.   81

COLLINS Con't
Susan 137
Thomas 15,32,111
Thomas R. 92
Walton 4
William 51,63,81,109

COLLOHAM
Ann 64

COLONA
Edmund B. 138
George D.H. 131
Molly 149
Robert W. 142

COLONNA
Abel B. 92
Susan Jane 156

COLLONA
Wm C. 138

COLLUNOR
Benjamin 109

COLLYER
Adalene 113
Maria 121
Polly 5
Sarah 143

CONALD
Henrietta 71

CONKLLIN
George W. 148

CONAWAY
Lewis S. 123
Maria 37
Susan A. 153

CONNAWAY
Margaret 140
Margaret R. 143

CONNELLEY
John H. 149

CONNER
Amelia 65
Charlotte 95
Edward T. 106
Elizabeth 12,53
Elizabeth W. 115
Frederick 29,32,44
George 28,140
Isaac B. 141
John W. 82
Levin 17,38
Levin H. 142
Maria 105
Mary A. 139
Matilda 61
Nancy 36,89
Sally 15, 48
Samuel J. 103
Zilpha 64

CONNERLY
Betsey 36

CONOLY
Henny 53

CONOLLY
Charles 43

CONOWAY
Curtis S. 113
Hester 118
Isaac A. 141
Thomas 116

COOPER
Benjamin 110
Henry 75,115
Jane 121
John 10,51,72,137
Maria E. 129
Martha 90
Mary Ann 110
Nancy 78

COPES
Beverly 43
Jiles 24
John 43
Nancy 67
Parker 65, 56
William H.H. 148

CORBEN
William 60

CORBIN
Amelia H. 136
Ann 36
Ann Maria 62
Arintha D. 139
Eleanor 69
Eliza 125
Elizabeth 16
Elizabeth D. 127
Esther 59
George 67
George W. 156
Harriett 51,89
James 41
John 16,21,24,
  54,81,155
Levin P. 125,138
Margaret 36
Mary 52
Molly 24,25
Peter C. 125
Peter S. 8
Ralph 36
Rebecca 111
Sally 64
Sarah E. 97
William 29,48
William S. 36

CORD
John R. 38
Patsey 112
William 95,134

CORE
Levin L. 114
Sarah A.C. 135

COSTEN
Nancy 56
Peggy 2
Susan 32

COSTON
Ezekiel 53
Henrietta 148
Henry 112
Henry T. 108
Peter 60
William 22,42

COTTINGHAM
Annie H.L. 152
Anthony 90
Daniel 2
Eliza 92
Elizabeth 38,72
Experance Grant 51
Grace 6
Henry 10 22
Hetty 25
Isaac 6
James 6,141
Janet 2
John 59,60
Jonathan 19
Joshua 62
Littleton 40
Mary 29
Milcah 62,105
Nancy 31,72
Nathan 76
Peter D. 124
Priscilla 44, 122
Sally 27
Sarah 65
Sarah M. 126
Susan 32
Susannah 23
Thomas 2
Virginia A. 110
William 32

COTTMAN
Elizabeth B.C. 102
Joseph S. 77
Lazarus 3
William 10
William S.B. 54

CORDRY
James C. 122
William 138

COULBORN
Rhoda 135

COULBOURN
Betsey 70
Catharine 12,36
Hetty Ann 100
James 33
Polly 52
Robert 52
Riley 73
Sampson 70
Samsom 65
William 53
William H. 79

COULBOURNE
Ann 42
Henny 105
Henrietta 99
John 49
Josiah 89
Mary 83
Mary S. 104
Sally E. 131
Sarah E. 129
William 104
William T. 93

COULBURN
Caroline 137

COURDRY
Jacob 108

COVINGTON
Elizabeth 13
Elizabeth Ann 63
Isaac 62
Sarah 153
Sary 41
William 7

COWLEY
Comfort J. 151
Elizabeth 76
Henrietta 62
Samuel 88
Samuel J. 152

COWLY
Samuel 16

COX
Joseph B. 130
Margaret D. 152
Thomas 17
Tubman 34

CRAFFORD
Sarah 13

CRAFT
William 43

CRAIG
Jane E. 97

CRAMMER
Abraham W. 131

CRAWFORD
John 76

CRIPPEN
Ann 40
Eliza 49
Hetty 36
Mary Ann 59
Nancy 69
Sarah 13

CRISP
Andrew 139
William E. 145

CROCKETT
Caroline F. 115
Maria A. 152

CROPPER
Andesiah 6
Catharine 38,62
Catty 12
Charlott Ann 84
Cornelius 9,47
Edmond 60
Edmund T. 15
Edward 33
Eleanor 152
Eliza 53,63
Elizabeth 43,85
Elizabeth A, 108
Elizabeth B. 107
George 108
Gertrude 21
Harriet 147
Henrietta 139
Hester 83
Hetty 10,42
James 78
James E. 155
James P. 139
Jesse 24,30,81
John 32
Jonathan C. 50
Josiah 45,49
Juliana 115
Kendall 12,73
Leah H. 18
Levin 20,20,102,141

Margaret 59,88
Maria 55,77
Mary 11,37,80,85
Mary Ann 87
Mary E. 133

CROPPER Con't
Nancy 12,46,90
Nehemiah 13
Polly 21
Rachel 27,68
Rebecca 51
Rhoda 12
Richard 121
Robert 119
Sabra 90
Sally 3,34
Samuel 91,130
Sarah 42
Selvina 5
Sophia 9,11
Thomas M. 14
William 30,31,111
     154
William D. 125
William P. 33

CROSDALL
George 51

CROSWELL
Eliza A. 108
George E. 127
John H. 126

CROUCH
Joshua 56

CRUFF
Darius 30
Julian 83

CUEST
Richard 47

CULENA
William T. 120

CULLY
William 20

CULVER
Charlotte A. 128
Richard 19

CUMMIN
Rev Charles 18

CUNNAN
Thomas 31

CURMEAN
Margaret A. 108

CURTIS
George 98
George R. 112
James 130
John 60,120
Rev John D 95
Mary A. 130
Sally 128
Sarah H. 141
Susan M. 71

CUSTEN
Sally 43

CURTIS
Edmund R. 44
Elizabeth 68
Sally M. 120
Sally W. 116

CUTLER
Ann Eliza 138
Elizabeth 34
George W. 107
Margaret I. 123
Rachel 2

Sally A. 148
Samuel 56

CUTTER
Rosanna 67

DAILEY
David   41
Sally   8

DAILY
Samuel 96,137

DAISEY
Mary Ann 139

DALBY
William   31

DALE
Adeline 68
Betsey 35,62
Benjamin T. 68
Charlotte 68,86
Eli 82
Elijah M. 25
Eliza A. 145
Elizabeth 55
Hannah 50,63
Hetty 66
Isaac 73,96
Isaac A. 38
Jacob 8
James 15, 24,102
James S. 138
Jane 63
John 24,25,50,
     55,62
Kitty Young 53
Leah Elizabeth 107
Leven 96
Margaret 4
Martha 55
Martha Jane 148
Martha M 1
Mary 44,47
Mary Ann 83
Milbourne M. 56
Nancy 13,44
Patty 36
Peggy 45
Pierce Ann 113

DALE Con't
Rachel 50
Rhoda C. 90
Sarah C. 70
Sarah E. 117
Sophia 12
Thomas 19
William 8,14

DALLY
George R. 154

DAMNAL
Jacob   53

DANIEL
Betsey   38

DARBY
Lovey 80
Margaret E. 120
Mary 32
Mary Ann   140
William 18,19

DARCY
Joseph F.   44

DARSON
William T.   121

DASEY
Elizabeth   97
James   111

DASHIEL
Col George   7

DASHIELL
Betsey 26
Charles 29,32
George H. 56
John 22
Levin M.   108
Nancy 19
Polly 16
Sarah 8

DASHIELS
John Jr.   26

DASKY
Eliza Jane 94

DAUGHTERS
Gilliss J.   121
Nancy   109

DAVY
Sally   103

DAVIDSON
David 74,107
George W. 131
John   62
Julianna   100
Margaret Ann 150
Mary J.   114

DAVIS
Abijah 1
Abisha 12
Alexene 106
Amanda S. 104
Amelia 14
Andesiah 19,54
Andrew 47
Ann 95,104,131
Anna 13
Ann Eliza 82
Ann Elizabeth H. 78
Ann Maria 154
Aralanta 61
Arsissy   57
Barnaba   34
Benjamin 19,63,127,155
Betsey 4,9,16,17,21,34
       52
Betsy   38
Betty   37
Catharine 11,32,102
Catherine 22,25
Charles 45,89,94,101
        155
Charles T. 123

DAVIS Con't
Charlott 131
Charlotte Ann 114
Chaney 43
Clarrecy 44
Comfort Rackliffe 21
David 77
Ebenezer 69
Edward 11, 23, 27
Edward E. 113
Edward J. 154
Elenor 22
Eli 59
Elijah 11, 40
Elisha 19, 142
Eliza 61, 65, 69, 76
Eliza E. 149
Elizabeth 24, 41, 55, 68
 87, 90, 114, 117
 118, 143
Elizabeth A. 116, 118, 120
Emily 79
Esme 140
Eunice 4
Frederick 7
George 14, 32
George M. 96
George W. 96, 120
Gertrude 48, 49
Handy 4
Hannah 12, 46
Henny 31
Henrietta 77, 145
Henry 17, 44, 106
Henry E. 155
Hessie 133
Hetty 35, 46, 58, 87
Hetty C. 154
Hezekiah 52
Isaac 43, 63, 84
 121, 130, 134
Ishmeal 84
James 3, 3, 39, 48, 50
 58, 74, 75, 76
 103, 151
James A. 112
James E. 99

DAVIS Con't
James Jr. 55
James M. 82
Jane 99, 111, 126
 138
Jesse 17, 127
John 12, 34, 46, 52
 72, 94, 113
John B. 36
John H. 135, 141, 155
John S. 132
Johnson H. 97, 103, 123
Jonah 17
Jose 19
Joseph 24, 68, 74
Joshua 50
Joshua J. 151
Josiah 14, 91
Joyce B. 128
Julia A.D. 106
Julian 76
Juliann 60, 66, 81
Kendall 96
Kendall B. 102
Lemuel 69, 153
Lettitia 130
Levi 20
Levicia 35
Levin 37, 63
Levin H. 152
Littleton 10
Littleton B. 109, 140
Littleton D. 141
Littleton T.C. 139
Lodawick 34, 136
Lodowick F. 99
Lorenzo 87
Lorenzo D. 91, 115
Mahalia 48
Maranda 77
Margaret 53. 148
Margaret Ellen 149
Maria 91, 91
Maria C. 125
Martha 7, 24, 40, 49
 88, 100, 114

DAVIS Con't
Martha S. 125
Martin A. 5
Mary 7, 7, 20, 27, 49
 60, 61, 70, 70
 91, 96, 106
Mary Ann 80
Mary E. 90
Mary Elizabeth 151
Mary H. 141
Mary Jane 133
Mary W. 97
Matthias 4
Milly 52, 73
Mineva G. 154
Molly 59
Mordeca 41, 113
Moses 24
Nancy 20, 20, 46, 54
Nehemiah 1
Patty 10, 60, 90
Peggy 12, 43
Peter 42, 47, 55, 104
Peter L. 96
Polly 20, 23, 39, 43
Rachel 63, 65
Robert H. 44
Rownds 32
Sally 3, 56, 79, 103
Sally M. 130
Sally T. 39
Sampson 10, 24, 106
Samuel 10, 45
Samuel C.S. 129
Samuel G. 138
Samuel J. 98
Sarah 31, 33, 37, 94
 102, 106, 143
Sarah Ann 85
Sarah E. 156
Sarah Elizabeth 94
Sarah L. 147
Scarborough 81
Senah 17
Silas 23
Silas W. 123

DAVIS Con't
Soloman 27
Stephen P. 143
Susan 40
Sylvester H. 116
Thomas 13,17,40,
    69,70,104
    133
Thomas W. 119
Turner 3,28,62
Warrington 6,25
William 6,17,18
    20,32,53
    55,63,108
    133
William A. 149
William D. 125
William J. 134,142
William T. 145
Wilson 143
Zeporah 28,49
Ziporah C. 120

DAVISON
Nancy 51

DAVORIX
Mary 46

DAWSON
Major S.J. 156

DAY
James 114

DAYZY
William 100

DAZEY
Emeline 121
Joseph 71
Polly 52

DEAL
Gatty 63

DEAN
Elizabeth 59

DEAR
Jesse 30

DEMIS
Elizabeth 28

DEMPSEY
William D. 71

DENNIS
Ann 82,86,90
Areada 14
Benjamin 19,25,28
    125
Charlotte 133
Charlotte E.B. 125
Daniel H. 137
Ebenezer 150
Eleanor 12
Elijah 100
Elizabeth 19,120,155
Elizabeth A. 77
Elizabeth U. 108
Ellen 153
Ephaim 154
Francis H. 132
Garrison 133
Gatty 104
Gertrude E. 153
Ginetta 43
Henny 109
Henrietta 116
Henry 15,16,42,45,
    89,99,101
Henry Emerson 121,151
Henry J. 119
Hester A.H.J.P. 127
Hetty Ann 126
Hiram J. 53, 155
Isaac 53,55,134
Isaac W. 65
James 18,28,92
James M. 130
Jane 111
John 59,79,109
John H. 87

DENNIS Con't
John M. 136
John P. 115
John Of Thomas 84
John U. 89
John V. 125
John W. 55,102,103
Johnson 42,128
Jonathan 125,137
Julia 92
Julia J. 131
Leah 12
Leah J. 149
Lemuel 67
Lemuel J.S. 131
Levin D. 96
Levina 14
Littleton Q. 2,37,108
    125
Littleton Z. 67
Louisa C. 93
Margaret A. 148
Margaret E. 138
Maria 74
Martha E. 125
Mary 63,100,104
Mary Ann 102
Mary C. 108
Mary E. 156
Mary G. 51
Mary Jane 131,149
Mary M. 117
Mary W. 113
Milly J. 125
Mina 82
Nancy 15,15,82,
    104,133
Nelly 33
Peggy 96
Peter 55
Polly 37.42
Priscilla 145
Robert 37
Rufus J.M. 151
Sally 30
Sampson 112
Sarah 17

DENNIS Con't
Thomas 115, 140
Thomas H. 109
Valentine 144
Wheelty 13
William 6, 154
William H. 142, 148
Wm 63

DENNY
James 31
John 49

DENSON
Levin 35

DENSTON
Benjamin 114
Elizabeth 111
John 59
Leah 13
Levin 107
Mary A. 111
Matilda A. 112
Milby 49
Samuel 104

DERICKSON
Catharine 45
Eleanor 99
Isaac 36
James 52
John 47
John C. 64
Levin I. 112
Mary I. 111

DEVENX
Mary 140

DEVEREN
William 70

DEVERAUX
Joseph 148

DEVEREAUX
Littleton 78

DEVEREUX
Caroline 156
Charlotte A. 125
Elizabeth 121
Mary Ann 146
Thomas 128

DEVERIX
Elizabeth S. 116
Hetty 61
James 27

DEVERIUX
Matilda J. 141

DEVIRIX
Purnell 75

DEVORIX
James 64
Thomas 65

DEVRIX
John 71

DICKERSON
Catherine 56
Cornelius 17, 46
Cornelius Jr. 18
Edward 85
Edwin C.P. 136
Elisha 93
Elizabeth 16, 19, 49
    92, 111, 119
Esther 18
Henry 24
Isaac 36
James 61
James M. 120, 143
Jane E.A.B. 127
John 16, 73, 74, 105
John F. 126
Joseph J.G. 100
Margaret H. 82
Martha B. 2
Martha E. 144

DICKERSON Con't
Mary 130
Mary A. 144
Mary Elizabeth 91
Mary R. 4
Merrill 71
Nancy 41
Oma 123
Parker 45
Peter 59
Polly 44
Salonia 79
Sarah 103
Susanna 6, 23
Thomas 127
William 7, 81, 92, 110
    115
William Hosier 52

DICKINSON
Harry J.R. 140
James T. 143
Marietta 149
Merrill 81
William S. 135

DICKS
George 18
Harriet 99
Pierson 14

DICKSON
Clarissa 65
Hewet ? 65
Margaret 60
William 64

DIDIEY
John D. AREY 134

DIKES
Esther 14
George 7
Leah 3

DINTY
Sally 40

DIRICKSON
Elizabeth 147
Emma C. 142
Mary Ann 80
Matilda R. 121
Rachel R. 111

DISHAROON
Charlotte E. 119
Frances 15
Grace 46
Isaac 127
James 15, 46, 154
James H. 154
Jane 107, 133
John 13, 130
Levin 140
Mary 76
Mary E.A. 102
Mary Jane 96
Nancy 66
Polly 2, 10
Sally Ann 97
Sarah 26
Tampy 31
Thomas L. 62
Ursula C. 141
William 77
William T. 131

DIX
Ann P. 40
Catharine T. 97
John H. 114
Levin D. 120
Mary E.S. 114
Mary W. 86
Sarah 81
Tabitha W. 111
Trafanny G. 61
William W. 81

DIXON
Ann 45
Ann Elizabeth 120
Anna 34
Anna Maria 109

DIXON Con't
Curtis 45, 125
Edwin 125
Eleanor 27
Elizabeth 14
George W. 140
Henny 24
Hewell Nutter 13
Huet N. 26
James 29
John H. 91
Leah A. 130
Leah Ann 131
Louisa K. 152
Margaret 75, 106
Maria 66
Martha 76
Mary Ann 96
Mary D. 33
Mary Ellen 132
Mary Nutter 16
Milly 78
Nancy 30, 102
Samuel 34
Sarah 76
Sarah A. 134
Sarah Jane 101
Sarah Lane 18
Susan 38
Tabitha 9
Wesley 95, 137
William 3, 53, 109
William C. 155
William Q. 37

DODD
William 23

DOLLEY
John C. 106

DOLLY
Nathaniel 72

DONAWAY
Isaac 56
Oma 135
Peter H. 151
Polk 155
Polly 40
Rhoda 118

DONOHO
Eliza 81

DONOHOE
Eleanor T. 87
Joshua 36, 69
Mary 89
Nancy 69
Teague 4

DONNEY
Nevey P. 121

DONOWAY
Ann 96
Catharine 100
Clarissa 112
Elizabeth 90, 114
Henry 114
Louisa 115
Martha 107
Mordecai 107
Thomas O. 142
Thos. W. 88
William 113

DONNAWAY
William 9

DORETY
James 61

DOREY
John 31

DORFUER
Andrew 143

DORMAN
Ann 44
Elijah 14
Elizabeth 30
Hetty 35
Hezekiah 57
James 33,156
James H. 149
Jane 29
John H. 113
John Henry 86
Leah 65
Mary 83,109
Mary C. 141
Matthew 14
Nehemiah 64,92
Parker 19
Peter 41
Sally 101
Samuel 10,43
Sarah 5,150
Susan 78
Tabitha 21,22
Thomas 26
William 38
William P. 121

DOROTHY
Elizabeth 82
Nancy D. 86
Thomas 11

DORSEY
Ellen 112

DOUBERY
Thomas 100

DOUBLIN
Thomas 87

DOUGHERTY
Lydia Jane 134
William 116

DOUGHTY
Ann Maria 59
Margaret 90
George W. 140
Elizabeth S. 151

DOUGLAS
Margaret 36

DOWNAY
Powell 104

DOWNES
Priscilla 17
Sally 15

DOWNING
Elizabeth 62,65
Henrietta M. 115
James W. 114
John R. 109
John W. 61
Julia 89
Margaret D. 46
Matilda 92
Nancy A. 118
Sarah Jane 142
William I. 53

DOWNS
Isaac 123
Joshua 43
William 153

DRAYTON
James H. 86

DREADEN
Isaac 4

DREADIN
James 8

DRESKILL
Ann 59
David 59
Elijah 44

DREYDEN
James 42

DRISCAL
John S. 149

DRISKELE
Lotte 2

DRISKELL
Benjamin 30
Ebenezer 145
John 11
Molly 16
Polly 68
Rowland 18
Thomas 38

DRISKILL
Benjamin 40
Ebenezer 21
Elizabeth 52
James P. 121
Joshua 83
Philliss 70

DRISKLE
Elgate 2

DRUMIS ?
Sally B. 85

DRUMMONED
Sally 91

DRUMMOND
David S. 109
Elizabeth Susan 79
George 30
Maria I. 92
Richard B. 108
William 55
William W. 111

DRYDEN
Addie O 146
Amelia 8
Benjamin 67
Betsey 31
Catharine 1
Drucilla 143
Elanor 135
Eleanor C. McA 109
Elisabeth 41
Elizabeth 35,127,133
Elizabeth J. 154
Ephraim 18
George W. 94
Henrietta 42
Henry 87,101
Isaac 46,56
Isaac Jr. 56
Isaac T. 153
Isaac W. 138
James 17,22,58
 62,132
James H. 138
James M. 104
James P. 109
Jane 130
Jesse 119,129
John 33,59,82
John H. 153
John S.S. 132
Joshua 29,52
Littleton 51
Littleton T. 150
Louisa 119
Maria 57,76,118
Martha 145
Mary 76,99,108
Mary Ann 104,128
Mary E. 151
Mary Jane 105
Matilda G. 72
Milby John Slemmone
 86
Milly 54
Nancy 22,42,100
Noble 138
Peggy 18

DRYDEN Con't
Polly 17,37
Priscilla 151
Rachel 4
Robert 88,103
Robert Houston 14
Sally 68
Sally H. 153
Sally J. 120
Samuel M.H. 137
Sarah V. 151
Sewell 15
Stephen 1
Susan 72
Susanna 45
Thomas 42,81
William 15,25,35,40
 69,81,87,

DUBBER
Mary Ann 64

DUBERLEY
Mary 48

DUBERLY
Thomas 146

DUBLEY
William 89

DUER
Esther 41
Harrett 21
John H. 121
Littleton J.M. 118
Margaret 47
Mary 34
Nancy 47
Sally 31

DUFFEY
Tabitha 30

DUFFIELD
John 30
John T. 51
Nancy Handy 95

DUFFY
James S. 134
James Thomas 126
John J. 155
Zadok 156

DUKES
Amelia A. 126
Benjamin 74
Betsey 27
Charlotte 23
Eleanor 75
Elizabeth 51,130
Elizabeth A. 131
Elizabeth J. 145
Frederic J. 145
Frederick 73
Gatty 56
Henny 80
James 100
John 8,24,54
 91,100
Lemuel 81
Littleton 66,103
Martha E.A. 106
Mary 40,101,109
Mary Ellen 144
Matilda 71
Melvin 41
Nancy 100
Parker 16,24
Patty 74
Polly 6,111
Robert 75
Sally 129
Sarah E. 137
Sarah W. 129
Severn 40
Thomas 80,84,100
 110

DUNCAN
Amelia 26
Cabel 88
Catharine 38
Charlotte 68,93
Drucilla 66

DUNCAN Con't
Eliza 53,129
Eliza M. 99
Euphamy 40
Fanny 62,86
Gertrude 56
Hannah 6
Harriet 124
Henry 42
Hiram 85
Hiram B. 108
James 44,62,63
James M. 49
Jane 16
John 79
Josiah 1,48
Laura Ann 89
Lemuel J. 131
Levi 4
Margaret 49
Mary 79,103
Mary C. 120
Milby 19
Nancy 22
Polly 18,64
Rachel 16
Rachel A. 150
Sally 30
Sally 36
William 5, 104

DUNKIN
Drucilla 22

DUNNAWAY
Harriett 62
John 65
Joseph 60
Molly 61
Oma 156

DUNSTON
Leah 6

DUNTON
Catharine 64
Catharine S. 69
James 139
James S. 63
Levin 100
Maggie 149
Maggie S. 151
Pattie A. 148
Thomas K. 77

DURHAM
James 155

DUSK
Henry 70

DUSKEY
John S. 134

DUSKY
Ann 74
Elexine 130

DYER
Sally 25

DYERS
Mary 27

DYES
Priscilla 98

DYKES
Ann 117
Anna 2
Arthur 55
Benjamin 71
Ebenezer 109
Elinor 137
Elizabeth 46
Ephraim 26
George 67,85

DYKES Con't
Henry 122
Hetty 75
James 125
James W. 69
John Edward 136
Kellaem 36
Kellam 132
Martha 122
Mary 115,141
Mary A. 130
Mary E. 133,156
Michael 28,49
Nancy 52
Peter 43
Phulis 45
Sarah 50
Selby 117
Stephen T. 119
Susan 97
Thomas 111
William 141

DYMOCK
Betsey 19
Hannah 1
Julia Ann 59

EASHAM
Hamman 13
Robert Henry 114
William 17

EASHUM
Collins 24
James 2
Mary 35
Sally 24,25

EAST
Peter 86

EASTERLY
Mary E. 40
Sarah 41

EDMUNDS
Anna Maria 65
Elizabeth B. 127
James W. 151

EDWARDS
Isaac J.S. 130
John A. 108

EGNEW
Robert 26

ELLEGOOD
Elijah 36
Robert H. 62

ELLENSWORTH
Elizabeth 97
William 76

ELLIOTT
Brinkley 77
Brinkley F. 154
Elizabeth 146
Hulda 149
Hulda Ann 137
James W. 37
John 137
Joseph 128
Leah Ann 134
Levi T. 144
Margaret E. 125
Sally 151
Sally R. 100
Teackle 111

ELLIS
Albert P. 135
Ann 111
Betsey 28
Charles 74
Emeline 114
George J. 129
Hannah 73
Henny M. 150

ELLIS Con't
Hetty 120
James 83
Jesse 98
John H. 126,139
Joseph R. 121
Josiah 39,58
Leah J. 144
Maria 123
Martha Ann 135
Mary Elizabeth 122
Matilda 105,108
Nancy 39
Rachel 57
Rebecca 25
Robert W. 146
Sally 38,104
Sally E. 144
Samuel 126
Susan 117
William 45,54,135
William H. 146

ELLISS
Caroline 89
Levi 36

ELSEY
Leah Ann 149

ELZEY
Sally 4

EMBERSON
John 24

ENNALLS
John 47
John William 107

ENNIS
Archebald 51
Ann M. 128
Booz 14
Covington 89
Donna 156
Elijah 10,29,70, 81

ENNIS Con't
Elizabeth 77,126
Elizabeth H. 122
Elizabeth J. 121
Elizabeth P.M. 71
Ellen 155
Gatty 116
Gilbert T.J. 141
Gilly 69
George 124
Isaac 57
Isaac H.F. 73
Isaac H. 82
James 60,101
Jane 130
Jesse 21,63
John 80
Joseph 34
Joseph I. 106
Joseph J. 123,128
Joshua 124
Levi 53
Levin 68,70
Louisa 145
Margaret 76,106,127
Martha 44
Mary 49,112
Mary Ellen 112
Matilda 145
Michjah 37
Milly 101
Nancy 8,24,63
Nelly 107
Nicy 87
Outten 5,74
Rachel 27
Richard 85
Sally 117
Samuel 6,9,46
Samuel R. 132
Sarah 2,30
Sarah M. 111
Stephen 34
Stephen W. 98
Susannah 9
William 40,103,105 118,128
Zepporah 40

ENOS	EVANS Con't	EWELL Con't
Abraham 29	Isaac 30,42	Josephine E.B. 148
	Jacob 32	Leah 65
ESHAM	James 77,108	Margaret 60
Catharine 115	James R.E. 104	Maria 40
Charlotte 31	James W. 136	Mary Ann 60
Elijah 77	Jane 122	Sallie M. 152
Elinor 71	Jesse 28	Sally 109,123
Elizabeth 51	John 34,37,76,	Solomon D. 149
Gatty 52	129,136	Thomas 102
Geo W. 153	John E. 156	William 35
Hamilton B. 103	John J. 118,149	William S. 91
Harriet 62	Joshua 4	
John 25,118	Leah 39	FACKS
Margaret 62,134	Leml. 88	Frederick 45
Martha 27	Martha 1	
Mary 57,72,141	Martha W. 89	FAIR
Nancy 71	Mary 46,78,84	Thomas 15
Parker 71	Mary C. 31	
Rachel 63,97	Mary H. 153	FAIRBROTHERS
Rhoda 70	Matilda 141,145	Maria 119
Rhoda J. 148	Molly 47,105	
Robert 36,71	Nancy 60,106	FAREBROTHERS
Sally P. 60	Nancy S. 133	Edward 105
Samuel 32	Peter 2,23,26	
Thomas 78	Priscilla 105	FARLEW
	Rowland J. 152	Benjamin 80
EVANS	Sally 22,57	
Andasia 51	Sarah C. 154	FARLOW
Andesiah 64	Solomon 74	Benjamin B. 95
Annamias 8	Thomas 38,39,75	Benjamin G. 122
Catharine 73,114	William 57,109	Benjamin W. 131
Cornelia S. 116	William F. 118	Billy F 40
David of Wm. 59	William H. 47	Billy F. Jr 119
Edmund 4	William Levinas 105	Billy H. 114
Eleam 67	Zipporah 68,76	Daniel J. 115
Eliza I.M.		David 31
Elizabeth 49	EVENS	David B. 133
Elizabeth Ann 110	Dolly 7	Gatty 125
Ellen 144		Gatty M. 116
Esther 5,95	EWELL	George 59
E,W. 142	Charles 40,47	George R. of Geo
Gamage ? 98	Coventon 20	139
George H. 151	Esther 144	George R. 114
George T. 111	James 130	Hannah E. 121
Hannah 39	John S. 69	Hiram W. 152
Harriet 117		
Henry 54		
Hester 134		
Hetty 20		
Indiana 140		

FARLOW
James H. 132,134
Jesse 3
Jonathan S. 115,123
Julia A. 129
Mahala E. 118
Mary 81
Mary E. 137,142
Nancy 59
Nancy D. 150
Priscilla E. 118
Sarah A. 134

FARREL
Ana 71
John 134
Lydia M.A. 136

FARRELL
Ann W. 108
Elizabeth L. 104
Isaac 98
James 57
John 12
Martha 57

FARROW
Emma S. 144
Jane 77
Julien M. 65
Mary I. 75
May C. 156

FASSETT
Ann E. 78
Correlius 84
Elijah 39
Elizabeth 12,19,54
Fanny 57
James 19
John 8,34
John B. 83
Juliana 49
Lucretia 79
Margaretta 44
Nancy 20
Sarah 8,22

FASSETT Con't
Thomas 8
Thomas S. 34
William 55,70
William of Jno 82
Zepporah P. 23

FASSITT
Charles H. 119
Edward B. 114
George W. 115
Hetty 117
James 119
John F. 57
Julia A. 152
Louisa 81
Lydia 58
Mary 102
Mary C. 104
Mary E. 153
Matilda 82
Molly 39
Nancy 24
Sally A. 132
Sarah 131
William 63
William 63

FASSITTE
James 37

FASQUE
Mary 111

FAULKNER
Jonathan 146

FAVOUR
John 45

FEDDEMAN
Amanda O. 147
Ann 104
Attlanta 56
Catharine J. 155
Henry 20
Levin J. 155
Michael 20
Olivia 123
William M. 127

FEEMAN
Isaac 72

FELDMAN
Mary 7

FERGUSON
William 4

FERMAN
Eunice 36

FERRILL
Sarah 37

FICKETT
Priscilla 41

FIDDEMAN
John 122
Maria 67

FIELD
William B. 85

FIELDS
Anthony B. 100
Charlotte E. 151
Mary J. 152
William 68

FIGGS
Benjamin T. 142
Elijah R. 147
Gillis 72
Gilly 119
Hetty M.E. 143
Jesse J. 152
Levema E. 126
Levin W. 143
Mahala E. 152
Margaret A.M. 122
Mary 126
Minos 135

FIGS
Ann Mariah 136

FINNER
Polly 17

FINNERY
Peggy 11

FINNEY
Eliza U. 34
John T. 146

FISH
Bennet 58
William J. 135

FISHER
Deborah 15
Elizabeth 2
Esther 32
Francis E. 153
Harriet J. 132
Hannah 72
Henry P. 55
Hetty 100
James 44
Jane 129
John 22,142,147
John J. 144
John Thomas 126
Joseph 77
Levi 91
Louisa 72
Margaret 97
Margaret S. 100
Mary 60
Mary A. 150
Mary J. 144
Matilda 123
Nathaniel 67
Polly 10
Samuel P. 103
Sarah E. 148
Stephen 99
Sophia 91
Susan 88
Thomas B. 71
William 156

FISJAREL
Elizabeth 12

FITACHETT
Margaret 127

FITCHET
Esther R. 105
Laura S. 147
Nathaniel 66
Severn 25
Susan 66

FITCHETT
Emeline 77
Patsy 92
Sarah 93
William J. 144
William S. 147

FLEETWOOD
William 143

FLEMING
Atta 82
Eleanor A. 76
Joshua 13
Littleton 43,72,82
Robert 46
Sally 41
Mary 55

FLEMMING
Alexene 109
Alfred 150
Anna 4
Daniel L. 144
Isaac 124
John F. 94
Nelly 7
Robert 99
William T. 91

FLETCHER
Fanny 40
Margaret W. 110
Polly 72
Sally 59
Thomas R. 108
William 39

FLOID
Emeline 54
William 103

FLOYD
Betsy 33
Betsey B. 38
Frederic 149
John 28,74,100
Mary 53
Mary E. 131
Moses 52
Peggy 40
Sally A. 131
Shepard B. 64
Smith W. 138
Sophia 43

FLOYED
Nancy 28

FOLIO
William 106

FOMMONS
Stephen E. 15

FOOKES
Pressa 44

FOOKS
Abigale 59
Amelia E. 121
Anna 68
Ann Elizabeth 126
Benjamin 149
Betsey 35
Cannon 67
Charles 13,37
Daniel 16,29,36
Delila 26
Dewit C. 122,135
Ebenezer H. 99
Eleanor 70
Eleanor Gray 59
Eliza 78
Elizie A. 145
Fane 149

FOOKS Con't	FOOKS Con't	FRANKLIN Con't
George 10,136	Sally M. 138	Andy 131
George N. 75,78,96	Samuel H. 140	Benjamin 23,71
Geo W. 152	Sarah 15.40	Betsey 20
Gertrude 48	Sarah Caroline 97	Comfort 38
Hance 76	Seth 20.26	Elinor 20
Handy 93	Unice 66	Francis 83
Henrietta 65	Uriah 68,102	George P. 99,114
Henry 79	Uriah E. 121	Henry 48
Hetty 121	William 68,87,154	Henry J. Jr. 57
Irving 123	William R. 50	James 14
James 12,16,76	Zepporah 29	Jane 114
James of D. 77,95		Littleton P. 124
James M. 82	FOREMAN	Louisa 64
Jane 69,149	Daniel J. 81	Martha 18,126
Jehu 69	John 51	Mary 75
Jesse 85	Sarah E. 112	Mary F. 79
John 70,131		Milcah E. 62
Jonathan 8,78	FORMAN	Molly 17
Jonathan of E. 61	Alfred 69	Mutey ? 10
	Edwin 52	Nancy 14,17
Julia T. 153		Nancy M. 69
Julian 55	FOSKEY	Peter 30
Juliann 98	Daniel 91	Polly 5,21
Leah 61	Mary 132	Rachel 45
Letta 50	Sabra 108	Rebecca 30
Liticia 123		Robert 46
Louisa 146	FOSSEY	Sally 23
Margaret A. 128	James 53	Sarah 38,44
Maria 82		Sarah M.O. 103
Maria Ellen 145	FOUNTAIN	Selby 6
Martha 81	Henry 12	Tho. 2
Mary 36,50,122	Levin Irvin 16	William 4
Mary Ann 93	Leah Washington 58	William Jr. 53
Matilda Ann 81		
Matty 131	FOX	FRAZIER
Nancy 37,67	Babel 87	Thomas T. 135
Peggy 59	Thomas 38	
Phebe 72	William 83	FREANY
Polly 10		Sarah 87
Polly R. 54	FOZWELL	
Rachel 23	Elzey 48	FREEMAN
Ritcher 85		Ann Mariah 153
Robert 70	FRANKLIN	Betsey 60
Saborouh 17	Alexander 3	Hester 155
Sally 23,32,71	Amelia 62	Isaac I. 152
	Andasiah 30	John 147
		Mary 132
		Sophia 74

FREENA
Richard 28

FREENEY
Elijah 145
John 11
John W. 139
Laura Ann 139
Mary Jane 139
William 62

FREENY
Amelia A. 144
Joshua J. 138
Richard 59

FRENEA
Milly 24

FRESHWATER
Nancy 5

FROST
Sally 31

FULWELL
Maria Amelia 48

FURBUSH
Peter 103

FURKIS
Mary 87

FURNACE
Matilda 141

FURNESS
Charlotte 50

FURNIS
William 13

FURNISS
James 30
Louisa 67
Polly 23
William 55

GAFFORD
James 119

GALE
Samuel 148

GALT
Mary 9

GAOTTEN ?
Sally 80

GARDNER
John 61
William 23,59

GARETTSON
Nancy 36

GARMAN
Ananias 62

GARMON
William 59

GARRETSON
Sally 62

GARRISON
Betsey 87
Elizabeth 89
Jane 111

GARROSON
Jonathan 20
Lavinia 111

GARWELL
Henry 5

GASKINS
Maria 57
Mary 138
Milcah 81

GAULT
Archibald 94,136
David 104,123
David W. 151
Eliza A. 146
Elizabeth 23,26
113,118
James 55
Jane 131
Jenkins 118,123
John 65
John P.W. 122
Mary 143
Obed 40
Peggy 10
Rhoda 16
Sally M.J. 104
William 46,109

GEE
Edward 28
Nancy 39

GEORGE
Mary 43

GERMAN
George 65

GEWELL
Charles 114

GIBB
Elisha 8
Elizabeth 155

GIBBONS
Eliza 133
John 61
Margaret 133
Sarah H. 110

GIBBS
Abraham 18,42
Betsey 3
Caroline 134
George 106,134
Hetty, 52,144
Jane 29
John 28,110
Joseph 63
Mary 30
Nancy 11,94
Stephen 77
Thomas 143
Wealthy 21
William 52

GILCHRIST
Eliza 58

GILLETT
Elizabeth 15
John 55
Louisa 65
Major 60
Mary M. 81
Robert H. 142
Sarah 2
Sarah Ann 156
Wealthy 20

GILLIS
Maria A.P. 32
John A.B. 78
John P.P. 137
Joseph 13

GILLISPEE
Peter J. 109

GILLS
Mary I. 137

GILROY
William 154

GIMMELL
Hugh 14

GINES
Nancy 36

GIVAN
Ephraim 66
Hiram 83
James 86
Joseph D. 77
Leah 69
Margaret 51
Mary 45
Mary M. 124
Noah 126
Polly 26
Robert 44
Sarah 17
Thomas 34
William 32

GIVANS
Eliza 82
Elizabeth 27
George 26,87
Henny 87
Hetty 7
Jacob 34
James 3
Joshua 31
Martha Ann 119
Mary 50,74
Nancy 33,50
Peggy 28
Peter 77
Polly 24
Rachel 10
Robert 1,4
Sally 33,63
William 12,14

GIVEN
Robert 13

GIVINS
Peter 118

GLADDEN
Edmund 24
Elizabeth 112
George 40
George W. 90
Henry 41
James H. 141
John 47,87,99,108
Leah 79
Luther 85
Maria 91
Mary Q. 147
Polly 5
Sally 91
Sarah Ann 57

GLADDING
George W. 134
Harriet 100

GLASS
Anna 20
Thomas 68

GLASSBY
Mary 91

GLEN
Margaret 39

GODDEN
Joseph 49

GODFREY
Ann 90
Ann Maria 6
Balitha 115
Belitha 62
Charles 60
Charlotte 76
Charly H. 143
Cornelius 61
Drucilla 147
Ellen 154
Elizabeth 50,78
Henry 97
Hety 69
James 28,39,116
John 23,35,58
Joseph 78,106

GODFREY Con't
Joshua 145
Levin 2,103
Martha E. 142
Mary 61,142
Mary A. 128
Mary Ann 128
Matthias 90
Mehala 54
Nancy 36,52,92
Peter 61
Priscilla A. 110
Robert 132
Samuel 133
Samuel M. 142
Sarah 8,73,78
Sarah Jane 155
Sopha Ann 115
Stephen M. 140
Susan 116
Thomas 112
William J. 129

GODWIN
John 89
Martha A. 156
Susan H. 113
Vianna 49

GODY
Sally 73

GOFFIGON
Sally R. 96

GOODNY
Sarah 105

GOOTEE
Elizabeth 17
John 135
Polly 2
William 123

GOOTON
William 105

GOOTY
Sally 103

GORDY
Aaron 31
Amelia E. 136
Benjamin H. 35,85
    125
Burton 101
Elijah 106
Emeline 75
Garritson 63
George W. 129,145
Gertrude 112
Harriet H. 79
Henrietta 120
Hetty Ann 101
Isabella 134
James R. 113
John H. 102
John P. 47
John S. 121
John T. 137
Julia Ann 116
Laura A. 155
Lavinia E.B. 1,129
    129
Lemuel D. 150
Leonard 71,76
Levi D. 145
Levin 2
Levin W. 131
Mahalia 83
Maranda C. 116
Maria B. 115
Margaret J. 151
Martha 77
Mary E. 101,112,115
    145,154
Mary Jane 116
Nancy 68
Nelly 72
Noah 54
Olevia E. 156
Sally A.W. 118
Sally E. 70

GORDY Con't
Sarah C. 122
Southey 71
Spicer 67
Thomas 27,40
Thomas B. 136
Thomas J. 70
Wesley 63
William 4
William G. 122

GORE
Comfort 22
Sarah Ann 152

GORMAN
Gertruce 67

GORNELL
Sally 26

GORNWELL
Mary 66

GOSWELLING
Stephen 149

GOUTEE
John 49

GOUTY
John 8
Mary 106

GOWTEE
John 2

GRAVENER
Sarah Elizabeth 99
William 138

GRAVENOR
Allison 145
Benton C. 128
Ebenezer 141
Elisha 156
Elizabeth 15

GRAY
Adeline 118
Ananias 84,106
Ann 42,132
Anna R. 101
Ann Elizabeth 61
Asa 118
Betsey 11,12,37,51
Bridget 34
Burton 46
Catharine 78
Charlotte 19
David 47
David H. 102
David Long 14
Drucilla 97
Easter 47
Ebenezer 136
Eliza 79
Elizabeth 88,93,124
Err 53
Ev T. 138
Fanny 51
George 39
George Howard 9
Hannah 14,18
Henry 53,124
Hetty 150
Jacob 65
James 27,29,41,87
Jane 127,147
Jesse 5,22,149
John 13,89
Johnson 36,93
Joseph 65,96
Julian 86
Julianna 137
Leah 57
Levin 96
Littleton 7
Louisa 126
Mahalia 42
Margaret A, 112
Martha 40,71
Martha I. 40
Mary 21,46,85

GRAY Con't
Mary Ann E. 63
Mary E. 108,142
Mary E.M. 96
Milby 132
Mitchell 31
Molly 29,34,90
Nancy 156
Patty 9,12
Peter 42
Phenette 55
Piercey 1
Polly 15
Rachel Jane 122
Robert 37
Rouse 1
Sabrah 53
Sally 10,30,139
Samuel 7
Sarah Catharine 95
Sarah C.M. 142
Sheppard 136
Stephen R. 138
Terena 73
Thomas 19,44,112
Tubman 47
Walton 70
William 121
William J. 144
William W. 19

GREEN
George 36
George Teackle 24
John 3
Molly 14
Nancy 24,25
Polly 19

GREER
Moses 62
Wealthy 75

GREW
Peter 14

GREY
James 90
Nancy 57

GRIFFEN
Belitha 1,9
Betsey 40
Charlotte 4
William 94

GRIFFIN
Belitha 91
Caroline 92
Charlotte 44,86,94
Edward 133
Henry 31
Hetty 87
Isabella 117
Jane 92
Lambert 87
Mahala A. 143
Mary 39,104,141
Mary A. 137
Milby 87.131
Nancy 49,118
Rebecca 136
Sally 132
William T. 124

GRIFFITH
Isaac 55
Milby 80

GRENNEL ?
Polly 41

GRIMMALDS
Thomas J. 108

GRINNALDS
Thomas I. 108

GRINOLES
Elizabeth 38

GROLTON
Thomas 132

GROTEN
Mary 111

GROTON
Catherine E. of Va.
　　　　137

GROVE
Augustus G.　85

GUNBY
Amelia　67
Ann O.　31
Benjamin　2
Esther　3
George S.　29
James　19
John　5,59,110
Kirk　6,12
Louisa　138
Mary　23
Mary Ann　63
Mary H.　49
Mary Miles　55
Sally W.　57

GUNN
Leah　6
Nancy　25
Polly　9

GUNTER
Elizabeth A.　156
Edward M.　149
Laban　80
Mariah　84
Nancy　41

GUTHERY
Charley　151
Elizabeth　1
George　150
Hannah　4
James　124
Jesse　14
John　96
Severn　23
William　124

GUTHRIE
John　79
William　94

GUTRY
John　42

HACK
Cave J.M.　86
Thomas U.　69

HADDEN
Eleanor　106
Polly　22

HADDER
Catharine　5,54
Elizabeth　21
Fanny　47,54
Gertrude　36
John　18
Lemuel　36
Mary E.　136
Nancy　28
Patty　23
Polly　13
Sally　22
Stephen　150
Stephen D.　125
Thomas　46
Warren　3
William　61

HADDOC
Isaac　152

HADDOCK
James H.　108
John　152
Mary　124
Milly　116

HADDOK
Joshua　77

HADDOR
Caty　27

HADOCK
William　135

HAILES
Mary　102
Mary Jane　105
Stacey　30
William　99

HAINS
Levin　82

HALE
Lemuel A.　116

HALES
Comfort　54
Elizabeth　88
Ellen　140
Harriet　70
Henny　85
John　140
Margaret　62
Matthias　139
Matthew　40
Sarah　82
William　53,95
William J.　132

HALEOCH ?
William　76

HALEY
Elizabeth　119

HALL
Alberta H.　146
Ann　130
Benjamin　42
Bridget　128
Edward　118
Elisha　144
Eliza　129
Elizabeth　60,65,98,124
　　　　135
George　1.20,25,35
　　　　97,129

HALL Con't
Harriet 64
Harriet E. 154
Henry 64, 81
James 16, 38, 39
 65, 96, 123
Jeanetta 113
Jerome B. 121
John 60, 75
John C. 104
John R. 152
Joseph S.B. 140
Joshua 147
Lambert A. 155
Laura A. 141
Lemuel 19
Lemuel A. 58
Littleton 96
Louisa 81, 102
Mary 33, 80
Mary M. 117
Major T. 114
Milly 101
Nancy 50, 110
Nelson 129
Peggy 28
Peter 19
Philip W. 119
Polley 22
Polly 60
Priscilla 131
Richard 47, 67, 70
 74, 123
Robert 80
Sally 10
Sally R. 134
Samuel 74 100
Sarah 100
Susan A. 129
Thomas 16, 91
William E. 109
Zadok 62, 113

HAMAN
Houten Jas. 134

HAMBLIN
Benjamin M. 115

HAMBLIN Con't
Clarissa 138
George W. 126
Henry H. 130, 152
Hetty Ann 113
James B. 108, 130
John 102
Joshua 59
Joshua J. 131
Julia 133
Julia C. 145
Marshall 11
Mary E. 131
Tingle 152
Wm S. 155

HAMDEN
Marshall 37

HAMMOND
Ann 63
Benjamin 2, 24
Billy 88
Bowden 5
Bowdoin 58, 77
Catharine 58
Charlotte 34
Clarinda 145
Dinah 36
Edward 1, 2, 7, 142
Edward of Chas.
 56
Eleanor 79
Ellen R. 155
Elizabeth 65, 92
Exeline 85
George W. 112
James 58
Jane 89
Jesse 70
John 82
Jonathan 7
Josiah 115
Leah 9
Martha 7, 123
Martha 7, 123
Martha A, W. 119

HAMMOND Con't
Mary 1, 34, 42, 51
Mary C. 146
Mary H. 87
Minos 139
Molly 14
Nancy 32, 38, 66, 85
Nelly 18
Rachel 41
Rhoda 72
Sally 12, 84, 86
Sally A. 140
Sampson 106
Stephen R. 108
William 3, 20, 62, 77
 142
Wm 13
Zedekiah 79

HANMMONDS
John T. 103

HAMMONS
Polly 37

HAMON
Abel 39

HANCOCK
Amanda W. 120
Ann J. 117
Cordelia 123
Eliza 121
Elizabeth 152
George W. 121
Isaac 133
James 132
Laura A. 150
Leonard W, 126, 142
Louisa 124
Mary 3
Mary Ann 116
Mary E. 155
Mary G. 135
Peter 131
Peter W. 154
Sydney 142
Thomas P. 153

HANDCOCK
Amelia P. 147
Andrew 150
Arailanta 101
Betsey 33
Daniel 57
Eleanor 69
Elizabeth 115
Elizabeth C. 140
Gertrude 81
Harriet 139
Isaac 130
James 9
Jane 97
John 52, 82
John E. 140
Lavinia 130
Lydia 55
Major 69, 104
Mitchell 65
Nancy 21, 88, 106
Peter 97
Sally 13, 69, 128
    133
Whittington 57
William 27, 78

HANDLEY
Margaret 33

HANDY
Anna R. 12
Betsey 4
Charles N. 96
Eliza 43
Elizabeth 4
Elizabeth G. 54
George 78
Harriet 13
Harriet G. 17
Hetty G. 47
Isaac William 93
James 50
James H. 32
Leven 91
Littleton D. 81
Margaret 28
Mary D. 39

HANDY Con't
Mary King 29
Nancy 6
Nelly A. 90
Priscilla 14, 27
Priscilla W. 99
Robert J.H. 9
Sally 8
Saml. 27
Samuel Jr. 52
Samuel W. 38
Sarah 30
William W. 57

HANLY
Caroline 80

HANNON
James 110

HARDIS
Ezeriah 79
George 90

HARDISH
Louisa 146

HARDY
James 50

HARGES
Nancy 29

HARGIS
Elizabeth Anne 133
Euphamy 46
Harriet H. 115
James M. 36
Levin H. 113
Lydia 44
Margaret 16
Mary 21
Mary W. 118
Nancy 69
Peter 39
Stephen 30

HARGIS Con't
Thomas 28, 33, 111
Thomas M. 45
Thomas W. 84, 110
William 33, 55, 70

HARGROVE
Sally 38

HARINGTON
Mary 109

HARLES
John 34

HARLEY
Albert 136

HARMON
Abel 32
Caroline 152
Comfort 35
Daniel 26
Elizabeth 123
Euphemia 101
James 96, 128
Joshua 54
Mary 33
Nancy 54
Nathan 19
Nathaniel G. 35
Rachel 31
Sally Mary 109
Sarah 30

HARMONSON
Francis 133
James 73
John 52
Littleton 54

HARNSBY
Sally 47

HARPER
Bridget 20
Catharine 50
Gertrude 9
Joseph 32

HARPER Con't
Mary 60
Samuel D. 55
William 26,92
William P. 128

HARRESON
James 72

HARRINGTON
Samuel 41

HARRIS
A. Amanda 134
Anelo 98
Charles 2,11
Eliza A.C. 89
Elizabeth 4
George B. 117
Harriet E. 127
Isaac 51,54
Mary 62
Mary A. 147
Mary M. 132
Nancy 16
Sally A. 125
Sarah 84
Thomas 2
Thomas L. 111
Tubman 37

HARRISON
Charlotte 67
Edwin G. 129
Elizabeth 96
Isaac 96
James 78
Julia 118
Margaret E.M. 97
Robert C. 101
Rouse 21
Sarah M. 102
Seth 64
Zepporah 67

HART
Betsy 68
Sally 40

HARTHWAY
John 146

HARVEY
Levi D.

HASTED
Henry 107

HASTEN
Lambert 104

HAISTINGS
Henry 109

HASTING
Caroline L. 142
Eleanor 67
Elijah 84
Eliza 81
Jane 141
Julia 90
Martha 94

HASTINGS
Anna Marie 125
Bettie 155
Daniel E. 147
Elizabeth J. 154
Fanny 93
Handy 93
Isaac H. 120
John 91,97
Joseph 154
Joshua 104
Kendal W. 124
Lawrenson 117
Major 40.116
Maria J. 148
Mary 145
Mary Elizabeth 139
Mary J. 153
Matilda A. 123
Michael J. 124
Rena 154
Richard 94,113
Sally 133
Sarah 106
Sarah E. 154
Susan 94
Warner
William 82

HASTINGS Con't
William A. 89
William N. 125
Winder H. 98

HASTY
Joshua 152
Matilda A. 123
Warren I. 152

HATHAWAY
William 135

HAUBERT
Frederick 125

HAY
Edward 49

HAYES
Elizabeth 65

HAYMAN
Daniel H. 155
Dan'l I. 78
David I. 86
Eleanor L. 116
Elizabeth 23
Emily F. 147
Francis A. 153
Francis O. 121
Handy 137
Harriet 133
Jacob H. 75
James W. 112
John 78,117
John H. 94
Johnson 14
John T. 126
Josiah 67
Leah A. 140
Levin 14,81
Maria Ann 63
Maria C. 154
Martha 25
Martha J. 123
Matilda 96

HAYMAN Con't	HEARN Con't	HENDERSON
Matilda C. 91	Esther 109	Amanda C. 116
Mary 28	George 44	Amelia A. 94
Mary Ann 89	George W. 129,131	Anna 15
Mary H. 133	Hetty 27	Anna H. 126
Rebecca 109	Hiram W. 123	Ara 33
Rebecca E. 106	Irena 127	Barnaby 4,13
Sally Ann 122	Irena F. 123	Benjamin 111
Stephen R. 150	Isaac 62	Betsey 13
Susanna 49	Isaac H. 133	Catharine 17,110,125
Theodore 111	Isaac T. 134	Charles 41
William 62	James 27	Charlotte 24
William W. 101	James R. 91	Curtis 13,53
	John 34	Denard 136
HAYS	John L. 109	Elanor Ann 88
James 24	Joseph 64	Elizabeth 47,128
John 48,50	Joseph W. 144	Elizabeth M.W. 74
	Nancy 54,75	Elvira W. 94
HAYWARD	Peter 92	Esekiel 66
Ann 105	Rachel 128	Esther 11
Elizabeth 124	Renattus 99,111	Ezekiel 1,133
Harriet Mary 124	Tabitha E. 138	Gertrude 26
John 52	Thomas M. 82	Harriet 65,98
John E. 47,141	William P. 139	Harriet H. 44
Susan W, 93	William T. 126	Hannah 39,58
		Henry 46
HAZZARD	HEARNE	Henry B. 142
Amelia 57	Handy 88	Irene 92
Charlotte 59		Isaac 3
Cord 18	HEATH	Isaiah 23
Cove 45	Comfort 26	Jacob 9,9,40
Sally C. 93	John D. 110	James 43,73,80
	Lewis D. 83	97,106,112
HEARN	Polly 26	James L. 107
Benjamin 38,73		Jane 106
Benjamin G. 91	HEBAND	Jesse 9
Betsey 45	Joseph H. 150	John 1,58,68,125
Brinkley A. 118,154		John R.P. 129
Clement C. 127	HECKMAN	Joseph F. 112
Ebenezer 5,35,45	Elizabeth 51	Josiah 25
Elijah 48		Leah 32
Eliza 67	HENCOCK	Lemuel 25,45
Eliza S. 113	Wealthy 60	Leven 92
Elizabeth 64,119,140		Levi 13,25
Elizabeth L. 101	HENDCOCK	Levin 11,42,60,88
Elizbth 88	Tabitha 46	Levin S. 148
Eleanor R. 136	William 47	Littleton S. 147

HENDERSON Con't
Lydia 33
Margaret 33, 84
Margaret Jane 137
Martha Ann 125
Mary 9, 41, 62, 126, 153
Mary Ann 75
Mary E. 107
Mary I. 72
Matilda 60
Molly 57
Nancy 9, 50
Noah 47
Rebecca 18
Sally 8, 18, 23, 48
Sally Ann 138
Sally L. 39
Sarah 10, 76
Sarah E. 132
Sarah M. 117
Scarborough 32
Tabitha 20
Thomas 55
Thos. 69
Warner W. 133
William 14, 27, 32, 55
William H. 9
Wm 17

HENMAN
Colemore C. 69
Elizabeth 108
John H. 156
Luther 65
Lydia 71
Mary J. 5
Nathaniel 74, 116

HENDMAN
Ann C. 128

HENRY
Adaliza 95
Ann 30
Charles R. 49
Dorotha Esther Waters 63

HENRY Con,t
Elizabeth 41
Elizabeth G. 140
Erexine 46
Gertrude 27
Harriet 142
Hozey 71
John 69
Laura Ann 70
Margaret C. 63
Mary 63, 64, 124
Robert J. 30, 39, 106
Sarah 56
Sarah A. 136
Zadok 55
Zadok P. 112
Zadok P. Jr. 147

HERINGTON
Nancy 48

HERMAN
Sally 46

HERRINGTON
Mahalae 92
Nelly 38
Sally 89

HICKMAN
Abil 6
Anna M.S. 109
Bayly 85
Catharine 93
Charlotte 43
Demirah B. 99
Edward 101
Eliza 140
Elizabeth 37, 39, 96, 127
Elizabeth C. 117
Esther 117
Francis 140
George 69
James 69, 91
Jane 88
Jesse 53

HICKMAN Con't
John 77, 99
John S. 140
John T. 127
Joseph 47
Josiah 22, 30, 55
Lemuel D. 120
Margaret 110, 129
Margaret T. 58
Mary 18, 26, 98
Mary A. 114, 144
Milby 78
Parker J. 144
Polly 9
Richard 135
Sarah 128
Sarah H. 100
Siner 113
Sophia Ann Elizabeth 103
Walter H. 121
Zebina 12

HICKS
Eliza 71

HICKSON
Polly 47

HIGGIN
Henrietta B. 123

HIGHT
Thomas 57

HILL
Ann 138
Ann Mitchell 71
Anasaline 134
Arthur W. 99
Betsey 11, 84
David 125
Dempsy 46
Eleanor 121
Elenor R.W. 98
Elisha 8
Elizabeth 56, 92
Elizabeth Jane 71

HILL Con't
George 94,115,135
          146
Gilbert 73
Henny   45
John 10,88
John H.   8
John J. 125,140
John R. 114
John T.   89
Johnson   27
Josiah   5
Laben   59
Levin   146
Levin Jr. 5
Levina   14,49
Major   107
Mary 23,33,57,
         64,83
Mary Ann 70
Mitchell 75
Molly   62
Nancy   21
Nancy Derickson 44
Patience 25
Patty   68
Peggy   34
Purnell   31
Rachel   88
Rebecca 6,54
Rhoda   56
Sally   61
Sarah   84
Sarah T. 109
Severn 53,93
Severn I. 100
Stephen 31,35,36
          145
William 6,30,37
William C. 121
Zechariah 70

HILLMAN
Hetty   37

HILMAN
Leah   70

HINDMAN
Margaret 147
Sally   28

HINMAN
Aquilla E. 140
Elizabeth H. 138
James   5
Jane   110
Rachel   105
Ralph   18
Samuel M. 106

HITCH
Ann   10
Henry W. 112
Irving   132
Joshua W. 60,63
Samuel   50

HITCHENS
James   25
Nancy   27

HITCHINGS
Sarah E.

HOBBS
Pamelia   99

HODGSON
Betsey   20

HOESKINS
Fleety S. 25

HOGSHIER
Thos.   33

HOLADAY
Benjamin 152

HOLDER
Hester E. 103

HOLDZKOM
James   153

HOLLAND
Amanda   123
Amelia   80
Ann 44,87,113
Ann S.   47
Benjamin 95,117
Betsey   13
Betsy   55
Caroline 138
Clarissa 101
Drucilla 99
Edward 95,106
Eleanor   73
Elizabeth 11,62
         65,84,112,116
Esther   5,97
George T. 117
Harriet   55
Helena W. 129
Hester   128
Hester E. 122
Hetty 53,66,77,137
Isaac 65,103
Isaac J. 135
James 20,34,57,118
James M. 69,99
James W. 154
Jesse 119,146
John 51.102
J.John   1
John S.D. 97
Kendall 21,43
Laura   138
Leah   51
Levi   18
Levin 15,58,61,68
Louisa Jane 89
Mamy   96
Margaret 88,110
Margaret J. 128,149
Maria 54,109
Martha   11
Mary 48,84
Mary Ann 116
Mary E. 147,149
Nancy 3,27,31
Nehemiah 2,33
Patty   3

HOLLAND Con't
Peter 25,96
Peter J. 139
Polly 24
Rosa M. 144
Sally M. 101
Samuel 137
Sarah 66
Sarah Ann 67
Sarah L. 125
Stephen 64
Stringer 150
Tabitha 135
Thomas D. 76
William B. 34,41,70
75,144
William H. 107,118
William J. 106,125
William T. 120

HOLLMAN
Susan 110

HOLLOCK
Comfort 26

HOLLOWAY
Aaron 53
Abisha 21
Adam 25
Andetiah 66
Ann 81
Armel Showele 6
Betsey 35
Daniel 97,146
David 66
David A. 121
Elihu 33
Elisha 92
Elisha Q. 155
Elizabeth 5,146
Fanny 53
Gatty 89,95
Hannah 46
Henry 100
Hetty 22,35
Jacob 56

HOLLOWAY Con,t
Jacob M. 122
Jane 38
John 16,39,61
69,83
Joseph 28
Joshua 12,29,81
98
Joshua J. 131,154
Leml. 34
Lemuel 84
Levin 45
McKimma B. 118
McKemmy 111
Mary 7,80,108
Mary A.E. 142
Mary G. 153
Mary Jane 140
Mordecal 79
Nancy 11,25,34
38,111
Patty 3,41
Samuel 54,116
Sarah G. 135
Sarah J.P. 155
Sophia 25
Stanton 137
Viny 64
Wm H. 139

HOLSTON
Adaliza 148
Ann 99
Benjm. 91
Charlotte 40
Cordelia 145
Dolly 8
Elizabeth 71,136
George 74
James 103,135
John of Levin 55
Joshua 70, 76
Levin 90,76
Mary Ann 78,89
Molly 46
Sally 71
Sarah 138
Sarah M. 135
Zadok 113,142

HOLT
Mary D. 141

HOLTON
Benjamin 71

HOOK
James 10
John 26
Zadok 28

HOOKE
Betsey 8

HOOLE
Luther T. 113

HOOLT
Marand 107

HOOP,
Belitha 13

HOOPER
Eleanor 87
Fanny 118
John 36,65
Maria L. 61
Mary 63
Thomas H. 105

HOPE
John 49
Margaret A. 107
Narcissa 27
Sally 17
Sibbel S. 150
William 117
William T. 85

HOPKINS
Amelia 26
Benjamin B. 48
Elizabeth 72,97
Esther A. 96
Hannah 13
Henry 72
Isaac 74

HOPKINS Con't
Josiah 9
Mary 114
Mary A. 153
Mary A.M. 119
Polly 27
Rhoda 33
Stephen 100
Tabby 108
Wolsy B. 145
William 17

HORNSWAY
Priscilla 37

HORSEY
Adaline W. 115
James B. 68
Levin 41
Martha 12
Mary 27
Ursula B. 142
Dr. William S. 116

HOSIER
Catharine J. 148
Charlotte 41
Elizabeth 118
Henrietta 140
Joshua 143
Martha 32
Rebecca 142
Sophia A. 121

HOSHER
Joshua 64

HOSHIER
Eli 15
Eliza 62
Elizabeth 60,66
Gatty 92
Gertrude 70
Hetty 48
John 28
Joshua 36
Lemuel 6
Mary 28

HOSHIER Con't
Miracle 70
Polly 47
Samuel 39,66
Samuel Jr. 66
Sarah 19
Sophia 74
Tabitha 82
Viny 25
William 4
Zepheniah 12

HOSTON
George 76

HOUGHTON
I.S. 116

HOUSTON
Amelia 18,56
Anamariah 51
Betsy 54
Caleb 4
Eliza 58,77
Elizabeth H. 68
Elizabeth R. 45
Emeline 99
Esther J. 124
George 3,12
Gertrude 47
Isaac 13,37,77,
James 10,11,20,61
  68,93
John 20,21
Joseph 1,34,57
Kitty 18
Leven B. 90
Levin D. 56
Marcellena 137
Margaret K. 71
Martha 77
Mary 3
Mary Ann 82
Priscilla 25
Sally 10,46
Samuel 82,152
Sarah 6
William J. 9

HOZIER
Betsey 21
John 57

HOZIOR
Maria 85

HOVINGTON
Elijah 70
Jesse 145

HOWARD
Abigail 1
Allen Bowie 107
Caroline 100
Eleanor D. 56
Elizabeth 26
Elizabeth Leah 113
Emily Francis 148
Ezekiel 90
Henry S. 52
Hester Ann 130
John 53,97,135
John H. 127
Julian 76
Mary 146
Nancy 2,94
Samuel 29
T.C.B. 110
William T. 155

HUBBEL
Josiah 11

HUBBELL
Edward 122
Eliza G. 53
Polly 20
William 21

HUDSON
Aaron 70
Abaline 57
Alexine 104
Anna 68,147
Annanias 9
Annanias F. 108
Ann Maria 144
Ann P. 42

HUDSON Con't
Arthur 3,6
Belitha 88
Benjamin 2,42,80
    109
Betsey 16
Catharine 84
Cora Ann 149
Cornelia 143
Dennis 1
Drucilla 133
Drucilla W. 147
Edward 26
Eleanor 59
Eleanor A. 137
Eli 8
Elizabeth 15,40,65
    71,75,78
    89,122
Elizabeth D. 79,80
Elizabeth T. 72
Ephraim 84
Evans 24
Eyedlite 144
Geo. 92
George 59,80,80,99
George W. 113
Gertrude A. 29
Hannah 134
Harriet 78
Harriet Jane 114
Henrietta 13,87
Hester Jane 149
Hetty 28,55
Hetty M. 119
Hulda 29
Irena 148
Isaac 70,110
James 28,73
James A. 113
Jane 123
Jane E. 116
Jane M. 88
Jesse 8,10,20,138
John 15,26,69,80
    86,92
John H. 119

HUDSON Con't
John L. 100
John Of Sam 13
John T. 107
Jonathan 6
Joshua 30,61,143
Josiah 117
Julia Ann 89
Laban 34,75,106
Lavisa 119
Leah 26,48
Leah W. 132
Leonard 13
Levy 7
Littleton 38
Louisa E. 121
Lovey 27
Lovey B. 120
Luritta 25
Major 21
Margaret 30,94,103
Margaret Ann 132
Margaret T. 121
Martha 99
Martha H. 39
Mary 81,91,91,111
    114,151
Mary A, 105
Mary E. 146
Mary Elizabeth 106
Mary Jane 113
Mary P. 136
Matilda 45,52
McKenny 1
Merridy 105
Michael 16
Milby A. 52
Milby R. 114
Molly 79
Moses 13
Moses J. 153
Nancy 2,72
Nancy C. 133
Patty 22,116
Peggy 7
Phillip 91,123

HUDSON Con't
Polly 37
Priscilla 19,39
Priscilla A. 146
Purnell 21
Rebecca 7
Richard 108,127
Robert 2,16,26
Samuel M. 146
Sally 26,33,36,46
    47,70,88
Sarah L. 1,121
Sarah H. 115
Selby 12,23
Seth 94,105
Sophia N. 44
Susanna 10
Thomas 48
Unice 15
William 5,7,12,28
    29,52,56,85,10
William C. 104,132
William D. 81
William Of L. 130
William S. 104
Zipporah 121

HUDZON
Gertrude 41

HUGHES
Hannah 28
Isaac T. 110
James 7,84,97,119
John 134
Josephine 155
Nancy 68
Patty 90

HUGHS
Henny 54
Lotty 53
William 3

HUMPHREYS
Cathell 102
Humphrey 79

HURLEY
Charles A. 147

HUSK
James 105

HUSTED
Henry H. 142

HUSTON
Elizabeth 75
Hester 142
Isabella 102
Margaret A. 149

HUTCHESON
Catharine R. 84
John G. 121
Joseph 41,56

HUTSON
Ann D. 57
Isaac 17
James H. 11
John 8
Peter 51
Richard 8

HUTT
Eliza 48
George 48
Major 49
Moses 15
William 101

HYLAND
Polly 44

HYSELUP
Margaret S. 119

HYSLOP
John W. 149

INGRAHAM
Edward D. 56

INSLEY
Elizabeth 92

IRONS
Comfort 8
Timothy 5,10

IRVING
Levin G. 63

JACKSON
Benjamin 121
Charlotte 88
Charlotte Ann 147
Elizabeth 122
George K. 134
Handy 61
Henny 61
Henry 77
Henry P. 134
Hetty 146
Hetty Amelia 152
James R. 84
James Thomas 61
John 2,18,45,72
Lambert 39
Levina 136
Maria 61
Mary 60,80,87,133
Molly 48
Nancy 82
Polly 21,73
Purnell 96
Rachel A.A. 84
Sally Mary R. 136
Sarah 125
Stephen 18
Thomas 137

JACOB
Teackle W. 88

JACOBS
Annie B. 146
Curtis W. 96
Eliza 87
William B. 102

JAMBLIN
John 63

JAMES
Ann Eliza 73
Branson 52
Catharine 77
Charlotte 85,92
Ellen J.S. 125
Emely 104
Ezekiel 35
Jane 80
John 46
Leah 41
Levin S. 151
Mary Ann 83
Robert 77
Thomas 64

JAMIESON
Jesse M. 83

JARMAN
Anania 76
Anna 94
Annanias 68,87
Anna Maria 114
Belitha 2
Benjamin 3
Cornelia 154
Drucilla 82
Fanny 53
Francis L. 147
Hannah 12
Henry 38
Isaac 39
James 10, 145
Jesse 18,106
Job 106,140
John 13,83
Joshua 82
Lavinia 151
Leah 107,138
Leonard 144
Littleton 61
Margaret Ann 117
Martha 82
Martha A. 129

JARMAN Con't
Mary 120
Mary A. 129
McKenny 77
Polly 59
Rachel 12,73
Rachel Ann 152
Rosina Andasia 147
Sally 97
Samuel H. 130
Sarah 15
Thomas 97
William 72,82,85
William H. 129,131,143

JARMIN
Elizabeth 94
Henry 48
Jesse 66
Kendall 68
Mary 116

JEARMON
Patty 45

JARRELL
Polly 19

JARVIS
Cornelia 138
Edgar H. 136
Elizabeth 68
Ellen A.R. 154
George 156
Harry 130
Henry W. 73
John E. 97
Kendal 87
Margaret 98
Mary E. 129

JEFFERSON
Samuel 39
Warren 17

JENKINS
Leah 42
Mary A. 120
Mary Ann 115
Nicholas B. 140
Sarah 32,58

JENNOR
John G. 16

JERMAN
Louisa 58

JESTER
Avery 140
David 89
Elizabeth 16
Isaac 131
Julia Ann 130
Leah 143
Michael 99
Parker 119
Tinny 83
William 151

JOHNS
Lucy 83

JOHNSON
Affradazy 23
Ann 38,46,64
75,156
Anne 36,36
Ann E. 94
Ann Maria 115
Aralanta 82
Arintha E.S. 126
Aurelia 94
Benjamin 8,92,98
119
Benjamin B. 104
Benjamin T. 146
Betsey 8,20,21
45,54
Catharine S. 103
Catharine M. 117
Charles D. 132

JOHNSON Con't
Charlotte 56,79
Comfort 25
Daniel 64
David 44,129
Denard W. 140
Dolly 8
Drucilla 108
Edward F. 107
Eleanor 5
Eleanor P. 51
Eleazer 28
Eliakem 6,20
Eliza 82,105,119
Elizabeth 27,52,64,
73,83,99,108
Elizabeth D. 50
Elizabeth N. 116
Elr 7
Emeline 102,111,146
Esther 10
George 22,68,122
Gilly 97
Hannah 61
Henny 19,48
Henry 67
Henry B. 140
Henry T. 105
Hetty 6,92
Isaac 23,36
Isaac S. 32,65
Jacob 5
James 3,14,84,119
Jane 68
Joanna 5
John 3,15,15,22,32
39,40,42,46,74
101,120
John E. 150
John P. 117,124
John T. 100
John W. 133
Joseph S. 136
Joshua 110,139
Joshua C. 110
Josiah 86
Julian 83

JOHNSON Con't
Lambert   93
Leah   26
Leonard   1
Levin H.   61
Littleton S.   117
Louisa   90
Malissa   149
Margaret   36,67,73
          80,138
Margaret E.   131
Mary   34,74,80
       81,110,128,144
Mary Ann   114
Mary E.L.   139
Mary Grace   84
Milly   44
Molly   29,37
Nancy   8,26,57,62
        64,67
Nicey   127
Patty   15
Patuna A.W.   68
Peter   34,81,87
Peter W.   120
Philis   46
Phillip J.   122
Polly   3,18,24,27
Polly N.   24
Priscilla   58
Purnell   23,25,56
          113
Rachel   2
Robert   21,26,29,97
Robert H.   52
Sally   8,23,35,37
        53,65,84,118
        128,145,147
Sally A.   127
Sally G.   37
Sally M.   56
Samuel   25,46,61,74
         97,118
Sarah   5,39
Sarah F.   113
Selby   67,97
Severn   36

JOHNSON Con't
Smith   67
Susan C.   99
Susan E.   153
Tabitha   3,62
Thomas C.   46
Thomas D.   74
Thomas Z.   149
Thos   33
William   41,48,66
          70,124
William C.   137
William S.   116
William of Samuel
              156
Wm.   18

JOHNSTON
William W.   83

JOINS
Margaret   94

JONES
Abel   76
Adlinee   135
Alfred T.   128
Amelia   5,54
Ann   54,83
Annania S.   70
Ann E.   138
Ann M.   116
Benjamin   60, 139
Betsey   21
Burton   105,140,146
Cabel   17
Catty Purnell   8
C,C.   155
Charlotte   23
Comfort   31
Daniel   13,16,126
Diadanna   64
Drucilla   74
Edward   20,130
Edward H.   116
Eliakem   69,97
Elihu   79,82

JONES Con't
Elisha   15,54,88
Eliza   69,78
Eliza K.   70
Elizabeth   27,45,52,74,
            75,76,85,96
            105
Elizabeth A.   127
Ellenor   89
Emma   153
Emma C.   147
Ephraim   93
Esme   106
Esther   53
Euphamy   5
Ezekiel   82
Fanny   96
Francis P.   153
Gatty J.   126
Geo   35
George   10,39,58,102
         115
George T.   122
Giles   52,102
Griffith   78
Handy   9
Hannah   10
Harriet Ann   56
Henny   53
Henry   60,100,120
Henry C.   128
Hetty   92
Hetty A.   119
Hezekiah   120,137
Huldah   58
Isaac   51,65,73
Isaac D.   122
Isaac R.   77
Isaac S.   98
Jacob   36,43
Jacob F.   54
Jacob H.   100
James   24,35,40,66,70
        99,102,112,156
James E.   139
James H.   136
James Hall   4

JONES Con't
James N. 128
James S. 102,129
Jane 154
Jane E. 133
Jesse 27,91,116
Jesse L. 34
Jesse S. 107
Jiles 20
Joanna J. 135
John 15,22,27,28
    29,36,49,65
    84,85,89,90
    91,127
John F. 131
John J. 108
John M. 145
John P. 89
John W. 127
Joseph 18,
Joshua 34,34,42,43
Josiah 44
Julia 114
Julia Ann P. 80
Julian 83
Kendal 56
Leah 78,86,106
    120
Lemuel 156
Levenia H. 148
Levey A, 155
Levi 1,50
Levin 40,109,124
Levin J. 10,104
Lewis 56
Littleton J. 139
Major W. 96
Margaret 55,81,97,119
Margaret A. 120
Margaret M. 112
Margaret W. 81
Maria 91,120
Martha A. 116
Martha C. 145
Martha P. 46
Martha W. 126
Mary 8,13,51,54
    57,58,66,86
    110

JONES Con't
Mary A. 113
Mary Ann 69,93,108
Mary E. 120
Mary J. 104
Mary Jane 102
Mary M. 119
Matthew 5,15,23
May 87
Moses 57
Moses U. 35,145
Nancy 22,25,30,34
    35,40,44,47
    50,54,101
Nancy C. 141
Nicholas 49
Obed 49
O. Wilson 134
Patience 110
Patty 20
Peggy 50
Peran E. 145
Peter 31
Peter S. 66
Polly 6,35,48
Purnell J. 68,118
Rachel 11,28,51
Rebecca 11
Rhoda 19
Rodah T. 42
Riley 41,49,56
Robert 52
Rosa F. 141
Rosa S. 143
Rosey O. 31
Sally 11,33,51,60
    102,127,,142
Sally of Isaac 123
Sally James 60
Samuel F. 132
Samuel Tindle 57
Sarah 3,16,27,34
    39,45,51,59,94
    154
Sarah A. 120,124,128
Sarah Ann 90, 98,98
Sarah W. 156

JONES Con't
Stphen 57
Tabitha 2,26,39
    43,106
Thamer 17
Thomas 13,32,53,67
    123,127
Thomas B. 61,108
Thomas H. 105
Tubman 81
Walty 32
Waters 85
Wealthy 61
Whittington 15,82,101
William 5,13,14,27,
    42,64,80,82
    89,104,107,11⸳
    133,133,151
William H. 103,111,14⸳
William Henry 60
William J. 141
William P. 143
Wm 14,32,33
Visa 51

JORDON
Sophia Elizabeth 131

JOSTURE
John 43

JOYNES
Edward G. 89
Elisha 87
Elizabeth 121
Mary 78
Melinda C. 83
Nancy 37
Robert 26

JUSTICE
Jesse 54
Littleton 144
Mary 94
Polly 29
Rosa A. 155
Sallie P. 141
Sarah A. 135
Tenney 19
William 130

JUSTON
Sally 22

KANNY
Samuel 43

KAYLOT
Mary 155

KEENRIGHT
Andrew J. 109

KELLAEM
Betty 24
Elizabeth 20
Peggy 7
Rebecca 40
Sophia A. 84
Tabitha 19
Thomas 77

KELLAM
Allen D. 62
Ann Maria Parker 48
Bettie A. 146
Curtis 6,95
Ella E. 151
Francis 109
James L. 96
Julietta S. 105
Martha E. 132

KELLEY
Asberry 141
Charles 47
John H. 148
Margret 47
Polly 38
Sarah 135
Tabitha 134
William 46

KELLY
Benjamin 67
Charles 125
Daniel 109
Davis 122
Elijah 85,108,112 121
Elizabeth 124
Emeline 101,134
George 125
Henry 40,46
Huldah 45
James 40
James Colbourne 111
John 118,153
John C. 141
Julia 129
Julia Ann 127
Luckey 40
Mahala 70
Margaret 112
Martin 155
Mary 142
Mary S. 126
Milly 34
Molina 87
Nancy 51
Patty 19
Polly 122
Richard R. 100
Sally 45
Samuel 73,133,152
Thomas 108
Thomas H. 153
Walter 60
William 64,79,98,115

KELPIN
John 100
Sarah Ann 146

KENDALL
Mariah

KENNARD
Sarah Ann 94

KENNETT
Leah C. 9
Nancy 3

KENNETT Con't
Polly 12
William 7

KENNY
Barsheba 85
William K. 69

KER
Hugh 123
Samuel

KERBY
Robert 20

KERR
Elizabeth C. 52
Milly 50

KERNYL
Nancy 1

KILBY
Elijah 55
Letta 25

KILLAM
Leah 37

KILLAEM
Tabitha 15

KILLEY
George 38

KILLIAM
Jermina 25
Mary 22
Nancy 26
William G. 52

KILMAN
Thomas W. 115

KILLMAN
Sarah Ann 137

KILPIN
Handy 44

KING
Elizabeth 67
Esther A. 142
Gede 30
Hetty 96
Hugh I. 142
James 3,94
Jesse P. 79
Martha 73
Mary 74
Milly 97
Sarah 85
Sarah P. 147
Thomas 15.121

KINNIKIN
Isaac 95

KIRBY
Charlotte 2

KITCHEN
Oliver 102

KNAPP
John 130

KNOCK
Ann 12
Elijah 105
John 94
Margaret Ann 105

KNOX
Albert 114
Comfort 5
Edward 30
George 5
Isaac 16,54,124
James 12,19,25,29
  59,71,94,96
James H. 119
James P. 99
John 50
Jno, M. 9
Margaret 4,83
Molly 92
Nancy 36

KNOX Con't
Patty 16
Priscilla 125
Robert 37
Wm D. 155

LAMBERSON
Amelia A.E. 147
Anne 33
Betsy 37
Eliza 80
Euphame 56
Famy 63
Henry 129
Isaac 146
John 22,40,76,115
John J. 123
Julia Ann 115
Levi 71
Levi M. 151
Polly 48
Sally 63,74
Samuel 104
Schoolfield 23,55,77
William T. 143

LAMBDEN
Ann 76
Edward 4
Edward H. 154
Elizabeth 156
Emeline 107
Esther S. 63
Harriet Hester 148
Harriet Jane 123
Levin M. 117
Maria 61
Nancy 49
Robert 44,45
Robert J. 121
Samuel 128
Sarah 90
Thomas 106

LAMBDON
Edwd. 20
James 26
John 22
Samuel J. 117

LAMDEN
Emily F. 140
Mary 4.101
Sally 72
Susanna 6

LANDEN
Margaret 80
Thomas 33

LANDON
Mary 47
Rachel 73
William D. 71

LANDING
Cordelia W. 136
Frances 126
George 30
Isaac B. 117
James 86
James H. 136
Mary A.V. 154
Mary E.W. 129
Sally 120
Samuel T. 85

LANE
Betsey 16
Eliza A. 123
Fanny 61
Francis 67,130
John 10
Mary A. 124
Nancy 22
Sally Dennis 7
Sarah 91
Sydney 153
Thomas 59
Thomas G. 90
William 24

LANGSDALE
George 75
John H. 89

LANK
Cannon 6
George W. 129
John T. 141

LANKFORD
Ann 95
Anna 51
Edward J. 135
Edward K.B. 144
Elizabeth 94
Henrietta 32
John H. 116
John S. 124
John T. 127
Joshua H. 89
Kellaem 15
Margaret 55
Mary W. 153
Sevasten 1

LARKIN
Joel 54

LARKINS
Joseph 110
Nancy 85

LATCHAM
Isaiah 36
John 45
Obadiah 16

LATCHOM
Isaiah 48

LATCHUM
Ary Catharine 117
Dolley M. 98
Elizabeth 103
Joseph 46
Levina 41
Nancy 43,50
Seth 133
Seth W. 99
Tabitha 38
Thomas 69
Thomas J. 122

LATEN
Rachel 39

LATHBURY
Arthur 98
William 122

LAW
Margaret E. 146
Sally 9
William 2
William L. 135

LAWRENCE
Sarah 5

LAWS
Ann 58
Anna 49
Charlotte M. 137
Clarissa 97
Daniel 44
Elijah 63
Elizabeth 130
Gatty E. 117
Isaac H. 47
James 138
John 41
John W. 145
Jonathan 98
Joshua 39
Leah C. 113
Lizzie A. 152
Lurany 96
Margaret Ann 96
Martha 43
Mary 13,89
Mary Jane 102
Polly 40
Sarah 3
Sarah E. 98
Sarah W. 102
William 55, 56
William Jr. 55
William L. 128

LAYFIELD
Catharine 8
Elizabeth 73
Elizabeth S. 124
Esther 13,15
George 85,95,148
George W. 145
Isaac 22,51
Jane 29
James 112
John 56,72
Levin 5,40
Maria 79
Martha Jane 149
Mary 90,136
Mary E. 130
Mary W. 152
Nancy 11,16
Nancy M. 99
Phoebe E. 154
Polly 5
Robert 29
Robert H. 156
Sarah 1
Thomas 79
Thos. 21
Thos. Jr. 7
William 8
William Q. 89
William W. 83

LAYTON
Elizabeth 67
Leah 75
Levin 72
Mary E. 126
Milbourn 152
Thomas J. 132
William 82,112

LEAKEY
Betsey 77
Isaac 74
Mary 87

LECATS
Catty 69
Nancy 51

LECOMPT
James 83
Mary Ann 69
William 103

LECOMPTE
Margaret 85
William 85

LEKATS
Eleanor 97

LEKIERTZ
Jesse 105

LEKITTS
Sarah E. 148

LENDON
Hetty 30

LENDZEY
Betsey 3
Harriet 57
Matthias 6

LENOX
Mary 56

LEONARD
Benjamin 43
Cyrus 57
Elzy 145
Joseph 39,70,100
Joshua 28
Mary E. 148,150
Polly 83
Sally A. 145
Sarah A. 82,123
Syrus 66

LESTER
John T. 72
Peter 7
Polly 5

LEVINGSTON
Benjamin 3,75
Elizabeth 55,71
George M. 58
Leah 89
Lorenzo 74
Nancy 29,44
Sally 33
William 56

LEWIS
Alfred 146
Anna 26
Betsy 43
Charlotte E. 152
Clarasa M. 147
David S. 154
Eliza A. 149
Elizabeth 93,100,143
 146
George 33
Henry P. 110,143
Hiram 138
Isaac 8,126
Isaac J. 144
Jane 133
James 43,128,140
 143
John 33,48
John E. 133
Joseph J. 149
Leah 135
Leven 96
Luke 146
Margaret 107
Margaret D. 152
Mary 83
Mary C.W. 140
Mary E. 143
Mary Jane 144
Milbourne S. 150
Milly 95
Nancy 29,50,63,104
Nancy E. 143
Polly 15
Priscilla 34
Rachel W. 130

LEWIS Con't
Raymond 153
Rhoda 153
Rosy 95
Sally 42,48,102
Sally Elizabeth 138
Sally W. 90
Sarah 140
Stephen 47
Stephen J. 34
Susan Ann 149
William 12,62,76
 86,110
William J. 147
William S. 117
William T. 139
Wm H. 153
Zadok S. 119
Zetta 11

LILLISTON
James 61,96
Robert 138
Sally 30

LINCH
Alfred 109
Marggaret 91
Wrixom 26

LINDALL
John 30

LINDSEY
Cora A. 140
Henry C. 146
Thomas S. 140

LINDSY
Mager 6

LINDZEY
Elizabeth 91

LING
Edward Tingle 120
Sally 110

LINGER William 54	LITTLETON Con't Samuel J. 118 Sarah 125	LOKEY Con't Harriet W. 148 Henrietta 120
LINTON Thomas 30	Sarah C. 151 Sarah J. 110,123 Thomas 92,131	James 121 John 13 Julina 112
LINZEY Hetty 31	Thomas Of E. 123 Thos. 15 Tully 84	Major 64 Margaret 117 Priscilla 105
LION Ethen 65	Vicy Quinton 99 Vine 15 William B. 110	Sally 112 Thomas 51
LISTER Cord H. 79 Molly B. 69 Sally 3 William 27	LIVINGSTON Edith E. 153 Elizabeth A. 152 Geo. 9 James 138	LONDON Hetty 29 LONG Ann 57 Arintha Ann 93
LITTLETON Abraham 12 Albert 133 Amelia 82 Charles 46 Charlotte 104 Clarissa 128 Edward 129 Eliza 94,111 Eliza J. 141 Handy H. 101 Harriet 138 Irving S. 128 Irving Spence 106 Isaac 72 James 86,154 John 139 Martha C. 144 Martha E. 147 Mary 111 Mary J. 143 Matilda 103 Matilda M. 155 Milly 125 Minos 124 Miranda 146 Molly 92 Nancy 156 Sally 91	John 96 John H. 67 Mary 85 Mary E. 153 Peter 134,152 Samuel S. 118 Susan 98 LLOYD Christopher C. 140 LOCKERMAN James 83 LOCKMAN John 26 LOEKEY John 64 Nancy 60 LOEK Priscilla 54 LOKEY Benjamin 8 Betsy 88 Dingley 98 Elizabeth J. 144	Catharine 36 Colbourn 46 Coulbourn 7 Coulbourne 9 David 10,46 Elizabeth 38,77,81 132 Hampton 20 Harriett 61 Henry W. 86 Isaac 4 James 91 Jess 42 Jesse 81,103 Jesse L. 101 John 26,33,39 Josiah 10 Levi 54 Malinda 93 Margaret C. 29 Mary E. 80 Molly White 9 Nancy 23,40,80 Rachell 1 Robert P. 101 Rosanna 37 Rosey 37 Sally 12,19,54 Samuel 51,60,63

LONG Con't
Sarah 1
Sarah Elizabeth 150
Shada Ann 107
Susan 60
Sydnum 112
William J. 116,136
Zadock 2

LOOKERMAN
James 83

LORD
Alexander 154

LOREMAN
James F. 110

LOW
Alexander 4
Edward 153
Kendal 50
Purnell 97

LOWE
Alexander 30

LOWS
Elijah 47
Tubman 10

LUCAS
Hetty 20,84
Parker 2,30
Rachel 87
Samuel T. 60
William S. 109

LUCAS
Elizabeth 38

LUKER
Margaret 53

LUMBER
Samuel 33

LYNCH
Ebbe 65
Elizabeth 99,118
Hetty L. 148
James H. 140
John R. 120
Joseph 106
Levin 155
Mary 131
Purdy 144
Ritta 156
William 116,126

McALLEN
Alexander 24
Arthur 25
Elizabeth 87
George W. 108
Leah Jane 87
Levin B. 112
Margaret A. 139
Robert 22,53
Sally 22
Sarah 92
Sarah E. 101
William A. 82

McBRIETY
Joshua 106

McCABE
Bartine T. 116
Charlotte 93
Elisha 143

McCAIN
Peter 148

McCAULEY
Peter 38

McCLAIN
James 35
Joseph 35
Purnell I. 97

McCOLLIER
Alexander 57

McCOLLOM
Alexander 38

McCOLUM
Jennetta 124

McCOLLY
John 19

McCORMACK
Thomas 6

McCORMICK
Comfort 14

McCREADY
Maria 57
Mary Jane 99
Sarah E. 116

McCREADDY
Stephen 63
Sophia Ann 75

McCREDDY
Polly 2

McDANIEL
David 3
Elizabeth 56
Henry 72
John 7
Kerdon ? 37
Polly C. 34
Stephen 149
William H. 112

McENTASH
Joseph 100

McFADDEN
Ann 71
Elizabeth 71
James 14,113
John 22,48
Maria 110

McFADDEN Con't
Rachel 37
Sally 67

McGEE
Betsy 24,105
James 55
Joseph 102
Julian 95
Maria 128
Mary Ann 128
Sally 92
Samuel 49
Sarah 35
Sarah Ann 118

McGRATH
James 138
John 20
Josiah 136
Julian 76
Rachel J. 122
Thomas 111
William 87,155

McGRAUGH
William 65

McGRAW
William 47

McGREGGER
James 139

McGREGOR
Elizabeth 34
James 50,111
Margaret 34
Mary 60
Nancy 63
Wm. 33

McGREGORY
Martha 42

McGRIGOR
Mary A. 119

McHENRY
Betsey 75
Hetty 91
John 134
William 63

McJEW ?
Henry 14

McKABE
Isaac 94

McKEE
George 137
John W. 134
Stephen 56
William J.C. 137

McKNEEL
George W. 61

McLANE
Elizabeth 120

McMASTER
Anna 92
Charlotte 35
John 120
Mary A.C. 140
Samuel 12,30,94

McMATH
Mary E. 149

McNAMAR
John H. 147

McNAMARRA
John 116

McNATT
Nathaniel 31

McNEIL
Ede 41
Elizabeth 72
John 18
John Henry 20

McNEILE
Catharine 101

McNEILL
Dolly 12
Polly 18
Sarah 24
Wilson 108

McNEILLE
Martha 65

MacCREADY
Harriet 86

MacKEY
Elizabeth 30
William D. 141

MacKLIN
Elizabeth 79
Matilda 124
Sally 109
Thomas 52

MacLIN
John 98

MACKMOTH
Sally 52

MADDOCKS
Mary E. 127

MADDOX
Benjamin 81
Hetty C. 74
Samuel 41

MADDUX
Alley 126
Ann 40
Ann E. 113
Charlotte 28
Daniel 47
David 90
Eleanor 110
Elijah 100,126

MADDUX Con't
Elijah S. 102
Elizabeth 132
Henrietta 69
Hester J. 144
Hezekiel 86
James 10,104,129
John H. 141
Lazarus 12,53
Levin D. 149
Louisa 145
Mahala 106
Mary 72,75,90
Mary Ann 106,122
Mary C. 151
Sally 43
Sally A. 147
Sarah 18
Thomas 19
William G. 136
William T. 84

MADLOCK
Elizabeth 145

MAGEE
George 62
John 16
Kitty 100

MAGRATH
Elizabeth 49

MALCOMB
George 38

MALLET
George 145
James 35
Samuel 119
Thomas 130

MALLETT
Edward 139
Isaac 125
James 144
John 88
Priscilla 139
Sally 88
Wealthy 52

MALONE
Alexander 154
Anna Maria 101
David 46,55
Mary Elizabeth 124
Nancy 97
Robert 55

MAPP
Indiana F. 149
James C. 147
James T. 133
Mary E. 150
Victor A. 149
William T. 149
Wm E. 149

MARCHANT
John 6
Mary A.E. 143
Mary Ann 80

MARCINDER
Major 21

MARNER
James 32
Leah 33

MARRELL
Henry 74

MARRILL
Levin 113

MARRETT
Elizabeth 49
Matilda 66
Nancy 31
Susanna 12

MARINER
Edward I. 137
George Bowman 112
Maria 80

MARRINER
Betsey 53
Louisa 135

MARRITT
James 11

MARSH
Hetty 24
Mary 68
Mary A. 38
Nancy 103
Philip 4,109,114
Sarah P. 16
Theodore 66
Thomas 134

MARSHALL
Albert G. 153
Ann 68,142
Anna 138
Charles W.B. 147
Clarissa 54
Dolly 42
Driucilla 84
Dr. Edward W. 125
Eliza 57,64,149
Eliza O. 63
Elizabeth 59,138
Elizabeth Ann P. 64
Elizabeth P.P 46
Euphame 7
Euphemia 78
George Esme 65
Isaac 5
James 10
Jermiah 152
Johannah 45
John 20,75
John E.H. 70
John H. 85
John P. 15,20,42,
72.89

MARSHALL Con't
John P. of Zadok
          83
John T. 86
Josiah 77
Lizor ? 42
Margaret B. 119
Martha 67
Mary 12,14,51,78
     98,151
Mary A. 127
Mary P. 41
Matilda 31,128
Michael 76
Nancy 48
Peggy 33
Peter 80
Rachel 9
Robert H. 94
Rosy 72
Sally 53
Sampson 53
Sarah 34.66
Sarah Ann 81
Sarah E. 145
Stringer 53
Susan 93
Sylvester J. 140
Thomas 13
Thomas E. 134
Washington 60
William 23,69,102
          110
William H. 148
Wm 14
Zachariah 68
Zadok 2,67,88
Zepporah P. 70

MARTIN
Abner 155
George H, 97
Margaret N. 115
Mary 14,41,62
Mary K. 122
Sarah 5,18

MARTIN Con't
Sarah S. 117
Smith K. 101
Thomas E. 138

MARTON
Abner 100

MASON
A ? Jane 135
Amelia 104
Ann 100
Ann M. 71
Ara 95
Ayres 23,69,129
Bagwell 11,24,52
Betsey 70
Charles 32,88
Charlotte 128
Daniel 93
Edward 111
Elijah 26,38
Elizabeth 54,117,139
Gideson 123
Harriet A. 133
Henry 72
Irving 130
James 60,83,86
John 87
John E. 148
July Ann 137
Lela 77
Lewis H. 97
Martha 134
Mitchel 133
Peter 51,121
Polly 89
Preason 79
Rachel 32,85
Rebecca 76
Rosa 139
Sally 75,150,152
Sarah 17
Stephen E. 132
Stephen T. 137

MASON Con't
Teakle 40
Thorogood 127
Thomas 133,145
Upshur 28
Wealthy J. 120
William 61,105
Wilson P. 106,141
Ziroabel C. 119

MASSAY
Julian 143

MASSEY
Alexander 15
Betsy 48
Caleb H. 35
Caroline 142
Catharine 38
Catharine Ann 86
Daniel 57
Elipher 23
Elizabeth 116
Elizabeth 70
Ephraim 69
James 69,93
James A. 74
John 55
John K. 112
Julia A.P. 151
Julian 143
Kendal Jr. 83
Louisa 67,133
Maria H. 106
Mary 70
Mary E. 152
Nancy 72
Purnell 25
Rachel I. 93
Ramsey 99
Rhoda 40
Sally 21
Sally L. 144
Sally M. 108,144
Samuel J. 148
Sarah 18

MASSEY Con't
William Chaille 98
William H.   113
William Shelly 94
Wm.   155

MASSON
Ellen A.   134

MATHEWS
Levina A. 89

MATTHEWS
Bartholamew 111
Betsey 65
Daniel 59
Drucilla 133
Eliza 67
Elizabeth 55,56,71
Elizabeth S. 102
Ellen A. 129
Ephraim 65
Henrietta 74
Henry 36,94
Hetty 76,100
Irving T. 115
Isaac 27,65
James 58,93
Jane 33
John 58,86,143
John S. 114
Joseph 135
Leah 60
Levi 71
Levin 5
Levina A. 89
Louisa 132
Maria 98
Maria Jane 100
Martha J. 149
Mary A. 88
Mary Ann 104
Mary Elizabeth 107
Meshack 57
Nancy 38,78
Rebecca A. 118

MATTHEWS Con't
Sally 40,50,111
Sally E. 141
Samuel 97
Sarah 138
Thomas 45
Washington 152
William 28,44,65,148
William H. 114
William S. 151
William W.   133

MATTHESS
Peggy 42

MATTHIS
George 105

MAWK
Peter   41

MAY
Susan 28
George S.   134

MEARS
Arthur T. 149
Catharine 102
Elijah B. 156
Henry 66
Hester A. 140
Hester Ann 119
Joseph W. 151
Lorenzo D. 84
Margaret 128
Robert 85
Saphronia E. 147
Sarah Ann 105

MEDCALF
Susan   109

MEER
Maria 109

MEGRATH
William 108

MEIRS
Henry 38

MELBOURN
Nancy 45

MELBOURNE
John 49

MELONE
Alexander 119

MELSON
Ann 100
Benjamin S. 78
Burton C. 118
Daniel F. 100,124
Eleanor S. 102
Elijah 72
Hannah 53
James 59,75,87
Joseph 23
Levin D.   66
Lovey 36
Margaret 91
Maria 86
Mary 75
Mary E.L. 108
Matilda G. 102
Peggy E. 28
Phebe Ann 82
Polly 33
Priscilla F. B. 99
Sally 64,71
Samuel M. 91
Shatty 83
William H. 106

MELVIN
Adaline 131
Agnes   3
Director 36
Elizabeth 60,94
Henrietta 73
James 38
James A.   141
James Walker 25

MELVIN Con't
John 9,54
John B. 98
John Smith 110
John W. 79
John Westley 50
Leah 20
Littleton 76
Maria 109
Mary B. 101
Nancy 30,63
Polly 1,23
Samuel 83,118,126
Samuel D. 134,154
Sarah 5
Sarah A. 146
Sophia 5
Thomas 32
Thomas B. 99
William 9
William Handy 66
Wm Jr 15

MERRELL
Elizabeth H. 20
Kendall 14
Sarah 52
Thomas 52
William 15

MERRILE
Levi 5

MERRILL
Albert J. 146
Alfred D. 123
Ann B. 30
Catharine 52,52,97
Catharine A. 69
Charlotte 32,40,59,67
Eleanor 27,35
Elijah 57
Elizabeth 8,45
Elizabeth Ann 96
Elizabeth P. 49
Ellen A. 107

MERRILL Con't
Esther 24
George 46,52
George S. 59,138
Handy 19
Harriet 52,71
Henry H. 147
Henry Long 130
Henry Thomas 109
Hetty 5,26,30,97
Irving W. 136
James 67
James R. 58
John 33,54,83
John S. 106,141
Julia C. 121
Leah 11,43
Lei 58
Levin 54, 98
Levin A. 132
Levin H. 134
Margaret 18,53
Margaret A. 96
Maria 60
Mary Ann 66
Mary E. 128
Namcy 16,20,44,66
Polly 4
Rosanna 4
Rosena 87
Sally 28
Sally A. 117
Samuel 10
Sarah E.A. 151
Sarah P. 35,93
William H. 52
William H.S. 118
William James 116
Wm 40

MERRITT
Francis 132
Hesse 8
Polly 3

MESICK
Thomas 87

MESSICK
Charles E. 138
Clara 153
Drucilla 149
Elmira W. 138
Jane 145
Jeremiah 34
John W. 155
Mary E. 102
Sarah 10

MEZICK
Aaron 26
Ann 105
Ebenezer 64
Elizabeth 100
Francis 65
James 74
Jane 120
Jeremiah 28
Nancy 135

METCALF
Thomas W. 76

MIDLETONS
Levinia A.M. 135

MIDDLETON
Hesse 29
Hester 126
Isaac 57
James B. 154
Maranda 138

MIERS
Sally 101
Sarah 16

MILBOURN
Deborah M. 68
Jacob 42
Kittusah 16
Rachel P. 4
Thomas 6
Thos. 33
William 28

MILBOURNE
Charlotte 92
Elizabeth 103
Henry 105
Isaac 88
James 56
Margaret 80
Margaret E. 103
Mary F. 68
Mary M. 133
Nancy 102
Nathan 117
Sally 67
Samuel 150
William 93,109
Zadok 69
Zadok T. 117

MILBY
Cora 122

MILES
Drucilla 150
Elijah 60
Eliza A. 43
Elizabeth 90
George I. 131
Handy Jr. 46
Rosey Ann 71
Sally Ann 144
Samuel 9
Severn P. 124
William 18,100

MILLER
Alexine 147
Elizabeth 144
Esther J. 148
Francis D. 62
James 23
John 97
Joseph 17,36
Joseph H. 86
Martha 31
Nancy 37
Polly 2
Sarah 38

MILLIR
Mary F. 136

MILLINER
Eliza 75

MILLS
Amelia E. 126
Betsy 4
Chole 29
Daniel H. 135
David 56,107
Ebby 17
Eliza 48
Elizabeth 28,82,92
Elizabeth E. 112
Elizabeth S. 66
George T. 82
Handy 16
Hannah 4
Henry L. 48
Hetty 64
Jacob U. 144
James 127
John D. 99,151
John S. 91,102
Jonathan 3
Joseph L. 149
Lavica 77
Leonard C, 101
Levin 28,106
Lydia 1
Margaret 58
Mary Jane 150
Mary R. 26
Nancy 17,30,31,84
Orando G. 156
Peggy 34
Polly 20
Robert 82
Sally 47,91
Samuel 13,18
Samuel M. 122
Sarah 2,77,92
Sarah Ann 86
Susan 113,115
Thomas J. 113
William 26

MILLS Con't
William A. 108
William Henry 98
W.S. 156

MILVEN
Ann 126

MINSON
Rachell 149

MISTER
Dowe 143
Mary 144

MITCHELL
Amelia 73
Ann Maria 94
Caroline 81
Dymock 27
Elizabeth 7,144
Elizabeth Ann 103
Eunice 49
George 101
Hannah 86
Harriet 72
Harriet E. 116
Henny 26
Hetty 39
Isaac 12,35,56,87
James 15,52,62
108,139
James H. 50
John 37,65,90
Joshua 117
Josiah 90
Julian 34,88
Keasey 112
Leah 71
Levin 62
Littleton P. 119
Margaret 53
Margaret C. 113
Mary 30,67
Mary H. 118
Mary Margaret 95
Mary P. 84
Nancy 10,25,73

MITCHELL Con't
Nathan 126
Phebe 75
Poly 4
Priscilla 51
Priscilla J. 156
Rebecca 62
Robert 4, 45, 63
Rufus K. 49
Rufus W. 104
Sally 28. 117
Sarah 37
Stephen 37
Susan 110
Washington 135
William 28
William C. 112
William T. 107, 110

MITCHELE
Betsey 4

MONGAR
Bable 22

MOOR
Adam 13
Hetty 85
Jenett 20
Polly 4

MONUDER
Mari 73

MOORE
Abraham 23, 27
Amelia J. 129
Caty 25
Darkey 53
Dorcus Ann 104
Eliza 105
Elizabeth 101
Erixene 121
John T, P. 142
Levin J. 146
Maria 131
Mary A. 121
Mary H. 131

MOORE Con't
Matthew 33
Matilda 74
Nancy 57
Rufus 92
Samuel E. 53
Stephen 48
Stephen P. 121
Thomas 59
Thomas F. 56
William 38
William P. Jr. 80
William S. 115, 129

MORE
Ann 46
James J. 109

MORAND
Alfred L. S. 143

MORGAN
William 25

MORIS
Rackliffee 44

MORRIS
Amelia 19
Andesiah 24
Benjamin 108
Betsy 110
Caleb 24, 37
Catharine 104
Catherine 11
Ceasar 30
Charlotte 46
Clarissa J. 154
Darkey 49
Edward 1, 15
Elijah W. 149
Eliza 129
Eliza E. 147
Elizabeth 78, 80
Elizabeth A. 123
Elizabeth T. 141
Esme P. 70
Esther 84

MORRIS Con't
Francis 137
Gatty 132
Harriet 98
Henry 149
Holladay 26
Isaac 83, 127
James 29, 144
Jeptha 42
Jeremiah 24
John 33, 47, 84, 110
John S. 13
Joshua 93, 147
Julia 84
Leonard 59, 111
Levin 31
Lucretia L. 123
Martha A. E. 146
Martha Ann 86
Martha J. 135
Mary 32
Mary A. 129
Mary Ann 77
Mary Elenor 106
Matilda 111
Nancy 34, 69
Peggy 14
Peter 52
Peter S. 38
Phillip 1, 6, 33
Polly 12, 87
Polly R. 18
Priscilla 55
Rebecca 67
Sally E. 119
Sarah A, 127
Theadore D. 141
Thomas 20, 40
Thomas C. 145
Thomas J. 114
Toy 37
William 50, 50
William B. 151
William R. 127
Zepporah 26
Zilpha A. 118

MORRISON
Hannah 27
Obediah H. 125
Samuel 40

MOROW
Michael M. 95

MULLENDER
Enock 107

MUMFORD
Anna 156
Charles P. 154
Charlotte 118
Comfort 52
David 28
Denny 35
Dilly 48
Elijah 72
Elizabeth 4, 98
Emily D. 140
Evans 9
George 112
Henry 52
Isaac 59
James 19, 28, 59
  60, 76, 81, 120
Jesse 3, 24, 41, 62
  84
John 23, 41, 56
Josiah 106
Julia 90
Littlen 17
Margaret 70, 83
Margaret A. 148
Martha 89
Mary 30, 50, 93, 128
Mary Ann 99, 143
Mary E. 128
Nancy 1, 99
Peter O. 51
Polly 10
Priscilla A. 134

MUMFORD Con't
Retta 81
Risdon 39
Robert 146
Samuel 132, 139
Tetia 47
Thomas 128, 139, 142
Thomas M. 156
Wilson 112,
William 20, 73, 80, 92
  95, 97, 117
William R. 125
William W. 88, 119, 124
Zebram 91
Zebulon G. 66

MURCHEON
Simom 77

MURPHY
Esther Ann 96
Mary 26

MURRAY
Charlotte 111
David 50
Edward 63
Elijah 100
Elizabeth 98
Francis 75
George R. 89
Hetty 14
Hetty D. 116
James 11, 88
John 99, 134
Joseph 66
Kendal 90
Lovey 113
Lydia 121
Maria 98
Mary 106
Rufus 104
Sarah C. 143
Stephen W. 98
William 21

MURREY
Ann 116

MURROE
Molly 59

MURRY
Francis 8

NAIRN
Sarah 2
Nancy 7

NAIRNE
Eleanor 27
Mary L. 92
Robert 6, 84
Sally 47

NARS
Charlotte 53

NEAL
Cyrus 153

NEBOLDS
Sarah Ann 7

NEILL
Edward D. 110

NELMO
Frankey 1
Nancy 7

NELSON
Benjamin W. 133
Betsey 4
Betsy 42
Caroline P. 112
Elijah 5
Eliza 64, 77
Elizabeth 36, 63
George 31
Grace 32
Hannah 9
Harriet Z. 116
Henrietta 77
Henry 76
Henry S. 144
John A. 73

NELSON Con't
John M. 66
Josephus H. 129
Josiah 2
Laura A.W. 132
Levi 4,59,120
Margaret 82
Mary 62
Mary P. 50
Mary Priscilla 149
Mary S. 79
Polly 16,58
Robert 87,93
Sally E.H. 127
Samuel M. 91
Stewart 71,99
Susan 114
Tabitha Smith 76
William 3,5,80

NEWBOLD
Sarah Ann 72
Thomas 5

NEWMAN
Hetty 39
Nancy 26
Nelly 20
Samuel 80

NEWTON
Comfort 16
Hetty 84
Horace M. 32
Mary E.D. 117
Nancy 25
Polly 11
Priscilla 14
Prisy 111

Sarah 26
William 23

NIBBLET
Charles H. 117
William L. 118

NIBLET
Richard 127

NICHOLS
Annanias 69
Betsey 19
Catharine A. 121
Cora Ann 152
Elizabeth 45
Isaac 90
John 94
Lauretta 86
Leah Jane 151
Letta 59
Maria 112
Mary 68,82
Nathaniel 59,130
Phillip 121
Polly 34

NICHOLSON
Amelia A. 155
Denny 73
Elijah 125,129
Frances Catharine 156
John 144
Joseph 96
Joseph Brittingham 86
Levin 90
Mary Ann 102
Nancy 26
William G. 147

NICKERSON
Betsey 16
Catharine 83
John 66
Lotty 38
Martha 57
Mary 49
Sally 62

NICKSON
James 12

NICOLSON
Joseph 21

NOBLE
Amelia A. 108
Ann 51
Hannah 2
Hetty 69
James 6
John 27
Mary 13
Nancy 28,62
Rosanna 28

NOCK
Albert 126
Aralanta P. 120
Edward 57,111
Elijah 115,117
Elizabeth 64
Esther E. 129
Gillet 98
Hetty 122
James 105
James T. 143,151
John 126
John B. 130
John C. 118
John W. H. 150
Julia R.E. 95
Littleton 53
Mary 78
Mary Ann 126,151
Mary R. 126
Nancy 98
Nehemiah W. 112
Sally 5,8,83
Susan P. 132
William 89,104
William J.T. 128

NORTHAM
Amrist 81
George J. 151
James 54
Rebecca 55
Sarah F. 125

NOTTINGHAM
Addison 83
Benjamin F. 152
Margaret 113
Thomas 83

HUSMAN
Aartha 79

HUTTER
Mary Ann 76
Nancy 9
Sally H. 90
Thomas E. 7
William 45, 73

ODELL
David B. 62

OLIPHANT
Eliza E. 150

OLIPHER
James 88

OLIVE
Elizabeth 83

OLIVER
Levi 7

ONLEY
Henry T. 114
John H. 139
John Thomas 80
Margaret 102

ONLY
Esther 9
Thomas 103

ORAM
Charles A. 89

OREM
William M. 95

OSTON
Polly 6

OTWELL
Patty 15

OUTEN
Revel 98
Purnell F. 151

OUTTEN
Benjamin 45
Esther 67
Euphemia 103
Mary 40
Mary A. 130
Peter 103
Polly 13, 16
Purnell T. 64
Revel 120
Sally 10
Sally T. 51
Tabitha 20
William 109

OUTTON
Nancy 101

OWENS
David 35
Ephaim 31
George C. 131, 137
John 146
Joshua 137
Mary 46, 133
Peter 89
Samuel 88
Sarah 137
Uriah 146

PAINE
Nancy 10
Wealthy 2

PAINTER
Mary Ann 83
Sally 76

PALMER
Elihu 63, 75
Elizabeth 97
John 116
John J. 152
John O. 146

PALMER Con't
Joseph Thomas 149
Mary 126
Mary Jane 124
Nancy 115
Sally 116
Sally A. 129
Thomas 78

PALMORE
James T. 107

PALSBURG
Kessy 100

PANMORE
Henrietta Virginia 124

PANAWELL
Peter S. 135

PARADIS
Lucitta 138

PARADISE
Catharine 15
Elizabeth 101
John 104
Kendal 131
Lauretta 155
Milby 96
Nancy 107
Thomas 66
William 40

PARIS
Peter 16

PARKER
Alce 58
Amelia 1
Ann 74
Ann C. 118
Ayres 49
Ayres B. 73, 126
Bavquilla 6

PARKER Con't
Benjamin 110
Betsey 10,28
Betsy 24
Charles 3,30
Charles Jr. 129
Charles W, 149
Charlotte 86,102
Charlotte A. 152
Clarissa 114
Clement I.B. 77
Comfort 21
Daniel 49
Delilah 2
Eleanor 44
Elisha 77,95
Elisha P. 97
Elisha Purnell 56
Eliza 77,113
Elizabeth 66,69,79 97
Elizabeth S. 124
Emeline E. 112
Gatty 70
George 33
George A. 76
Gertrude 20
Harriet A. 91
Henretta 27
Henrietta 75,122
Henry 33
Hester E. 145
Hetty 35,56
Hetty Jane 100
Hiram D. 118
Huldah 95
Isaac H. 109
Jacob 107,117
James 16,53,122
James H 128
Jane 86
Joanna 155
John 2,29,48,62
John H. 148
John P. 128
John S. 144
John W. 156
Joshua R. 116
Julia A. 90

PARKER Con't
Lavinia A. 139
Lemuel 14
Levica H. 51
Levin W. 103,150
Lucinda 108
Margaret 42
Margaret H. 141
Maria 62,68
Maria Ann 113
Maria E. 142,152
Martha J. 151
Mary 6,43,62,71
Mary C. 154,154
Mary J.W. 152
Mary P. 143
Matilda 50
Matilda A. 140
Matty 90
Milly Ann 127
Minos F. 132
Nancy 2,3,4,45,54
Nelly 32,107
Patty 19
Peter 23,131
Polly 39
Pressey 32
Rachel 57
Rebecca 35,109
Sally 4.29,52
Sally E. 148
Samuel 72.
Sampson 102,115
Sarah 54,59,69
Sarah Ann 108
Selby 20
Severn C. 54
Sophia 29
Susan 39
Tabitha 114
Theodore 115
Thomas 78,97,118
Thomas D. 84
Thomas H. 119
Thomas P. 76
William 10,21,27,38 41,135
William A. 79

PARKS
Charlotte 83
Elizabeth B. 103
Elizabeth M. 156
Ellen 89
Hetty C. 147
John 20
Margaret 77
Robert C. 67

PARMER
John 121
Thomas 70

PARMORE
Elizabeth 7

PARR
James 41

PARRAMORE
Edward L. 151
James H. 71
Mary 10

PARSONS
Adam 119
Amelia H. 147
Ann 66
Ann Maria 124
Benjamin 75
Benjamin S. 140
Betsy 72
Caleb T. 96
Catharine 92
Charles 134
Charlotte 156
Clarissa 154
Daniel F. 120
Daniel J. A. 141
David B. 107
Eli 115
Elijah 46,57,116
Elisha 56
Eliza J. 134
Elizabeth 31,79,145
Elizabeth A. 120
Elizabeth Ann 154

PARSONS Con't
Elizabeth S.   118
Emeline 116
Emma V. 150
Ephraim W. 98
Gatty Elizabeth 137
George 11,46,68,153
George B. 67
George L. 66,153
George W. 148
Hannah 10,115
Hannah G. 127
Henrietta 50,120,137
Hester A. 139
Hiram D. 120
James 7, 31,47
James A. 115
James H. 154
James S. 113
Jehu 148
John 19.124
John A. 60,95
John B. 108
John F. 120
John J. 127
John W. 153
John W, B. 26
Jonathan 24
Jonathan Stevens 44
Josiah 96
Julia Ann 123
Julia J. 153
Lambert W. 137
Laura A. 137
Leah 93
Levi C. 135
Levin 147
Margaret A. 155
Martha 152
Martha A. 152
Mary 54,114,128,135
Mary Ann 138
Mary E. 145
Mary Elizabeth 146
Mary G. 117
Milly 41
Mordica G. 120
Nancy 29,55,140

PARSONS Con't
Nancy Carolin 135
Nathaniel P. 66
Patrick W. 89
Peter 40
Peter P. 48
Peter R. 98
Peter T. 116
Priscilla Eleanor 86
Purnell 98
Rebecca 48
Richard L. 121
Sally 117
Samuel 25,76
Sarah 43,65,86,99
       100,118,119,154
Sarah E. 136
Sheda 32
Temperance 62
Thomas 94
William 45,49,60
        63,88,119
William of Saml 132
Zephaniah 34

PASTERFIELD
Jeremiah 129

PATEN
William Jr.   84

PATEY
Elizabeth 75
Jane E. 107
Kendal J. 129
Kendall 27
Powell 34
Sally 137

PATTEY
Fanny M. 130
John M. 116
Nancy 62

PATTY
William 74

PATY
Elizabeth 42

PATRICK
Polly 18
Thomas 18

PATTERSON
Anderson 20
Ann 56
Bridget 1
Caroline P. 109
Charles 66
Elizabeth 53,60
George 8
George W. 120
Henry 85
James 48
John 18, 66
John R. 48
Juliet Ann 88
Margaret A. 103
Mary 45
Nancy 51,84
Sally M. 82
Samuel 60
Priscilla 121
William 34

PAYDEN
Ann Mills   31

PAYDON
William 129

PAYNE
Adline 135
Benjamin O. 128
Betsey 23,33
Catharine 20
Catharine J. 133
Charlotte I. 141
Drucilla 111
Drusilla 96
Easther 91
Edward 132
Eleanor 27
Eleanor W. 109
Elizabeth 6,110,154
Emeline 98
Esther 58

PAYNE Con't
Esther J.   140
George 92
Ira 142
Jacob 6,22,78,108
James 36,76,102
John 7,63,78
John I.   116
John S.   125
John W.   140
Joshua 31
Leah 63
Leah E.   145
Levin 45
Littleton 120
Mary 74
Mary A.   133
Moses 40,49,54,134
Nancy 80,146
Nancy W.   125
Narissa 73
Nelly 78
Rebecca 53
Rixon 105
Rounds T.   140
Samuel A.   73
Samuel H.   117,137
Samuel J.   150
Sarah 49, 117
Stephen 97
Susan 78,137
William 27, 105
William H.   130,140
Wrixham 42
Zila Ann 106

PAYNTER
James 64
Mary Ann   85

PAYTON
Anne B.   142
Henrietta   139
Jane 153
John 107
John W.   147
Mary F.   142
Sarah E.   140

PEACOCK
Ann 81
Sarah M.   92

PEARSON
William T.   119

PENAWELL
Noah 135

PENDLETON
Edmond 46

PENEWELL
Mary Ann 136
Wesley 129
Zeporah 109

PENEWILL
Elizabeth 131

PENN
Thomas 125

PENNAWELL
Caty 14
Thomas 15

PENNEWELL
Annanias 66
Ann Maria 104
Aralanta 102
Arralanta 26
Betsey 17
Caroline 99
Charlotte 37
David 36
Eliza 54,74,94
Gatty 88
Henry B.   111
Hetty 66,91
Isaac 15
John 71
Luke 91
Mary Ann 81
McKimmy 16
Milby 50
Mitchell 77

PENNEWELL Con't
Nancy 1,76
Nelly   43
Peter 80
Priscilla S.   133
Rachell 64
Sally 122
William 123
William I.   88

PENNIWELL
Elizabeth 150
Isaac G.   143
James 133
John 31
Mary A.   154
Purnell 27
Purnell M.   152
Rachel 20
William L.   139

PENNEWILLE
Ara 145

PENNYWELL
Elias 85

PEPPER
Ann 56
Nancy C.   119
Naomi 15
Patsy 7
Rebecca 1
Winder 123,127
Zachariah 33

PERDUE
Elijah C.   25
Elijah L.   99
Elizabeth E.Y.   19
George 14
Gertrude J.   135
Henrietta 130
John B.   66
John Kendall Hebrun
                         14
Lambert G.   128
Lemuel H.   115,131

PERDUE Con't
Martha 26
Mary 115
Miranda F. 120
Sabra 16
Sally Ann 93
Sally E. 121
Sarah Ann 118

PERKING
Mary 56

PERKINS
Esther 128
George 22
Nancy 16
Peggy 11
Robert 116, 122

PETERSON
Amos 143

PETIT
John 115
Sarah 125
Thomas 151

PETITT
David 122
Emaline 128

PETTIT
Ananias 121
Anna 12
David 138
Elias 147
Leah 133
Martha 43
Mary A. 132
Polly 16

PETTITT
Henry W. 71
Hetty 29
Mary 33
Rhoda 28

PEUZEY
Parker 17

PEWSEY
Thomas 58

PHILIPS
Ann 93
Isaac B. 127
John T. 118
Phebe Ann 114
Sarah 132

PHILLIPS
Aralanta 106
Handy 48, 122
Harriet 99
Hetty M. 117
Hiram 115
Isaac 21
James 88, 93
James A. 150
Joshua 19, 73, 124
Kendall 19
Major M.C. 137
Mary 68, 107, 124
Nancy 66, 122
Sarah C. 142
Thomas F. 136

PHIPS
John 155

PHIPPIN
Mary J. 142

PHIPPS
Absalom 151
John 89

PILCHARD
Althea J. 137
Ara 101
Aurena 150
Denwood 73
Devin 10
Donard 133

PILCHARD Con't
Elijah 55
Elizabeth 46, 126, 145
Ellen 129
Emerst W. 122
Erastus 117
Henry L. 136
Hetty 55
Jepthah 33
John 64
Lemuel 95
Levi 12
Mary 155
Mary Ann 107
Molly 78
Moses 6, 68, 85
Ome 12
Peter T. 155
Rixon 100
Rosetta 144
Sally 32
Sarah 10
Stephen 102
Stephen Pope 23
Susan 51
Susanna 24
Tabitha Jane 82
Thomas 152
William 21, 150
Wriseham 68
Wrixham E. 147

PILCHER
Catharine 35
Stephen 12

PINCHIN
Alfred 141

PINKETT
Elijah 92
John 143

PIPER
Mary 50

PITTS
Catharine 38
Edward T. 113
Elizabeth 13,82
Elizabeth H. 49
Elmira 117
Henrietta C. 102
Hillary 40
Dr Hillary R. 148
Dr Hilliary 99
Hilliary R. 115
James 13,25,41,67
John R. 34,73,79,89
Laura 141
Maria 84
Mary Gatty 91
Mary Margareta 156
Molly Bratten 57
Nancy 49
Nancy P. 14
Polly 3
Robert 29,53,131
Sally Ann 156
Sarah G.S. 95
Thomas N. 108
William 8,47
William D. 89
William P. 102

POINTER
Catharine 1
Elias 26
Isaac 12,84
Milly 44

POLK
Charlotte C. 40
Eliza 45
Emerson G. 146
Susan 105
William 20
William S.C. 144
William T.C. 124

POLLET
Catharine 154

POLLETT
Eleanor Jane 64
Thomas 68

POLITT
Esther 49

POLLIT
Leasha 47

POLLITT
Ann Maria 110
Benjamin L. 116
Eleanor 100
Elizabeth 55
Henrietta 55
Jane 43
James A. 137
John 155
Jonathan 33,120
Josiah M. 109
Leah 48
Leah Jane 149
Lewis 71
Louis 154
Mary E. 122
Nancy 31
Nehemiah 36
Perry R. 155
Polly 29,36
Sarah 48
Sarah A. 114
Stephen 76
Titus 79
William 83

POLSON
Elizabeth 59

POOL
Emeline W. 109
John H. 101,124
William W. 112

POPE
Charlotte Jane 122
Emeline 103
Henry 104

POPE Con't
Henry Purnell 97
Josiah 27
Littleton 34,76,126
Margaret 126
Mary 147
Mary E. 124
Polly 30
Sinah E. 121
William 80
William J. 154

PORTER
Ann 57
Ayres 50
Catharine 20
Edward 117
Edward P. 89
Elizabeth 46
Emeline 107
George 74
George W. 144
Gustavus R. 72
Hannah 100
Isaac 31
James 64,67,148
James H. 150
Jane W. 104
John 12
John S. 64
Joseph 12,36
Kendall 39
Laura Ann 99
Levi 32,42
Louisa 85
McKemmy 4,77
Mahala 42
Margaret 36,51
Margaret G. 124
Mary 35,38,77
Mary P. 138
Molly 56
Nancy 27
Polly 26,46
Purnell 32
Rebecca 25,50
Rhoda 18
Rosena 114

PORTER Con't
Sally 13
Samuel 54,56
Samuel T.P. 149
Shephard 72
Thomas 109
William 1,44,133
William W. 34

POSTLY
Nancy 10

POTTER
Hosea 77

POULSON
Elizabeth A.B. 130
Thomas 121
Tuphany 130

POWDERS
Elizabeth 88
Mary 110
Nathan 31

POWEL
Batty 67

POWELL
Adelia K. 155
Ananias 82
Ananias W. 82
Annanias W. 92,113
Ann 45
Ann M. 133
Anna 36
Arthur 43
Benjamin 30
Betsey 52
Betsy 95
Brittingham 64
Caleb 1,20
Catharine 153
Catherine 15
Comfort E.H. 84
Drucilla 74
Ebenezer 22
Edward 156

POWELL Con't
Edward U. 85
Elawiza 97
Eleanor 58,74,98
Eli 19
Elijah 45,63,147
Elijah B. 56
Elijah M. 144
Elisha 59
Eliza 100
Elizabeth 44,51,98
        113,145,146
Elizabeth A. 96
Ellen 125
Emily A. 148
Ephraim 70
Fanny 11
Francis 106
George 145
George E. 133
Henrietta 63
Henry 10,42,54,73
        74,81,125
Hetty 32,81
Hugh S. 120
Isaac R. 123
Isaiah 143
Jacob 122
James 18,26,30,88
James B. 93
James M. 116,130
James R. 81
James of Solomon
        85
Jesse 7,29,30,108
John 11,21,35,49
        60,61,94,103
        112,147
John D. 111
John E. 83
John Hiram 99
John K. 147
John W. 85
Jonathan 17
Joshia D. 80
Julia A. 104
Julia Ann Pitts 88

POWELL Con't
Kezzier 15
Lambert 67
Lambert C. 107
Laura A. 143,153
Lauretta S. 109
Leah 65
Levi 22
Levin 22,29,74,128
Levin T.A. 148
Levin W. 95
Littleton 68
Lophus 92
Lorenzo 127
Lydia 80
Marandy 63
Mardecai J. 154
Margaret 100,122,144
Margaret D. 130
Margaret E.R. 92
Maria 93,98,102,155
Martha 14,15,35,89
Mary 48,48,80,100
        108,132
Mary A. 131
Mary Ann 104,109
Mary D. 109
Mary E. 121,139,147
Mary Elizabeth 91
Mary H. 142
Matilda 85
Milby 47 88
Minos H.F. 141
Modica J. 116
Nancy 14,24,25,37
        64
Nathaniel 111
Pattey 77
Peter 35,78,84,86
        101,104
Philip 111
Polly 2,18,23
Priscilla 130
Rachel 135
Rachel Gunby 33
Rebecca 81,119
Robert 52,104

POWELL Con't
Robert H. 86,113,134
Robert J. 126
Robert W. 135
Rosetta 144
Sally 23,76,86
Salley E. 150
Sallie E. 146
Sally E. 142
Samuel 104
Sandy 134
Sarah 76,99,153
Sarah M. 129,144
Solomon 38,112
Sophia 67
Susan 112,
Thomas 13,59,59
 132,138
William 20,50,52,52
 58,98,122,133
 140
William of Elisha 121
William H. 63
William J. 130
William R. 114
William T. 105
Wm 14,17
Zadok 72
Zadok Jr. 18
Zeno 14
Zepy 52
Zipporah C. 126

POWLSON
William T. 140

POYNTER
Isaac 13
Justus 15

PRATT
Henry 20

PREDEAUX
Eliza A.A. 29
Hetty 63
John 22
Nancy 33
Peggy 42
Polly 11

PREDUX
Sally 41

PRESCOT
Elizabeth 96

PRESLEY
John 54

PRICE
Ann 89
Ansy 79
Arthur B. 69
David 11
Ellen 150
John 38, 99
Levin B. 140
Mary 6
Patsey 20,27
Peter 75,98
Polly 30
Sarah 9,43
Soloman K. 4
William 6,67

PRIER
Betsey 98

PRIMROSE
Anna 147
Cynthia M. 135
James S. 155

PRIOR
Arnold 65
Caroline 60
Charles 83
David 78,90
Eliza 77
Elizabeth 94,138
Eloza 69
George 147
Margaret 107
Mary Ellen 111
Molly 43
Sarah Jane 147
Thomas 122
William P. 147

PRUIT
Sally 7

PRUITT
Charlotte 114
Comfort 119
David 82,111
Druscilla A. 133
Edward T. 127
Eleanor 119
Elijah 4,48
Elizabeth 127
Elizabeth J. 135
George 99,148,153
Harriet 93
James H. 130
John 76
John H. 60, 142
John S. 148
Lanta 28
Lazarus 75
Leah 105
Lemuel 55
Lemuel S. 106
Marcellus 154
Margaret 78
Mary C. 125,127
Mary E. 113
Mary P. 123
Nancy 42,46
Robert 111
Sarah 57,105
Selby 1
Severn 3,65
Severn J.M. 139
Thomas 122
Wincy 93
William 46.111,133
William C. 149
William M. 91

PUDDERY
Betsey 14

PURDEU
Robert Asbury 136

PURDUE
James B.W. 142

PURNELL
Amelia 75
Amelia H. 35,50
Andasia R. 56
Anna 12
Anna M. 115
Azariah 32
Betsey 14
Catharine B. 54
Charlotte 57,126
Charlotty 25
Delilah A. 152
Dolly 24
Elisha 14,73
Elizabeth 20.28,75, 144
Elizabeth M. 140
Ellen A. 154
Ellen J. 115
Elmira C. 132
Erexine S. 89
Esma 7
Esther H. 106
Esther R. 34
Euphamy 30
Francis J. 146
George 10
George G. 122
Georgianna C. 147
Henrietta W. 52
Hesse 13
Hessey 35
Isaac 90
Isaac B. 127
Dr. James B.R. 148
James R.S. 75
Jane 1,128
Jesse 83
John 4,48
John A. 95
John F. 56
John H. 115
John Hill 107
John J. 3
John M. 123
John R. 64,142
John S. 63

PURNELL Con't
July Ann 48
Leah 4
Lemuel 128
Levi 42
Levin 19
Littleton R. 129
Margaret 139
Margaret Spence 16
Martha 25,41
Martha A. 95
Martha H. 145
Mary 10,11,59,77
Mary Ann 93,94
Mary Elizabeth 111
Mary J. 56
Mary Jane 93
Mary Marshall 47
Mary O. 27
Mary S. 34,103
Matthew 40
Milby 1,18,61
Milley 28
Moses 28,51
Nancy 42,48
Narcesia 22
Parker 23
Patty 4
Peggy 15
Polly 12
Rebecca 76
Roan F. 38
Robert 9
Robert H. 38
Sally 25
Sally of Merrill 65
Sally E 148
Sally L. 91
Sally M. 53,112
Sally Maria 121
Sarah 11
Sarah Maria 35
Stephen 46,58,102
Susan 32
Thomas 13,31,41,45 61
Thomas D. 137
Thos. of Thos 32
William 35,60
WilliamH. 115

PURNELL Con't
William N. 55
William T. 103
William T. J. 102
Zadok 18,45,87,131
Zadok G.W. 134
Zadok Jr. 61
Zeporah 13

PUSEY
Betsey 110
Elihu J. 107
Eleanor A. 141
Emory A. 126
John F. 144
John P. 148
Leah M. 145
Levin T. 145
Louisa D. 150
Lydia 138
Marthenia 129
Mary 58
Mary A. 145
Narcissa 150
Purnell 128,135
Rebecca 124
Sarah Francis 110

PUZEY
Ann 77
David 54
Eleanor 89
Elizabeth W. 109
Ephraim 104
Isaac 61
James D. 108
Lankford 22
Leah Purnell 62
Levin 105
Mary 102
Mary Purnell 99
Mary W. 101
Matilda 105
Nancy 72
Nelly 54
Priscilla 38,97
Pusy 90
Purnell 39,104

PUZEY Con't
Rebecca 39
Sarah 107
Stephen 105
Tracey 64
Whittey 70
William 74
William Q. 102

QUILLEN
Charlotte A. 132
Ebenezer 81
Edward J. 153
Elizabeth 105
Fanny 122
Henry 138
Hillary P. 133
James H. 123
John P. 147
John P. I. 95
Joseph 93, 153
Lambert 65
Lambert J. 148
Levi 94
Lydia 12
Martha 101
Martha J. 118
Mary 95
Mary Ann 86, 115
Mary E. 141
Matilda 67
Nancy 72
Nancy C. 152
Nathaniel 78, 98
Obediah 10
Peter 67
Sally Mary 139
Sarah 129
Thomas 44, 84
William S. 118

QUILLING
Elizabeth 90
Martha C. 104
Peter 90
Rebecca 55

QUILLION
Thomas N. 110

QUINN
Virginia A. 146
William 76
William W. 152

QUINTON
Comfort E. 98
Elizabeth 28
Henrietta 6
Hetty 31
Nancy M. 55
P.W. 82
Polly 5
William 6

RACKLIFFE
Betty 1
James 44, 82
Mary 36
Mary Ann 56
Thomas P. 22

RADISH
John 7

RADDISH
Susan 101

RADNEY
William 46

RAIN
Betsey 63
Charlotte 75
Eliza 89
Gilbert 114
Gillis 96
Hetty 47
James 35, 70
John 88
Kesiah 6
Mary E. 126
Nancy 91
Nancy 8
Peter 76, 125
Sally 111
Selby 71

RAINE
Tomothy 142

RALEIGH
William 103

RALLION
Henry 95
Sally 136

RALPH
James 77

RANDALL
Henretta 27

RANKIN
Elizl 33
James 24
John 20
Mary 7, 45
Sally 48

RATLIDGE
Mary 117

RATLIGE
Jane 135

RAYFIELD
Ann J. 79
Tabitha H. 100

RAYN
Bassitt 106

RAYNE
Annie M. 155
James P. 131
John A. 128
John M. 147
Moses 56

RAYPHIELD
Mary 122

READ
Elizabeth 128
Eliza Maria 45
John 118

REDDEN
Altha 69
Catharine S. 77
Eleanor 46, 51
Hester 111
Isaac A. 70
James S. 144
John 4, 8, 77, 141
Laura Ann 131
Letitia J. 154
Margaret Ann 106
Mary 9
Nancy 50
Nehemiah 35, 78, 80
Olevia 150
Patsey 82
Peggy 52
Polly 59
Ronna 62
Rosena 88
Sally 54, 61
Sarah 44
Stephen 50, 101, 129
Stephen A. 129
William 133

REDISH
John 22
Lucretia 150

REDDISH
Ann 87
Elizabeth I. 97
Isabella 74
John 151
Lydia Jane 76
Mary 114
Sally 22
Sarah 125
William 29

REECE
Ephraim 49

REED
Ann 66
Anna 47
Betsey 9
Charlotte Ellen 155

REED Con't
Eleanor 45, 79
Eliza 113
Elizabeth 19, 88
Francas 47
Henry 85, 86, 95, 113
James 105, 136
Janette 32
John 40, 82, 106
John T. 125
Joshua 43, 47, 114
Leah 72
Littleton 128
Major 87
Margaret 61
Mary 49
Mary E. 143
Matilda 24
Pearce 72
Polly 7
Rachel 30
Rebecca 150
Samuel 144
Thomas 70, 101, 108
William 45
William Parker 47

REEDE
Henry 103
John 102

REESE
Esther 77
William W. 142

REGGAN
James 66
Nancy 45
Noah 16
Puzey 29
Sarah 4

REGGEN
Levi 35

REGGIN
Levin 20

REGISTER
Elijah 138
Samuel M. 154

REID
Betsey 51
James 4
Major 137
Milly 19
Mitchell 22
Nancy 17
Polly 21
Sallie M. 148

RENNALS
Martin 21
Wm 17

REVEL
Edward 129
Mary E. 120

REVELL
Charlotte 118
Nathaniel F. 94

REVILL
Edward A. 36
Sally 34

REW
Charles T. 92
James H. 72
Lovey D. 132
Revell 113

REYNALDS
Edmund 18

REYNOLDS
Elizabeth C 131
Hammond 80
Nancy J. 134
Thomas 3

RIAN
John 36

RICE
George 1
Mary 41

RICH
Jane 95

RICHARD
Joseph 19
Kendall 39
Rachel 28
William 11,43

RICHARDS
Barshaba 6
Benjamin 32
Caty 22
Charlotte 41
Charlotte C. 93
Elizabeth 51
Henrietta 118
Isaac 37
Jacob 4
Jane 97
John 8,12
John B. 150
Mary 52
Nancy 2
Polly 18
Sally 5,61
Schoolfield 55
William 21,43,115

RICHASON
Charles 119

RICHARDSON
Amelia A. 139
Andazia 110
Ann 96
Ann M. 106
Armell 83
Augusta C. 120
Benjamin 5,35,47
Benjamin J. 109
Benjamin T. 109,132
Betsey 3

RICHARDSON Con't
Betsy 108
Betsy M. 13
Catharine J. 108
Charles 48
Charly 143
Comfort 55
David 33,100
Edward A. 141
Ellanor 89
Elleanor A.D. 89
Elenor 107
Elizabeth 23,103
Esme 53
Fisher 11
George 12,27,54
George M. 142
George W. 94
Henry 110
Hester A. 79
Hetty 80,94,125
Hulda 28
Isaac H. 137
James 65,80,110,111
        127,149
James W.M.W. 153
Jeptha 80
Jethery 38,43
John 27,29,48,64,75
        79,80,125
John P. 91
John S. 110,136
John Thomas 149
Joseph 27,65,146
Joseph E. 136
Joshua 16
Levi 24
Littleton 74,101
Margaret 108
Maria 76
Martha 2,7
Martha J. 153
Mary 38,41,57,73
        77,85,92,125
Mary Ann 145
Mary B. 80
Mary J. 110
Mary M. 65

RICHARDSON Con't
Matilda 156
Nancy 9,24,30,47,
        60,63,148
Oma 11
Peter 10
Polly 1,10,16,30,42
Rachel 10
Rachel A. 153
Robert 57
Robert M. 10
Sallie M. 130
Sally 14,17,23,47
        56
Sally Ann 111
Sally E. 127
Samuel 48,72,92
Sarah Ann 69
Susan 96
Tabitha 98
Thomas 99
Thomas I. 115
Wilmor S. 117
William 23,60,77
        101,132
William C. 130
William H. 131
Zadok 58,145,148
Zadok H. 116
Zeporah 15
Zorababel 59

RICHIE
Thomas H. 154

RICKETTS
Mary 72

RIDER
Amelia 92
Charles 50
Hetty A.S. 137
James W. 148
John Byrd 96

RIGGAN
Amelia 17
Bayard 100
Benjamin 98

RIGGAN Con't
Elenker 54
Eliza 54
Emeline 76
Hamilton 118
Hannah 77
Jacob 49, 98
James 27, 39
John 75, 90
John T.W. 89
Leah 27
Lemuel 47, 98
Lucretia 24
Mary 73
Nancy 22, 27, 47
Olivia 103
Polly 73
Rachel 12
Sally 7, 51
Sarah 38
Steward 87
William 72

RIGGEN
Henrietta 156
Lavin 41

RIGGIN
Alfred R. 122
Alley W. 133
Dolly A. 144
Edward T. 103
Eleanor 101
Elizabeth A. 132
George H. 147
Hamilton 67
Irving 133
Jacob 38
Margaret A. 106
Margaret E. 154
Matilda 148
Nancy 18
Sally 93
Sarah 60
William C. 137
William J. 117

RIGGS
Nancy 13

RILEY
Anna 4
Ann C. 47
Catharine 13
Elizabeth 1, 54, 70
Elton Gray 72
Henrietta 73
Isaac 11
Jacob 48
James 18, 57, 138 145
James D. 120
Joshua 75
Julian 50
Leah 65
Littleton 2
Margaret E. 115
Mary Ann 73
Mary Jane 132
Mary O. 59
Molly 10
Nancy 115
Nancy T. 129
Nelley 143
Peter 76
Rachel 3
Relbaca 140
Sally 30
Samuel M. 112
Stephen 27
Thomas 46
William 27, 61
William B.L. 41
William F. 41
William H. 95
William T. 48

RING
Mary 98

RION
Elisha 124
Rachel 133
Thomas 139

RISLEY
William S. 119

RITCHER
John 156

RITCHIE
Emma 153
George W. 126
John 36
Thomas 39

ROACH
Betsey 5
Bossa 16
Eleanor 8
Henrietta 20
Hetty 35
James 35, 61
Nancy 41
Sally 11
Stephen 4, 92

ROAN
Betsy 38
Nancy 28

ROBERSON
John 112

ROBERTS
Alice 32
Catharine T. 121
Effy 25
Esther 37
Jacob 19
James 44
Mary Ann 107
Nancy 16, 19
Peter 25
Sarah 1
Susan 93
Sylvanus Uriah 2
Thomas L.B. 102

ROBERTSON
Alfred L. 115
Elinora C. 136
George 30
James 7
Joseph 34
Martha W. 138
Rhoda 49
Ruth 4
Sally 76
Thomas B. 113
William 110
Zadock P. 156

ROBINS
Anna 46
Attalanta 15
Bowdoin 51
Daniel G. 35
Eleanor H. 56
Eliza 24
James B. 56,124,154
John L.B. 56
John Purnell 83
John S. 130
Joseph 73
Leah 76
Lewis 93
Littleton Junr. 12
Margaret S. 53
Maria T. 13
Martha 34
Martha B. 42
Mary S. 61
Sarah E. 95
Susan 83

ROBINSON
Avary 148
Sophia 20

ROCK
John 4
Josiah 61
Maria L. 86
Nancy 30
Sallie E. 114

RODNEY
Annanias 122
Elizabeth A. 141
Emeline 153
John B. 156
Perry 99
Perry S. 91
Phillip 99
Schoolfield 17

RODGERS
Samuel J. 57
Walter 88
William 129

ROGER
William 37

ROGERS
America 14
Catherine 21
Elizabeth V. 98
Jacob 66
Jane 127
John 94
Mary J. 108
Soloman 48
Thomas 75, 104
Walter 73

ROLEY
William K. 136

ROSE
Levi 92
Mary Ann Elizabeth 132

ROSS
Charlotte 121
Dolly A. 155
Francis J. 144
Jacob M. 70
Margaret J. 148
Mary Ann 118
Nancy 101
Parker 95
Ralph 112
Sarah F. 156
William 101
William H. 144

ROSSE
Euphamy 35
Frances 28
Francis 33
Nancy 60
Richard 103
Sally 137
William 31

ROUND
Jacob 7
Julian 95
Nancy 51
Sally 82
Sarah 44
Thos R. 56

ROUNDS
Allison T. 141
Betsey 57
Daniel D. 128
George 130
Hannah 79
John R. 35
Mary 41,43,75
Mary A. 121
Polly 8
Thomas P. 145
William 74
William I. 141
Zaporah 3

ROWND
Edward 43
George 94
Joshua 34
Sally 66
William 19,31

ROWNDS
Jenkins 39
Mary 39
Peter 67,72

ROWLEY
Catharine 54
Coventon 22
Daniel 10, 69
David L. 96
Edmond 83
Esther 37
Henry I. 99
Hessey 33
James 71
James H. 33
James L. 97
John 49
John W. 101
Margaret P. 143
Mary 70
Mary Catharine 108
Nancy 30, 108
Polly 124
Salley 47
Sally A. 107
Samuel 47, 60
Sarah 23, 58
Sarah Ann 104
Susanna 15
Thomas 132
William 23
Wiliam A. 128
William H. 95, 118
Wm 38

ROWLY
Henry 20
Polly 21
William 20

ROYALL
John 126

RUARK
Adeline 143
Ann 19
Charley 56
Charlotte 90
Comfort 85
Daniel 39
Drucilla 143

RUARK Con't
Emeline 80
Ezekiel 25
Gertrude 153
Hannah 13, 151
Hetty Ann 151
Isaac 38
Jarrell 81
James 26, 125, 146
James W. 83
Jas. N. 87
John 40, 102, 130
Johnson 9
Joshua 92
Keturah 95
Leah 37
Margaret 95
Margaret J. 132
Martha 17
Mary 36, 71
Nancy 23, 65, 68, 127
Peggy 35
Peter 82
Priscilla A. 93
Rachael 143
Rachel 47
Samuel 151
Seth 8
Stephen 36
Stouton 16
William 58, 71
William J. 155

RUKE
Hannah 57

RULLEDGE
John P. 41

RUNNELS
Alfred James 112
Druscilla 72

RUNNELLS
Ann 86
Catharine 60
Epolita 75

RUSE
Sarah 111

RUSSELL
Anna 61
Daniel P. 100
Delight 68
Elizabeth J. 112
John 65, 81
Lybia 47
Mary 97, 107
Nancy 47
Robt. 35
Sally 55

RYON
Ann Maria 104
Elijah 104
Elizabeth 116

SALSBURY
Caty 90

SAMPSON
George 41
Julia Anna R. 59
Mary 27

SANDERS
William W. 107

SATCHEL
George T. 114

SAUNDERS
John A. 72
Mary A. 106

SAVAGE
Ann 66
Calvin H. 105
Catharine 138
Elizabeth 93
Emeline 83
Emmie S. 136
Esther B. 142
Griffen 50
John 13, 52

SAVAGE Con't
Dr John G.   108
Leonard B.   134
Lizzie H.   143
Mary 128
Mary A.   109
Mary E.   152
Mary J.   134
Mary K.   139
Peggy 129
Polly 7,27
Sally 60
Sally T.   99
Severn 131
Susanna 33
Tabitha 19
Tabitha W.   103
Thomas 47
Virginia M.   127

SAYAGE
Mary 100

SAYERS
Sarah Ann 121

SAYES
Mary 133

SCARBOROUGH
Ann 32
Ann A.   57
Betsey 19
Betsey 36
Edward 3,112,120
Eliza 81
Emily E.   95
Esther K.   48
George 43
Harriet 101
John 2
Juliet L.   79
Kendall 46
Mary 13,124
Mary Ann 111
Mitchell T.   138
Peter 80
Richard 52,68
Sally 99,155

SCARBOROUGH Con't
Sarah 1,5,34
Vienna 23
Wm. M.   45

SCHARBOROUGH
Elizabeth 127

SCHIRER
Frances E.   109

SCHOFIELD
William 1

SCHOOLFIELD
Catharine 16
Charlotte 110
Elijah C.   71,92
Elizabeth 53
Henrietta 108
Henry 39
Hilda 21
Isaac B.   12
Jane 93
John 64
Joseph 3,45,49
Margaret 90
Mary A.F. 100
Nancy 10
Nevett 68
Nevit H.   81
Patty 15
Rebecca 22
Rosey 76
Sallie A.   153
Samuel T. 146
Sarah 8,31
William 4,32,105
William M.   136
Zepporah 14

SCHURER
Charlotte A.   83

SCOTT
Adam 34
Benjamin 9
Edward R.   102
Elijah C.   136

SCOTT Con't
Eliza Ann 87
Elizabeth M.   103
Esther 105
George 68,100
James 110
John 28
John E.   95
Joseph 23
Leah 27
Levin 150
Martha 66
Mary 87
Mary A.   91
Mary Ann 89
Mary E.   112
Mary Elizabeth 153
Nelly 30
Patience 34
Peter 27,92
Sally A.   100
Sarah 107,153
Stephen 144
Susan 53
Susan W.   86
Thomas 48,48,103
Walter 93
William 44,70,90
William C.   140
William J.   103
William W.   103

SEALES
Thomas 57

SEARS
Carey Collier 90
John 18,81,115
Margaret E.   150
Rebecca 34

SELBY
Albert 94
Amelia 30,149
Anna 32,35
Asa 143
Attalanta 15
Betsey 65

SELBY Con't	SELBY Con't	SHARPLEY Con't
Caroline 49	Nathniel 121	Henry 85
Catharine 18	Olivia A. 136	John T. 154
Catherine 1	Outten 84	Joseph 79,87
Charlotte 69	Pamela 140	Martha A. 137
Comfort A. 127	Parker 15,65	Martin 136
Delilah 21	Patty 33	Mary Ann 93
Elizabeth 19,84,97	Polly 4,7,49	Nancy 93
107,134,135	Priscilla 29	Walter 71
Elizabeth A. 129	Rachel 39	William 140
Elizabeth D. 52	Sally 7,9,11,25	
George 4,31	60,92	SHARPLY
George P. 76	Sally A. 151	Henny 88
Harriet F. 69	Sampson 52	Henry 14
Henry 20	Sarah C.	John 137
Hetty 17,67,129	Tabitha 6	
Isaac 23,85,92	Thomas 28,45	SHAY
Jacob 74	Wealthy 42	Elijah 55
James 7,29,49,143	William 11,27,69	William 139
James H. 143	83,110	
James P. 74,143,148	William F. 27	SHELTON
James Q. 73	William P. 139	John 24
Jane 138	William W.112,119	
John 11,42	Zadok 78	SHEPPAM
John Jr. 20,28,32,33	Zadok O. 104,141	Rebecca 19
John of Dan 29		
John J. 21,29,33	SELMAKER	SHEPARD
John O. 84	John P. 27	Levenia L. 125
John W. 85,133,145		
Jno Jr 34	SERMAN	SHEPARD
Josiah 105	Mary E. 155	Stewart 138
Josiah T.133		
Lemuel 38	SEYMOUR	SHEPHERD
Levin 57	William 30	Elijah 59
Levinor 43	William D. 52	John 128
Lotty 38		Margaret J. 107
Major 25	SHADRICK	Martha A. 128
Martha 77	Mary 99	Mary E. 100
Mary 2,20,34,52		
69,87,126	SHALLEY	SHEPPARD
Mary A. 105,139	Polly Richardson 45	Elijah 128
Mary Ann 101,151		Martha E. 106
Mary C. 118	SHANAMAN	Priscilla A. 131
Mary E. 90	John 124	
Matilda 44		SHEPPERD
Milly 82	SHARPLEY	Sally 40
Molly 9	Charlotte 107	
Nancy 3,18,20,32,34	Daniel 63	SHERWOOD
Nancy C. 150	David 75	Augusten L. 105
	Eliza 85	
	George 148	

SHIELD
Elizabeth 117
Peter 67

SHIELDS
George S.D. 91

SHOCKLEY
Albert W. 141
Alison A. 109
Amelia E. 137
Ann 36
Ann Maria 154
Annis 129
Anniss 98
Atty M. 134
Betsey 11, 78
Burton 37
Elijah 41, 51
Elizabeth 14, 133
Elizbeth Ann 143
Frances A. 109
George W. 126, 131
Gibbs 124
Hannah 34, 110
Henry 134
Hezekiah Gibbs 97
Hildah 111
Ibba Jane 149
James H. 122, 135
James Madison 89
Jane 39, 128
John 27, 30
Jonathan 7
Joshua 76, 112
Leah 21
Lorenzo D. 144
Lucretia Townsend
    59
Margaret 155
Maria 103
Martha 8, 67, 124, 126
Mary 109
Mary A. 121
Mary Ann 135
Mary E. 118, 151
Milly 96
Nancy 85
Nelly 57
Peter 53, 60, 75

SHOCKLEY Con't
Polly 44, 58
Priscilla 59
Priscilla A. 106
Quinton 148
Richard 54
Riley J. 150
Sally 30, 123
Sally Kelleam 45
Sampson 79, 116
Solomon 60
Stewart 75
Susan J. 119
Uriah 129
Wise 74
William 104, 110
William L. 126
William Noble 55
William S. 60
Wm J. 155

SHOCKLY
Benjamin 22
Betsy 29
Eli 5
Isaac 42
John 27
Joshua 30
Mary 25
Molly 60
Nancy 44
Sally 25
Thomas 5

SHORT
Cannon 83, 130, 143
Daniel B. 102
Gilly C. 99
Obed 93
Phillip 17, 28
Purnell W. 86
William 104

SHOWARD
Hester Ann 110

SHOWELL
Henrietta 57
John 60
John D. 120
Josiah 63
Lemuel 51, 146
Mary Ann 64
Molly 25
Sally 73
Sarah 25
William 67

SHREAVES
Maria Ann 131

SHRIEVES
William 74

SILVERTHORN
Augenotte 150
Henry 36
John 22, 43
Robert I. 125
Robert J. 152
Sally 29
Tabitha 90

SIMPSON
Andrew 3
Elizabeth 26
Walter 12

SINGLETON
William H. 114

SLAUGHERY
Caty 26
Elizabeth 25
William 38

SLEMMONS
Francis Marion 146
John B. 25

SLOCOMB
Charlotte 85
Ida 154
Polly 55
Samuel 117
Thomas 12

SLOCUM	SMACK Con't	SMITH Con't
John 135	Martha 137	Dolly 72
Lavina C. 109	Mary 1,74,75	Edward M. 65
	Mary Ann 125	Elijah 8
SLOCUMB	Mary K. 59	Elenor 23
John 2	Molly 29	Elizabeth 18,73,143
William C. 96	Nancy 32	Elzey 15
	Patsey 52	Emeline 98,117
SMACK	Polly 6,35	Esther 141
Albert 70,92	Powell 51	Ezekiel 57
Andasiah 16	Purnell 17,58	Fanny H. 149
Andy 93	Riley 82	George 81
Ann 32,81	Sally 72,124,136	George F. 95
Ann M. 140	Thomas 47,139	George W. 150
Ann Z. 115	Thompson 127	George W.P. 132
Attalanta 14	William 80	Gidy 113
Betsy 22	Zedekiah 24	Harriet E. P. 151
Caty 11		Henny 69
Charlotte E. 135	SMASKY	Henry 61
Edgar 134	McKemmy 83	Henry J.B. 114
Ellenor 91		Hetty 47
Eliza 83	SMALL	Holland Smith 15
Elizabeth 15,96,101	Marcellus 156	Isaac 35,73
122	Solomon 66	Isaac P. 28
Emeline 152		Isaac W. 143
Fanny 138	SMALLWOOD	James 1,35,43,48
George 149	Rachel 7	James A. 151
Handy 86,138		James E. 107
Henry 81,101	SMART	James G. 101
Henry Jr. 74	Nathaniel 47,68	James W.T. 81
Hetty 52,110		Jane 80,128
Holland 5,7,51	SMASHY	Jediah 59
Isaac W. 136	James 26	Jesse 21
James 89	Samuel 85, 91	John 5,8,10,10,15
James S. 112		52,61,61,145
James T. 117	SMITH	John A. 141
Jane 152	Amanda J.R. 149	John D. 42
Jane E. 126	Anda Rebecca 110	John H. 147
Jesse 4,94	Ann McMaster 98	John W. 79
John 18.137	Anna P. 69	Josiah 156
Joshua 133	Anne 5,45	Josiah H. 111
Kendall 94	Archebald 1	Judah 13
Lambert 137	Benjamin D. 152	Julia C.C. 134
Lemuel 64	Benjamin Dingley 9	Julian 80
Leoisa 39	Betsey 11	Laura 139
Levi 6	Betsy 19	Leah 46
McKemmy 52,94	Charlotte 41	Letty 26
Maria 148	David 9	Levin 62

SMITH Con't
Levin S.H. 97
Lewis 84,128
Littleton 81,99
Maranda 64
Margaret 2,36,70
Marshall 8,93,141
Martha 68,141
Mary 1,2,23,56
  57,63
Mary A. 80
Mary Ann 1
Mary C. 103,150
Mary F. 85
Mary H. 119
Matilda 149
Merrell D. 78,89
Milby 46
Miranda 77
Molly 29
Moses C. 63
Nancy 24,44,53
Nancy Elizabeth Tabitha
  84
Nathaniel S. 141
Pattey 26
Patty 79
Peggy 7
Peter 54,107
Ritta 85
Robert 5
Rufus T. 153
Sally 80
Sally E.S. 97
Samuel 68
Samuel C. 115
Samuel R. 12,41
Sarah 36,119,123
Sarah C. 114
Sarah H.T. 113
Seth 26,58,81,134
Stoutten 7
Tabitha 16
Thomas 68,116
Vaughan 100
William 9,9,26,58,106
William L. 148
William P. 72,125

SMOCHY
Leah 16

SMORHEY
Justice 31

SMULLEN
Curtis 54
Edward 130
Elizabeth 2,95
Ephraim 37
Esma P. 148
Gilly 54
Humphrey 152
Isaac 51,95
James T. 141
Lambert 151
Lewis 39
Mary Ann 60
Peter 23
Randall 143
Sally 37,51,152
Stephen 38,47
Tabitha 51
Walter 43

SMULLIN
Jas 87
John 65
Maria 70
Rebecca 127
Sally 35
William 78

SMYTH
Elizabeth 69

SNEAD
Elizabeth 100,146
James 19
John 107
Molly 94

SNEED
Betsey 19
George D. 46
Hester 121
John 46
Thomas 19
Tully 47

SNIPE
William 87

SNOW
Walter P. 117

SOMERS
Eliza 105
Rachel M. 130

SPALDING
Mary 77

SPARKSMAN
George 37

SPARROW
Susan 60

SPEAKS
Elizabeth 44,77

SPENCE
Andesiah Rebia 16
Anne Maria 107
Ara 46,78
Betsey Washington 13
Bettie 115
Henrietta 103
Irving 53,124
John S. 35
Lemuel P. 29,62,67
Louise 110
Margaret Ann 83
Mary E. 92
Thomas R.P. 34

SPENCER
Allen D. 147
Ann Maria 114
Benjamin G. 146
Elizabeth W. 141
Frances 42
James T.H. 146
John 36,60,67
  John E. 123
Priscilla 55
Sally 31
Sophia 36
William 58

SPIEN
Catharine 14

SPION
Comfort 10

SPIRES
Polly 20

SPYKES
Claddy 62

STAKES
Wiliam S. 81

STANDFORD
Polly 43
William 16

STANFORD
Betsey 31
Constant D. 31
Richard 138
William 101

STANT
Edward T. 150

STARLING
Nancy 72

STATEN
Elizabeth 43
George 3, 33
Sally A. 151

STATON
Ann Byrd 95
Daniel J. 123
Elizabeth M. 101
George W. 103, 146
John W. 156
Joseph L. 142
Robert T. 119
Warner 45

STAUGHERTY
Wm 14

STAYTON
Elenor 37
Wise 38
William 81

STEEL
John 11

STEELE
Mary Elizabeth 91

STEPHENS
Amelia A. 147
Elizabeth 85
James 76

STERLING
Hannah 20
Southy 4
William 70

STERRIGE
Iza 57

STEVENS
Albert S. 151
Eliza Ann 112
Henrietta 72
James 51
John 13, 25, 33
Leah 105
Mary J. 130
Patience 12
Susan 83
William 50, 73
William W. 79

STEVENSON
Amelia 61, 155
Ann G. 84
Catharine 57
Charlotte 65
Cormo G. 17
Edward 7, 10
Edward W. 126
Edy 23
Elijah 11
Eliza 52
Elizabeth 4, 68, 123

STEVENSON Con't
Elizabeth C. 120
Elizabeth K. 68
Elizabeth W. 58
Esther 60
Franklin 147
Gertrude 38
Harriet 65
Henny 78
Henretta 52
Henry M. 96
Hugh M. 31, 39
Hugh S, 153
Isaac 64
Jabez 16
Jacob 151
James 63
James H. 83
James W. 60
John 6, 11, 20
John E. 57, 122
John H. 152
John S. 65
Jonothan 1
Joseph 4, 16, 23
Lydia 13
Margaret 45
Mary 58
Milcah 68
Nancy 22, 42, 46
Peggy 23
Polly 10, 17, 20
Priscilla 21
Rachel 48
Rebecca 34, 85
Robert 23
Rosey 68
Sally 19, 68
Sarah 30
Sarah A. 118
Tabitha 5
Thomas F. 130
William 7, 47, 67
William T. 68

STEWART
Ann 97
Emma E. 117
Harriet 90

STEWART Con't
John 110
John W. 88
Joshua G. 100
Levin 12
Mary 104
Robert 38
William 81

STIRGIS
Ephraim 92

STINSON
Hetty 73
Leah 63
Nancy 67

STOCKLEY
Sally 134

STOCKLY
Molly 8
Nehemiah 43

STRAUGHN
David H. 147

STRAYER
Webster M. 153

STRINGER
Benjamin C. 142

STRONGER
Peggy E. P. 81

STUART
Elizabeth 106
John 36

STUDLEY
Eliphalet C. 109

STURAIS
John Junr. 62

STURGES
Margaret 124

STURGIS
Ann 93
Ara 107
Aralanta C. 126
Barnaba 76
Betsey 13,28
Betsy Curtis 4
Catharine 68
Catherine 11
Charlotte 74
Comfort 18
Easther 134
Edith 101
Eleanor 64
Elenor 51
Elinor 23
Eliza 72
Elizabeth 61,67,78
  81,84,93,109
Ellen A. 145
Ellen R. 156
Erexine M. 143
Esther 2
Gertrude 49
Hancy Miles 50
Harriet 144
Henry 38,95
Hetty 92
Jacob 117
James 8,21,37,68
  79,
James D. 118
James E. 123
James W.L 69,95
Jane 50,53
Joanna 13
John 3,3,18,39,50
  64,90,93,111
John Jr. 54,74
John D. 64
Joshua 12,114
Joshua H. 116,131
Levin 8
Littleton 18
Littleton J. 129
Lutheran M. 64
Manervey 44
Maria 57

STURGIS Con't
Martha 50
Mary 39,41,53,61,80
  84,95
Mary A. 108
Mary Bell 31
Mary D. 65
Mary E. 113,126
Mary Esther 145
Mary J. 135
Mary W. 138
Matila 66
Michael J. 124
Milly 37
Molly 59
Nancy 7,79
Naomi 1
Patty 17,23,45
Peggy 21
Peter 27,111
Polly 6,13,92
Priscilla 28,110
Rhoda 37
Richard 6,21
Robert 117
Sally 3,31,44,50,73
Sarah 75,111,144
Sarah Amos 81
Thomas 114,116
Thomas E. 44
William 86
William H. 156
William J. 149
Zadok 63
Zipporah 105

SULLIVAN
Elizabeth 71
Parker 79
Samuel 139

SULLIVIN
Lydia Ann 139

SURMAN
John P. 101

SWIFT
Mary W. 155

SYMINGTON
James T. 90

TABBS
Eliza 91

TALBOT
Samuel 31

TANKARD
Philip B. 98

TAPMAN
Ann 101
Elizabeth 76
Emeline 103
Henry 128
Isaac 76
Matthias 17,57,63
            74
Sarah 109

TAR
Charlotte 78

TARPIN
Thomas S. 96

TARR
Anna 39
Ann Maria 108
Betsey 55
Betsy 29,94
Charles 31,89,132
          146
Charlotte 84,131
Dolly 59
Elizabeth 24,104,135
Frankey 91
George 81,85,122,140
Georgiana 139
Henrietta 149
Hetty 71
Isaac 93
James 71,79,95,138
James H. 86

TARR Con,t
Jane 86
J.H. 114
John 3,120
Lany 17
Levi 19.67
Major 8,57
Margaret 31,80,81
Martha 2
Mary 22,46,57,106
Mary Ann 68
Nancy 16,44
Nelley 97
Patsey 35
Peter 15.78,152
Peter W. 88
Presilla 87
Purnell 95
Rebecca 9
Sally 29,40.55,113
Sally A. 141
Samuel 19,30,56
Sarah Ann 113
Sarah H. 29
Sarah J. 155
Stephen 102
Tabby 58
Thomas 22,67
Uriah 73
Walter 84
William 4,53,90
          144
Willimore F. 144

TATHAM
Ayres 130
Charles 88,120
Samuel 72

TATMAN
John 43,145
Littleton 128
Sally 138

TATTMAN
John 77

TATUM
Ann W. 86

TAYLOR
Alfred J. 147
Amelia 53
Ann 89,133
Annaretta 7
Arthur 5
Arthur W. 124
Asa 155
Atalanta 16
Augustine C. 138
Augustine W. 107
Barnabas 86
Betsey 18,18
Charles 129
Charlotte 36
Colmar 156
Colmore G. 127
Collymore 122
Comfort 9
Cordelia 134
Cornelius T. 136
Covington 128
Drucilla 129
Easther 49
Ebenezer 43
Edwae 77
Edward 52,83,154
Elias 102
Elijah 65
Elisha 103
Eliza 55
Elizabeth 8,39,52,70
            93,106,112
            145,152
Elizabeth 154
Esme 37
Esther 25,74
Esther H. 140
Fisher 12
Geo 21
George 2, 17
George B. 148
Gillet 29
Hannah 105
Harriet E. 141
Harriett 61
Henrietta 141
Henrietta M. 140
Henry 75,120

TAYLOR Con't
Henry B. 71
Hesse 4
Hester Ann 120
Hetty 121
Hezekiah 23
Hope 6
Isaac 40
Jacob 60,69
James 1,39,41,55,58
    61,107,113
James A. 92
James H. 105
James S. 121
Jarman 23
Jeremiah 110
Jesse 137
John 2,14,19,23
    66,72,82,85,
    93,100,127
John F. 76
John Gibbs Jr. 4
John J. 150
John P. 94,104
John R. 132
John Skinner 134
John T. 14,74,75
Joshua H. 105
Josiah 90,131
Julia Ann 130
J.W.H. 153
Kendal D. 129
Kendall 74
Laura C. 149
Leah 70,85,115
Lemuel 73
Lemuel S. 69
Levi 143
Littleton 62,82,83
Lydia 127
Margaret 86
Maria 73,86
Martha 66,73
Mary 53,54,87,92
    98,123,124
Mary A. 120,154
Mary Ann 87,149

TAYLOR Con't
Mary A.P. 113
Mary B. 88
Mary C. 107
Mary E. 154
Mary F. 145
Mary Priscilla 145
Matilda 122
Matilda C. 118
Matilda S. 127
Merrene 49
Milly 42
Missouri 156
Molly 8,70
Nancy 1,3,8,20,26
    64,66
Nehemiah 44
Offy 50
Oliver H. 142
Patty 104
Peggy 22,23,28,42
Polly 5,8,16,18,24
    32
Priscilla 1
Prissey 53
Purnell 25,71,85
Rebecca 7,24,127
Ritta M. 137
Robert 79
Roger 53
Rose 22
Sacker 11
Sally 3,17,20,45,
    51,63,65,75,
    78,104,125
Sally E. 127
Samuel 51,51,103
    105,128
Samuel B. 90
Sarah 32,66,80
Sarah A. 146
Sarah Ann 66,70,130
Sarah E. 147
Sarah Eleanor 132
Sarah M. 121,152
Semore 35
Serena Jane 133

TAYLOR Con't
Severn 138
Sewell T. 103
Southey J. 153
Southy 55
Stephen 22,36,78,143
Stockely 126
Susan 78,123
Susanna 12
Tabitha 66
Teagle H. 125
Thomas 9,81,85,109
    139
Thomas T. 112
Thoeogood S. 117
Thorogood 145
Uphamy 46
Washington 49
Welthy 76
Whealthy 24
William 83,86,115,135
    138,144,,151
William H. 8
William L. 153
Wm. 8
Wrixam 123
Zadok 19

TEABRAIN
Shoiles C. 86

TEACHNER
James 73

TEACKLE
Abel 11

TEAGLE
Anny 41

TEAGUE
Caty 26
Comfort P. 62
Elizabeth 83
Elizabeth F. 54
Hetty 62
Jacob 3

TEAGUE Con't
Louisa 120
Maria J. 131
Mary 2
Sally 79
William 51
Zeporah R. 54

TEAUGE
George 106
John 36

THAMS
Margaret M. 124

THOMAS
Charlotte A. 152
Edward C. 90
Emily 131
Jane 102
John 109
Jno B. 69
Sophia S. 152

THORNTON
Edward 89
Elvisa 105
Henry 5
James 44
John 55
John H. 122
Mary E. 133
William 142

THORINGTON
Wm W. 153

TILGHMAN
Alfred L. 142
Ann 58
Anna 28
Cabel 10
Daniel 136
Elizabeth 114
Elizabeth I. 116
Esther 32, 57
George 77
George W. 135

TILGHMAN Con't
Hanah E. 135
Hetty 77
James 31, 51, 68
John 52, 60
John H. 130
John Sr. 93
Joshua 75
Julia A. 129
Leah J. 132
Louisa 142
Margaret 38
Mary 95, 132
Mary Ann 136
Mary J. 136
Nancy 40, 57, 87
Nancy P. 40
Noah 50, 132
Noah J. 117, 126
Oliver 96
Peter 72, 116
Polly 2
Rebecca 17
Sally 19
Samuel H.T. 119, 136
Sarah E. 115
Sophia Jane 137
William 58
William B. 68

TILLMAN
James 58
Richard S. 53
Richard T. 59

TIMMONS
Alexander 39, 83, 92
Ama 8
Amelia B. 78
Amelia E. 130
Anda M. 72
Andashiah 33
Anania 35
Ann 37
Anne 50
Bassett 18
Belitha 7

TIMMONS Con't
Benjamin 88
Caleb 70
Catharine 139
Charlotte 22, 123
Charlotte A. 131
Denny 51
Edward 123
Elijah 41, 74
Eliza 86
Elizabeth 3, 41, 55, 106
155
Elzey 100
Ephraim 3
George 26
Hannah 1
Harriet J. 142
Hester A. 151
Hester C. 125
Isaac 66, 136
James 106, 106
James B. 97, 111
Jane 119
Jenkins 152
John 30, 53
John B. 114
John S. 115
John T. 148
Kendall 93
Kesiah 53
Leah 85
Leml 89
Lemuel 29, 155
Lemuel I. 141
Leonard 10
Leonard J. 135
Levi D. 86
Lizy 18
Margaret 101
Martha 12, 34, 79
Martha L. 47
Mary 87
Mary Ann 143, 151
Mary E. 130
Matilda 89
McKemmy 92
McKimma 129
Milby 15

TIMMONS Con't
Nancy 57, 80
Nancy E. 103
Nehemiah 17
Patty 41
Peggy 19, 95
Peter 17
Polly 2
Rebecca 24, 28
Rhody 11
Sally 21, 53, 57, 67
Sarah 153
Schoolfield 44
Sophia 39
Stephen 28, 35, 78, 122
Stephen D. 104
Stephen P. 147
Thomas 37, 65, 90, 96
William 75, 100, 106, 125
William B. 146
Wm. E. 95

TINDAL
John 79, 85
Washington 152
William 79

TINDALE
Thomas 3

TINDALL
Ann 30
Elijah 19
Elizabeth 95
Harriet 95
James 149
Nehemiah 21
Peter 91
Samuel 16, 19

TINDLE
Isaac 35
Peter 143
Thos 33

TINEL
Peter 109

TINGLE
Benjamin D. 84
Catharine 74
Elizabeth D. 48
Gertrude 44
Harriet G. 65
Henry D. 103
Hetty Ann 71
Hetty Matilda 59
James A. 70
John 10, 53, 99
Maria 69
Martha 59
Nancy F. 25
Nathaniel R. 41
Sarah 7
Sarah M. 113
William 1, 60
Wm. 33
Virginia 136

TIRE
William 48

TOADVINE
Alse 25
Carolin H. 138
Eleanor 31, 86
Elicia Ann 94
Elijah 49
Eliza 29
Harriet 55
Harry 122
Henry 54
Isaac 32, 43
Isaiah 14
Isaiah M. 99
James 12, 122
John 28
John B. 94, 120, 130
Nancy 13, 68
Nelly 31
Outten 14
Polly 32. 111
Priscilla 58
Purnell 29
Rhoda 14
Stephen 46

TODD
George 39, 57
George W. 118
Robert S. 113
Spencer 47

TOMPKINS
Washington 94

TOPPING
Nathaniel 65

TOWNSEND
Amanda 146
Amelia 81
Amelia A. 125
Ann 27, 53
Anna 29
Anne 19
Ann M. 101, 141
Benjamin 67
Betsey 2, 3, 11, 15, 52
Caroline 150
Charles 44, 98
Charlotte E, M. 82
Drucilla 150
Easter 47
Edward 84, 104
Edward G. 130
Eleanor 55
Elijah 24
Elinor 21
Eliza 123
Elizabeth 6, 15, 16, 52,
   53, 82, 106, 146
Elizabeth A. R. 144
Emily R. 146
Ephraim 2, 37, 39 48
Ephraim T. 77, 82
Esther 22
Euphame 5
Frances 26
George 2, 45, 80, 97
Gilbert 6
Gora 48
Grace 38, 38
Hamutah 43
Hanna 36

TOWNSEND Con't
Henerietta 110
Henrietta 59
Hessy 45
Hester 129
Hetty G. 100
Isaac 36,92
Isaac W. 156
Isarael 87
Israel 105,154
James 6,24,25,44
    93,
James G. 54,57
Jane H. 127
Jenkins 51
John 45,80
John Francis 98
John W.A. 141
Joseph 12
Joseph H. 151
Josiah 150,151
Joshua 29,117,141
Leah Ann 71
Lemuel 24
Letty 106
Levin 7,19,46,64,
    81,154
Levin Henry 112
Levin T. 139
Littleton 43,55
Lucretia 10,64
Luke 24
Lyban 80
Lydia 107
Mahala 134
Major 76,138
Margaret 91,123
Margaret S. 133
Martha 4
Mary 7,12,13,33,70
Mary Ann 104
Mary G. 113
Mary W. 147
Milley 98
Muty 57
Nancy 7,14,17,21
    41,62,135
Nathaniel 87

TOWNSEND Con't
Peggy 26,55
Peter 38,38
Polly 11,20,53
Prieson P. 150
Priscilla 12,25,132
Priscilla A. 92
Rebecca 37,83
Rhoda 2
Rives R. 1
Robert 1,20,42,51
    76.77,98,124
Sally 2,37,43,44,
    75,105
Samson 123
Samuel J. 128
Sarah 18,78
Sarah Kirk 6
Sophia 72
Staphen 2,17
Stephen 68
Susan 117
Susanah 26
Susanna 33
Teackle 73
Thomas 104,131
Thomas S. 150
Thos. 16
Tricy Eleanor 149
Uphamy 19
William 8,24,28,38
William I. 115
William J. 141
Zadok 7,22
Zadok P. 131
Zillah 67

TRACY
Rebecca C. 154

TRADER
Alfred 148
Amaret J. 136
Ann 94
Arenia 94
Caroline 120
Charlotte W. 97
Eliza 79

TRADER Con't
Elizabeth 85,87
Elizabeth A.W. 100
Harriet 109
James 135
James H. 121,137
John 149
John R. 115
Joshua S.A. 64
Levin 129
Littleton 53,138
Mary 107
Mary Ann 76
Mary Elizabeth 150
Mary H. 148
Nancy 4
Nancy E. 124
Parker 46
Parker D. 142
Rosae A. 122
Rufus 104
Samuel 73,130
Samuel R. 136
Samuel T. 101
Sarah 7
Sarah E. 126
Sarah Jane 101
Stater 12
Susan G. 152
Teackle A. 45
William 155
William B. 82

TRAHEARN
Arthur H. 101
George 104
Mary 73
Samuel 33,93
Thrizey 70

TRAYHEARN
James 16
Julian 71
Martha 21
Matilda 78
Polly 9
Sally 21
Tabitha 21

TRAZY
Arthur 5

TREHEARN
Charrity 47
Cyrus 30
George L. 71
Maria 29
Nancy 28
Sally 73
Thomas J. 153

TREHEARNE
Harriet A. 143

TREYHEARN
Polly 30

TRINDELL
James 51

TRIP
James 1

TRIPPAND
James 11

TRONDLE
Naomi 18

TRUIT
Nancy 1

TRUITT
Adeline 90
Amos 25
Anderson 38
Ann 100
Ann T. 2
Benjamin 5
Betsey 57
Betsy 40
Burton B. 96
Caleb 109, 135
Catherine 17
Charles W. 138
Charlotte 8, 20
Clarissa 145

TRUITT Con't
Comfort 29
Cyre 11
David 28, 58, 64
David J. P. 138
Denny 14
Edward 86
Edward M. 86, 124
Eleanor 32
Elijah James 123
Elisha 9
Eliza 40, 96
Eliza M. 121
Elizabeth 6, 22, 35, 71
  93, 98, 114, 144
Elizabeth B. 67, 88
Elizabeth J. 94
Esther 99
Eyre 29
Gatty 67, 119
George 4, 5, 21, 25, 64
George K. 140
George I. 147
George T. 109
Handy J. 137
Hannah E. 128
Henny 49
Henny A. 81
Henrietta 83
Henry 49
Henry S.C. 140
Hester 85
Hetty 11, 31
Isaac 45
Isaac J. 124
Isabella 143
James 8, 24, 25, 43
  78, 127, 140
James H. 135
James P. 89, 94
James T. 93
Jesse 92
Jesse B.. 121
John 22, 34, 37, 42
John D. 121
John F. 86
John H. 124
John K. 2

TRUITT Con't
Joseph 31, 71
Joshua 49
Julia 88
Kendal 144
Kendall 58
Lauretta S. 72
Lemuel 52, 55, 75
Lemuel E. 147
Lemuel S. 117
Littleton 40
Lydia 85
Maranda 89
Margaret W. 146
Maia 79
Maria B. 132
Martha 32, 66
Martha E.J. 136
Mary 8, 32, 69, 89
Mary A. 141, 153
Mary Ann 119
Mary B. 88
Mary C. 131
Mary E. 151
Mary J. 126
Matthias 61
Melinda T. 140
Minos 105
Molly 28, 37, 65
Mordica 27
Nancy 16, 53
Narcissa 156
Nehemiah 18
Nelly 8
Patty 62, 70
Peggy 24, 34, 74
Peter 29, 51, 55, 57
  99, 121
Phebe 106
Polly 42, 60
Priscilla A. 154
Priscilla H.H. 117
Purnell 78
Rebecca 18
Rhoda 65, 129
Riley 37
Ritta 118
Robert 21, 29

TRUITT Con't
Rosa F.D. 132
Rose 130
Rufus M. 112
Sallie 149
Sallie M. 136
Sallie W. 136
Sally 4,4,41,42
   99
Sally E. 114
Sally L. 121
Samuel H. 114,126
Samuel P. 121
Saml H. 90
Sarah 47,94,119
Sarah E. 127
Selby P. 118,130,155
Silas 118
Sophia 16
William 15,17,58,128
William C. 66
William R. 84
William T. 131
Zadok 26
Zedekiah 117

TRULOVE
Eliza 135

TUBBS
Ann 66
Catharine 22
Henry M.H. 136
James 6,75
James R. 132
Jane Elizabeth 115
John 22,70
Kendall 22
Littleton 48
Littleton D. 57
Mary 94
Samuel 37
William 86
William J. 123
William R. 120
Wm. 17

TUERO
Maria Gracia W. 151

TULE
Andrew 6

TULL
Annanias 67
Benjamin 33
Catharine 23,85
Charlotte 134
Edward 90
Eliza M. 145
Elizabeth 30,102
Elizabeth Ann 85
Esther J. 139
Gatty 102
George 131
Gideon 130
Hannah 82
Harriet J. 154
Henry 89,109
Hesse 94
Hetty 8,119
James 13,21,37
   113,155
James T. 154
John 85,96
John Henry 98
Joseph 47,55
Joshua 40
Leah 3
Leah Jane 116
Levi 17,78
Levin 28,122,155
Mahala 103
Margaret 53,134
Maria 90
Martha 20
Mary 64
Mary Ann 109,124
Miles 147
Nancy Ann 95
Outten 100
Peggy 40
Peter 52

TULL Con't
Polly 17
Rebecca W. 125
Sally 39
Sally E. 125
Samuel 66
Sarah 9,44,92,112
Sarah E. 153
Sarah Ellen 134
Soloman 9,88,118,147
Tabitha 104,
William 25,70,76,106
   138

TUNNEL
Sallie A. 135

TUNNELL
John J. 142
Mary 22
Nancy 40
Rachel 21
Samuel 42
Scarborough 30
William 17

TUNNELS
John 2

TURLINGTON
Arthur J. 151
Francis 35
John W. 147
Louisa S. 123
Sarah 58

TURNELL
Richard 68

TURPIN
Emily H. 154
Henrietta 9
John 6
John L. 102
Sally 110
Sewell 1
Susan I. 112

TURNER
Andesiah 34
Aralanta 139
Caty 40
Charles Parker 113
Ebenezer W. 156
Elizabeth 57, 113
Emiline E. 146
Henry 19
Hetty A. 139
Hulda 40
Jesse 66
Jesse H. 141
John R. 23
Lancy 35
Lemuel 4
Lydia 9
Margaret Costen 33
Mary I. 140
Mary Polly 106
Mary S. 134
Polly 33
Rachel 3
Rhodah 51
Rosa 119
Rosea Jane 94
Sally 28
Samuel 3
Thomas 25
Walter 39, 121
William 11, 130

TURNTON
Mary 146

TWIFORD
Margaret 130
Revel 91
Robert 111
William 101

TWIG
James H. 98
John 97
Louisa 118
Maria 74
Robert H. 137

TWIG Con't
Saml. 28
William 39
William H. 119

TWIGG
John B. 127
Matilda 105

TWILLEY
George 78
Robert 21
Salley E. 155
William 99

TWILLY
Elizabeth 105
Mary Ann 82
Priscilla 38
Robert 109

TWINE
Zipporah 87

TYRE
Henrietta 94
Henny A. 133
Seth W. 127

TYLER
Dr George 111

TYLOR
Levin 27

TYRE
Anny 49
Sally 140
Sally A. 125

TYSON
Nathaniel 63, 72, 118
Mary Ann 118

UNDERHILL
Edmund W. 79
Rachel 74

UNDRILL
Betsey 67

UPSHUR
George M. 92, 140
Resina M. 83

URBUSH
Joseph 5

VADEN
Mary 92

VAGON
Nancy 98

VALLANDIGHAN
James L. 92

VANCE
Nancy 53
Peter O. 79
Sally 14

VANDAUM
Ann M. 117

VANDOM
Mary Jane 151

VANDOME
George 65
Mary B. 6

VANDUM
George 47
George W. 116

VATOPE
Nancy 25

VEASEY
Ellen 133
Isaac N. 134
Nathaniel 78
Rosa 133
William 110

VEAZEY
Hetty 72

VENABLES
James A. 148
John 8

VENSON
George 10
Samuel 35

VERDIN
Mary 49

VERNETSON
William 66

VESSELS
David B. 118

VESTER
David 51

VICKERS
Catharine 130
Eliza 103
Hamilton 144
Isaac T. 132

VICTOR
Anna. B. 59
Elizabeth 56
Holland 17
Sally 14

VIGUS ?
Elizabeth 88

VINCENT
Elizabeth 85,113
James H. 97,153
Joshua J. 132
Mary A. 78
Nancy 81
Olivia H.D. 141
Thomas H. 138
William 123

VINSON
Benjamin 55
George 52
Solomon 46

WADKINS
Thomas 35

WAGAMAN
Nancy 22

WAGGAMAN
Betsey 21

WAIGHT
July 104

WAILES
Betsey 58
Daniel 11
William H. 82

WAINRIGHT
Sally 41

WAINWRIGHT
Edward J. 103
Elijah 134
George 79,131
Hannah 43
Rosanna E.M. 91

WAIT
Ann A. 7
James 57
Nancy 57

WALEA
William 36

WALES
Elizabeth 67
Emily 102
Isaac 51
Lucretia B. 105
Matilda H,M, 74

WALKENS
Thomas 23

WALKER
Betsey 11
Elizabeth 144
George W. 148
Harriet 113
James 47
James K. 101
John 5,12
John P. 108
Levin 85
Margaret 133
Martha E. 151
Mary 94
Nancy 116
Samuel 131
Sarah Ann 97
Susan 102

WALLACE
Fanny J. 130

WALLER
Esme 4
Joseph 151
Mary 5
Sally 60

WALLOP
Comfort 104
David 66
George 93
Margaret M. 49
Mary A. 120
Mary H. 66
Mary R. 112
Rachel 31
Rozell 53
Sally 45
Sarah E. 120
Skinner 62

WALSTON
Anna 31
David 4
Ebenezer 77
Eliza 91
Elizabeth B. 57
Gatty M. 116

WALSTON Con't
George 75
Levin 32
Mary Jane 103
Nancy 58
Polly 34,50
Sally 81
William 66

WALTER
Eleanor 6
Esme M. 34
Isaac 12
Samuel 87

WALTERS
Hester Ann 109
Mary A.E. 111
William H. 153

WALTON
George 44
Stephen 7,48
William 47

WAPLES
Joseph 76
Wiliam A. 127

WARD
Benjamin 150
Caroline 132
Charlotte 136
Dial 93
Eliza 83
Eliza A. 127
Elizabeth 87,107
Elizabeth A. 122,136
Euphamy 22
Frederic Edward 149
George F. 156
George H. 126
Henry 50
Hugh 16
Isaac 50
Jackson 113
Jacob 32
James 17,124
James A. 80

WARD Con't
Jane 136
Jenkins 51,59
John 7,87,152
Joshua J. 119
Julianne 64
Laura J. 126
Levi 49
Luther 139
Lydia 52
Lydia D. 31
Mary 104,112
Mary Ann 74
Mary E. 141
Mary Jane 123
Moses 148
Octava 154
Priscilla 3,59
Rachel 9
Rebecca 92
Sally G. 76
Samuel 152
Sarah 116
Stephen 78
Susan 27
Thomas 128
William 62,78
William F. 155

WARE
Charles 29
Nancy Rice 34
Sarah 85

WARINGTON
Elijah 82

WARNER
George I. 97
Jacob 113
Levin Jr. 101
Polly 32
Sally 22
Sinah 142
Solomon 139

WARNOCK
Robert 17

WARREN
Adaline 68
Albert 126
Albert Henry 110
Anania 21
Ananias 22
Ebenezer 19,79
Eby 26
Edward 61
Euphama 87
Hillery 90
Isaac 11
James 55
Jane 129
John 129
Josiah 113,130
Maria 76
Margaret Jane 99
Martha 124
Mary 73
Mary Ann 146
Matts 7
Matthias 43
May 88
Nancy 42
Patty 54
Philip 90
Phrenetta 111
Polly 17
Robert 87,114
Sally 84
Selby 16
Thomas 73,77
Zilla M. 122

WARRENGTON
John B. 83

WARRENTON
Elizabeth 98

WARRICK
William 15

WARRINGTON
Harriet 111
Isaac 50
James 59,116

WARRINGTON Con't
Julia 119
Nancy 37
Peter 63
Sally 115
Samuel 39,139
Southy 100
Walter 16
William 148
Zeno 67,88

WARTERS
Charlotte 6
Joseph 136

WARWICK
William 7

WATERFIELD
Margaret 97
Mary 89
William 27

WATERS
Angelina 112
Betsey 48
Charlotte 129
George C. 83
James 87
James M. 103
Jessie 48
John 16
Joshua 156
Major 30
Margaret Jane 85
Margaret M. 101
Nancy 33
Nancy N. 132
Patrick 21
Polly 18
Qillian 6
Rachel 14
Richard T. 96
Sally W. 97
Tabitha 52
Thomas 64
Thos 88
William 7,54

WATSON
Agnes 10
Amanda 107,113
Benjamin 136
Betsey 35
Betsy 24
Covin 42
Elizabeth 102
Emily 151
Gillet 41
Harriet 123
James 39,55
John W. 136
Julia A. 119
Major J. 152
Margaret S. 101
Mary 79,130
Mary Ann 80
Minos B. 155
Mitchell 68,144
Patsy 93
Peter 154
Sally 23,42,105
Sarah 120
Thomas J. 107
West 28,123
William 46,102,150
Zadok 47

WATSTON
William 53

WATTER
Lemuel 24

WATTS
Elizabeth 45,97
Emily A.G. 131
Henry 26
Margaret 115
Peter C. 77
Rebecca 71
Sophia 86
William 13,54,59

WEATHERLY
Edward K. 69

WEAVER
Thomas 53

WEB
Rachel 82

WEBB
Amelia Jane 150
Andy 106
David 111
Ebenezer 78
Esme 94
Gatty 92
Harriet 91
Henny 64
Herny 91
Hiram 144
Isaac 80
Isaac A. 127
Jeptha 90
John 3,10,13
Margaret 99
Maria 99
Mary 9,89
Mary Ann 124
Mephibosbeth C. 132
Minos 142
Peter 49
Robert 27
Rose 57
Sally 33
Sarah 14
Susan 63
Thomas 7
Thomas Scott 16
William 38,81

WEBDELL
Isaac E. 61

WEBSTER
Samuel L. 131

WEEKS
Caleb 21
Harriet 35

WEIGHT
Nancy 124

WELBERN
William 45

WELBORN
Isaac D. 90

WELBOURN
John D. 70
William 31

WELBOURNE
Eliza B. 101
James 54
John D. 101

WELDON
Ebenezer 49
Nancy 9
Sally 39,103

WELDONE
Mary 33

WELLS
Cannon 117
Hetty 140
James 128
Lavinia 126
Mary 151

WELSH
Richard E. 43

WENELLS
Asa 105

WENRIGHT
Joseph Heath 43

WESCOAT
Joseph 127

WESSELLS
Ann 86
Emeline T. 117
Ephraim 93
J.W. 134

WEST
Cassey 43
Clara I. 95
Ebenezer 129
Elizabeth 28
Elizabeth H. 98
Francis 142
George 37,79
Henrietta V,C. 142
Hester J. 150
Indiana M. 114
Isaac 42
John W. 102
Kendall 31
Kendall V. 103
Lavinia 115
Leah 50
Maggie E. 148
Margaret E. 132
Maria J. 136
Mary 57
Mary J.H.H. 110
Mary S. 115
Minos B. 151
Nathan G. 108
Nancy E. 125
Peggy 29
Polly 79
Sally 79,110
Sally A. 132
Sarah H. 114
William 154
William H. 46,120,124
William T. 129
William W. 49

WESTCOAT
Catharine 81
John K. 101

WESTERHOUSE
Sally 9

WHARTON
Hetty B. 103

WHALEY
Hetty A.S. 96
Mariah C. 139

WHALEY Con't
Mary E. 115
Peter 41,139
Seth M. 99,137

WHAYLY
Nathaniel 24

WHAYLAND
William J. 107

WHEALTON
Ann 81
Charles S. 156
Eliza 96
Elizabeth 74,138
James 60
John H. 110
Maria 79
Mary 90.148
Mary G. 149
Michael 113
Rebecca 141
Sarah 85
Thomas 24,72
William 59

WHEATLEY
Henry J. 150

WHEELEN
Leah 29

WHEELER
Elizabeth 5
Henry 61
Hetty 83
Major 53,67
William 30
Wm. 20
Zadock 2
Zadok 14

WHEELTON
Polly 43

WHELTON
Oliver I. 134

WHERLOW
Henny 29

WHIRLOW
Harriett 65

WHITE
Ambrose 11
Amelia 63
Ann 108
Ann M. 128
Ann Maria 150
Archibald 44
Augusta 36
Aurelia W. 146
Benjamin 17,84
Charlotte 115
Ebenezer 149
Edward 146
Edward H. 99
Eli 68,84
Eliza 42,100
Elizabeth 17,23,27 73,113
Elizabeth J.S. 103
Elizabeth S. 69
Elizabeth Wise 79
Francis A. 140
Gatty J. 144
George 15
Gustavus A. 50
Harriet 52,58,75,
Henry 3,6,7,32,47 87
Hester 80
Jacob 6
James 19
James Henry 88
Jane 87
Jehue 136
John 7,12,44,57 117
Joseph G.B. 115
Joshua 20,43
King V. 156
Laura C. 116
Levin 115
Lewis 96
Margaret 104,116

WHITE Con't
Margaret Ann 73
Mary 43,45,45,50 142
Mary Ann 99
Mary A.S. 131
Mary E. 126
Milly 22
Nancy 12,59,65
Nat 9
Noah 71
Peter 28,50
Phillip 16
Polly 3
Rebecca 48
Sally 4,81
Sally E. 136
Samuel 64
Samuel J. 132
Samuel Q. 83
Sarah 58,81,88,111
Sarah Catharine 30
Sarah E. 124
Sidney 97
Spicer 72
Staphen 17
Stephen 18
Susanna 22
Tabitha 76,148
Thomas 2,27,34,106 146
Thomas H. 150
Thomas M.P.S. 113
Urbin J. 124
William 25
William B. 82
William Bell 12
William M. 51
William S. 2,34

WHITELOCK
Henrietta R.E. 72

WHITETASH ?
Wlisha ? 66

WHITNEY
Matilda 143

WHITTINGTON
Caty 7
Charlotte C. 79
Elizabeth 60
Leah 2
Martha 147
Mary 58
Sally D. 49
Sarah Ann 156
Sarah H. 59
William 30

WIATT
Elizabeth 57
Maria 113

WIDGEON
Cornelius 117
Elizabeth 128
Georgianna 144

WIGGEN
Sally 135

WILBUR
Charlotte 58

WILDEN
Elizabeth 76

WILDGOOSE
Jane 29

WILEY
Peggy 19

WILKERSON
Isaac 46
James 139
Jesse 66
Jesse P. 149
John 21, 119
Mary 111
Mary E. 152
Milkey 90
Peter 122
Solomon M. 117
Stephen 151

WILKENSON
Nathaniel 128

WILKINGS
Mary 58

WILKINS
Betsey 24
Hessey 25
Hetty 9
James L. 153
Jane 148
John 1
John Warner 136
Joseph 31
Lambert 137
Leah 101
Martha 148
Matilda 107
Molly 92
Rachel C. 147
Sally 133
Sophia 9
William 48,51

WILKINSON
Elizabeth 83
Jesse 91
Solomon 91
Sophia 32

WILL
Betsey 19

WILLACE
Sarah G. 110

WILLETT
Isaac R. 99
John 62

WILLIAMS
Amelia 46,76
Ann 7,108
Betsey 5,11,62,77
Betsy 38
Cabel 9
Caroline 90

WILLIAMS Con't
Charlott A. 136
Cyrus 89,95
Daniel J. 136
Denard 75
Drucilla 126
Eleanor 88
Eli 5
Elijah 33
Eliza 53,54
Eliza J. 154
Elizabeth 2,46,81,82 132
Emeline 76
Emily 130
Ephraim 86
Euphame 41
Ezekiel 40,40
Gertrude 55
Handy 72
Harriet Anna 155
Hassie 67
Henrietta 143
Hester 127
Hetty 9,90
Hetty H. 147
Huldy 58
Isabel 135
James 68,90
James F. 122
James L. 93
James S. 150
Jane 84
Jno 9
Joel 94
John 9,14,18,43
  45,85,99,116,*113*
John B. 31, 147
John D. 120
John F. 108
John H. 135
John W. 43
Josiah 118
Katy 55
Kendall 14,15
Kitty Ann 96
Lambert 77,82,98
Laura A.S. 142

WILLIAMS Con't
Lemuel 78,85
Major C. 152
Margaret Ann 100
Margret 43
Maria 53,62
Mariah 142
Martha 21,104
Martha J. 131
Martha T. 120
Mary 45,71,99
Mary A. 112
Mary Ann 70
Mary E. 124
Matilda 95, *84*
Matilda H. 69
Molly 78
Nancy 7,59
Narcissa Ball 61
Naron B. 79
Nathan 25
Peggy 14,17
Peter 14,51
Polly 5
Pressgrave 11
Purnell 7
Richard 103
Robert 35
Samuel 17,23,70
Samuel T. 126
Sarah 29
Sarah C. 30
Sarah Elizabeth 150
Sarah G. 83
Sarah Jane 43
Severn F. 154
Stewart 23
Theodore W. 119,132
Thomas 3,53,64,97
Thomas E. 151
Thomas N. 79,98
William 22,27,30,68,98
Wm. 87
Zilla 68

WILLIAMSON
Sally Maria 60
Stuart 23

WILLIN
Eleanor 12

WILLING
Major 8

WILLIS
Ame 90
Betsy 133
Caty 51
Charlotte 5, '67
Elijah 37
Elizabeth 42
George 7
Henny 74
John 37,62,86,135
Julia A. 124
Mary 100,114
Mary Eliza 112
Miranda 138
Molly 45
Nancy 52
Polly 38
Prisse 27
Sally 38
Sarah 49
Thomas 30
William 11
Zadok 58
Zilla 129

WILLISS
Macy 89
William 61

WILLS
John 9

WILSON
Ann Jane 117
Elijah C.T. 116
Elizabeth 15
Elizabeth H. 38
Ellen W. 129
Ephraim K. 8,31,124
Harriet 137
Henry J. 120
James Henry 110

WILSON Con't
James M. 87
Jane 14,18
Jemina 6
John 2
Leah 3
Lemuel D. 107,118
Levin 24
Mary 51
Mary G. 56
Nancy 22,35
Nancy J. 33
Piercey 79
Polly 6,25
Priscilla 78
Severn 43
Thomas 2
William H. 145
Zipporah 66

WIMBOROUGH
Henrietta 49
Lurenda 75
Peter 39
Thomas 51

WIMBRO
Catharine 141
Elizabeth 139

WIMBROW
Ezekiel 105
John I. 100
Mary E. 132
Moses N. 126
Robert T. 128
Samuel P, 116
William 76
William J. 100
William T. 132

WIMBROUGH
Elijah 75
Henrietta 134
James E. 133
John 70
Peter A. 118
Sarah E.H. 155
Zelpha A. 155

WINDER
Abel 89
Charlotte A. 120
James A. 141
John H. 22
John W. 145
Margaret 111
Mary 94
Richard B. 120

WINDSOR
Thomas 13,
Thomas A. 156

WINGATE
Alfred 134
Covington 151
Dolly 13
Elizabeth 44
Moses 33

WINSOM
John 55

WINTERBOTTOM
Tabitha 85

WINWRIGHT
Elizabeth 75

WISE
Betsey 79
Catharine 120
Tabitha T. 44
Thomas Evans 48

WISHART
Maria 35

WONNELL
Caroline 90
Elizabeth 15,104
Jacob 41,93
James 13,122
Mary 30
Nancy 17
Nancy James 76
Parker 26,62
Sally 16
Wheatley D. 75

WOODEN
Henny 61

WOOLFE
George 17

WOOLFORD
Stephen 39

WOOLRIDGE
John 99

WOOTEN
George 67

WORKMAN
Jesse 121
Joshua 100

WORRINGTON
Zeno 64

WOUND
Lyda 51

WRIGHT
Ann C. 61
Charles 112
Dennis 41
Eliza Ann 92
Elizabeth 6,67
Harriet 19
Hessy 10
James B. 99,107
Lott 5
Mary 49
Mary Ann 72
Sally 6,19,54,117
Sampson 11
Thomas 12

WYATH
Andrew B. 54

WYATT
Absolom 1
Caleb 153
Catherine 142
Esther 65
John 86
Mahala 139
Margaret 52
Minos 114
Nathaniel W. 113
Rebecca 135
Seth 131
William 145

YERBY
Annie 123

YOUNG
Ann 96
Anna 69
Betsey 68
Clarissa 156
Elizabeth 95
Grace 151
Hannah 30
Isaac 152
James 36,37,74
Jane 150
John 26,48
John H. 119
Joseph 20
Julia 139
Miss Mary 105
Mary H. 138
Polly 77
Rosa 125
Rosa J. 132
Samuel J. 127
William 42

www.ingramcontent.com/pod-product-compliance
Lightning Source LLC
Chambersburg PA
CBHW070729160426
43192CB00009B/1364